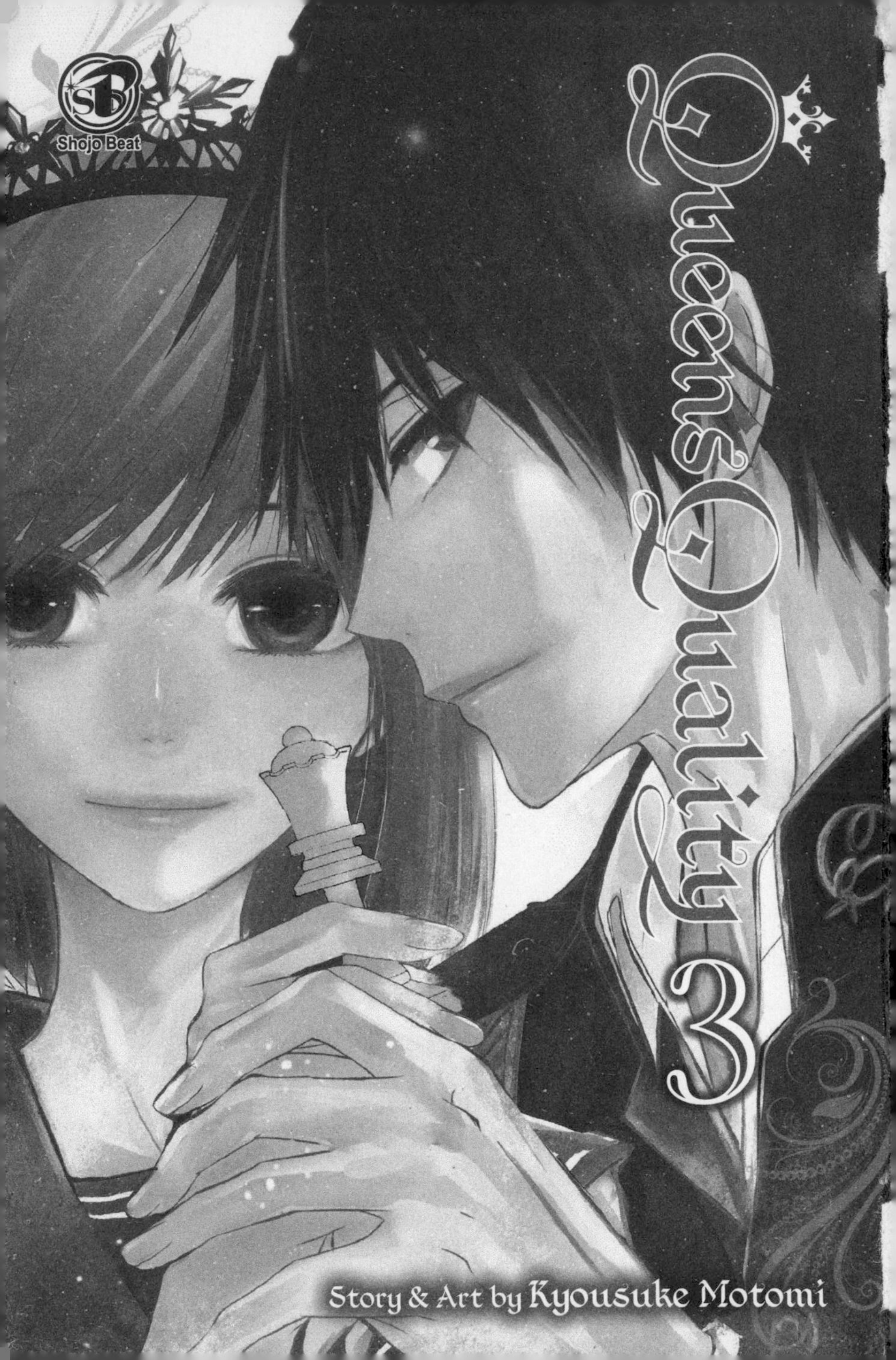
Shojo Beat
Queen's Quality 3
Story & Art by Kyousuke Motomi

Queen's Quality

CONTENTS

3

◇ Cast of Characters ◆

Fumi Nishioka

An apprentice Sweeper with the powers of a Queen, this second-year high school student dreams of finding her very own Prince Charming.

Kyutaro Horikita

A mind Sweeper who cleanses people's minds of dangerous impurities. He's incredibly awkward with people, but he has feelings for Fumi.

Ataru Shikata

A bug handler who uses bugs to manipulate people. He wants to ensure that Fumi awakens as a Black Queen.

Miyako Horikita

The prior head of the Genbu Sweepers. She can be both strict and kind, and she watches over and advises Fumi.

Koichi Kitagawa

The chairman of the school Fumi and Kyutaro attend. He's a Sweeper as well as being Kyutaro's brother-in-law.

Takaya Kitahara

A psychiatrist who's related to the Genbu Gate Sweepers. He's an expert with suggestive therapy, and he counsels Fumi.

◇ Story Thus Far ◆

The Horikitas are a family of Sweepers—people who cleanse impurities from human hearts. After seeing Fumi's potential, they take Fumi on as an assistant and trainee. But Fumi has the untapped, immense power of a Queen, and thanks to Ataru's scheming, that power has started to stir inside her.

Fumi discovers a Queen inside herself who's neither the Black Queen nor the True Queen, and she accepts the deal this Queen offers: each time Fumi draws on her Queen powers, she'll be compensated with the return of some of her lost memories...and if Fumi can endure everything that comes with those memories, she'll find the path to becoming the True Queen.

MONTHLY BETSUCOMI SALE DATE NOTICE ON TWITTER

CHAPTER 11

Kyutaro, where are you hurt?
Leave him alone, Fumi.
He hurt himself trying to protect you.
Sometimes the kindest thing you can do is look the other way. Protect his dignity.
Good job, Horikita!

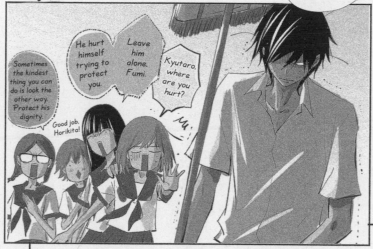

WHAT'S UP IN *QUEEN'S QUALITY* THIS MONTH?

(1) IT ISN'T STEALTH MARKETING.
(2) SMOKING CLEANING MAN (SECOND GENERATION)
(3) WE MISSED HIS VITAL SPOTS, SO HE SHOULD BE ALL RIGHT...PROBABLY.

YOU MIGHT SEE THE BEST JOB DONE BY THE QQ SWEEPERS IN CHAPTER 11!

I tweet things like that every month around when *Betsucomi* is released. You have to read the actual chapter for the tweet(s) to make sense. I also post new artwork sometimes, or older pictures, or just everyday chatter. Please check it out from time to time!
@motomikyosuke

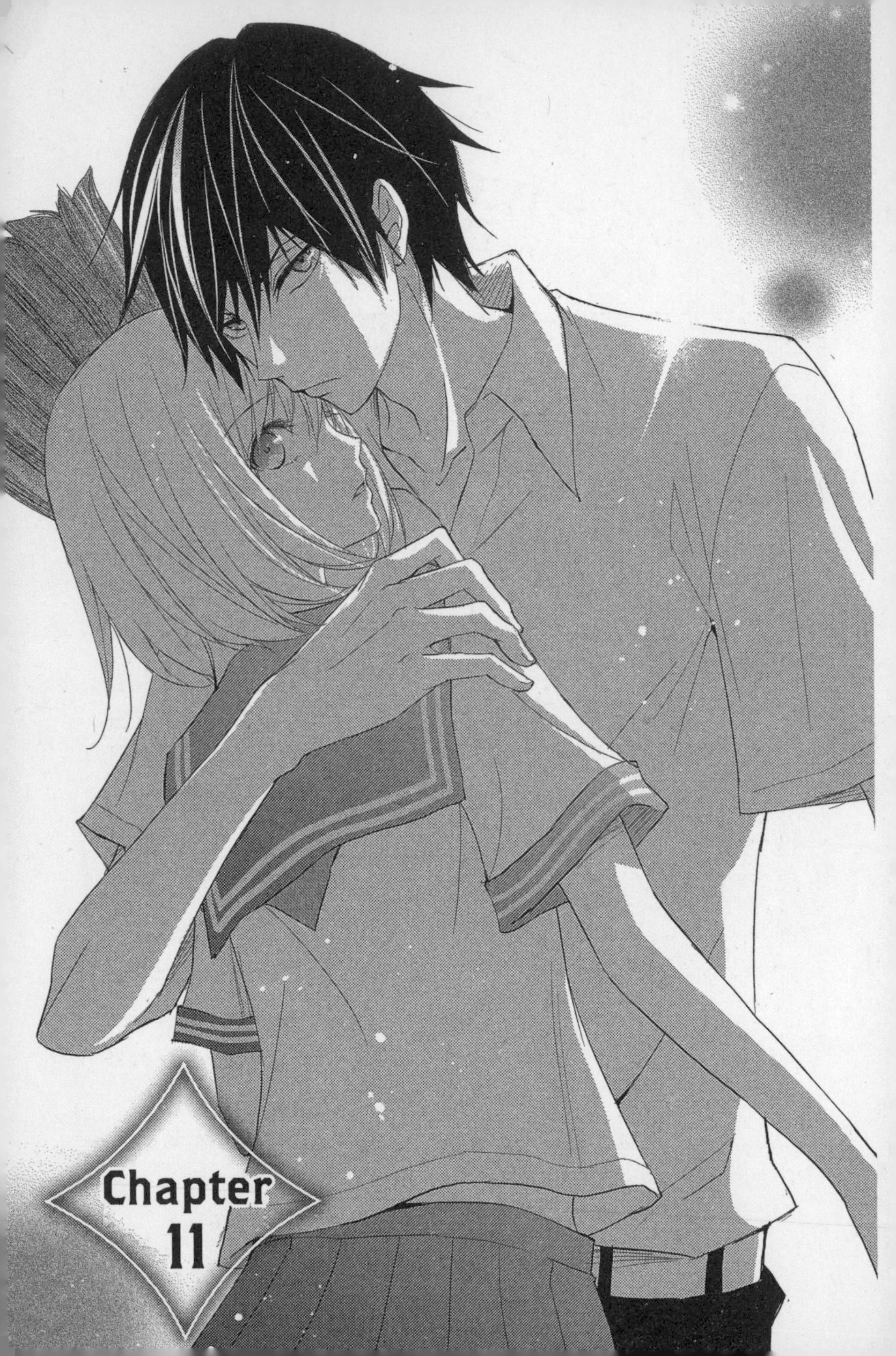
Chapter
11

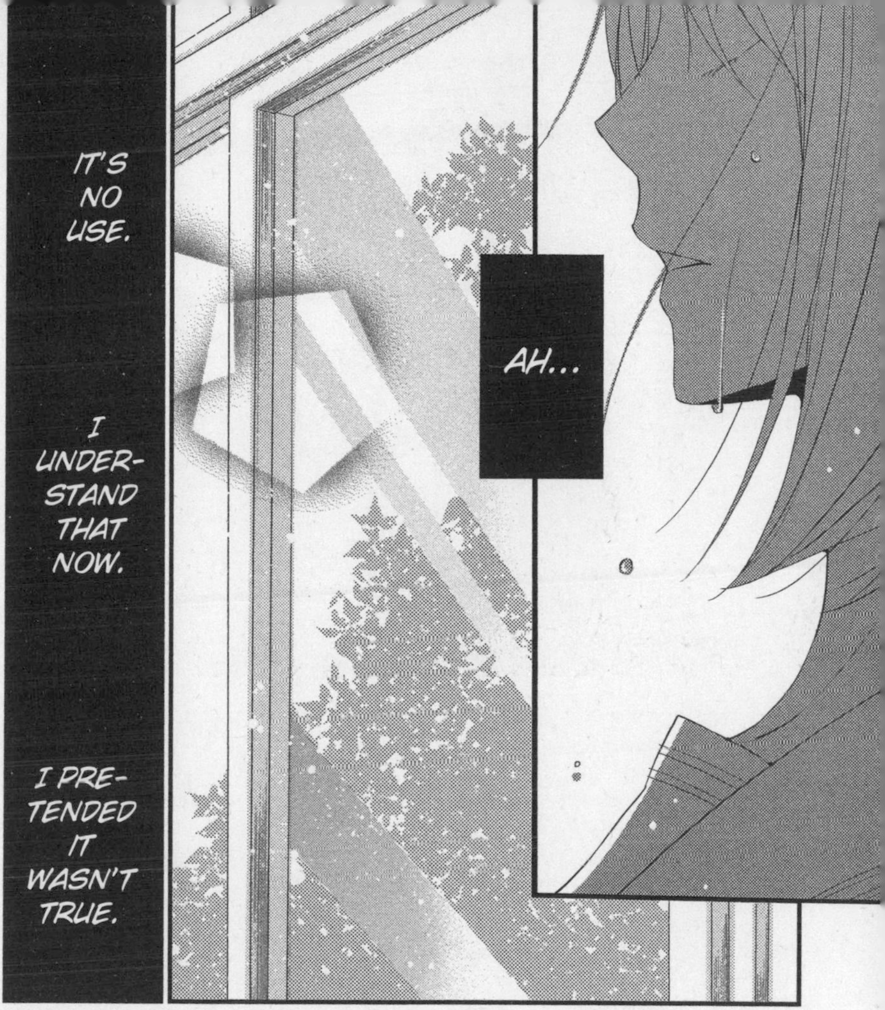
AH...
IT'S NO USE.
I UNDERSTAND THAT NOW.
I PRETENDED IT WASN'T TRUE.

Hello, everyone!
Kyousuke Motomi here.
Thank you for picking up volume 3 of *Queen's Quality*!
I'm so happy to reach volume 3, which is where my previous series, *QQ Sweeper*, ended.
New characters arrive and the tension mounts in this volume.
I hope you enjoy it!

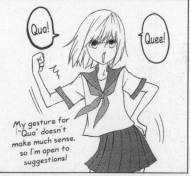

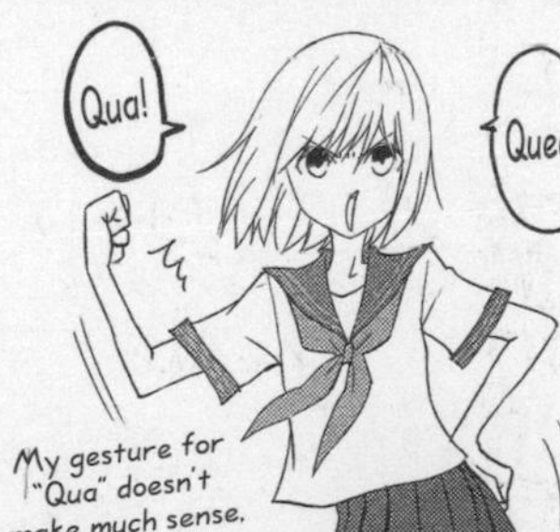
Qua!
Quee!
My gesture for "Qua" doesn't make much sense, so I'm open to suggestions!

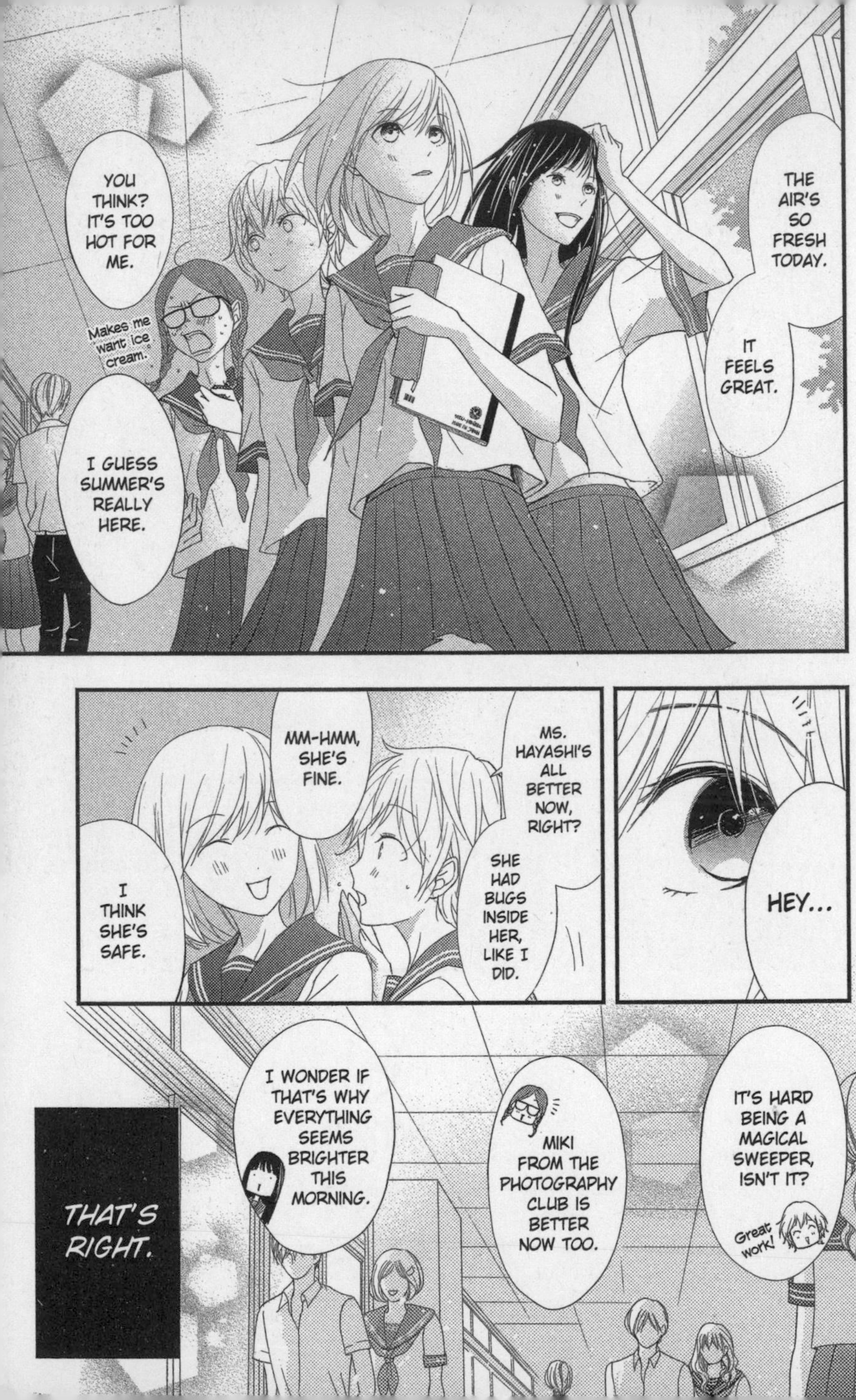
THE AIR'S SO FRESH TODAY.
IT FEELS GREAT.
YOU THINK? IT'S TOO HOT FOR ME.
Makes me want ice cream.
I GUESS SUMMER'S REALLY HERE.
HEY...
MS. HAYASHI'S ALL BETTER NOW, RIGHT?
SHE HAD BUGS INSIDE HER, LIKE I DID.
MM-HMM, SHE'S FINE.
I THINK SHE'S SAFE.
IT'S HARD BEING A MAGICAL SWEEPER, ISN'T IT?
Great work!
MIKI FROM THE PHOTOGRAPHY CLUB IS BETTER NOW TOO.
I WONDER IF THAT'S WHY EVERYTHING SEEMS BRIGHTER THIS MORNING.
THAT'S RIGHT.

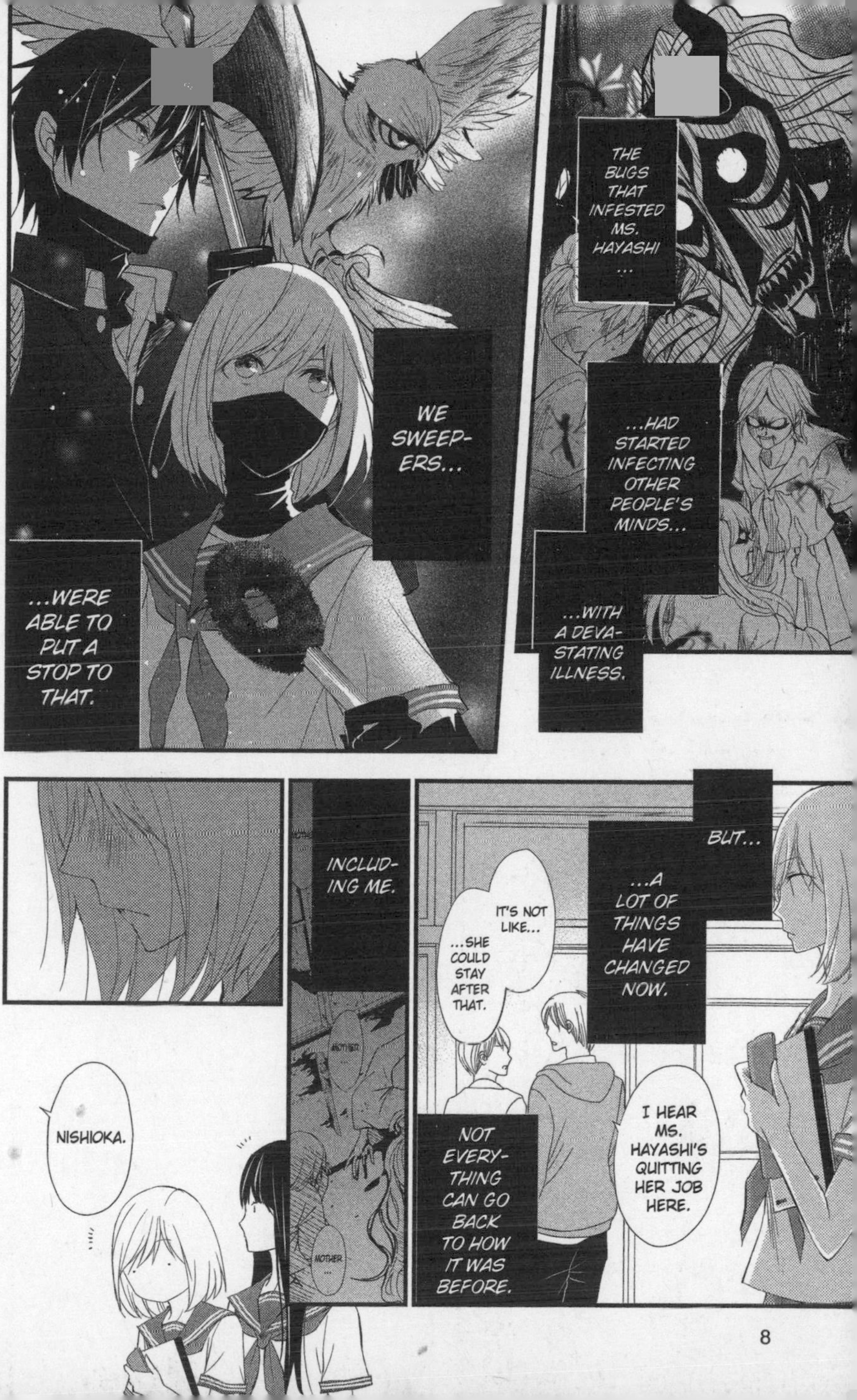
THE BUGS THAT INFESTED MS. HAYASHI ...
...HAD STARTED INFECTING OTHER PEOPLE'S MINDS...
...WITH A DEVASTATING ILLNESS.
WE SWEEPERS...
...WERE ABLE TO PUT A STOP TO THAT.
BUT...
...A LOT OF THINGS HAVE CHANGED NOW.
I HEAR MS. HAYASHI'S QUITTING HER JOB HERE.
IT'S NOT LIKE...
...SHE COULD STAY AFTER THAT.
NOT EVERYTHING CAN GO BACK TO HOW IT WAS BEFORE.
INCLUDING ME.
MOTHER ...
NISHIOKA.

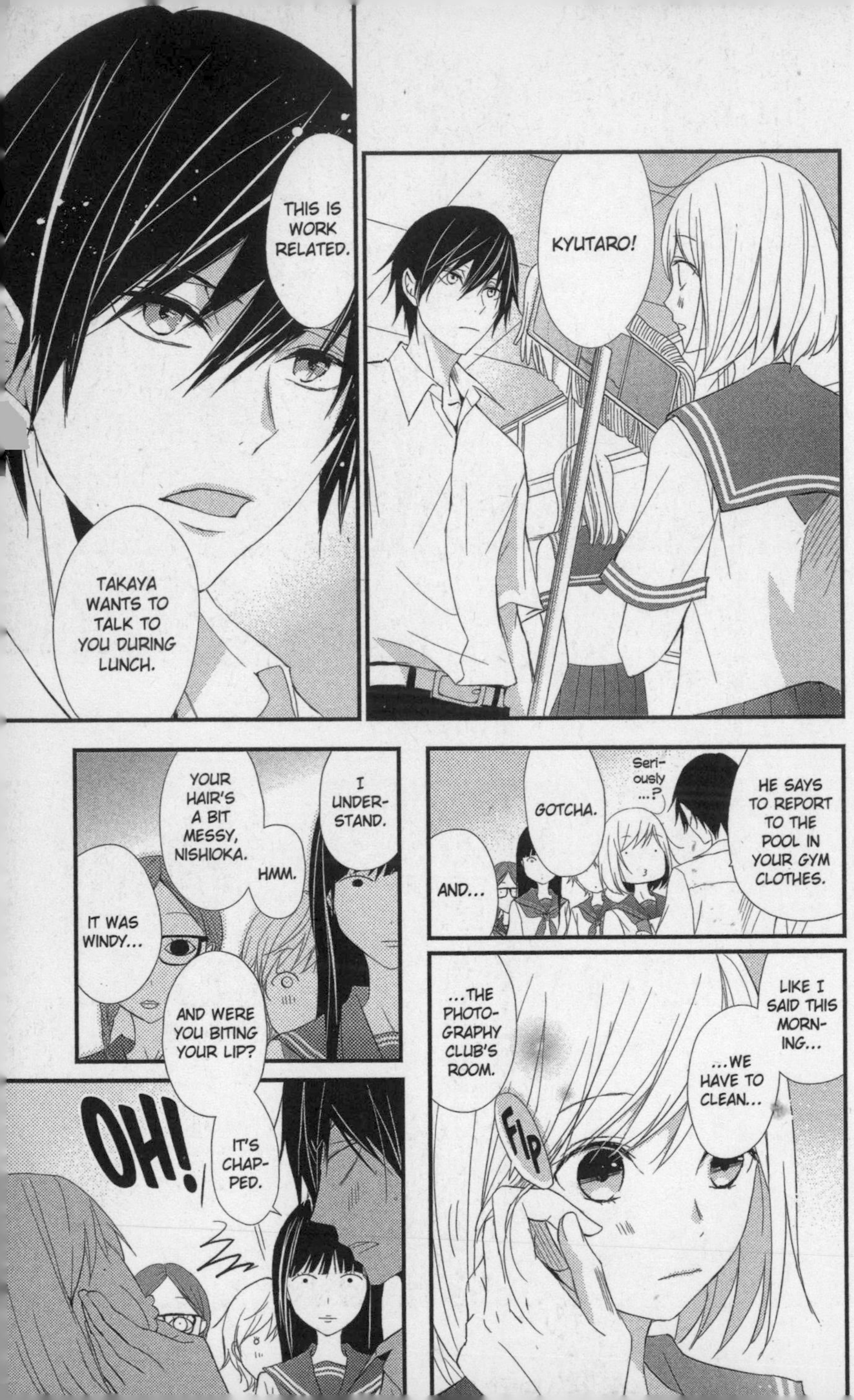
KYUTARO!
THIS IS WORK RELATED.
TAKAYA WANTS TO TALK TO YOU DURING LUNCH.
HE SAYS TO REPORT TO THE POOL IN YOUR GYM CLOTHES.
Seriously ...?
GOTCHA.
AND...
I UNDERSTAND.
YOUR HAIR'S A BIT MESSY, NISHIOKA.
HMM.
IT WAS WINDY...
AND WERE YOU BITING YOUR LIP?
LIKE I SAID THIS MORNING...
...WE HAVE TO CLEAN...
...THE PHOTOGRAPHY CLUB'S ROOM.
FLIP
IT'S CHAPPED.
OH!

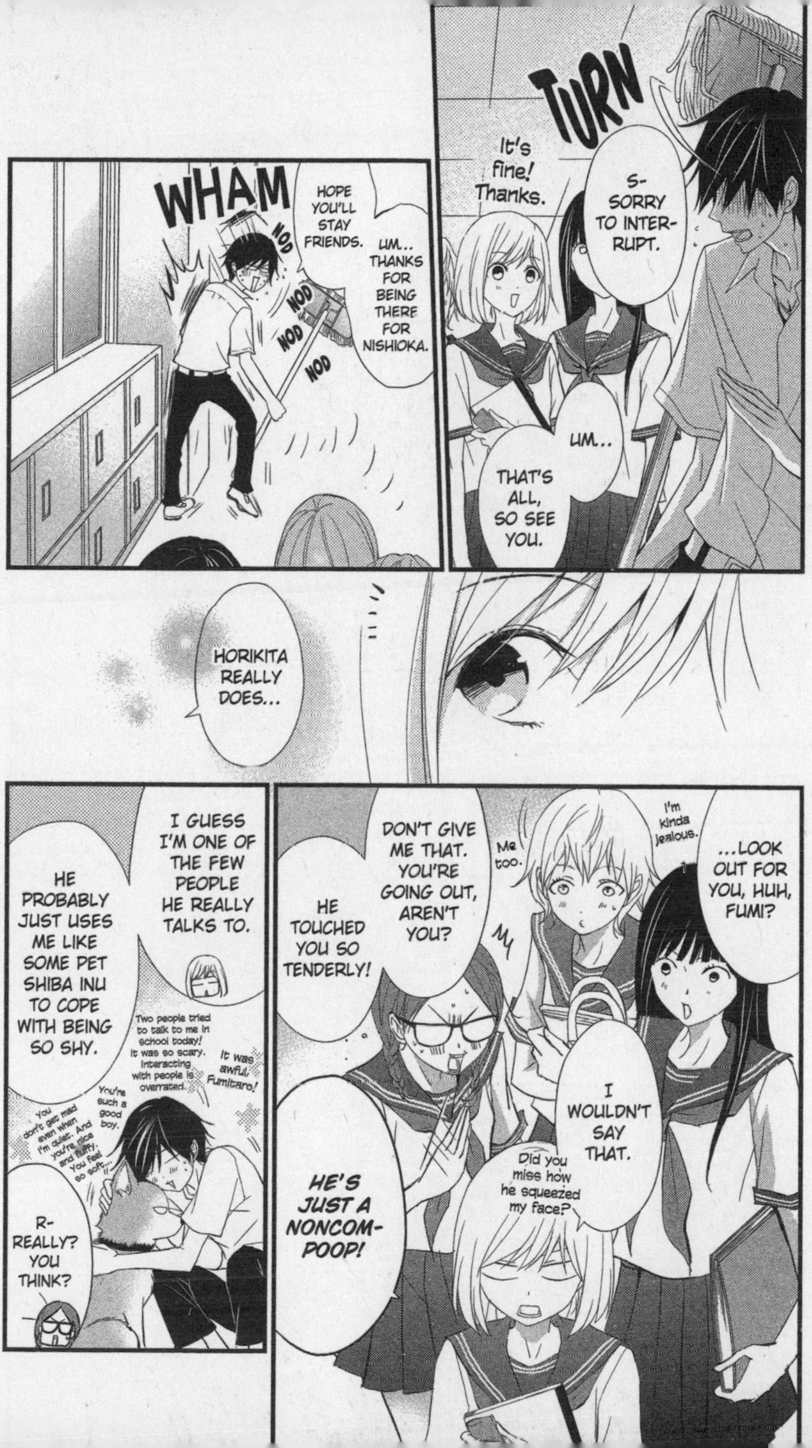
TURN
S-SORRY TO INTERRUPT.
It's fine! Thanks.
UM...
THAT'S ALL, SO SEE YOU.
UM... THANKS FOR BEING THERE FOR NISHIOKA.
HOPE YOU'LL STAY FRIENDS.
WHAM
NOD
NOD
NOD
NOD
HORIKITA REALLY DOES...
...LOOK OUT FOR YOU, HUH, FUMI?
I'm kinda jealous.
Me too.
DON'T GIVE ME THAT. YOU'RE GOING OUT, AREN'T YOU?
HE TOUCHED YOU SO TENDERLY!
I WOULDN'T SAY THAT.
Did you miss how he squeezed my face?
HE'S JUST A NONCOMPOOP!
I GUESS I'M ONE OF THE FEW PEOPLE HE REALLY TALKS TO.
HE PROBABLY JUST USES ME LIKE SOME PET SHIBA INU TO COPE WITH BEING SO SHY.
It was awful, Fumitaro!
Two people tried to talk to me in school today! It was so scary. Interacting with people is overrated.
You're such a good boy.
You don't get mad even when I'm quiet. And you're nice and fluffy. You feel so soft...
R-REALLY? YOU THINK?

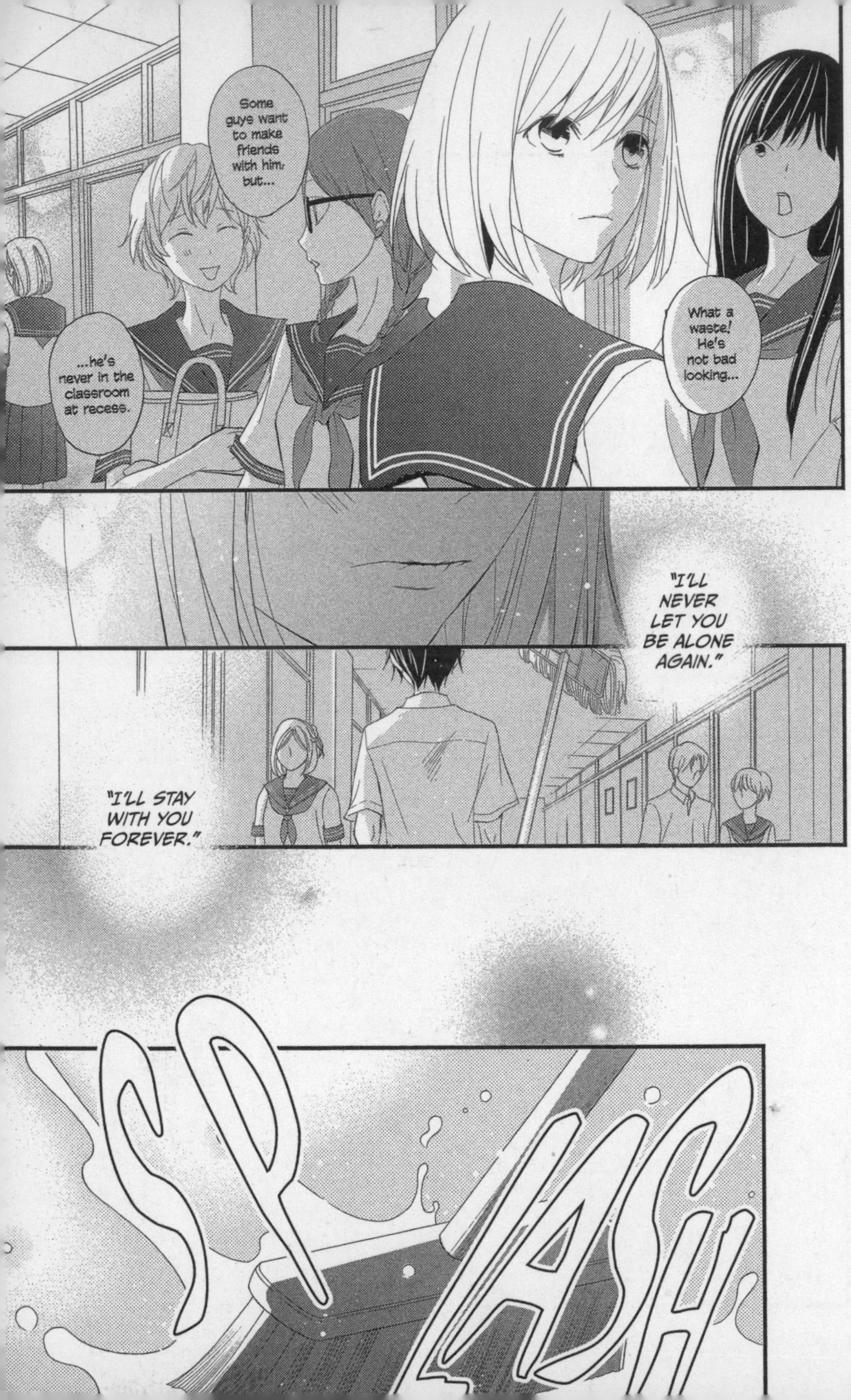
Some guys want to make friends with him, but...
...he's never in the classroom at recess.
What a waste! He's not bad looking...
"I'LL NEVER LET YOU BE ALONE AGAIN."
"I'LL STAY WITH YOU FOREVER."
SPLASH

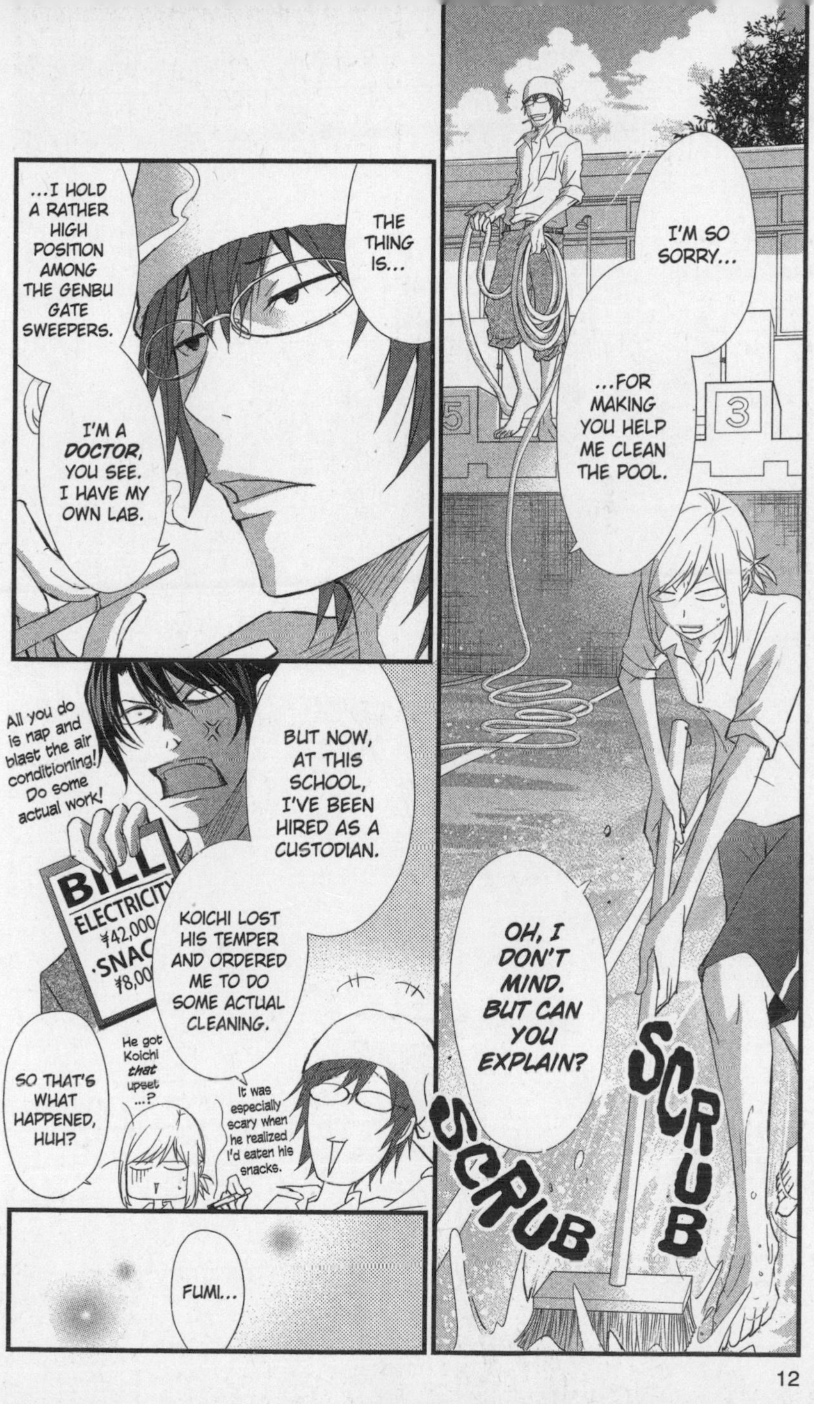
I'M SO SORRY...
...FOR MAKING YOU HELP ME CLEAN THE POOL.
OH, I DON'T MIND. BUT CAN YOU EXPLAIN?
SCRUB
SCRUB
THE THING IS...
...I HOLD A RATHER HIGH POSITION AMONG THE GENBU GATE SWEEPERS.
I'M A *DOCTOR*, YOU SEE. I HAVE MY OWN LAB.
BUT NOW, AT THIS SCHOOL, I'VE BEEN HIRED AS A CUSTODIAN.
All you do is nap and blast the air conditioning! Do some actual work!
BILL ELECTRICITY ¥42,000 ·SNAC ¥8,00
KOICHI LOST HIS TEMPER AND ORDERED ME TO DO SOME ACTUAL CLEANING.
It was especially scary when he realized I'd eaten his snacks.
He got Koichi *that* upset ...?
SO THAT'S WHAT HAPPENED, HUH?
FUMI...

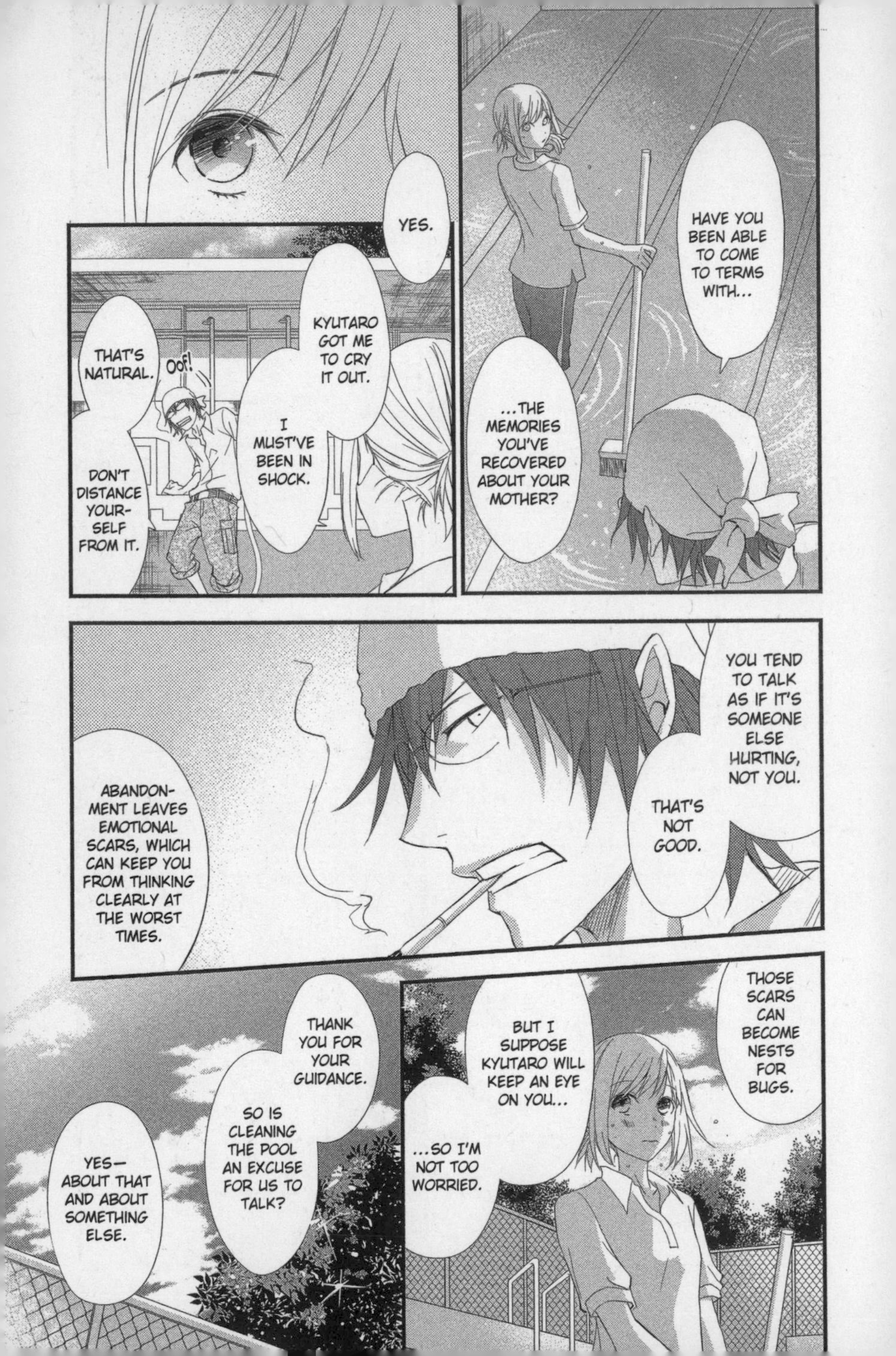
HAVE YOU BEEN ABLE TO COME TO TERMS WITH...
...THE MEMORIES YOU'VE RECOVERED ABOUT YOUR MOTHER?
YES.
KYUTARO GOT ME TO CRY IT OUT.
I MUST'VE BEEN IN SHOCK.
THAT'S NATURAL.
Oof!
DON'T DISTANCE YOURSELF FROM IT.
YOU TEND TO TALK AS IF IT'S SOMEONE ELSE HURTING, NOT YOU.
THAT'S NOT GOOD.
ABANDONMENT LEAVES EMOTIONAL SCARS, WHICH CAN KEEP YOU FROM THINKING CLEARLY AT THE WORST TIMES.
THOSE SCARS CAN BECOME NESTS FOR BUGS.
BUT I SUPPOSE KYUTARO WILL KEEP AN EYE ON YOU...
...SO I'M NOT TOO WORRIED.
THANK YOU FOR YOUR GUIDANCE.
SO IS CLEANING THE POOL AN EXCUSE FOR US TO TALK?
YES— ABOUT THAT AND ABOUT SOMETHING ELSE.

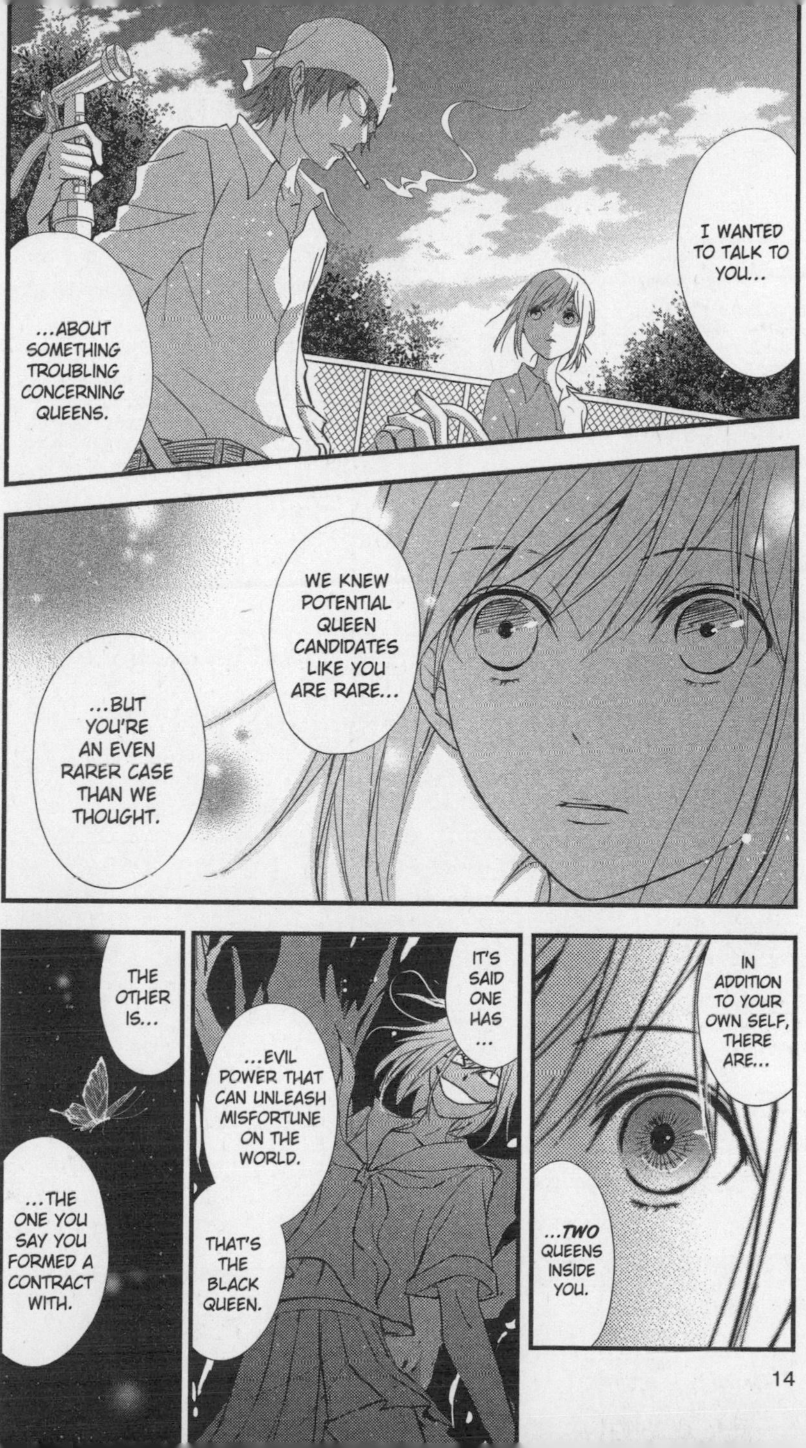
I WANTED TO TALK TO YOU...
...ABOUT SOMETHING TROUBLING CONCERNING QUEENS.
WE KNEW POTENTIAL QUEEN CANDIDATES LIKE YOU ARE RARE...
...BUT YOU'RE AN EVEN RARER CASE THAN WE THOUGHT.
IN ADDITION TO YOUR OWN SELF, THERE ARE...
...*TWO* QUEENS INSIDE YOU.
IT'S SAID ONE HAS...
...EVIL POWER THAT CAN UNLEASH MISFORTUNE ON THE WORLD.
THAT'S THE BLACK QUEEN.
THE OTHER IS...
...THE ONE YOU SAY YOU FORMED A CONTRACT WITH.

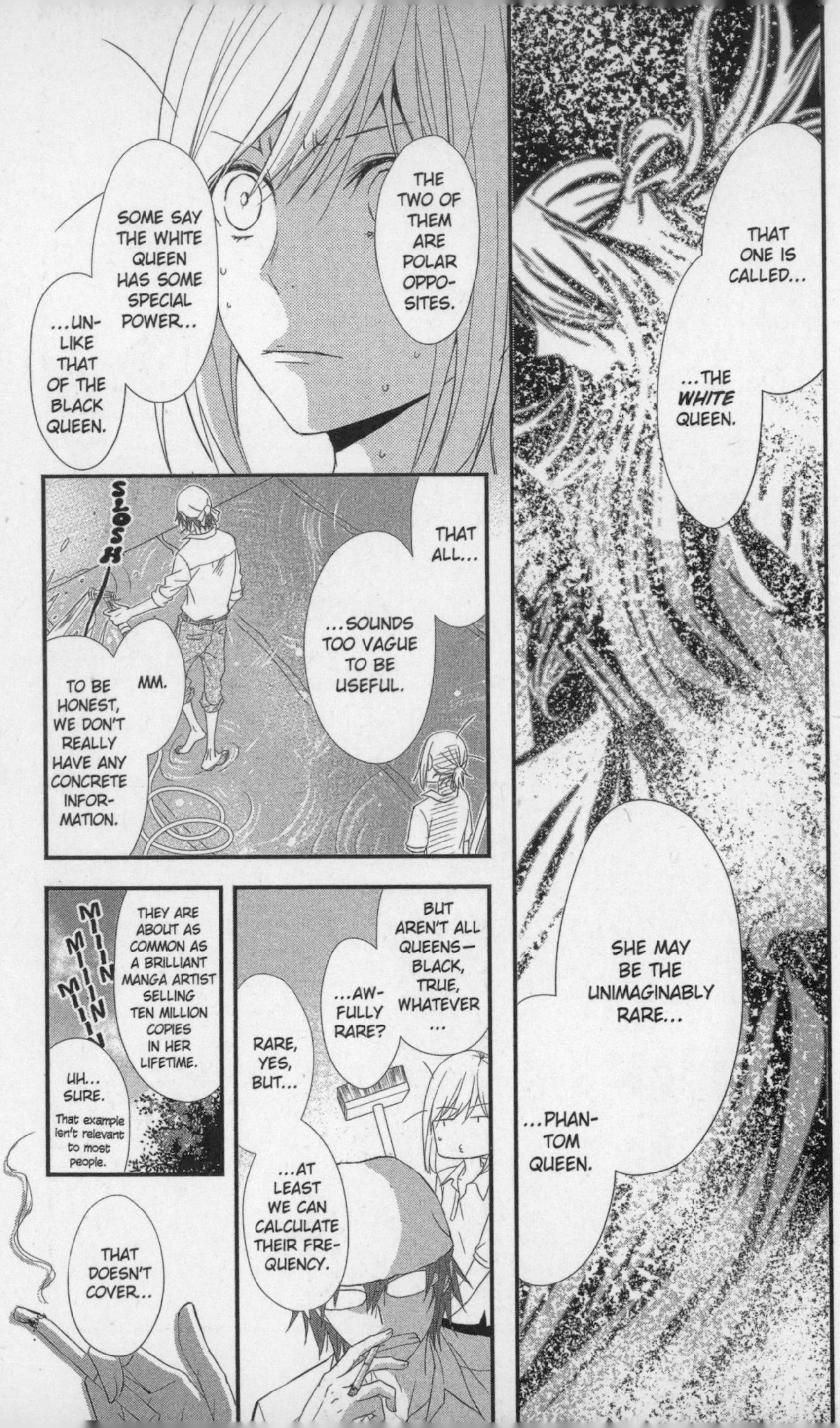
THAT ONE IS CALLED...
...THE *WHITE* QUEEN.
SHE MAY BE THE UNIMAGINABLY RARE...
...PHANTOM QUEEN.
THE TWO OF THEM ARE POLAR OPPOSITES.
SOME SAY THE WHITE QUEEN HAS SOME SPECIAL POWER...
...UNLIKE THAT OF THE BLACK QUEEN.
SLOSH
THAT ALL...
...SOUNDS TOO VAGUE TO BE USEFUL.
MM.
TO BE HONEST, WE DON'T REALLY HAVE ANY CONCRETE INFORMATION.
BUT AREN'T ALL QUEENS—BLACK, TRUE, WHATEVER...
...AWFULLY RARE?
RARE, YES, BUT...
...AT LEAST WE CAN CALCULATE THEIR FREQUENCY.
MIIN MIIN MIIN
THEY ARE ABOUT AS COMMON AS A BRILLIANT MANGA ARTIST SELLING TEN MILLION COPIES IN HER LIFETIME.
UH... SURE.
That example isn't relevant to most people.
THAT DOESN'T COVER...

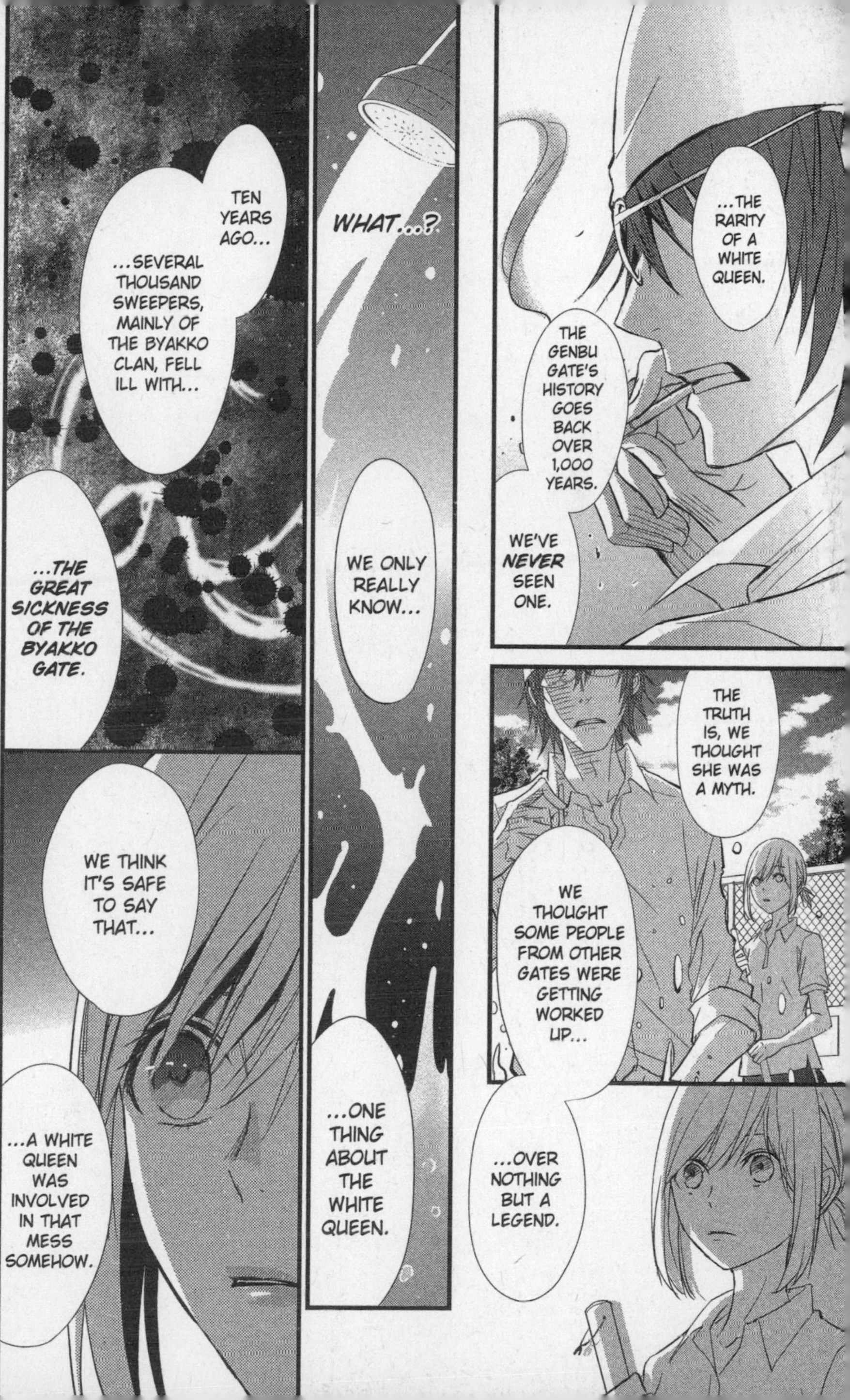
...THE RARITY OF A WHITE QUEEN.
THE GENBU GATE'S HISTORY GOES BACK OVER 1,000 YEARS.
WE'VE NEVER SEEN ONE.
THE TRUTH IS, WE THOUGHT SHE WAS A MYTH.
WE THOUGHT SOME PEOPLE FROM OTHER GATES WERE GETTING WORKED UP...
...OVER NOTHING BUT A LEGEND.
WHAT...?
WE ONLY REALLY KNOW...
...ONE THING ABOUT THE WHITE QUEEN.
TEN YEARS AGO...
...SEVERAL THOUSAND SWEEPERS, MAINLY OF THE BYAKKO CLAN, FELL ILL WITH...
...THE GREAT SICKNESS OF THE BYAKKO GATE.
WE THINK IT'S SAFE TO SAY THAT...
...A WHITE QUEEN WAS INVOLVED IN THAT MESS SOMEHOW.

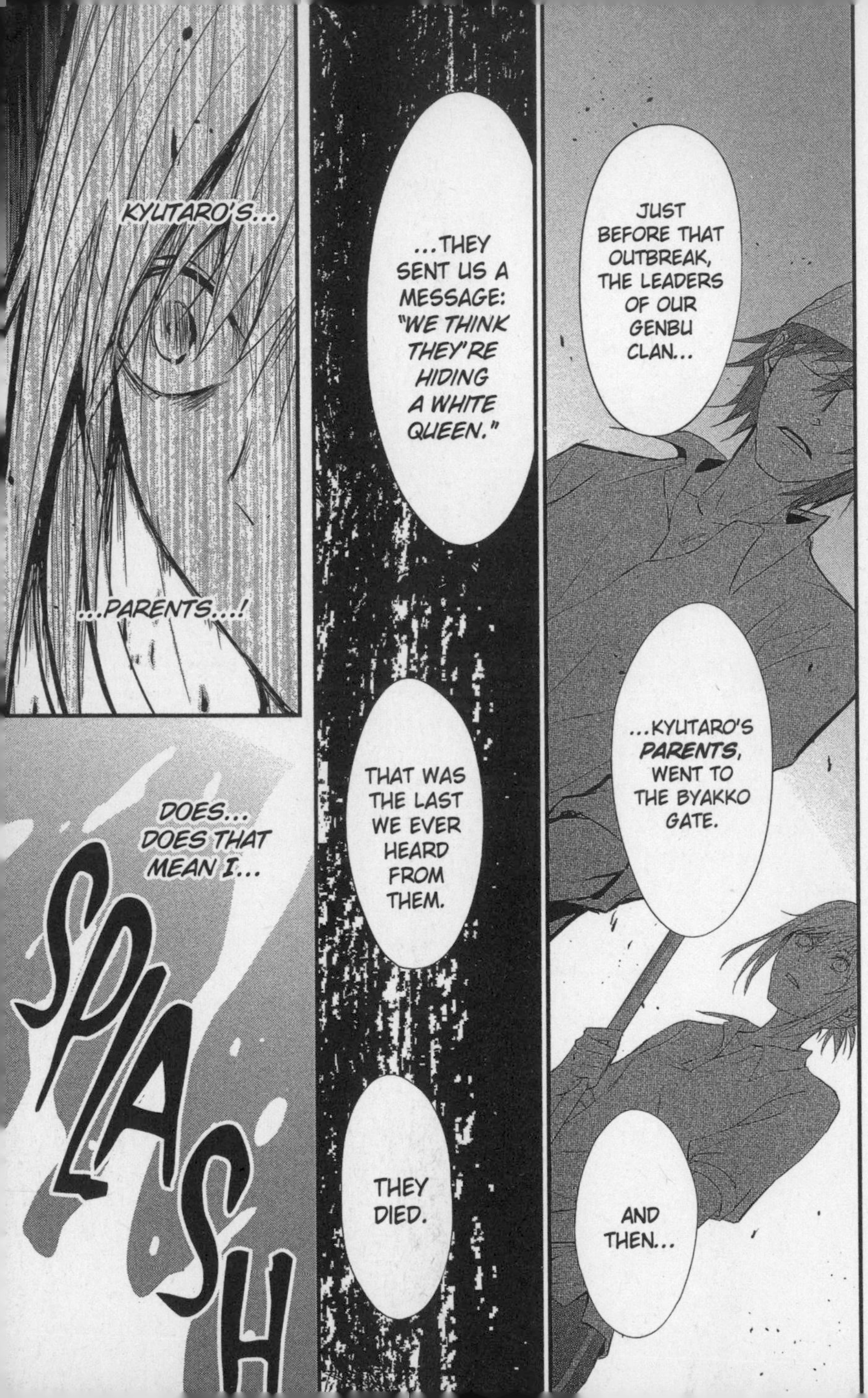
JUST BEFORE THAT OUTBREAK, THE LEADERS OF OUR GENBU CLAN...
...KYUTARO'S PARENTS, WENT TO THE BYAKKO GATE.
AND THEN...
...THEY SENT US A MESSAGE: "WE THINK THEY'RE HIDING A WHITE QUEEN."
THAT WAS THE LAST WE EVER HEARD FROM THEM.
THEY DIED.
KYUTARO'S...
...PARENTS...!
DOES... DOES THAT MEAN I...
SPLASH

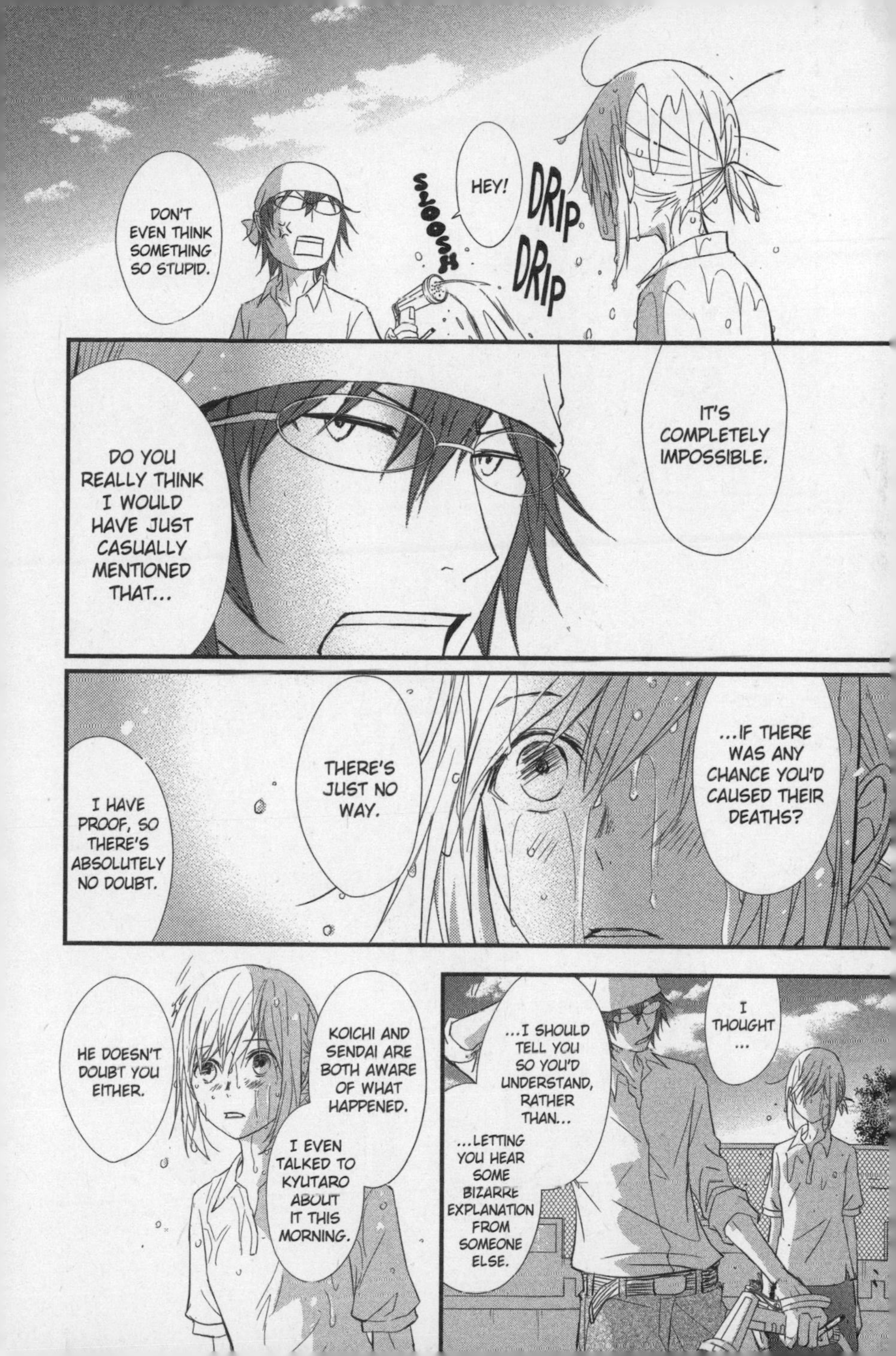
DRIP DRIP
HEY!
SLOOSH
DON'T EVEN THINK SOMETHING SO STUPID.
IT'S COMPLETELY IMPOSSIBLE.
DO YOU REALLY THINK I WOULD HAVE JUST CASUALLY MENTIONED THAT...
...IF THERE WAS ANY CHANCE YOU'D CAUSED THEIR DEATHS?
THERE'S JUST NO WAY.
I HAVE PROOF, SO THERE'S ABSOLUTELY NO DOUBT.
I THOUGHT...
...I SHOULD TELL YOU SO YOU'D UNDERSTAND, RATHER THAN...
...LETTING YOU HEAR SOME BIZARRE EXPLANATION FROM SOMEONE ELSE.
KOICHI AND SENDAI ARE BOTH AWARE OF WHAT HAPPENED.
I EVEN TALKED TO KYUTARO ABOUT IT THIS MORNING.
HE DOESN'T DOUBT YOU EITHER.

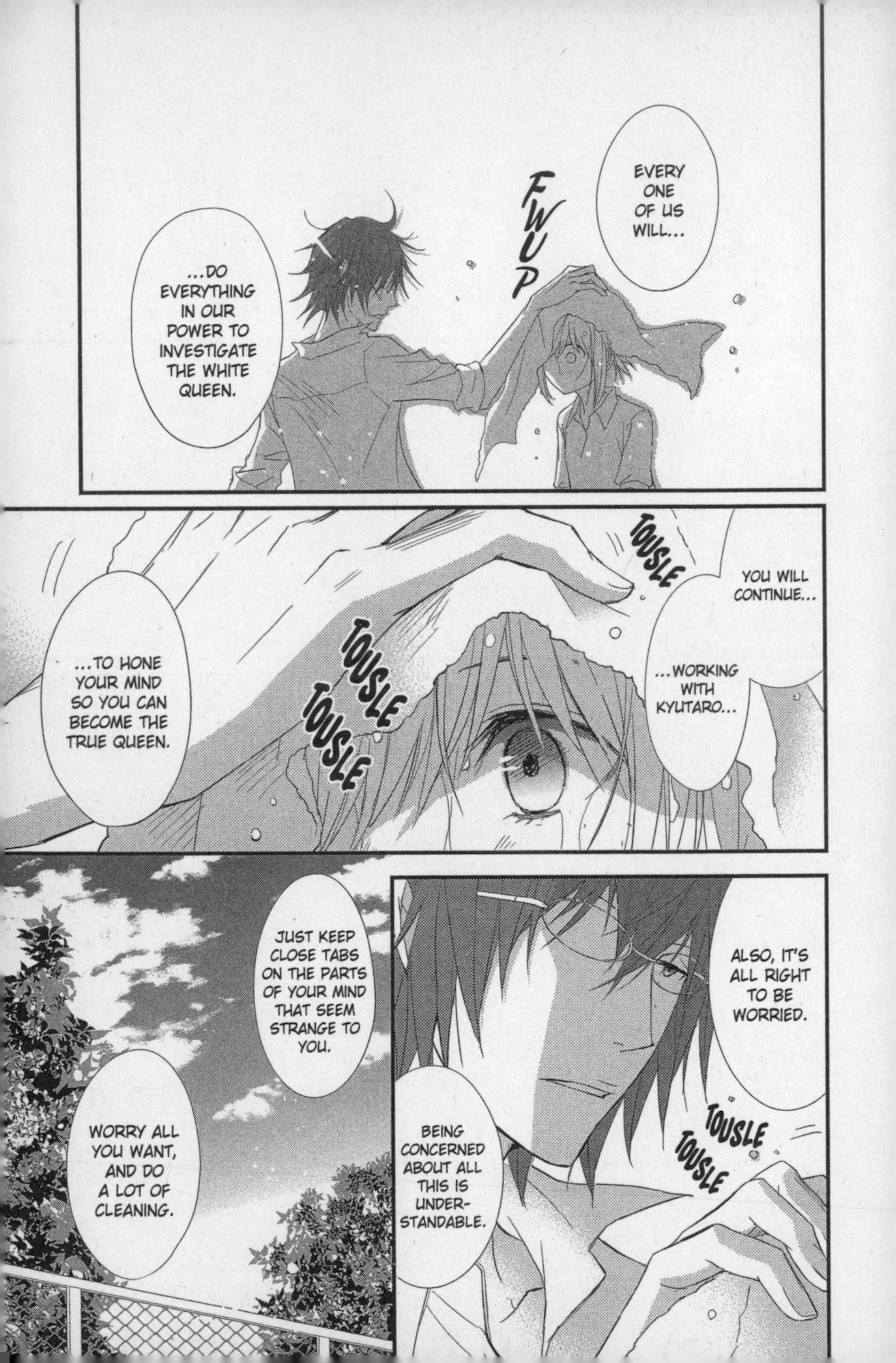
EVERY ONE OF US WILL...
FWUP
...DO EVERYTHING IN OUR POWER TO INVESTIGATE THE WHITE QUEEN.
YOU WILL CONTINUE...
TOUSLE
...WORKING WITH KYUTARO...
TOUSLE TOUSLE
...TO HONE YOUR MIND SO YOU CAN BECOME THE TRUE QUEEN.
ALSO, IT'S ALL RIGHT TO BE WORRIED.
TOUSLE TOUSLE
BEING CONCERNED ABOUT ALL THIS IS UNDER-STANDABLE.
JUST KEEP CLOSE TABS ON THE PARTS OF YOUR MIND THAT SEEM STRANGE TO YOU.
WORRY ALL YOU WANT, AND DO A LOT OF CLEANING.

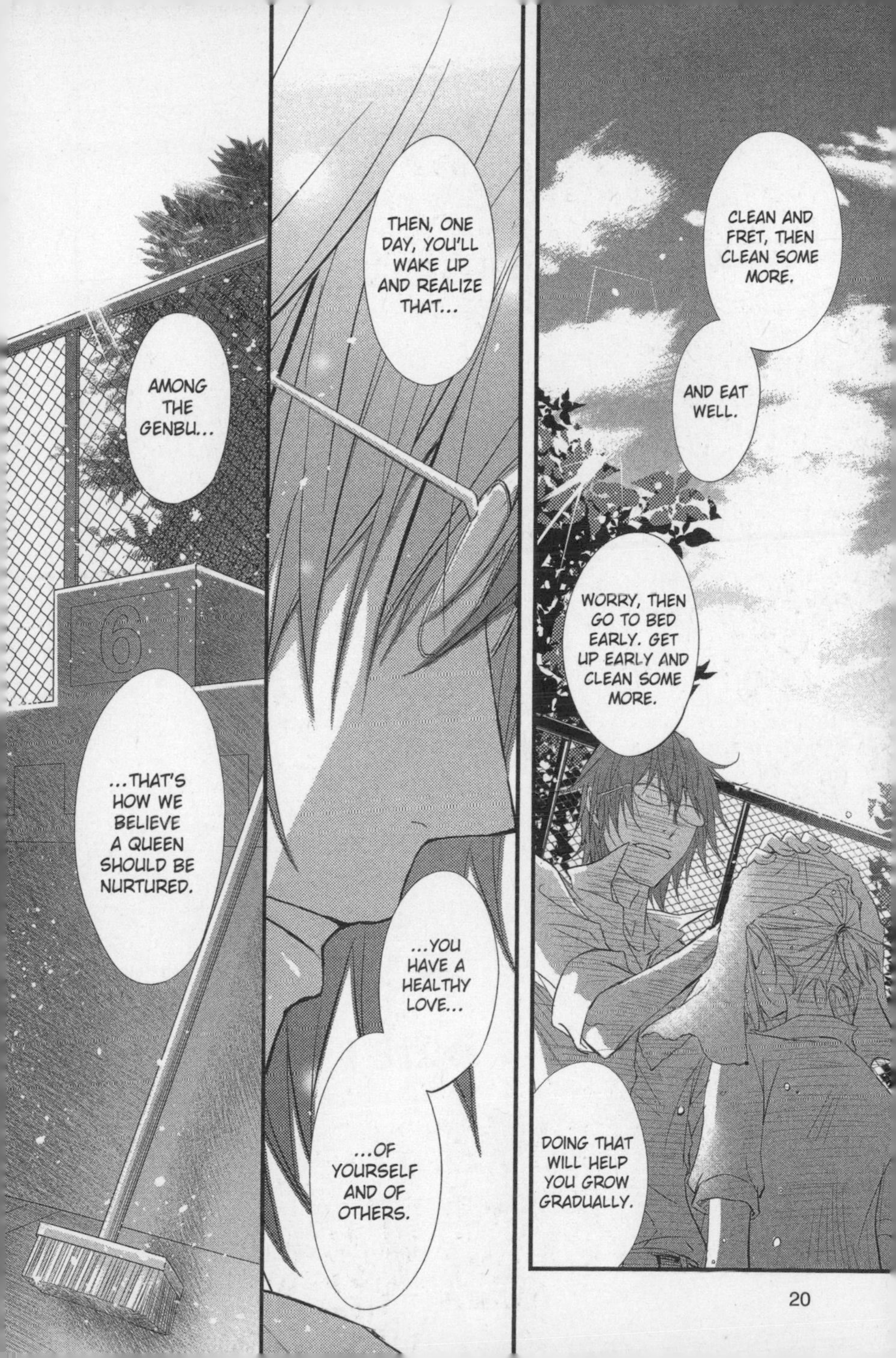
CLEAN AND FRET, THEN CLEAN SOME MORE.
AND EAT WELL.
WORRY, THEN GO TO BED EARLY. GET UP EARLY AND CLEAN SOME MORE.
DOING THAT WILL HELP YOU GROW GRADUALLY.
THEN, ONE DAY, YOU'LL WAKE UP AND REALIZE THAT...
...YOU HAVE A HEALTHY LOVE...
...OF YOURSELF AND OF OTHERS.
AMONG THE GENBU...
...THAT'S HOW WE BELIEVE A QUEEN SHOULD BE NURTURED.

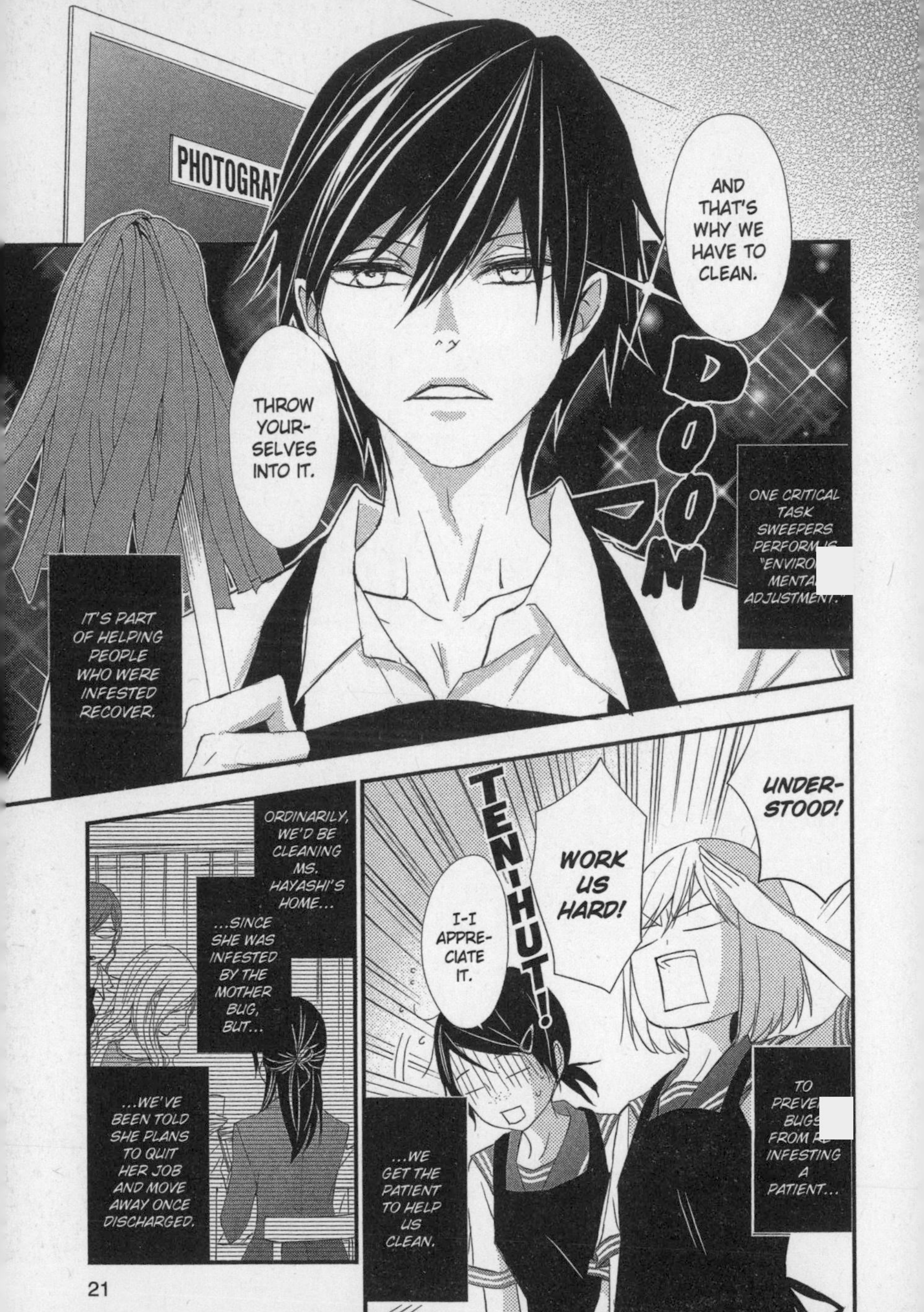
AND THAT'S WHY WE HAVE TO CLEAN.
DOOOM
ONE CRITICAL TASK SWEEPERS PERFORM IS "ENVIRO MENTA ADJUSTMENT."
THROW YOUR-SELVES INTO IT.
PHOTOGRA
IT'S PART OF HELPING PEOPLE WHO WERE INFESTED RECOVER.
TO PREVE BUGS FROM INFESTING A PATIENT...
UNDER-STOOD!
WORK US HARD!
TEN-HUT!
I-I APPRE-CIATE IT.
...WE GET THE PATIENT TO HELP US CLEAN.
ORDINARILY, WE'D BE CLEANING MS. HAYASHI'S HOME...
...SINCE SHE WAS INFESTED BY THE MOTHER BUG, BUT...
...WE'VE BEEN TOLD SHE PLANS TO QUIT HER JOB AND MOVE AWAY ONCE DISCHARGED.

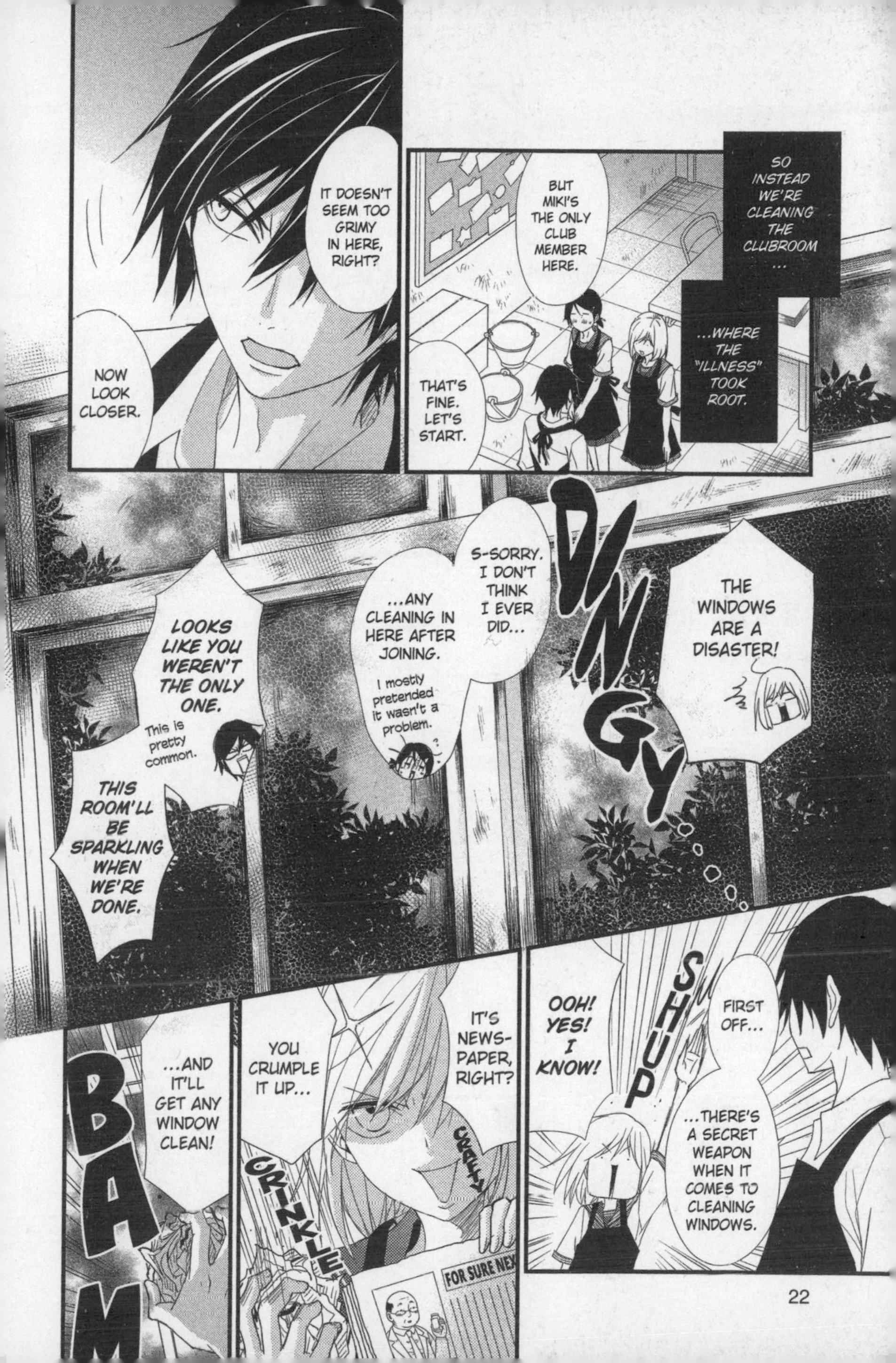
SO INSTEAD WE'RE CLEANING THE CLUBROOM...
...WHERE THE "ILLNESS" TOOK ROOT.
BUT MIKI'S THE ONLY CLUB MEMBER HERE.
THAT'S FINE. LET'S START.
IT DOESN'T SEEM TOO GRIMY IN HERE, RIGHT?
NOW LOOK CLOSER.
THE WINDOWS ARE A DISASTER!
DINGY
S-SORRY. I DON'T THINK I EVER DID...
...ANY CLEANING IN HERE AFTER JOINING.
I mostly pretended it wasn't a problem.
LOOKS LIKE YOU WEREN'T THE ONLY ONE.
This is pretty common.
THIS ROOM'LL BE SPARKLING WHEN WE'RE DONE.
FIRST OFF...
SHUP
...THERE'S A SECRET WEAPON WHEN IT COMES TO CLEANING WINDOWS.
OOH! YES! I KNOW!
IT'S NEWS-PAPER, RIGHT?
YOU CRUMPLE IT UP...
CRINKLE
FOR SURE NEX
...AND IT'LL GET ANY WINDOW CLEAN!
BAM

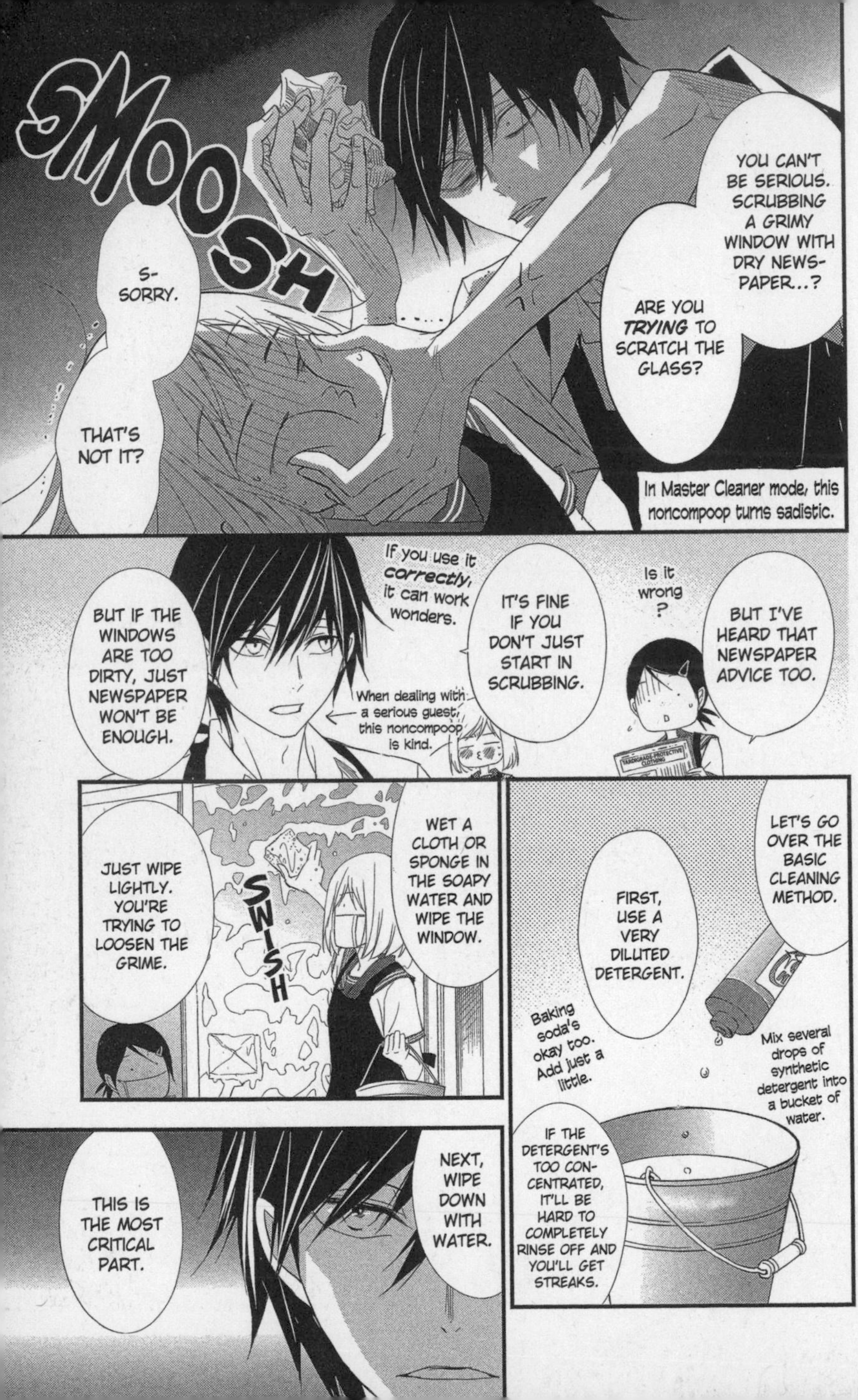

YOU CAN'T BE SERIOUS. SCRUBBING A GRIMY WINDOW WITH DRY NEWS-PAPER...?
ARE YOU *TRYING* TO SCRATCH THE GLASS?
In Master Cleaner mode, this noncompoop turns sadistic.
SMOOSH
.....
S-SORRY.
THAT'S NOT IT?
BUT I'VE HEARD THAT NEWSPAPER ADVICE TOO.
Is it wrong ?
TARDIGRADE-PROTECTIVE CLOTHING
IT'S FINE IF YOU DON'T JUST START IN SCRUBBING.
If you use it *correctly*, it can work wonders.
When dealing with a serious guest, this noncompoop is kind.
BUT IF THE WINDOWS ARE TOO DIRTY, JUST NEWSPAPER WON'T BE ENOUGH.
LET'S GO OVER THE BASIC CLEANING METHOD.
FIRST, USE A VERY DILUTED DETERGENT.
Mix several drops of synthetic detergent into a bucket of water.
Baking soda's okay too. Add just a little.
IF THE DETERGENT'S TOO CON-CENTRATED, IT'LL BE HARD TO COMPLETELY RINSE OFF AND YOU'LL GET STREAKS.
WET A CLOTH OR SPONGE IN THE SOAPY WATER AND WIPE THE WINDOW.
SWISH
JUST WIPE LIGHTLY. YOU'RE TRYING TO LOOSEN THE GRIME.
NEXT, WIPE DOWN WITH WATER.
THIS IS THE MOST CRITICAL PART.

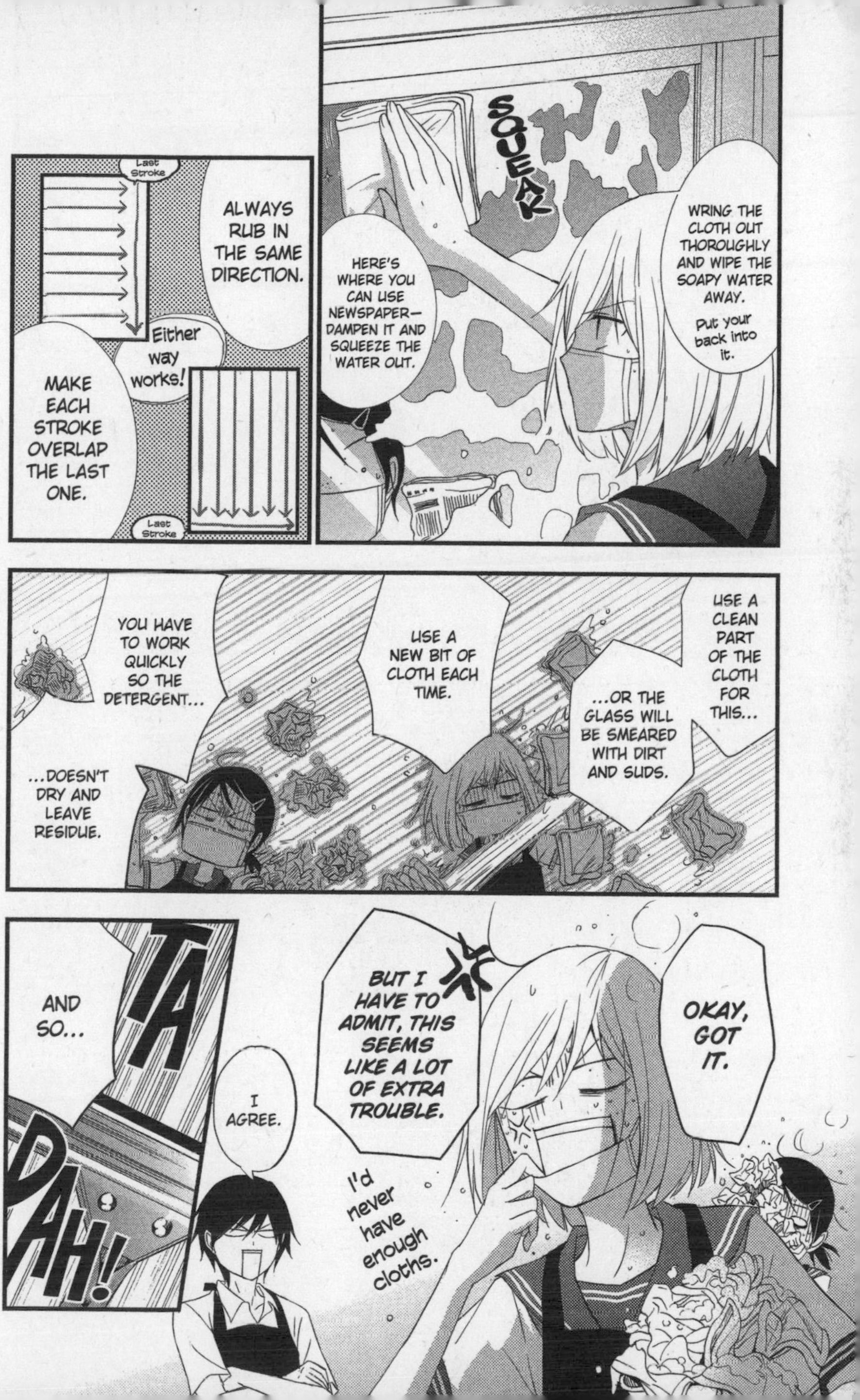
SQUEAK
WRING THE CLOTH OUT THOROUGHLY AND WIPE THE SOAPY WATER AWAY.
Put your back into it.
HERE'S WHERE YOU CAN USE NEWSPAPER—DAMPEN IT AND SQUEEZE THE WATER OUT.
ALWAYS RUB IN THE SAME DIRECTION.
Last Stroke
Either way works!
MAKE EACH STROKE OVERLAP THE LAST ONE.
Last Stroke
USE A CLEAN PART OF THE CLOTH FOR THIS...
...OR THE GLASS WILL BE SMEARED WITH DIRT AND SUDS.
USE A NEW BIT OF CLOTH EACH TIME.
YOU HAVE TO WORK QUICKLY SO THE DETERGENT...
...DOESN'T DRY AND LEAVE RESIDUE.
OKAY, GOT IT.
BUT I HAVE TO ADMIT, THIS SEEMS LIKE A LOT OF EXTRA TROUBLE.
I'd never have enough cloths.
I AGREE.
AND SO...
TA DAH!

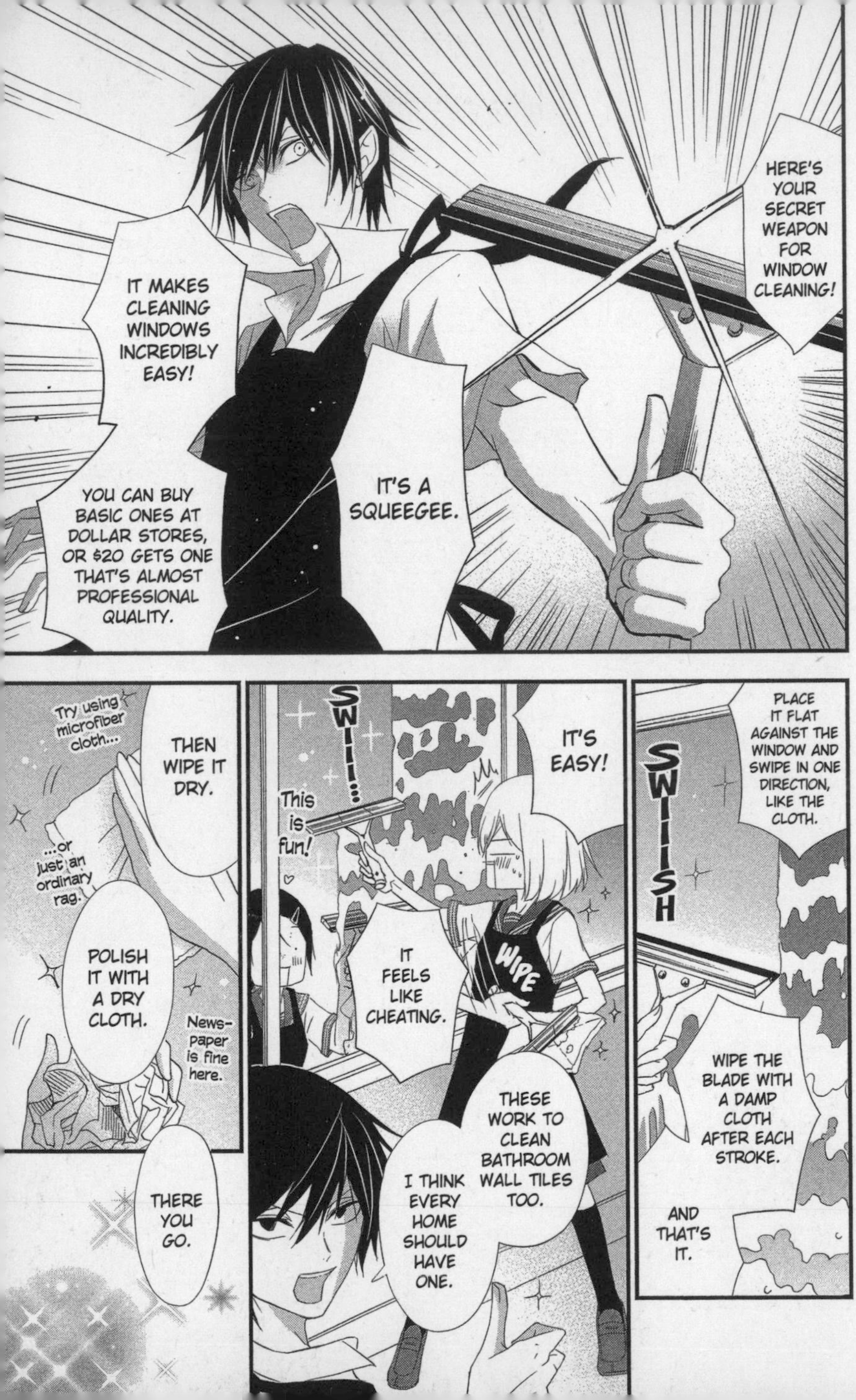
HERE'S YOUR SECRET WEAPON FOR WINDOW CLEANING!
IT'S A SQUEEGEE.
IT MAKES CLEANING WINDOWS INCREDIBLY EASY!
YOU CAN BUY BASIC ONES AT DOLLAR STORES, OR $20 GETS ONE THAT'S ALMOST PROFESSIONAL QUALITY.
PLACE IT FLAT AGAINST THE WINDOW AND SWIPE IN ONE DIRECTION, LIKE THE CLOTH.
SWISH
WIPE THE BLADE WITH A DAMP CLOTH AFTER EACH STROKE.
AND THAT'S IT.
IT'S EASY!
SWIII...
This is fun!
IT FEELS LIKE CHEATING.
WIPE
THESE WORK TO CLEAN BATHROOM WALL TILES TOO.
I THINK EVERY HOME SHOULD HAVE ONE.
THEN WIPE IT DRY.
Try using microfiber cloth...
...or just an ordinary rag.
POLISH IT WITH A DRY CLOTH.
Newspaper is fine here.
THERE YOU GO.

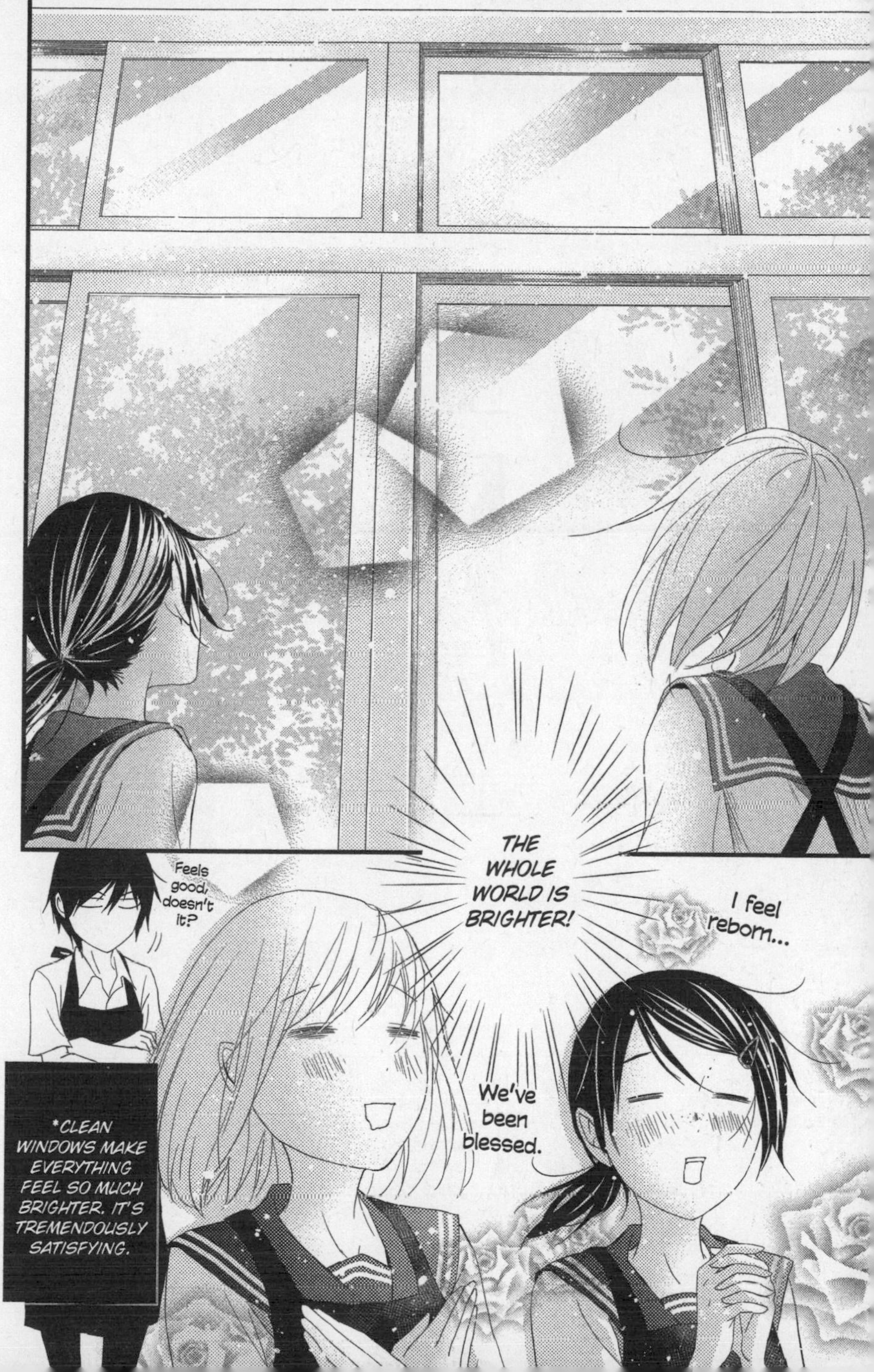
I feel reborn...
THE WHOLE WORLD IS BRIGHTER!
We've been blessed.
Feels good, doesn't it?
*CLEAN WINDOWS MAKE EVERYTHING FEEL SO MUCH BRIGHTER. IT'S TREMENDOUSLY SATISFYING.

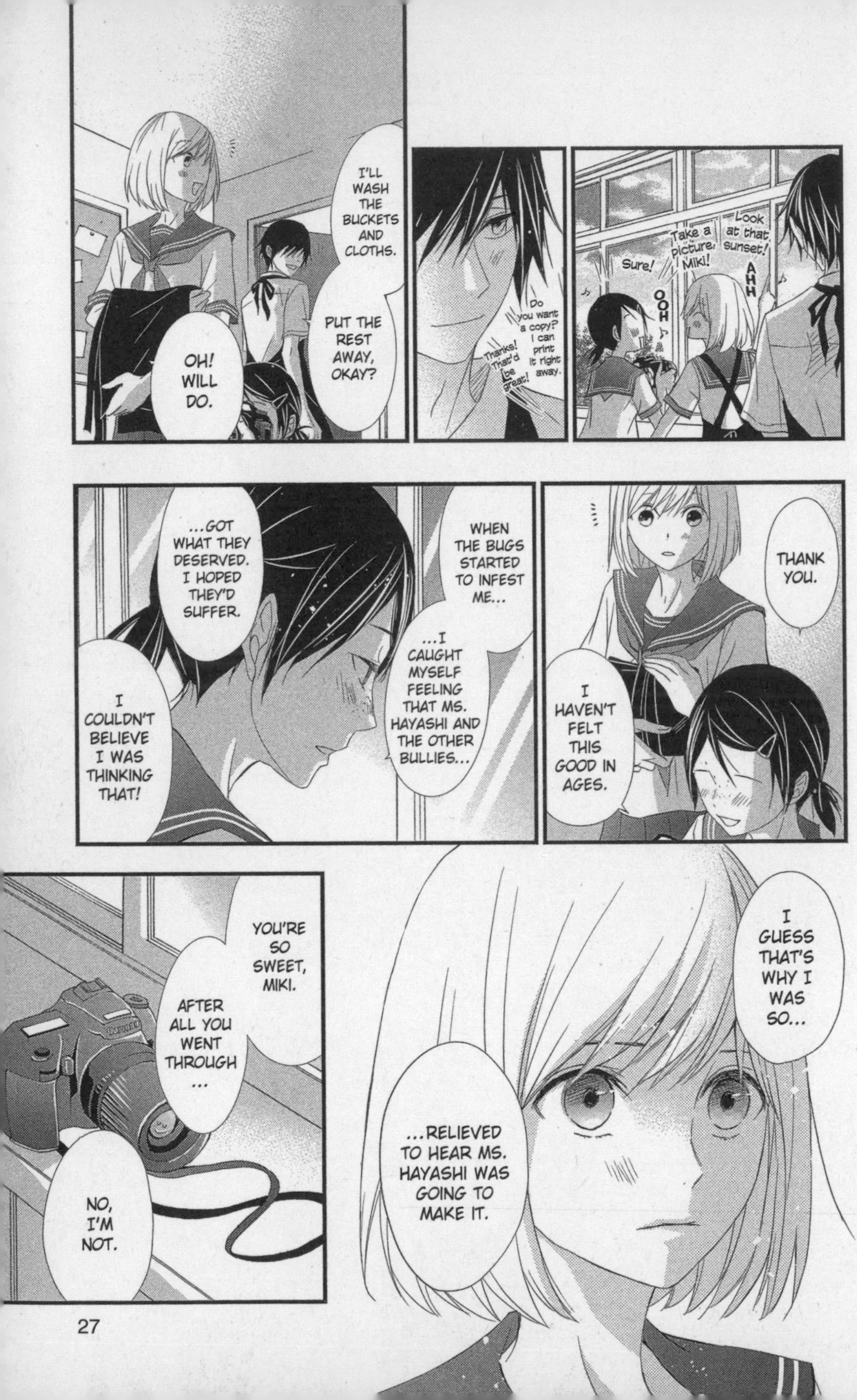
Look at that sunset!
AHH
Take a picture, Miki!
Sure!
OOH
Do you want a copy? I can print it right away.
Thanks! That'd be great!
I'LL WASH THE BUCKETS AND CLOTHS.
PUT THE REST AWAY, OKAY?
OH! WILL DO.
THANK YOU.
I HAVEN'T FELT THIS GOOD IN AGES.
WHEN THE BUGS STARTED TO INFEST ME...
...I CAUGHT MYSELF FEELING THAT MS. HAYASHI AND THE OTHER BULLIES...
...GOT WHAT THEY DESERVED. I HOPED THEY'D SUFFER.
I COULDN'T BELIEVE I WAS THINKING THAT!
I GUESS THAT'S WHY I WAS SO...
...RELIEVED TO HEAR MS. HAYASHI WAS GOING TO MAKE IT.
YOU'RE SO SWEET, MIKI.
AFTER ALL YOU WENT THROUGH...
NO, I'M NOT.

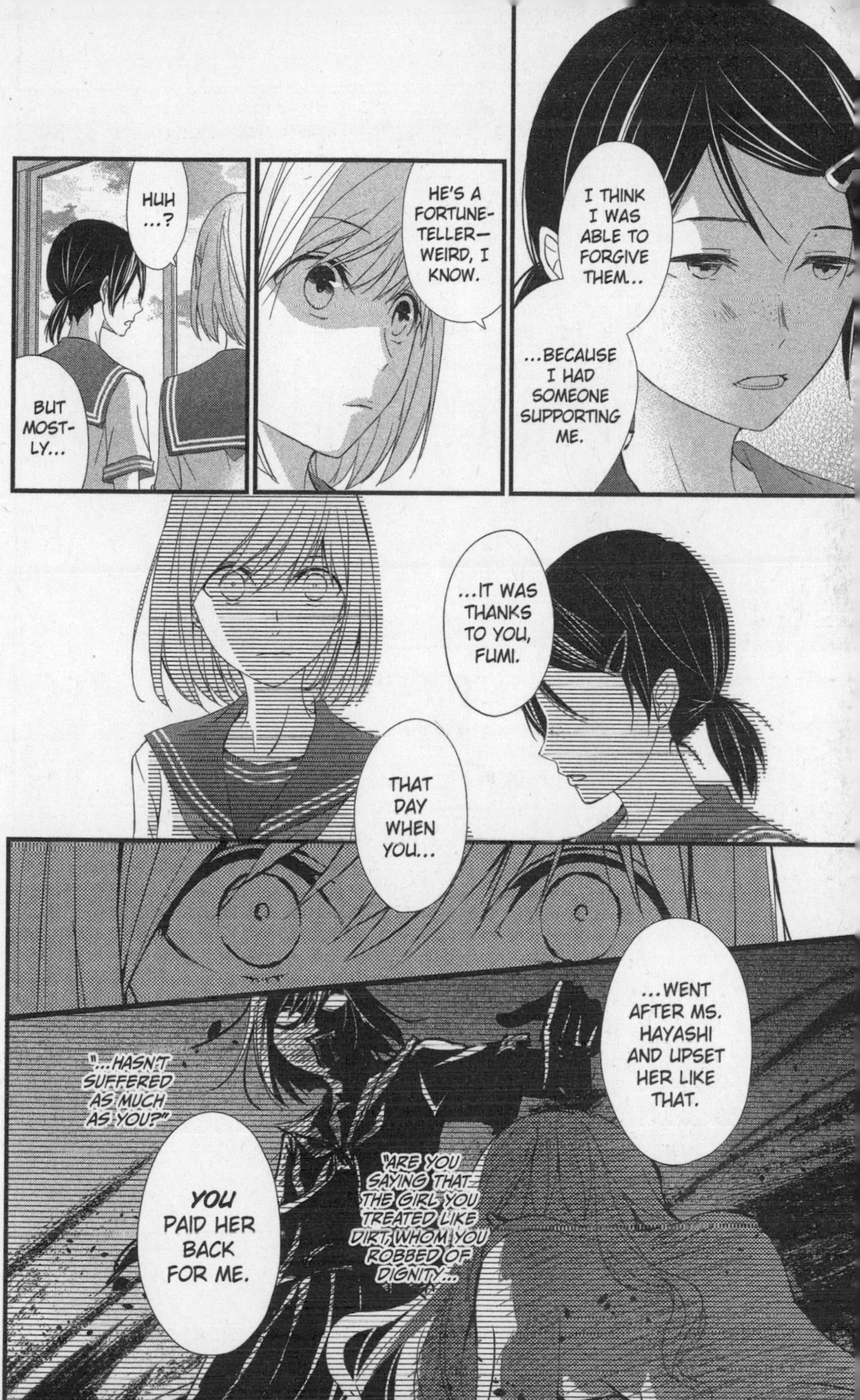
I THINK I WAS ABLE TO FORGIVE THEM...
...BECAUSE I HAD SOMEONE SUPPORTING ME.
HE'S A FORTUNE-TELLER—WEIRD, I KNOW.
HUH ...?
BUT MOSTLY...
...IT WAS THANKS TO YOU, FUMI.
THAT DAY WHEN YOU...
...WENT AFTER MS. HAYASHI AND UPSET HER LIKE THAT.
"ARE YOU SAYING THAT THE GIRL YOU TREATED LIKE DIRT, WHOM YOU ROBBED OF DIGNITY...
...HASN'T SUFFERED AS MUCH AS YOU?"
YOU PAID HER BACK FOR ME.

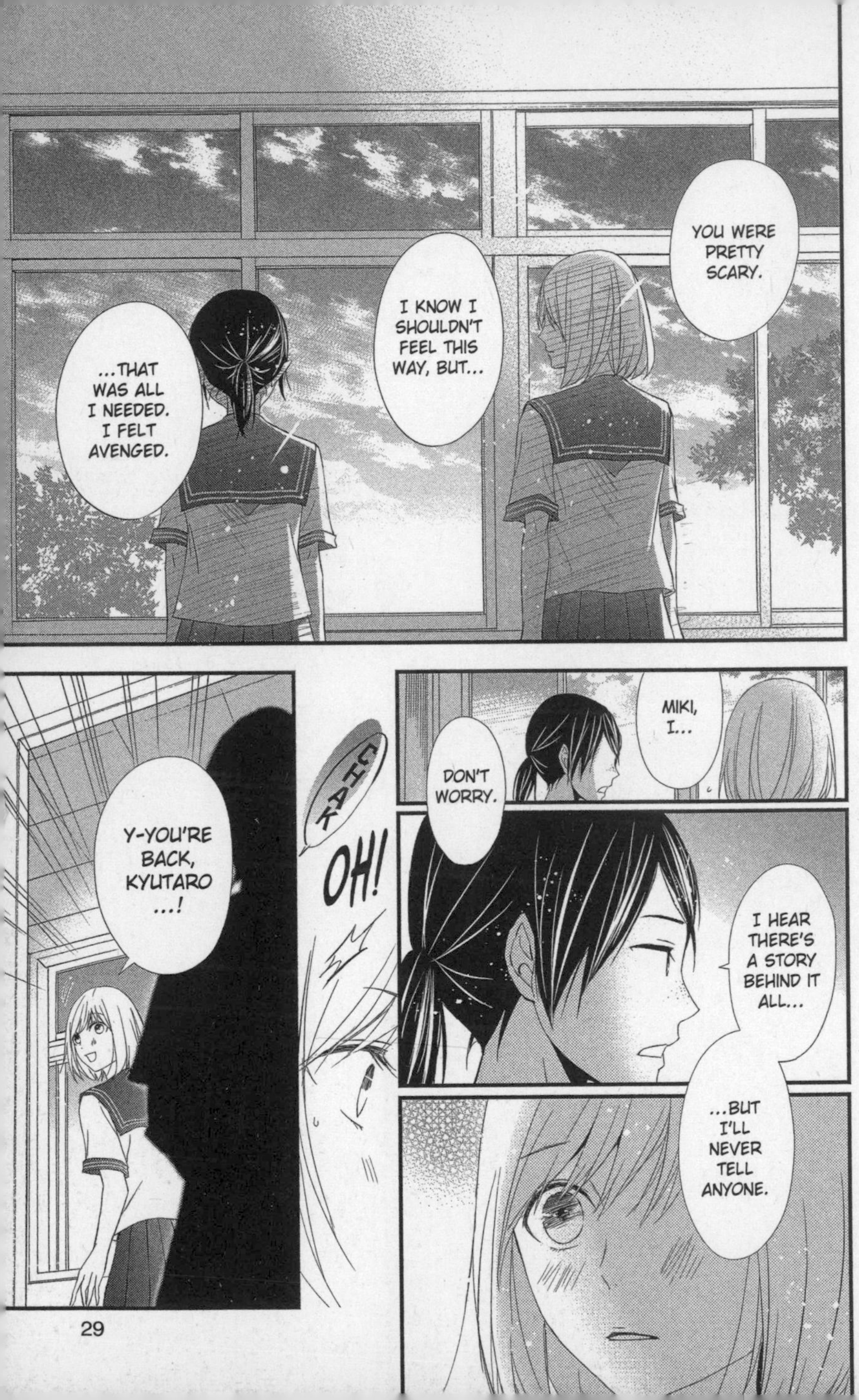
YOU WERE PRETTY SCARY.
I KNOW I SHOULDN'T FEEL THIS WAY, BUT...
...THAT WAS ALL I NEEDED. I FELT AVENGED.
MIKI, I...
DON'T WORRY.
I HEAR THERE'S A STORY BEHIND IT ALL...
...BUT I'LL NEVER TELL ANYONE.
CHAK
OH!
Y-YOU'RE BACK, KYUTARO ...!

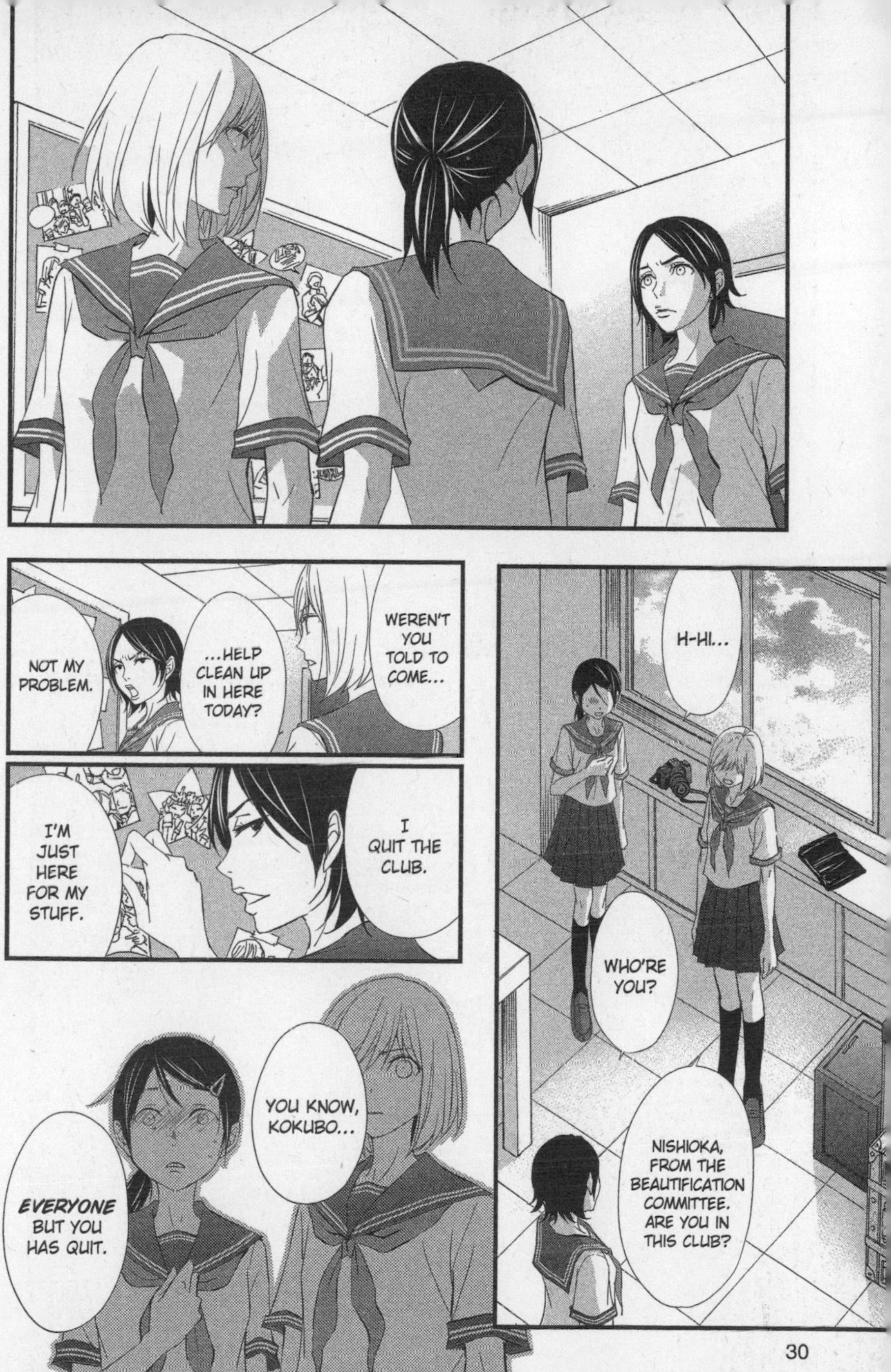
H-HI...
WHO'RE YOU?
NISHIOKA, FROM THE BEAUTIFICATION COMMITTEE. ARE YOU IN THIS CLUB?
WEREN'T YOU TOLD TO COME...
...HELP CLEAN UP IN HERE TODAY?
NOT MY PROBLEM.
I QUIT THE CLUB.
I'M JUST HERE FOR MY STUFF.
YOU KNOW, KOKUBO...
EVERYONE BUT YOU HAS QUIT.

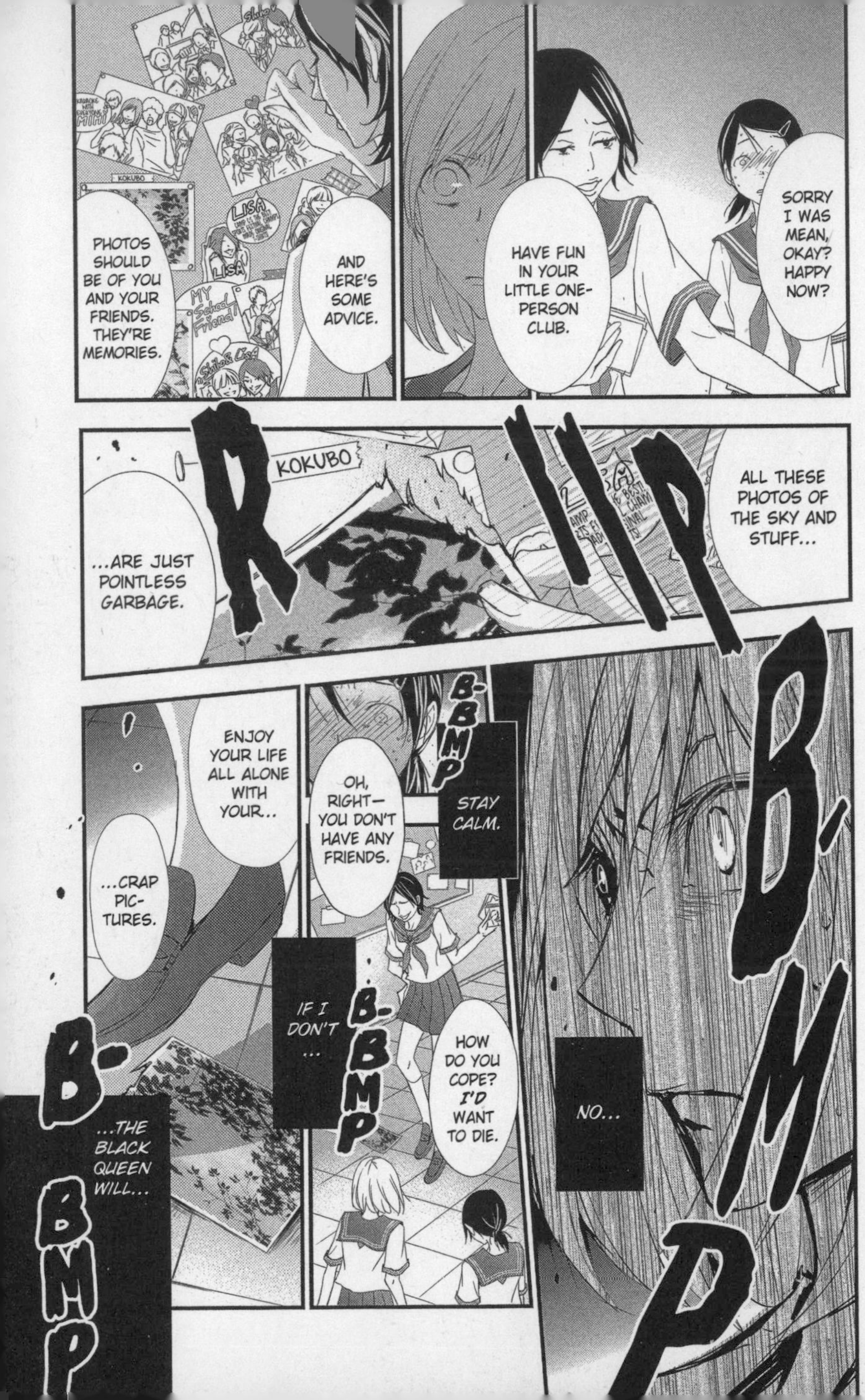
SORRY I WAS MEAN, OKAY? HAPPY NOW?
HAVE FUN IN YOUR LITTLE ONE-PERSON CLUB.
AND HERE'S SOME ADVICE.
KOKUBO
LISA
PHOTOS SHOULD BE OF YOU AND YOUR FRIENDS. THEY'RE MEMORIES.
ALL THESE PHOTOS OF THE SKY AND STUFF...
RIIP
KOKUBO
...ARE JUST POINTLESS GARBAGE.
B-BMP
NO...
B-BMP
STAY CALM.
OH, RIGHT—YOU DON'T HAVE ANY FRIENDS.
IF I DON'T...
B-BMP
HOW DO YOU COPE? I'D WANT TO DIE.
ENJOY YOUR LIFE ALL ALONE WITH YOUR...
...CRAP PICTURES.
B-BMP
...THE BLACK QUEEN WILL...

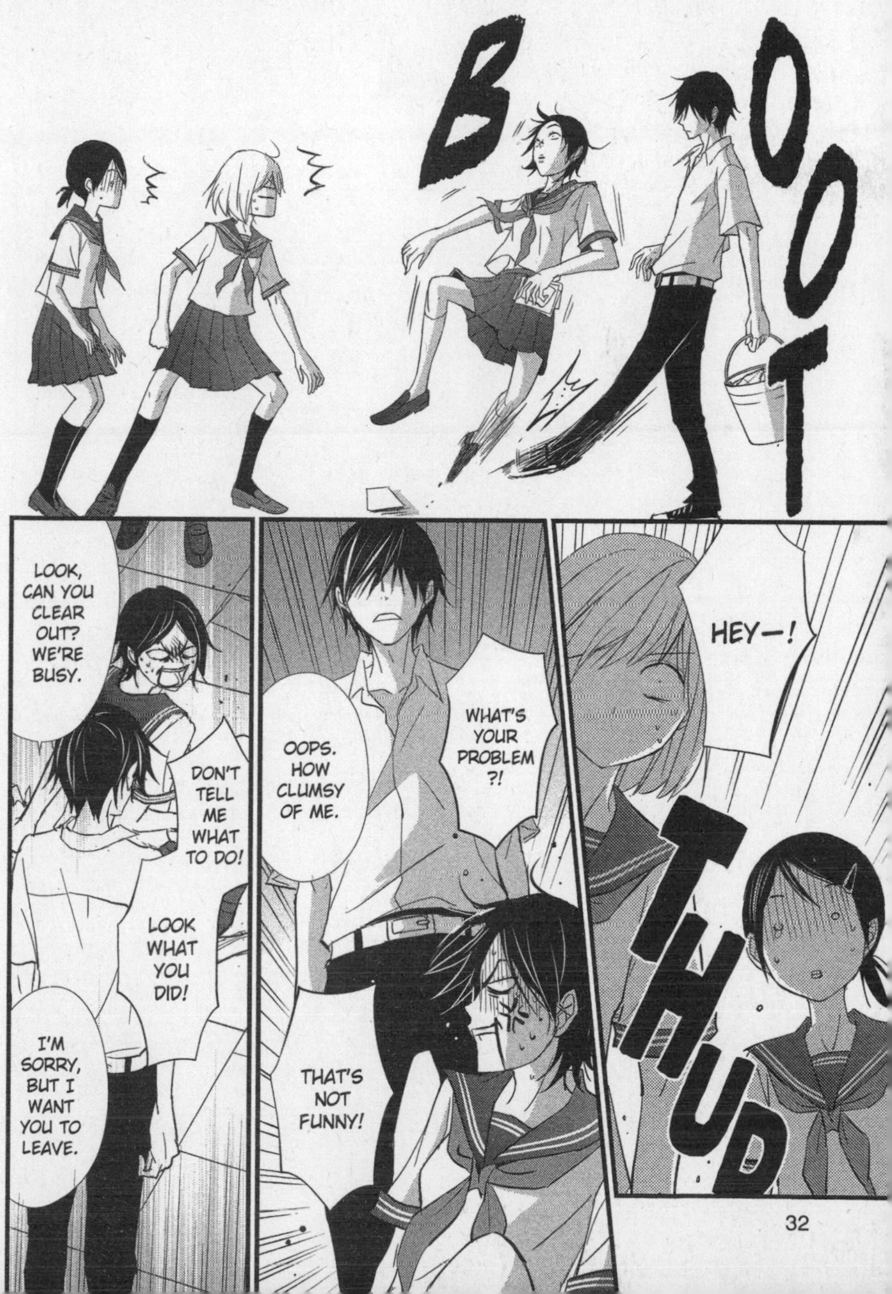
BOOT
HEY—!
THUD
WHAT'S YOUR PROBLEM?!
OOPS. HOW CLUMSY OF ME.
THAT'S NOT FUNNY!
LOOK, CAN YOU CLEAR OUT? WE'RE BUSY.
DON'T TELL ME WHAT TO DO!
LOOK WHAT YOU DID!
I'M SORRY, BUT I WANT YOU TO LEAVE.

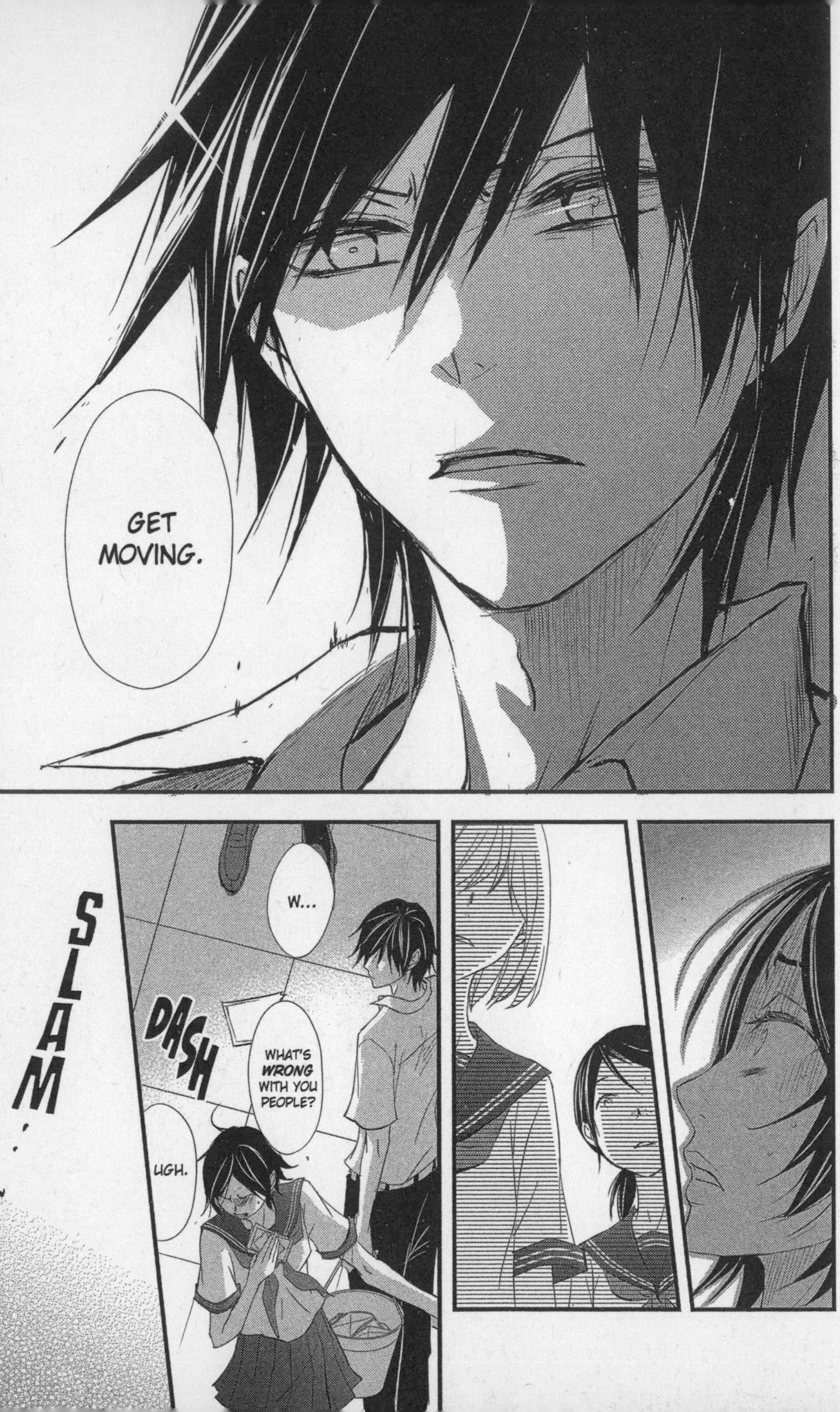
GET MOVING.
W...
WHAT'S *WRONG* WITH YOU PEOPLE?
DASH
UGH.
SLAM

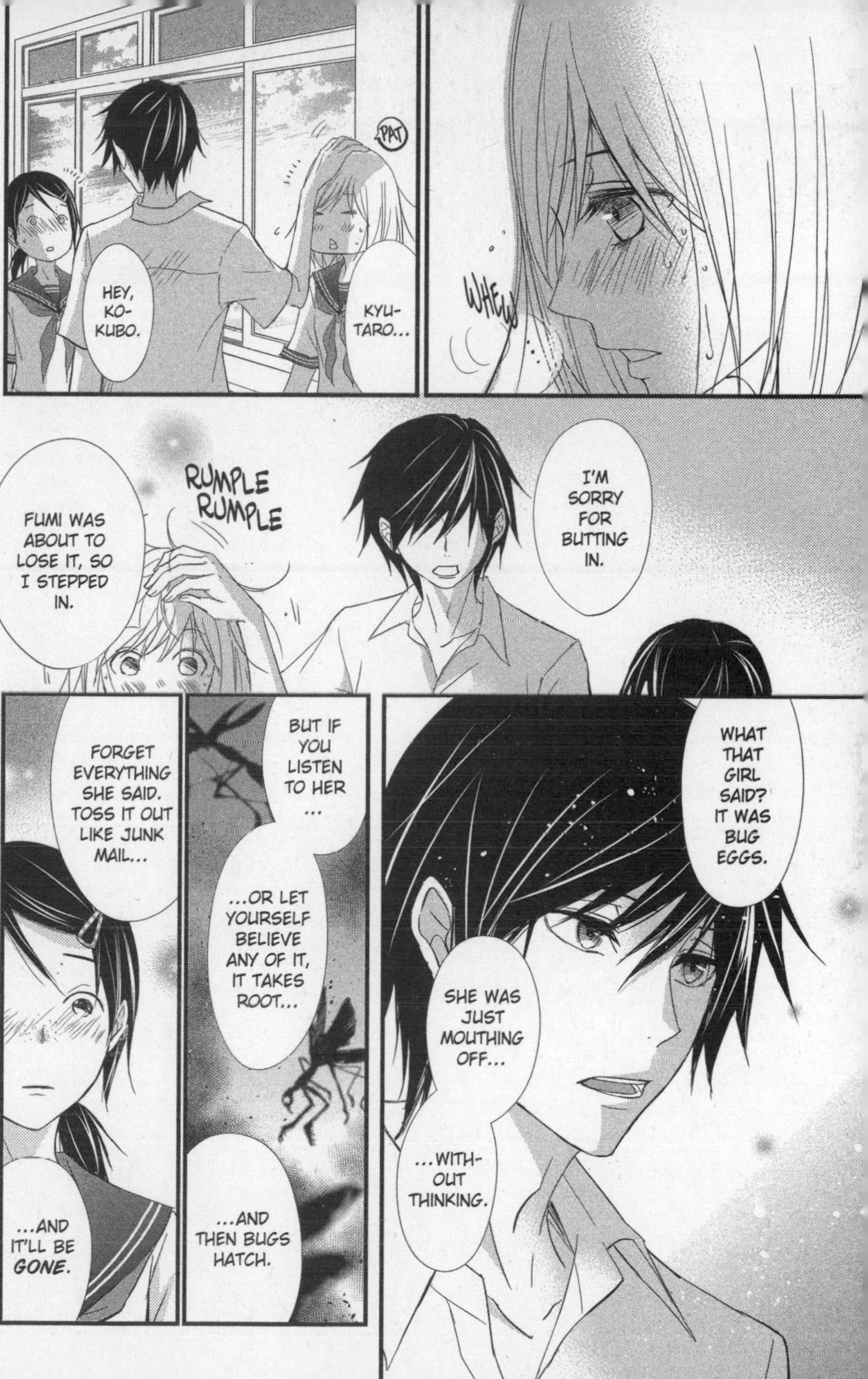
WHEW
PAT
KYU-TARO...
HEY, KO-KUBO.
I'M SORRY FOR BUTTING IN.
RUMPLE RUMPLE
FUMI WAS ABOUT TO LOSE IT, SO I STEPPED IN.
WHAT THAT GIRL SAID? IT WAS BUG EGGS.
SHE WAS JUST MOUTHING OFF...
...WITH-OUT THINKING.
BUT IF YOU LISTEN TO HER...
...OR LET YOURSELF BELIEVE ANY OF IT, IT TAKES ROOT...
...AND THEN BUGS HATCH.
FORGET EVERYTHING SHE SAID. TOSS IT OUT LIKE JUNK MAIL...
...AND IT'LL BE *GONE*.

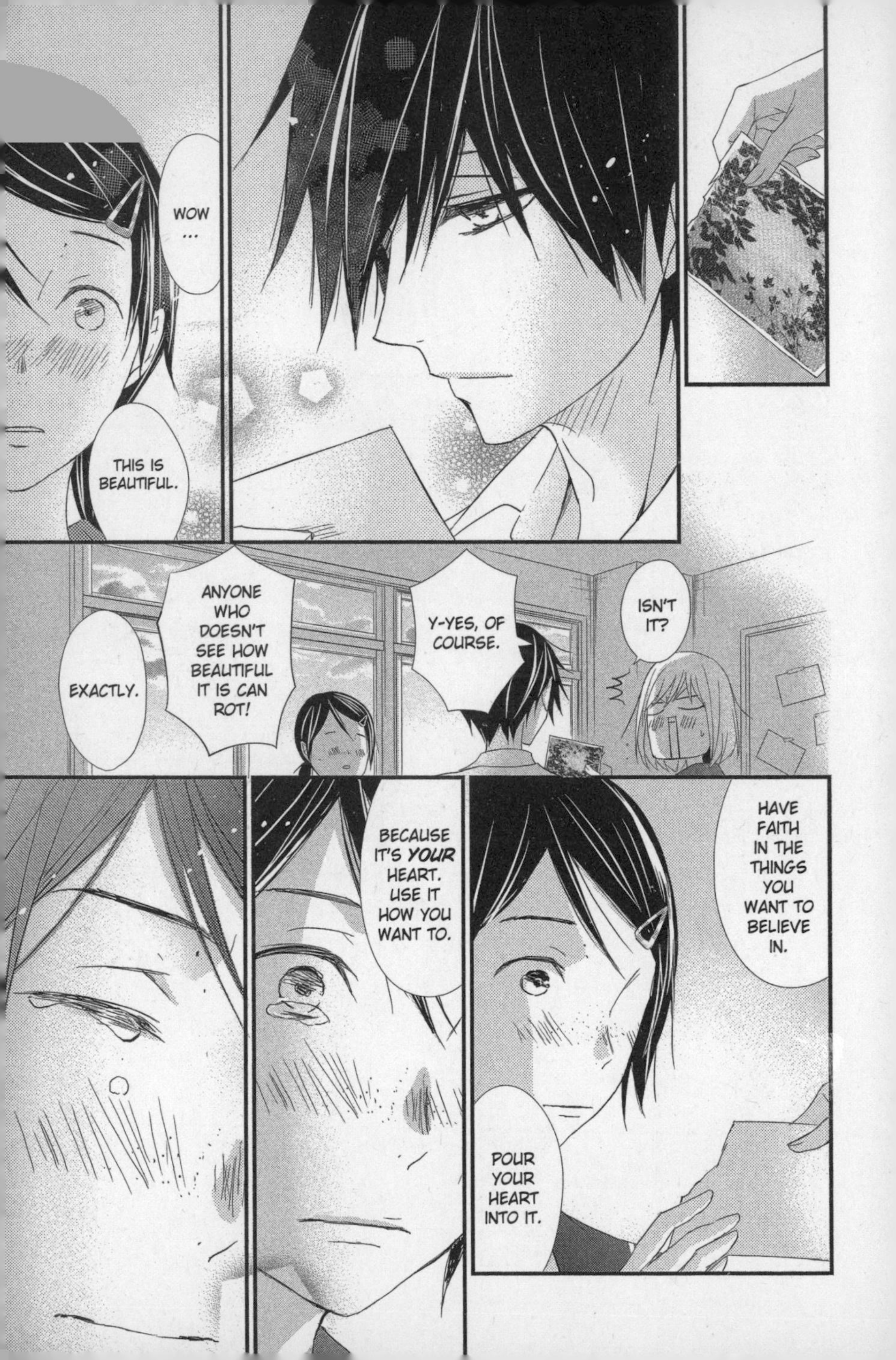
WOW ...
THIS IS BEAUTIFUL.
ISN'T IT?
Y-YES, OF COURSE.
ANYONE WHO DOESN'T SEE HOW BEAUTIFUL IT IS CAN ROT!
EXACTLY.
HAVE FAITH IN THE THINGS YOU WANT TO BELIEVE IN.
POUR YOUR HEART INTO IT.
BECAUSE IT'S *YOUR* HEART. USE IT HOW YOU WANT TO.

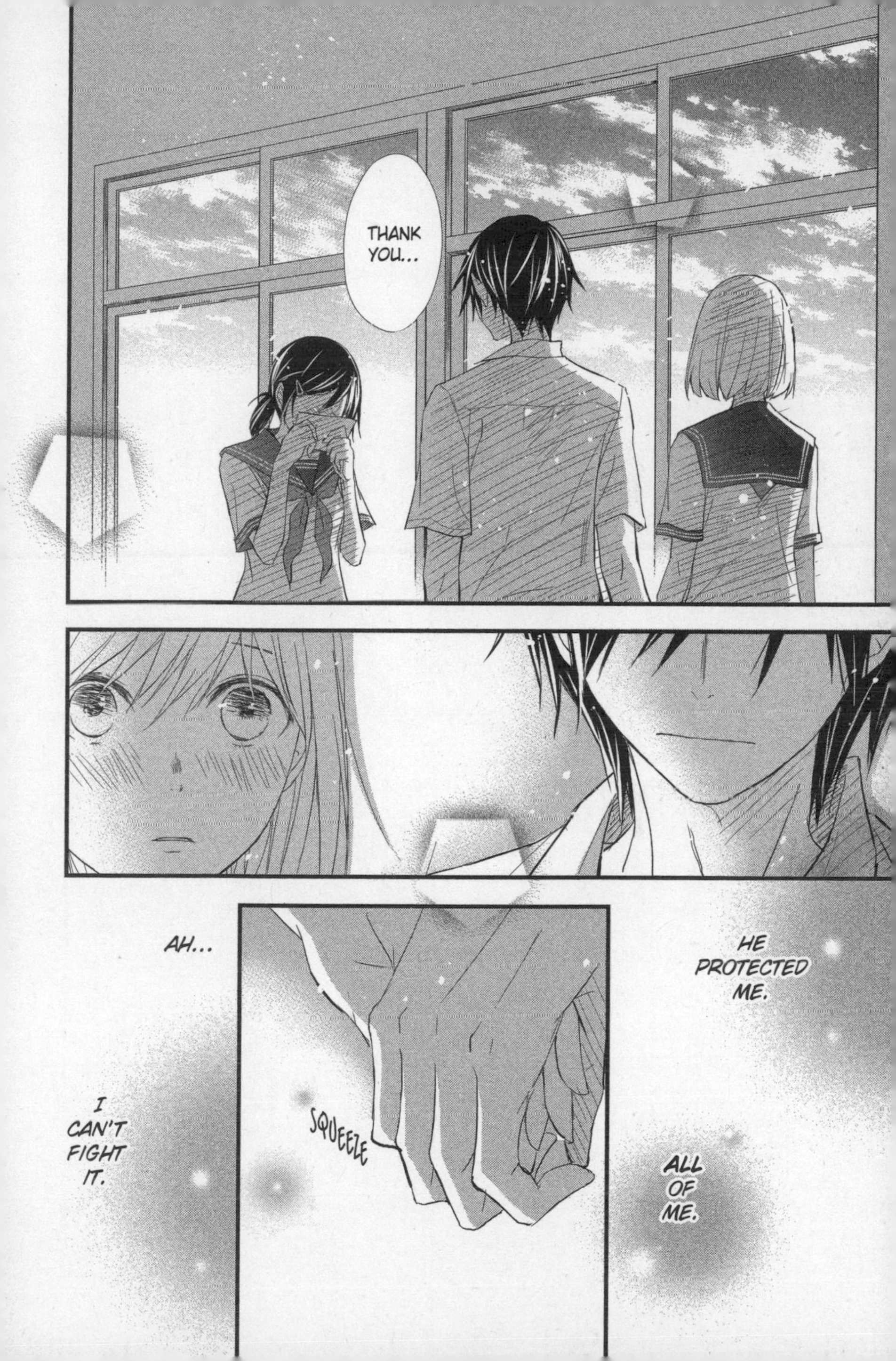
THANK YOU...
HE PROTECTED ME.
AH...
ALL OF ME.
SQUEEZE
I CAN'T FIGHT IT.

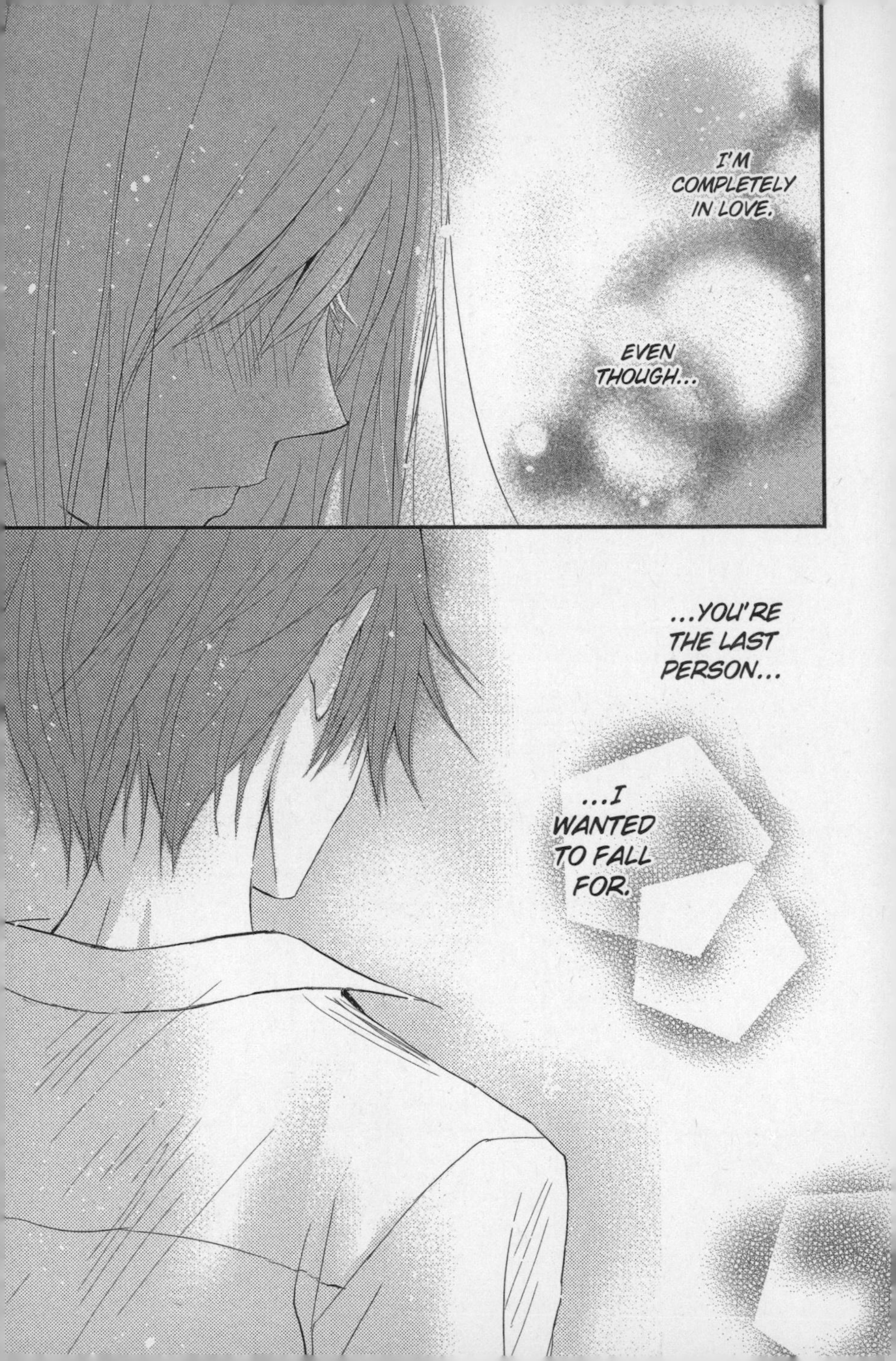
I'M COMPLETELY IN LOVE.
EVEN THOUGH...
...YOU'RE THE LAST PERSON...
...I WANTED TO FALL FOR.

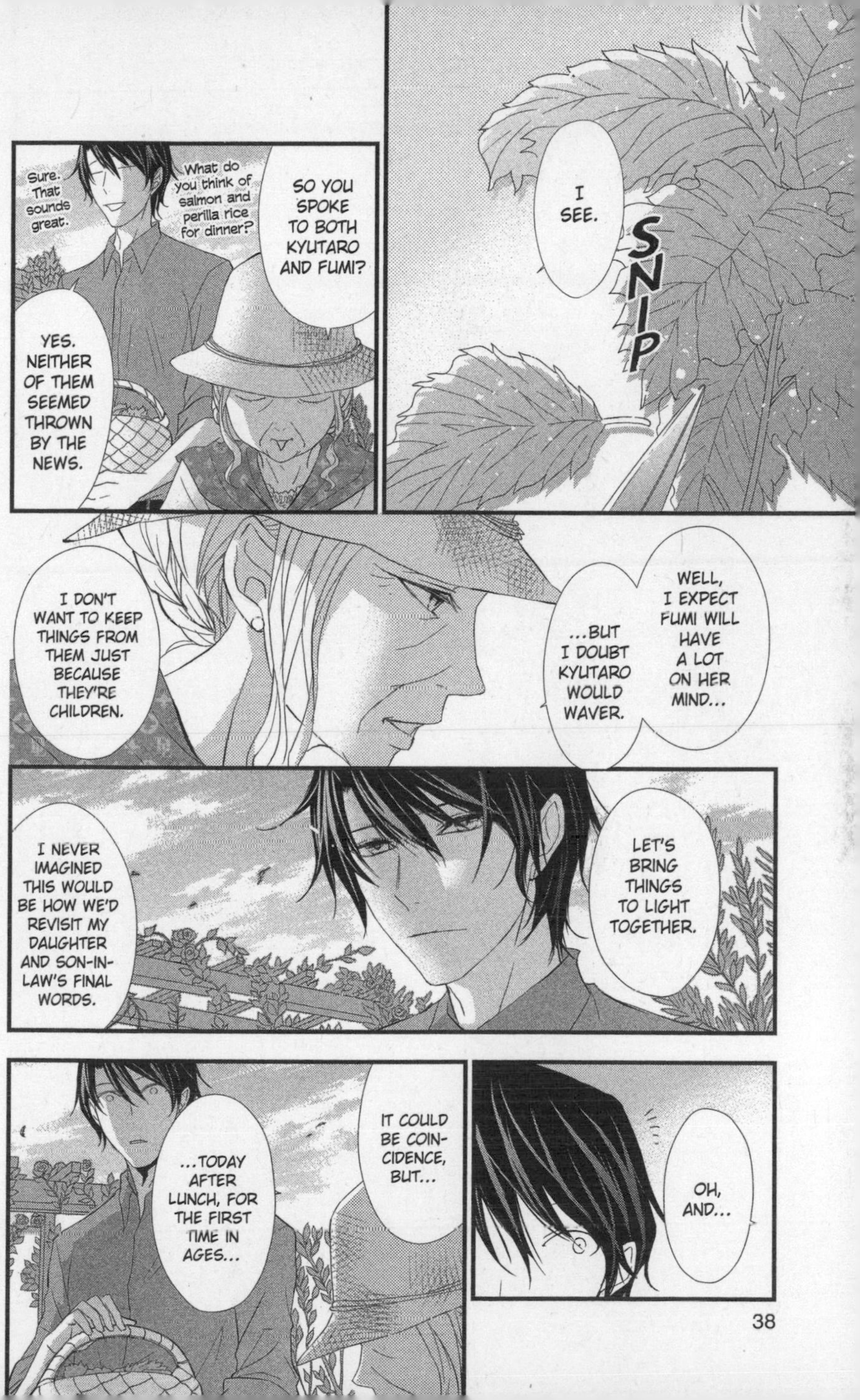
SNIP
I SEE.
SO YOU SPOKE TO BOTH KYUTARO AND FUMI?
What do you think of salmon and perilla rice for dinner?
Sure. That sounds great.
YES. NEITHER OF THEM SEEMED THROWN BY THE NEWS.
WELL, I EXPECT FUMI WILL HAVE A LOT ON HER MIND...
...BUT I DOUBT KYUTARO WOULD WAVER.
I DON'T WANT TO KEEP THINGS FROM THEM JUST BECAUSE THEY'RE CHILDREN.
LET'S BRING THINGS TO LIGHT TOGETHER.
I NEVER IMAGINED THIS WOULD BE HOW WE'D REVISIT MY DAUGHTER AND SON-IN-LAW'S FINAL WORDS.
OH, AND...
IT COULD BE COINCIDENCE, BUT...
...TODAY AFTER LUNCH, FOR THE FIRST TIME IN AGES...

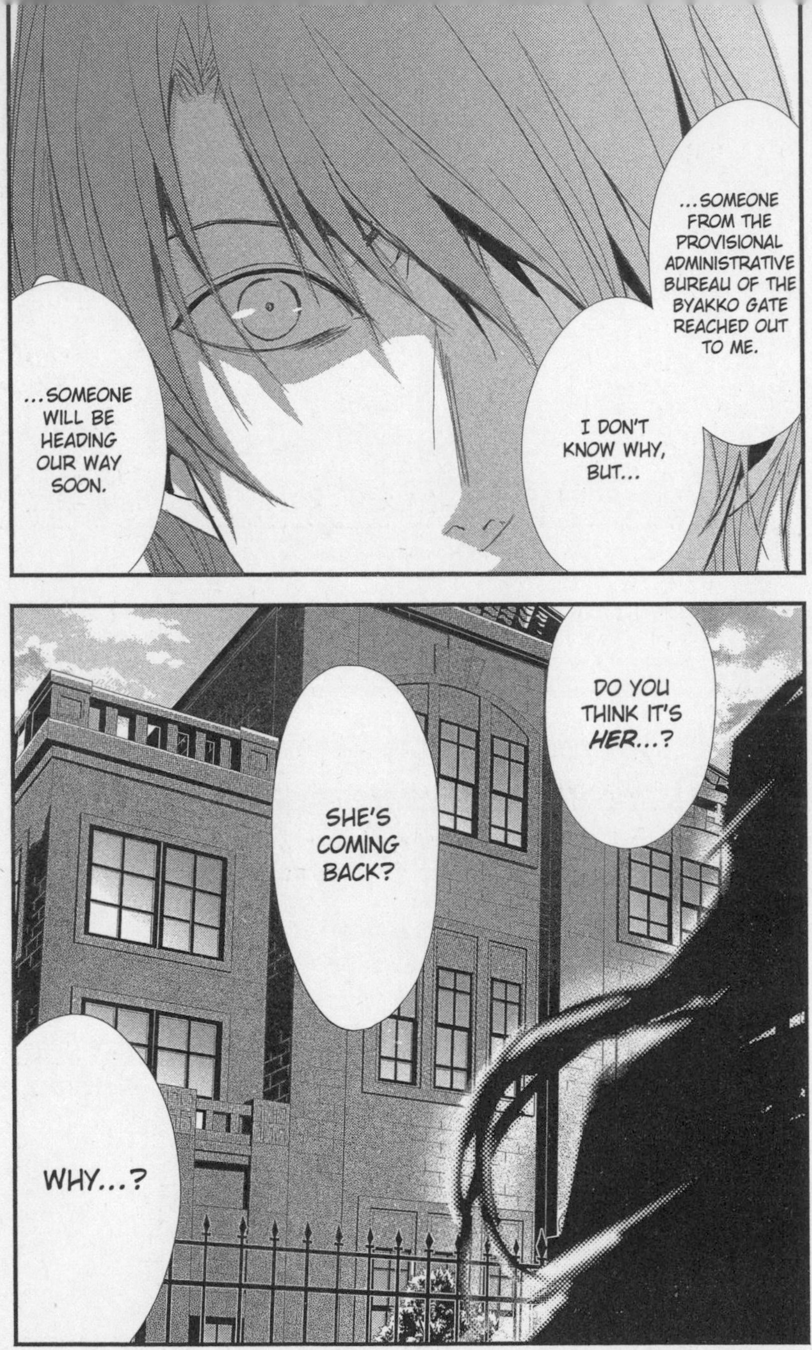
...SOMEONE FROM THE PROVISIONAL ADMINISTRATIVE BUREAU OF THE BYAKKO GATE REACHED OUT TO ME.
I DON'T KNOW WHY, BUT...
...SOMEONE WILL BE HEADING OUR WAY SOON.
DO YOU THINK IT'S *HER*...?
SHE'S COMING BACK?
WHY...?

Send your letters to: ♡

Kyousuke Motomi
c/o Queen's Quality Editor
VIZ Media
P.O. Box 77010
San Francisco, CA 94107

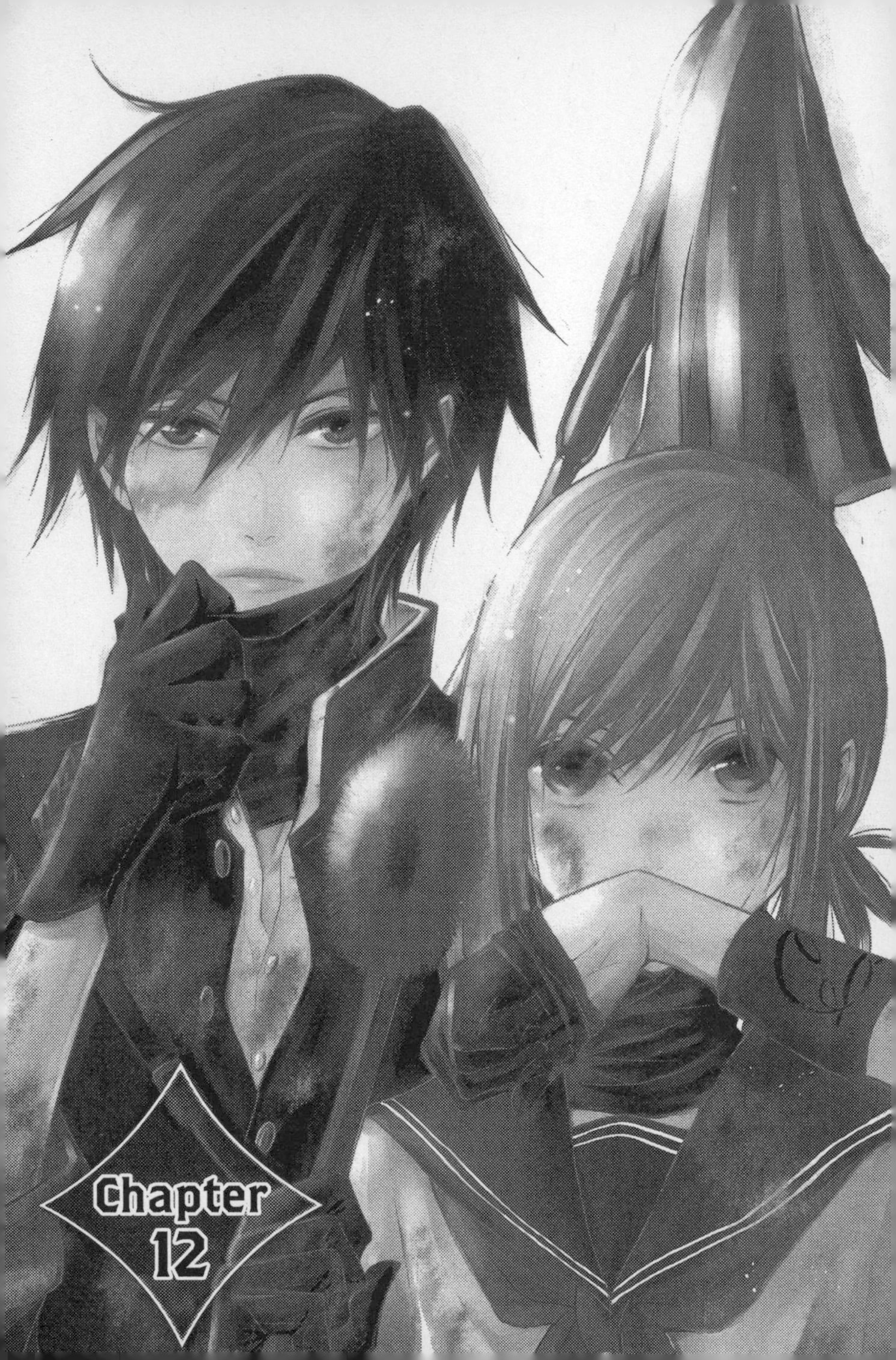
Chapter
12

MONTHLY BETSUCOMI SALE DATE NOTICE ON TWITTER

CHAPTER 12

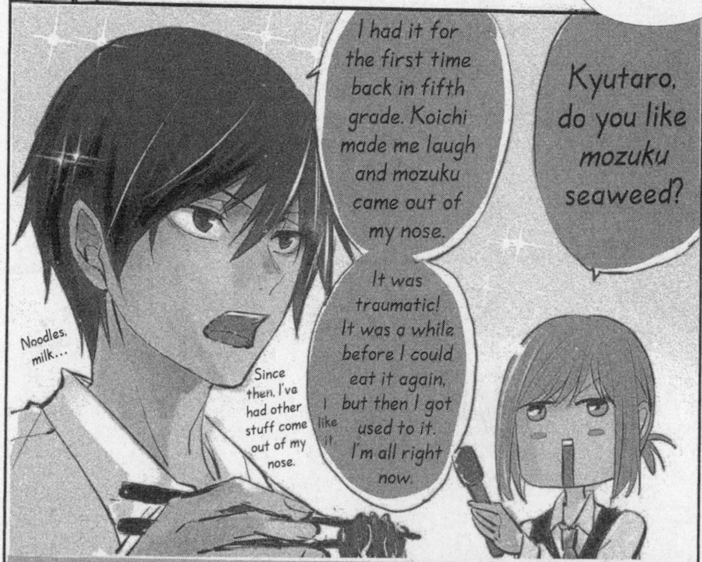
Kyutaro, do you like mozuku seaweed?
I had it for the first time back in fifth grade. Koichi made me laugh and mozuku came out of my nose.
It was traumatic! It was a while before I could eat it again, but then I got used to it. I'm all right now.
I like it.
Since then, I've had other stuff come out of my nose.
Noodles, milk…

↑ Based on the author's real-life experiences.
(Thanks to my dad.)

WHAT'S UP IN *QUEEN'S QUALITY* THIS MONTH?

(1) THE MORE SURREAL AN URBAN LEGEND IS, THE SCARIER IT SOUNDS.
(2) KOICHI'S SHIRT RUINS EVERYTHING AGAIN.
(3) NO OTHER MANGA THIS MONTH WILL PUSH *MOZUKU* SO HARD!

WE'LL HAVE A LOT MORE DARK SCENES IN THIS CHAPTER!

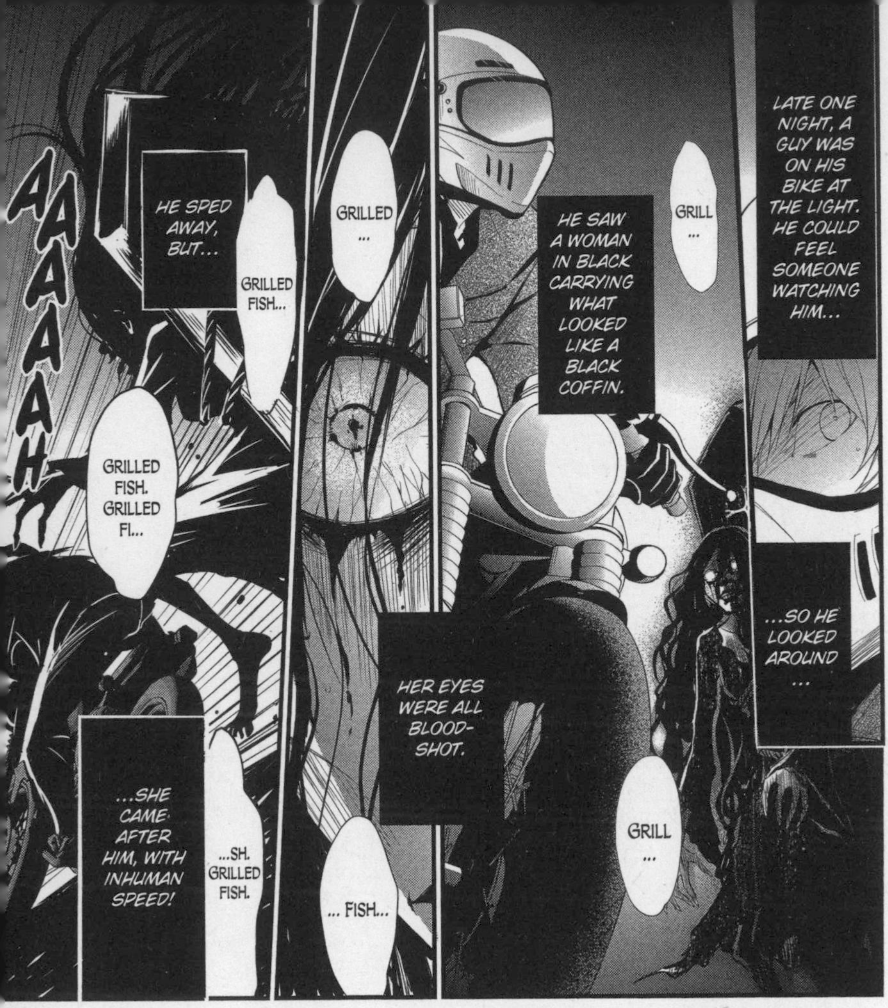
LATE ONE NIGHT, A GUY WAS ON HIS BIKE AT THE LIGHT. HE COULD FEEL SOMEONE WATCHING HIM...
...SO HE LOOKED AROUND...
GRILL...
HE SAW A WOMAN IN BLACK CARRYING WHAT LOOKED LIKE A BLACK COFFIN.
GRILL...
GRILLED...
HER EYES WERE ALL BLOOD-SHOT.
... FISH...
HE SPED AWAY, BUT...
GRILLED FISH...
GRILLED FISH. GRILLED FI...
AAAAAAH!
...SH. GRILLED FISH.
...SHE CAME AFTER HIM, WITH INHUMAN SPEED!

Chapter 11 was all about window cleaning, huh?
I cleaned my windows before starting in on that part. Washing your windows on a sunny day is so satisfying! I bought a pretty professional-looking squeegee and window washer and justified them to myself as research material for chapter 11. They made the chore a breeze. I could wash the windows and frames, then squeegee them dry in a jiffy! It was neat—a little like fighting with two swords.
Highly recommended!

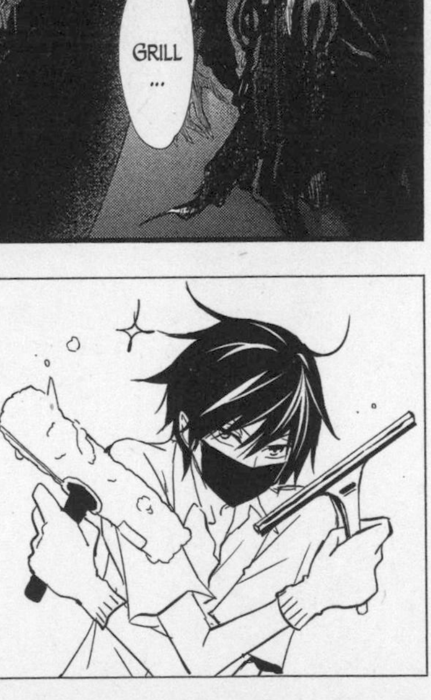

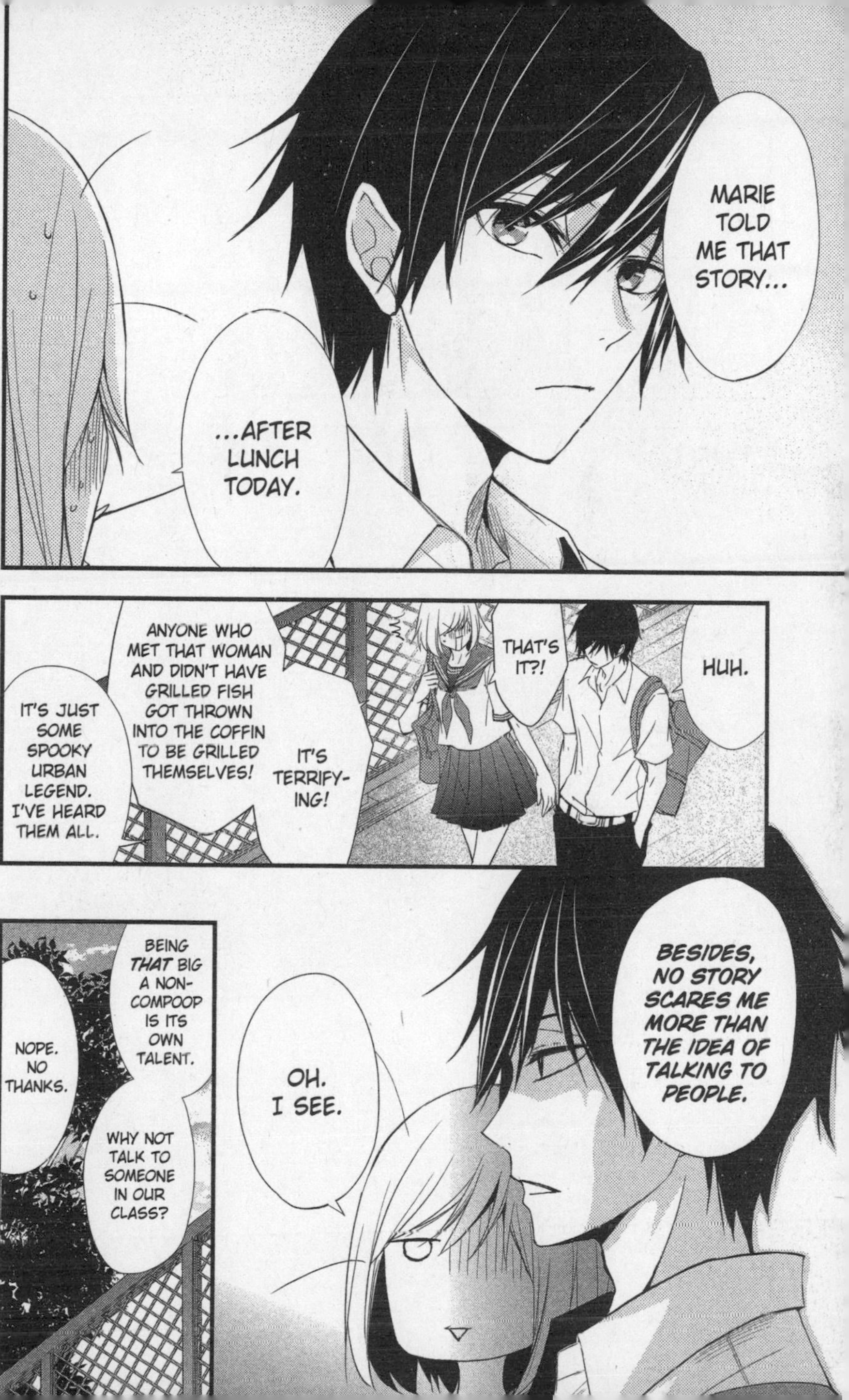
MARIE TOLD ME THAT STORY...
...AFTER LUNCH TODAY.
HUH.
THAT'S IT?!
ANYONE WHO MET THAT WOMAN AND DIDN'T HAVE GRILLED FISH GOT THROWN INTO THE COFFIN TO BE GRILLED THEMSELVES!
IT'S TERRIFY-ING!
IT'S JUST SOME SPOOKY URBAN LEGEND. I'VE HEARD THEM ALL.
BESIDES, NO STORY SCARES ME MORE THAN THE IDEA OF TALKING TO PEOPLE.
OH. I SEE.
BEING *THAT* BIG A NON-COMPOOP IS ITS OWN TALENT.
WHY NOT TALK TO SOMEONE IN OUR CLASS?
NOPE. NO THANKS.

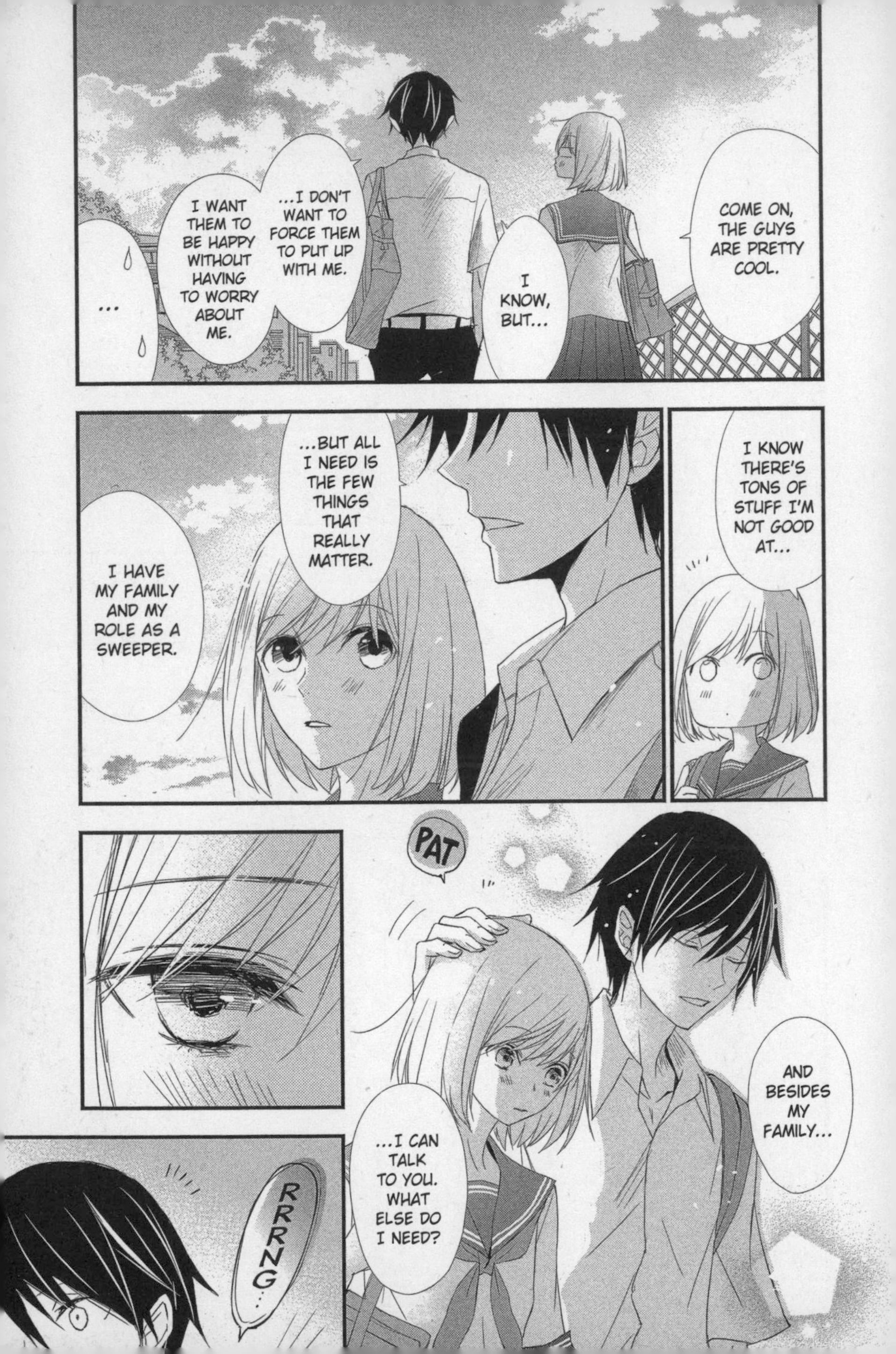
COME ON, THE GUYS ARE PRETTY COOL.
I KNOW, BUT...
...I DON'T WANT TO FORCE THEM TO PUT UP WITH ME.
I WANT THEM TO BE HAPPY WITHOUT HAVING TO WORRY ABOUT ME.
...
I KNOW THERE'S TONS OF STUFF I'M NOT GOOD AT...
...BUT ALL I NEED IS THE FEW THINGS THAT REALLY MATTER.
I HAVE MY FAMILY AND MY ROLE AS A SWEEPER.
PAT
AND BESIDES MY FAMILY...
...I CAN TALK TO YOU. WHAT ELSE DO I NEED?
RRRNG...

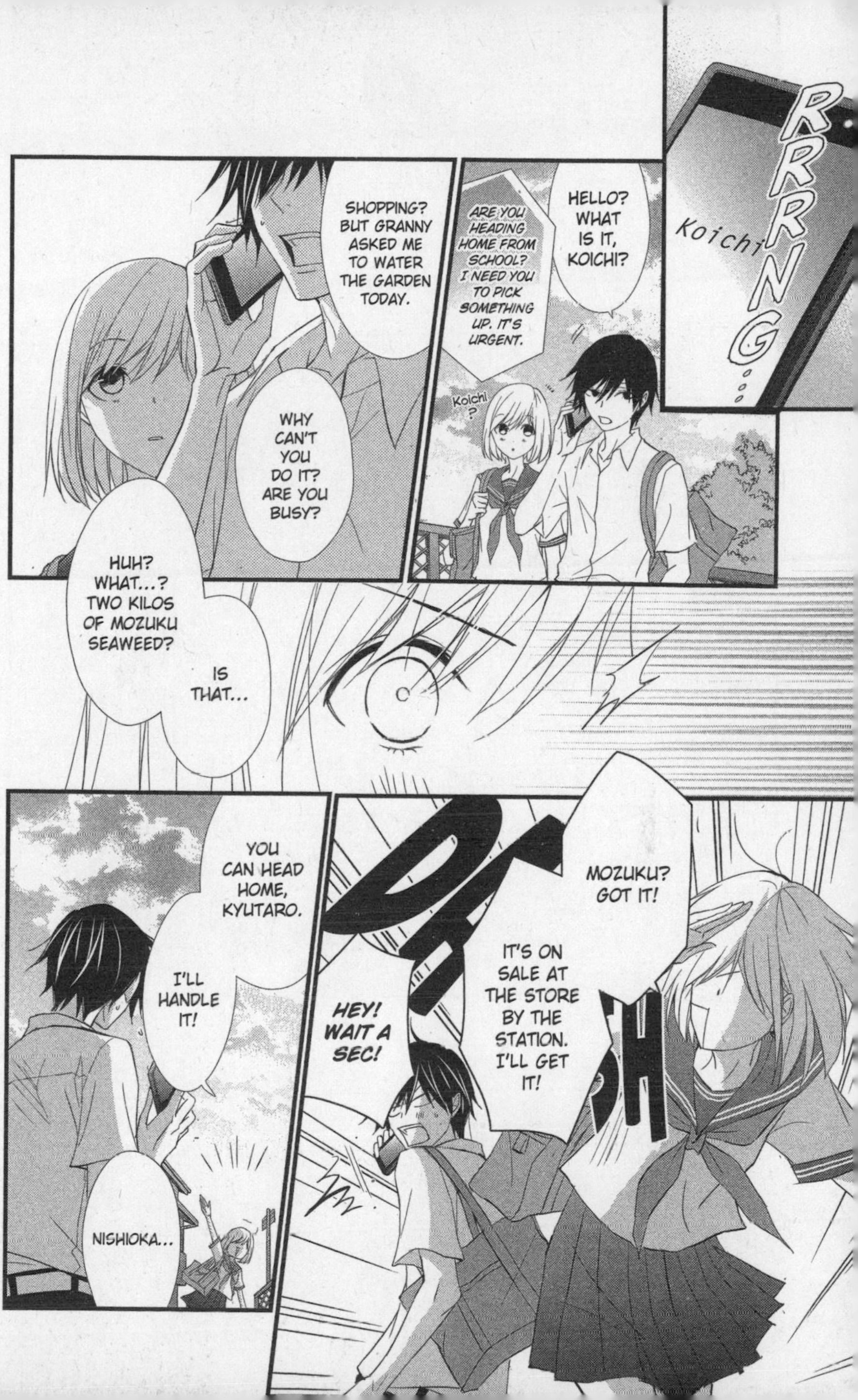

RRRNG...
Koichi
HELLO? WHAT IS IT, KOICHI?
ARE YOU HEADING HOME FROM SCHOOL? I NEED YOU TO PICK SOMETHING UP. IT'S URGENT.
Koichi?
SHOPPING? BUT GRANNY ASKED ME TO WATER THE GARDEN TODAY.
WHY CAN'T YOU DO IT? ARE YOU BUSY?
HUH? WHAT...? TWO KILOS OF MOZUKU SEAWEED?
IS THAT...
DASH
MOZUKU? GOT IT!
IT'S ON SALE AT THE STORE BY THE STATION. I'LL GET IT!
HEY! WAIT A SEC!
YOU CAN HEAD HOME, KYUTARO.
I'LL HANDLE IT!
NISHIOKA...

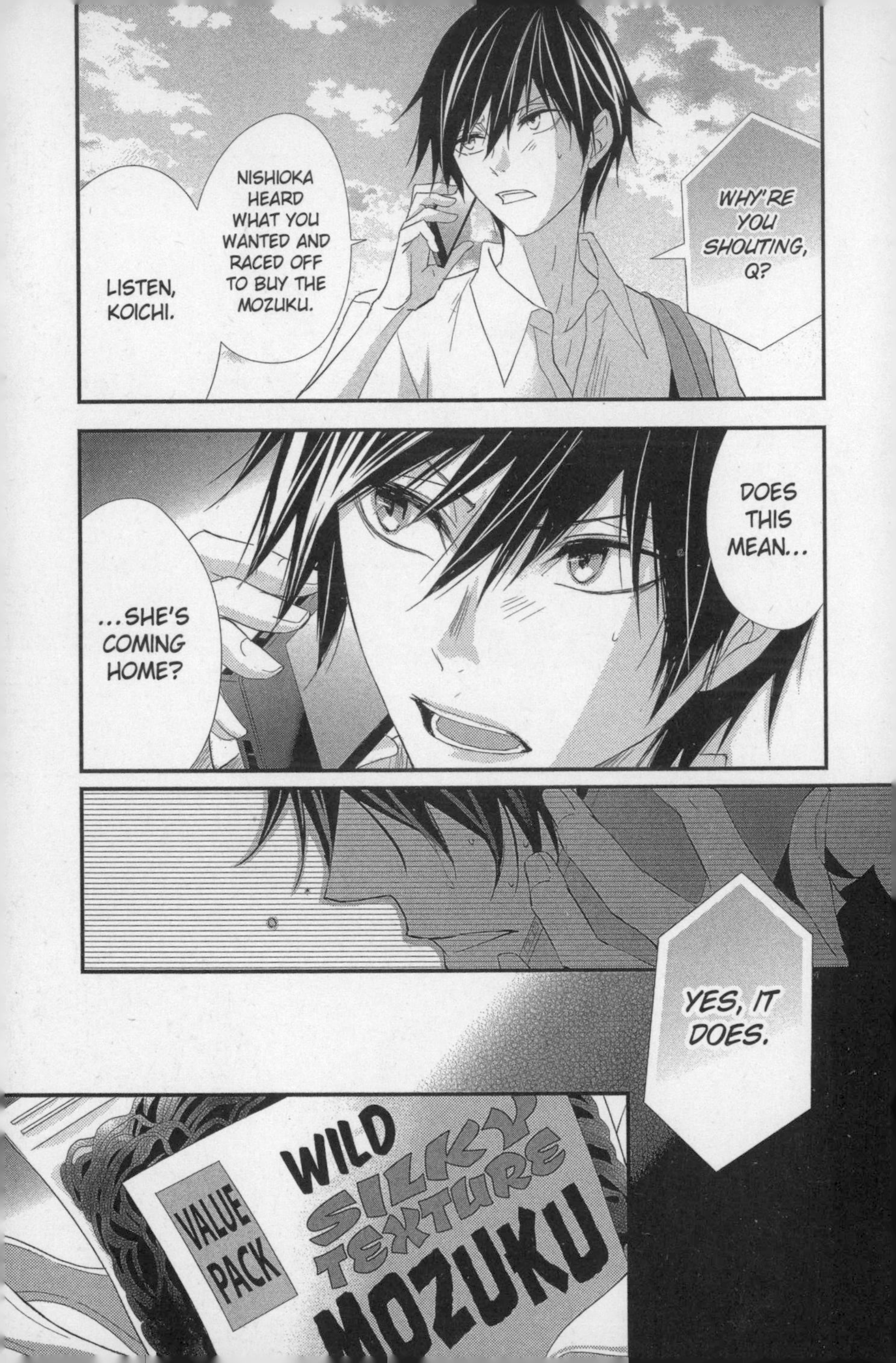
WHY'RE YOU SHOUTING, Q?
NISHIOKA HEARD WHAT YOU WANTED AND RACED OFF TO BUY THE MOZUKU.
LISTEN, KOICHI.
DOES THIS MEAN...
...SHE'S COMING HOME?
YES, IT DOES.
VALUE PACK
WILD SILKY TEXTURE MOZUKU

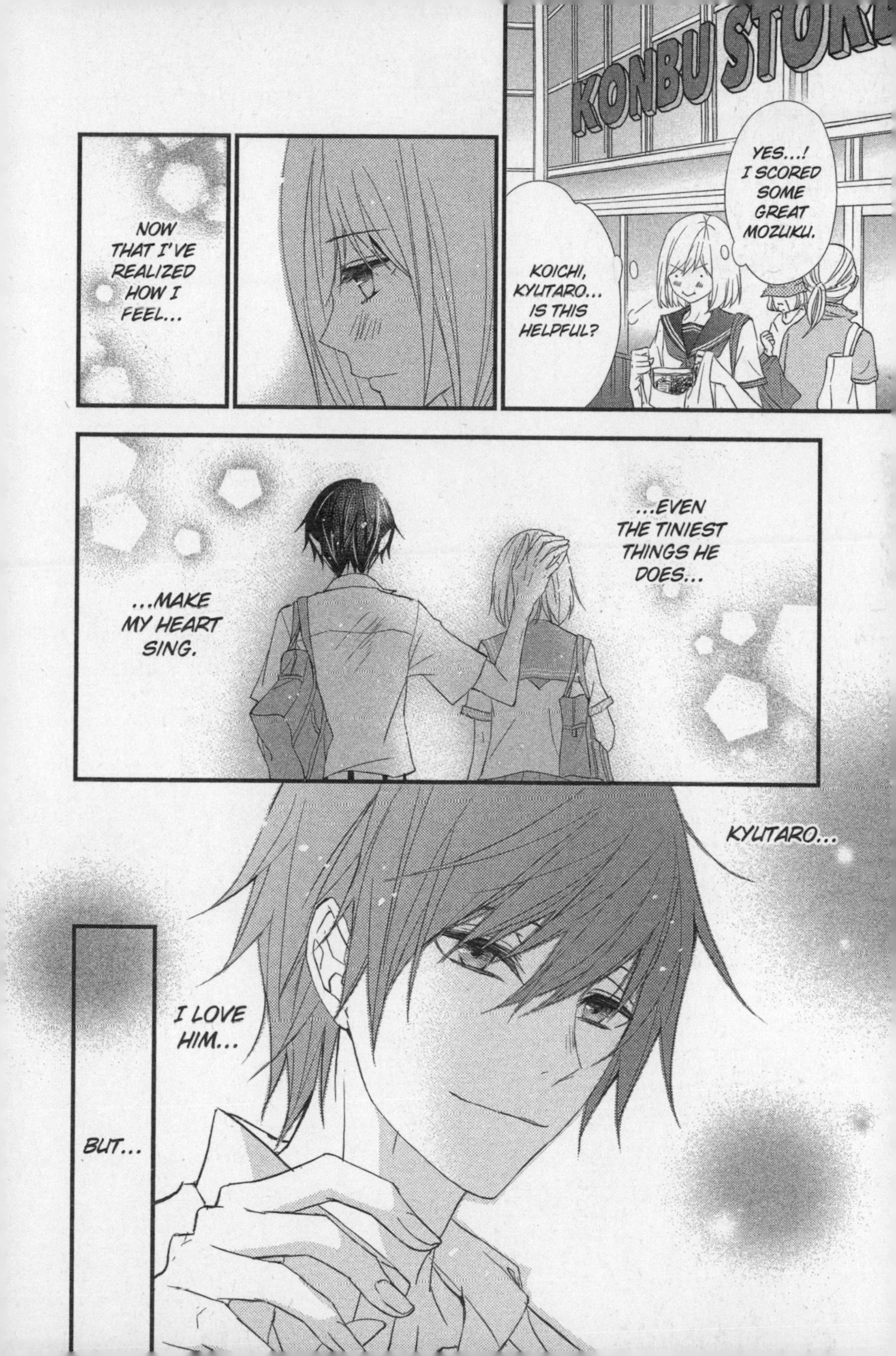
KONBU STOR
YES...! I SCORED SOME GREAT MOZUKU.
KOICHI, KYUTARO... IS THIS HELPFUL?
NOW THAT I'VE REALIZED HOW I FEEL...
...EVEN THE TINIEST THINGS HE DOES...
...MAKE MY HEART SING.
KYUTARO...
I LOVE HIM...
BUT...

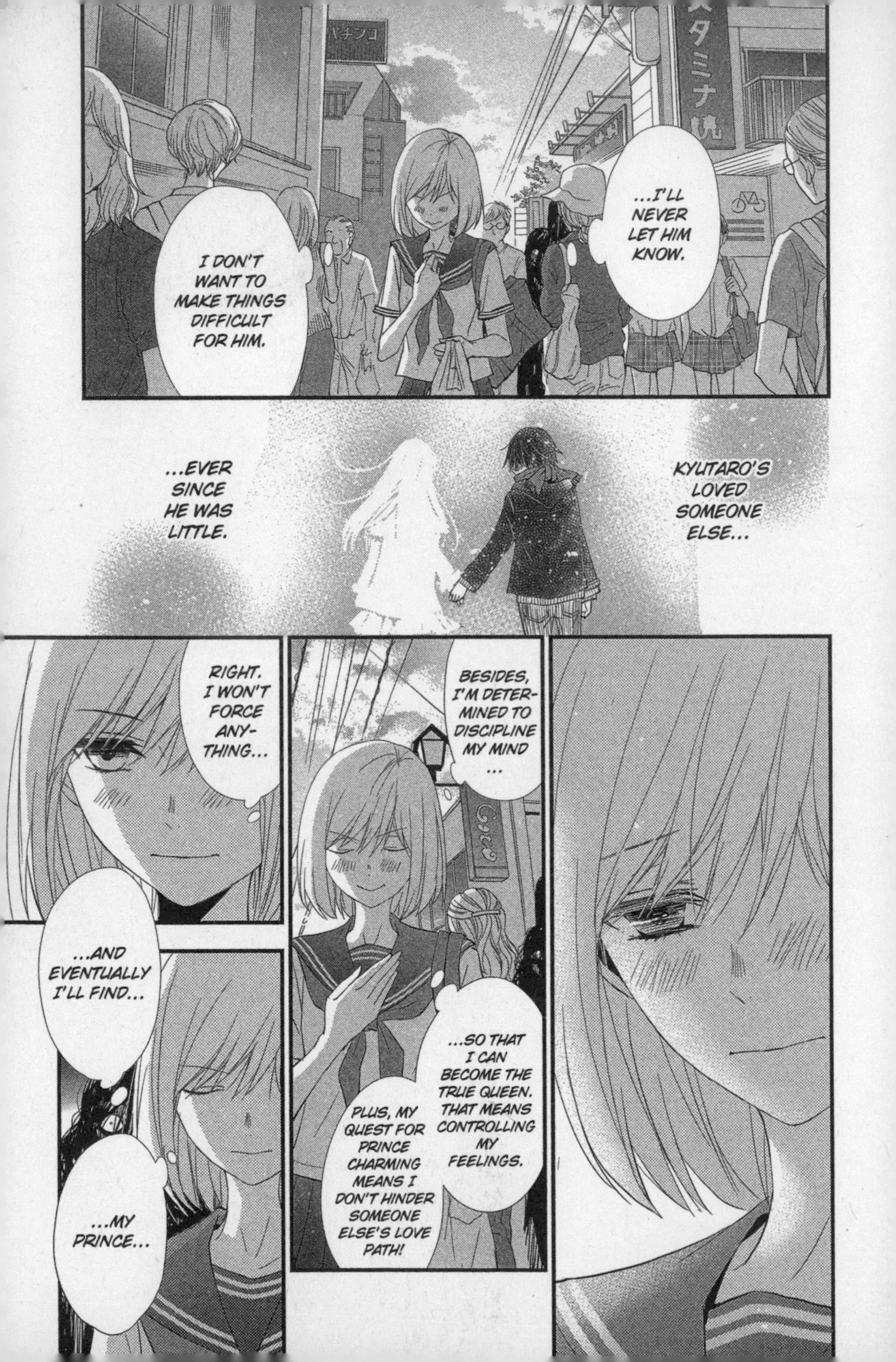
...I'LL NEVER LET HIM KNOW.
I DON'T WANT TO MAKE THINGS DIFFICULT FOR HIM.
KYUTARO'S LOVED SOMEONE ELSE...
...EVER SINCE HE WAS LITTLE.
BESIDES, I'M DETERMINED TO DISCIPLINE MY MIND...
...SO THAT I CAN BECOME THE TRUE QUEEN. THAT MEANS CONTROLLING MY FEELINGS.
PLUS, MY QUEST FOR PRINCE CHARMING MEANS I DON'T HINDER SOMEONE ELSE'S LOVE PATH!
RIGHT. I WON'T FORCE ANYTHING...
...AND EVENTUALLY I'LL FIND...
...MY PRINCE...

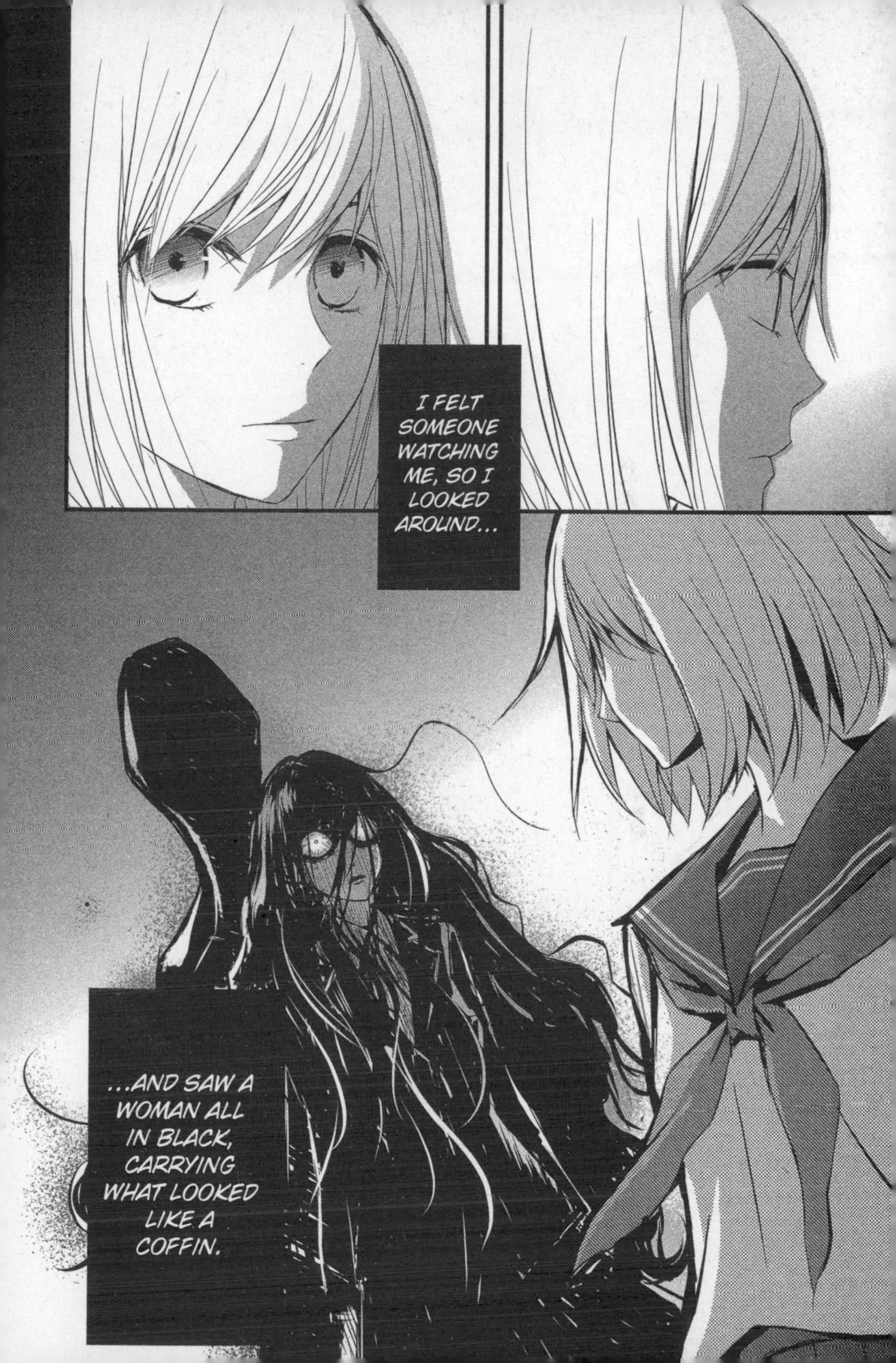
I FELT SOMEONE WATCHING ME, SO I LOOKED AROUND...
...AND SAW A WOMAN ALL IN BLACK, CARRYING WHAT LOOKED LIKE A COFFIN.

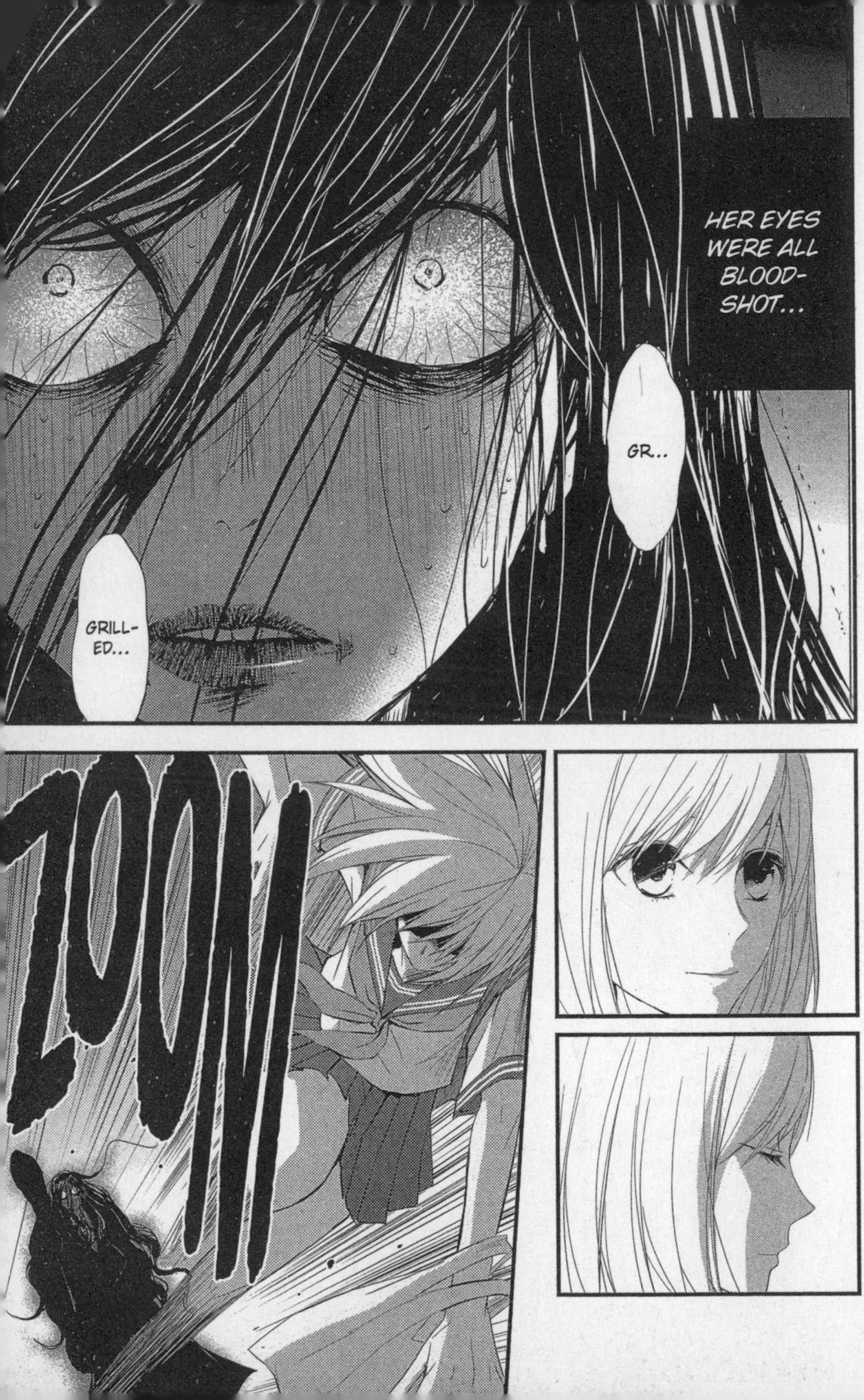
HER EYES WERE ALL BLOOD-SHOT...
GR...
GRILL-ED...
ZOOM

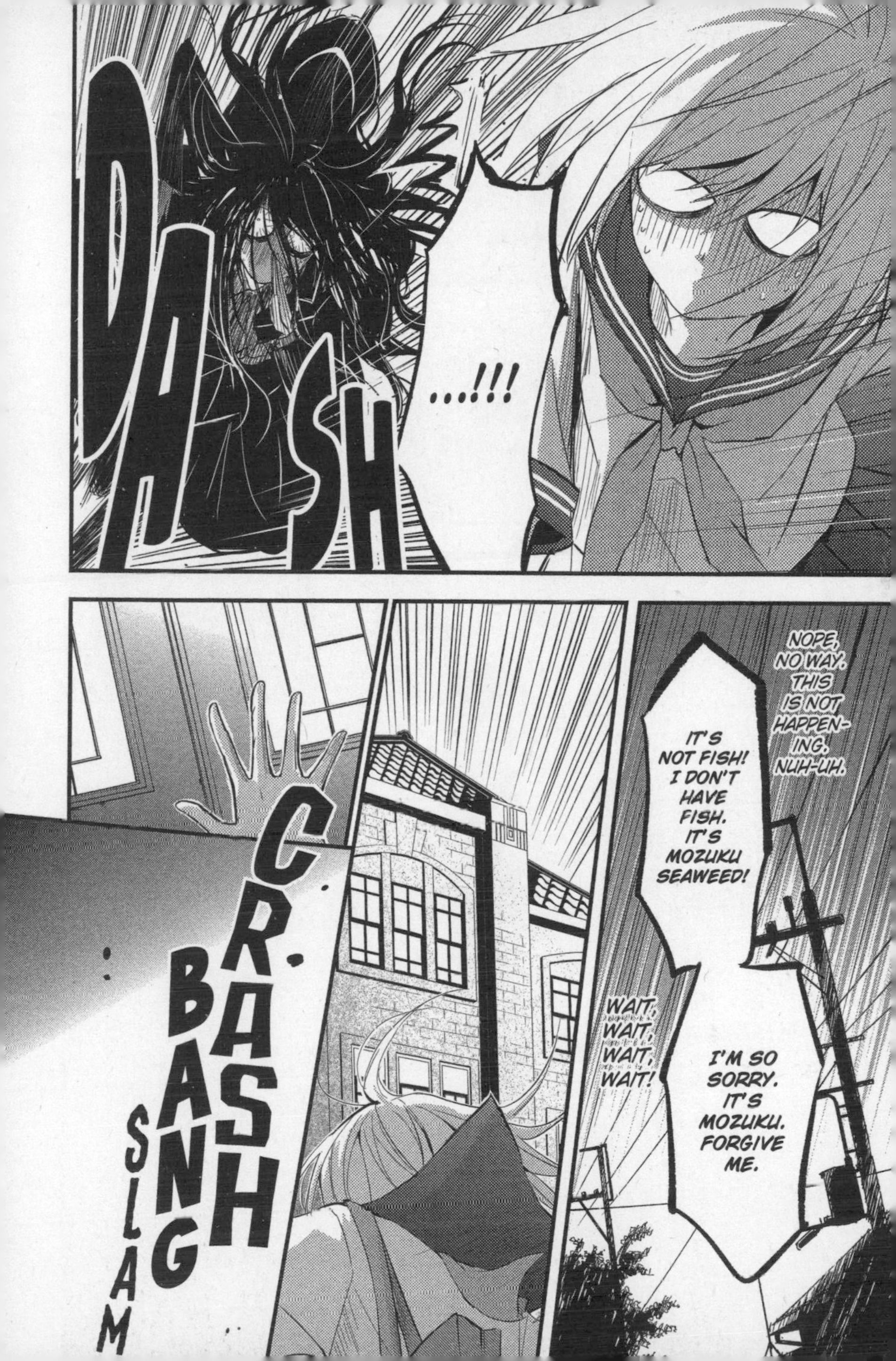
...!!!
DASH
NOPE, NO WAY. THIS IS NOT HAPPEN-ING. NUH-UH.
IT'S NOT FISH! I DON'T HAVE FISH. IT'S MOZUKU SEAWEED!
I'M SO SORRY. IT'S MOZUKU. FORGIVE ME.
WAIT, WAIT, WAIT, WAIT!
CRASH
BASH
BANG
SLAM

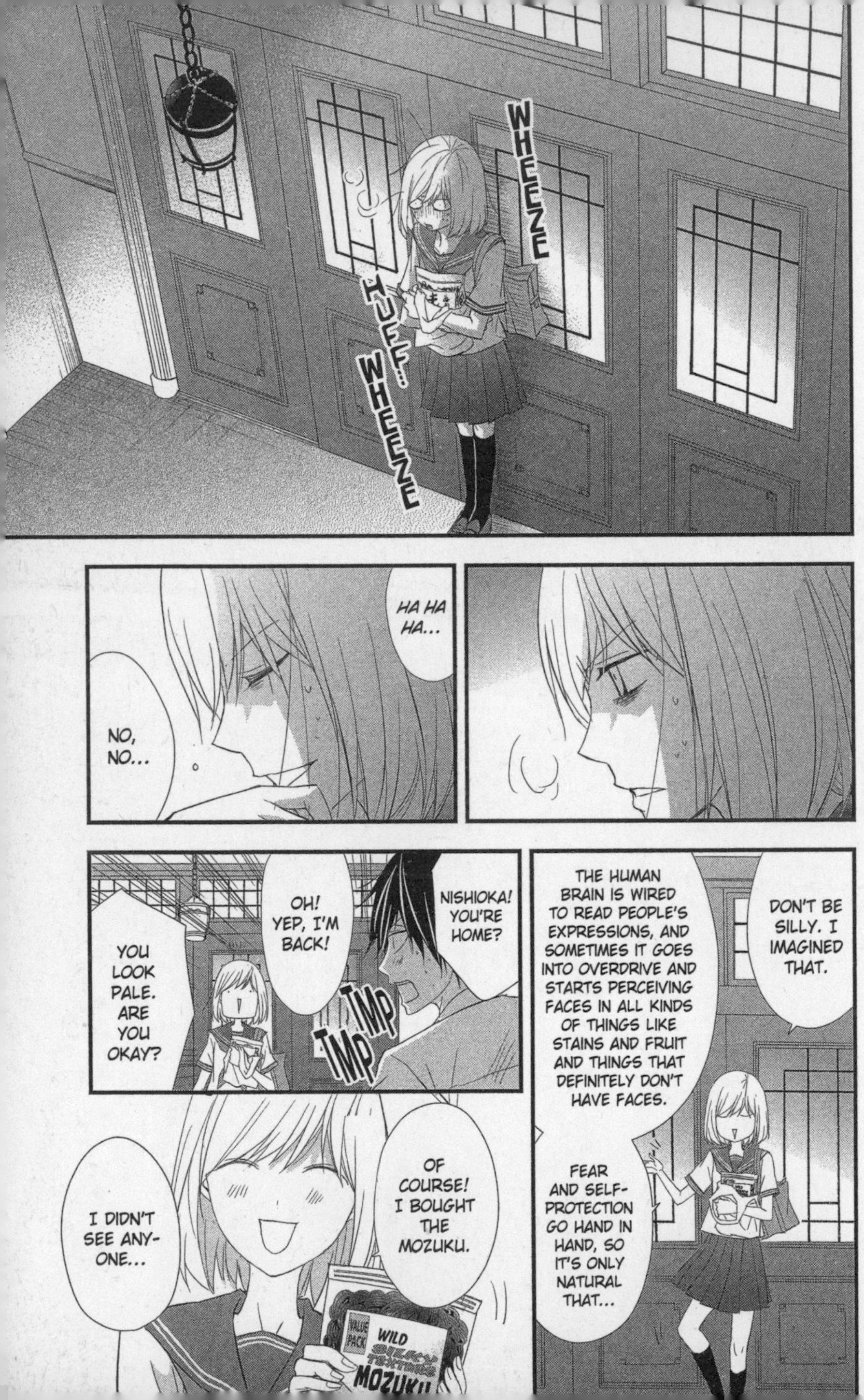
WHEEZE
HUFF...
WHEEZE
HA HA HA...
NO, NO...
DON'T BE SILLY. I IMAGINED THAT.
THE HUMAN BRAIN IS WIRED TO READ PEOPLE'S EXPRESSIONS, AND SOMETIMES IT GOES INTO OVERDRIVE AND STARTS PERCEIVING FACES IN ALL KINDS OF THINGS LIKE STAINS AND FRUIT AND THINGS THAT DEFINITELY DON'T HAVE FACES.
FEAR AND SELF-PROTECTION GO HAND IN HAND, SO IT'S ONLY NATURAL THAT...
NISHIOKA! YOU'RE HOME?
OH! YEP, I'M BACK!
TMP TMP
YOU LOOK PALE. ARE YOU OKAY?
OF COURSE! I BOUGHT THE MOZUKU.
I DIDN'T SEE ANYONE...
VALUE PACK
WILD
MOZUKU!!

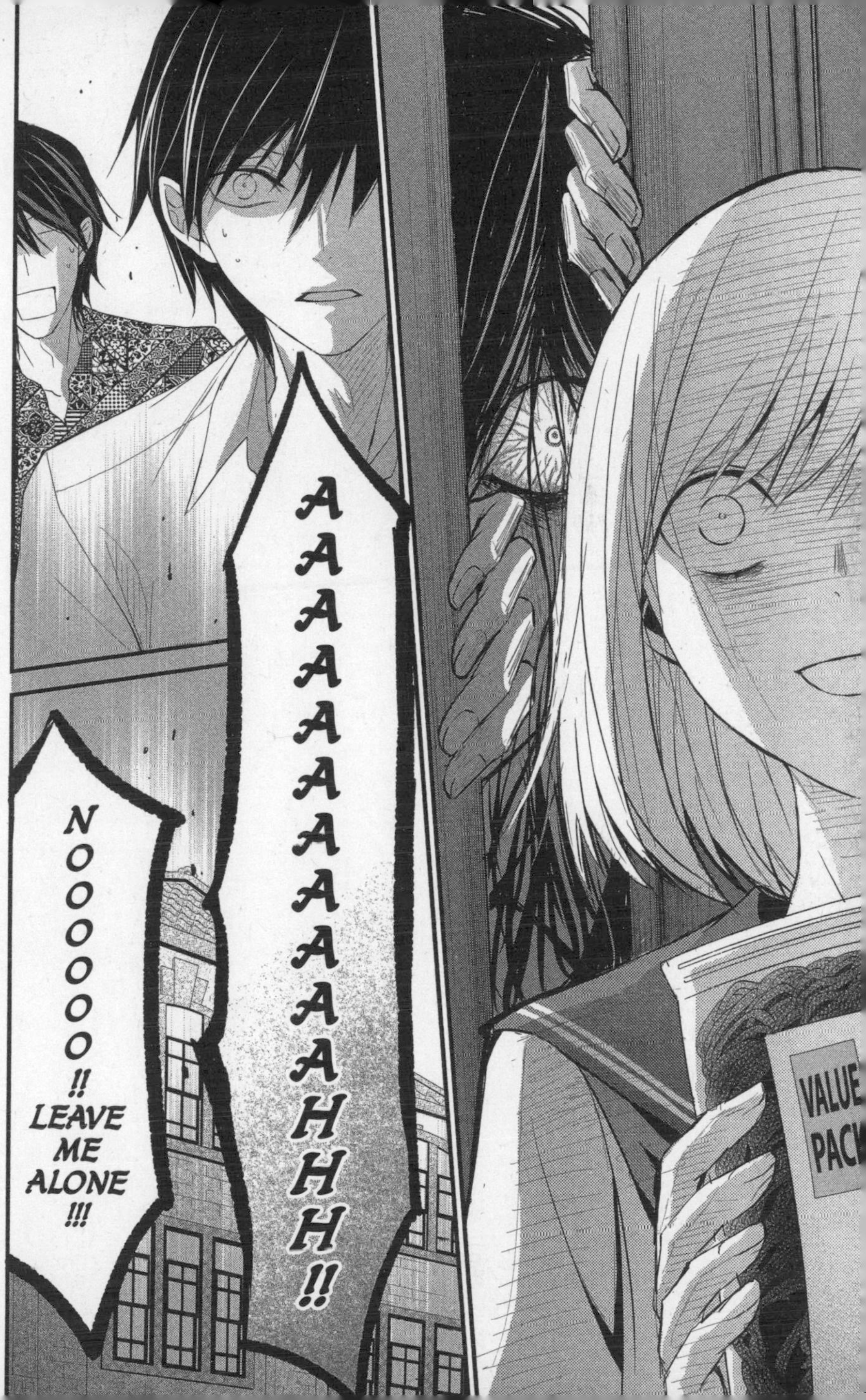
AAAAAAAAAAAAHHH!!
NOOOOOO!! LEAVE ME ALONE!!!
VALUE PACK

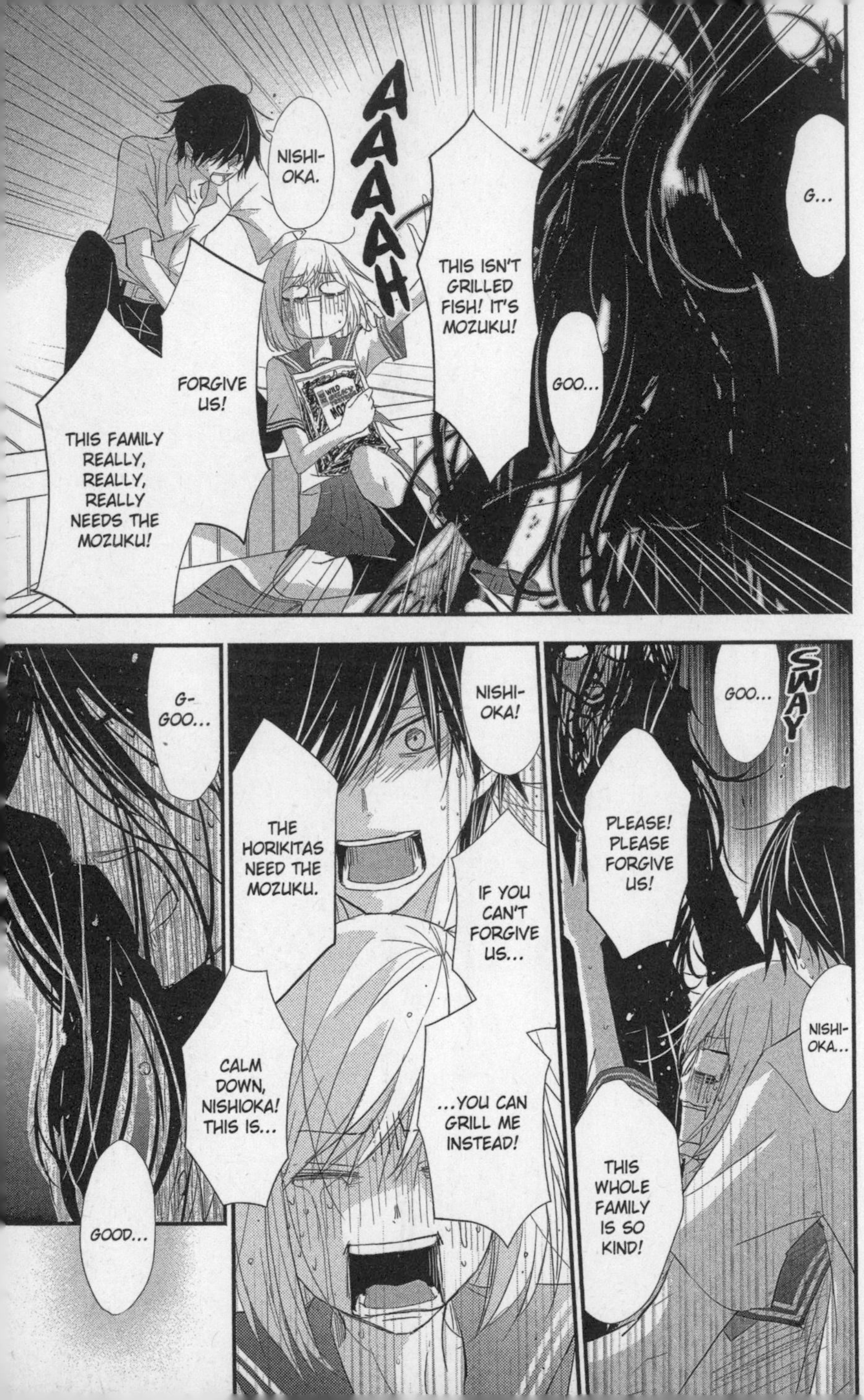
G...
GOO...
THIS ISN'T GRILLED FISH! IT'S MOZUKU!
AAAAH
NISHI-OKA.
FORGIVE US!
THIS FAMILY REALLY, REALLY, REALLY NEEDS THE MOZUKU!
GOO...
SWAY
PLEASE! PLEASE FORGIVE US!
NISHI-OKA...
THIS WHOLE FAMILY IS SO KIND!
NISHI-OKA!
THE HORIKITAS NEED THE MOZUKU.
IF YOU CAN'T FORGIVE US...
...YOU CAN GRILL ME INSTEAD!
CALM DOWN, NISHIOKA! THIS IS...
G-GOO...
GOOD...

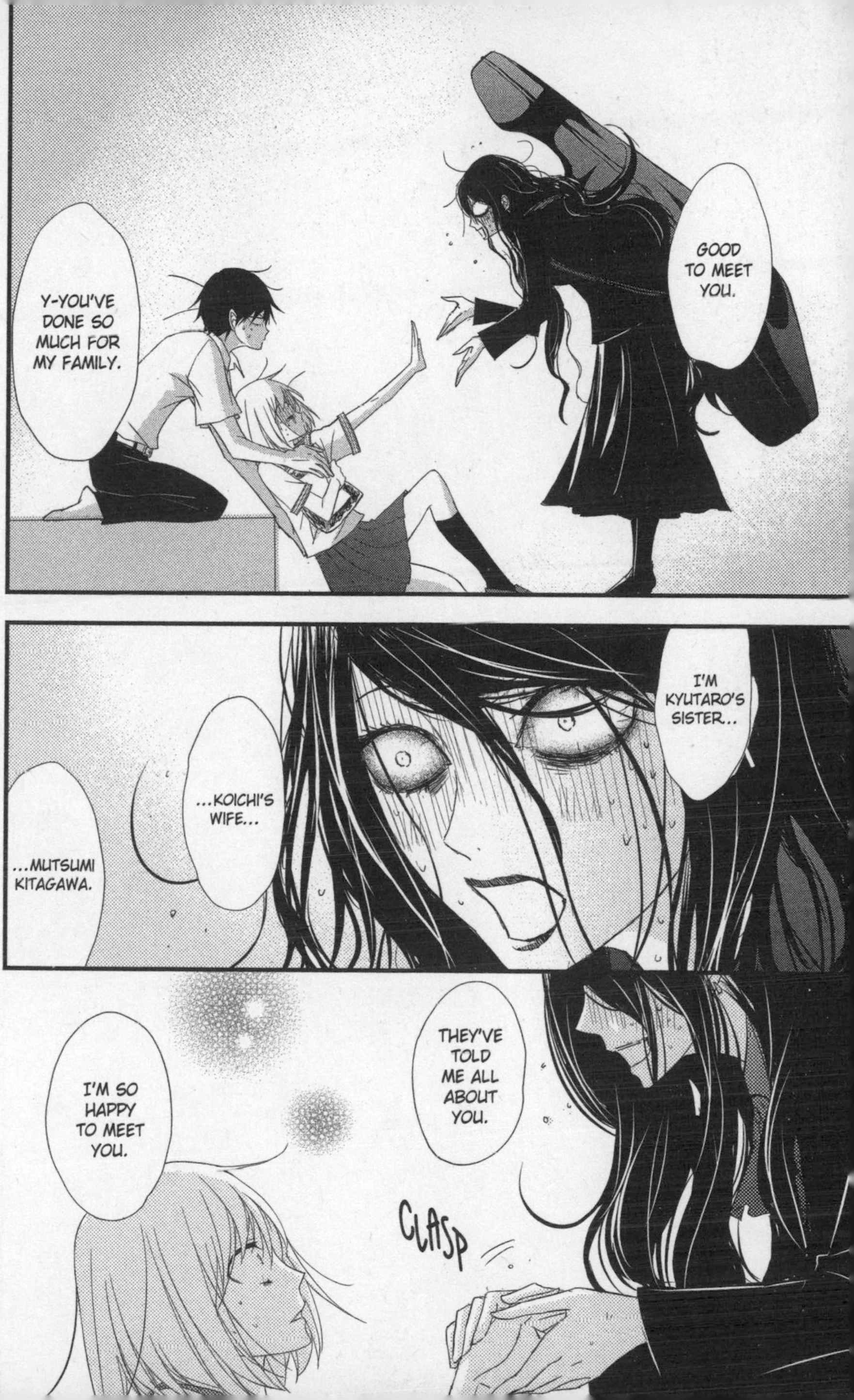
GOOD TO MEET YOU.
Y-YOU'VE DONE SO MUCH FOR MY FAMILY.
I'M KYUTARO'S SISTER...
...KOICHI'S WIFE...
...MUTSUMI KITAGAWA.
THEY'VE TOLD ME ALL ABOUT YOU.
I'M SO HAPPY TO MEET YOU.
CLASP

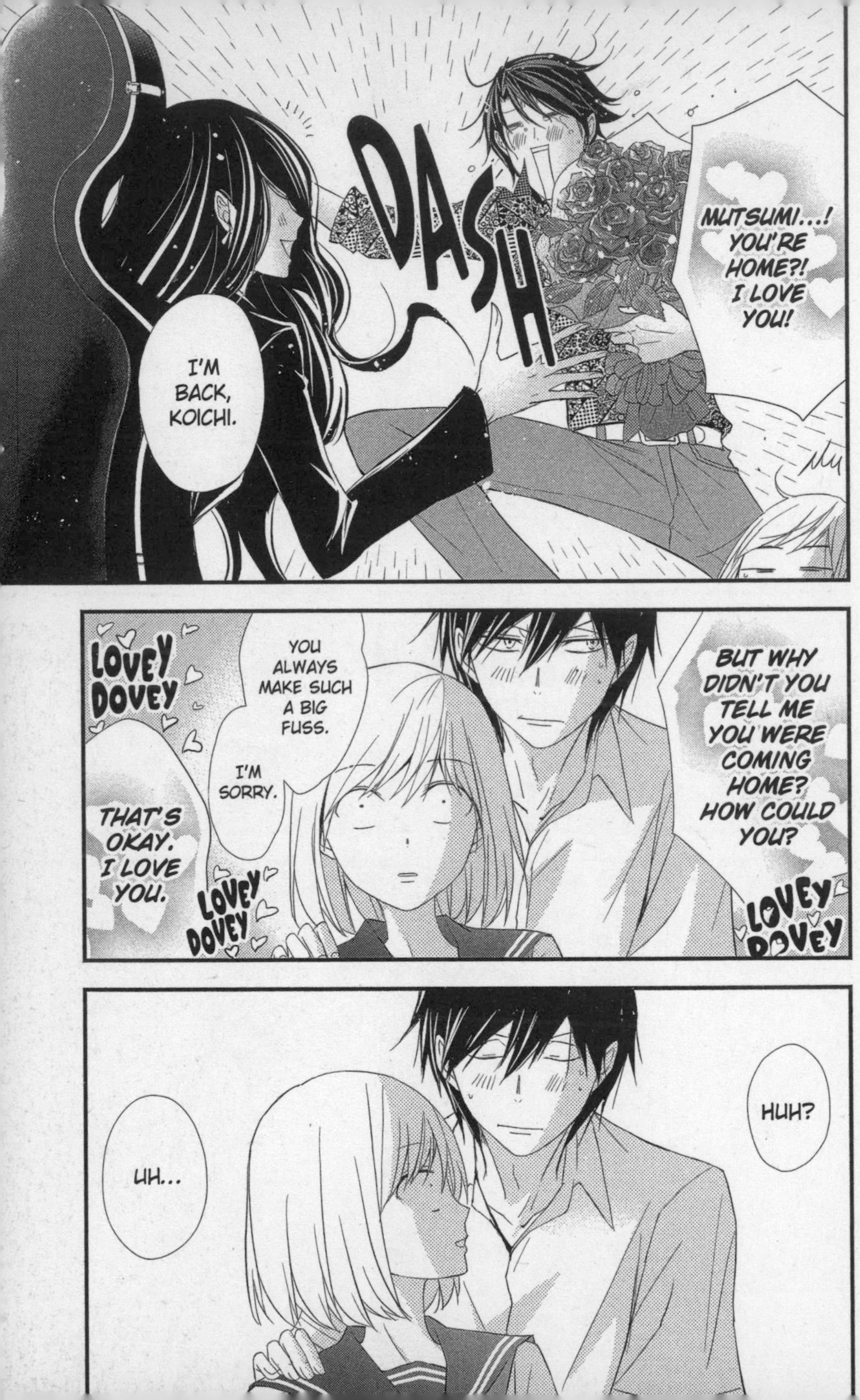
MUTSUMI...! YOU'RE HOME?! I LOVE YOU!
DASH
I'M BACK, KOICHI.
BUT WHY DIDN'T YOU TELL ME YOU WERE COMING HOME? HOW COULD YOU?
LOVEY DOVEY
YOU ALWAYS MAKE SUCH A BIG FUSS.
I'M SORRY.
LOVEY DOVEY
THAT'S OKAY. I LOVE YOU.
LOVEY DOVEY
HUH?
UH...

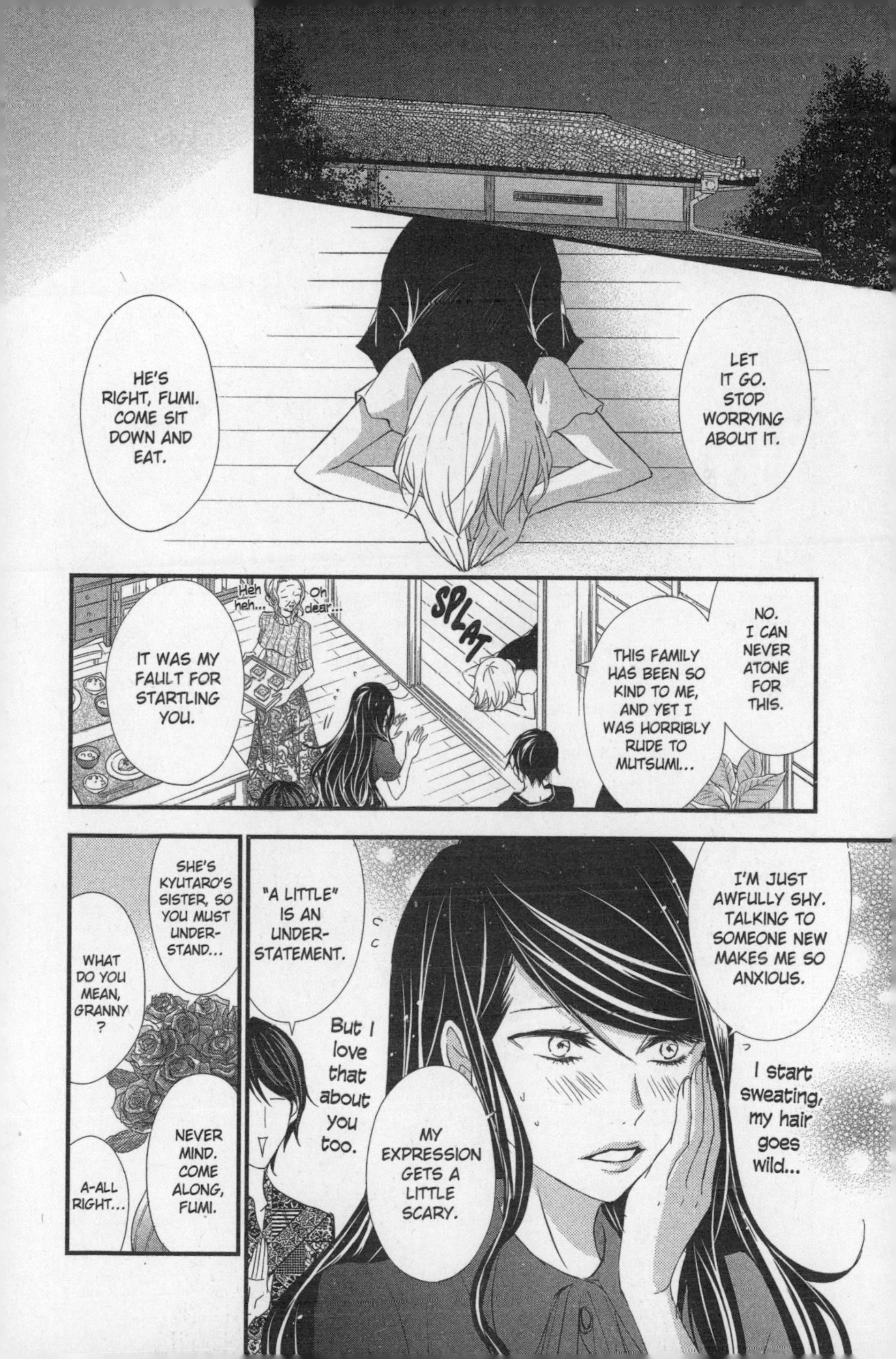
LET IT GO. STOP WORRYING ABOUT IT.
HE'S RIGHT, FUMI. COME SIT DOWN AND EAT.
NO. I CAN NEVER ATONE FOR THIS.
THIS FAMILY HAS BEEN SO KIND TO ME, AND YET I WAS HORRIBLY RUDE TO MUTSUMI...
SPLAT
Oh dear...
Heh heh...
IT WAS MY FAULT FOR STARTLING YOU.
I'M JUST AWFULLY SHY. TALKING TO SOMEONE NEW MAKES ME SO ANXIOUS.
I start sweating, my hair goes wild...
MY EXPRESSION GETS A LITTLE SCARY.
But I love that about you too.
"A LITTLE" IS AN UNDER-STATEMENT.
SHE'S KYUTARO'S SISTER, SO YOU MUST UNDER-STAND...
WHAT DO YOU MEAN, GRANNY?
NEVER MIND. COME ALONG, FUMI.
A-ALL RIGHT...

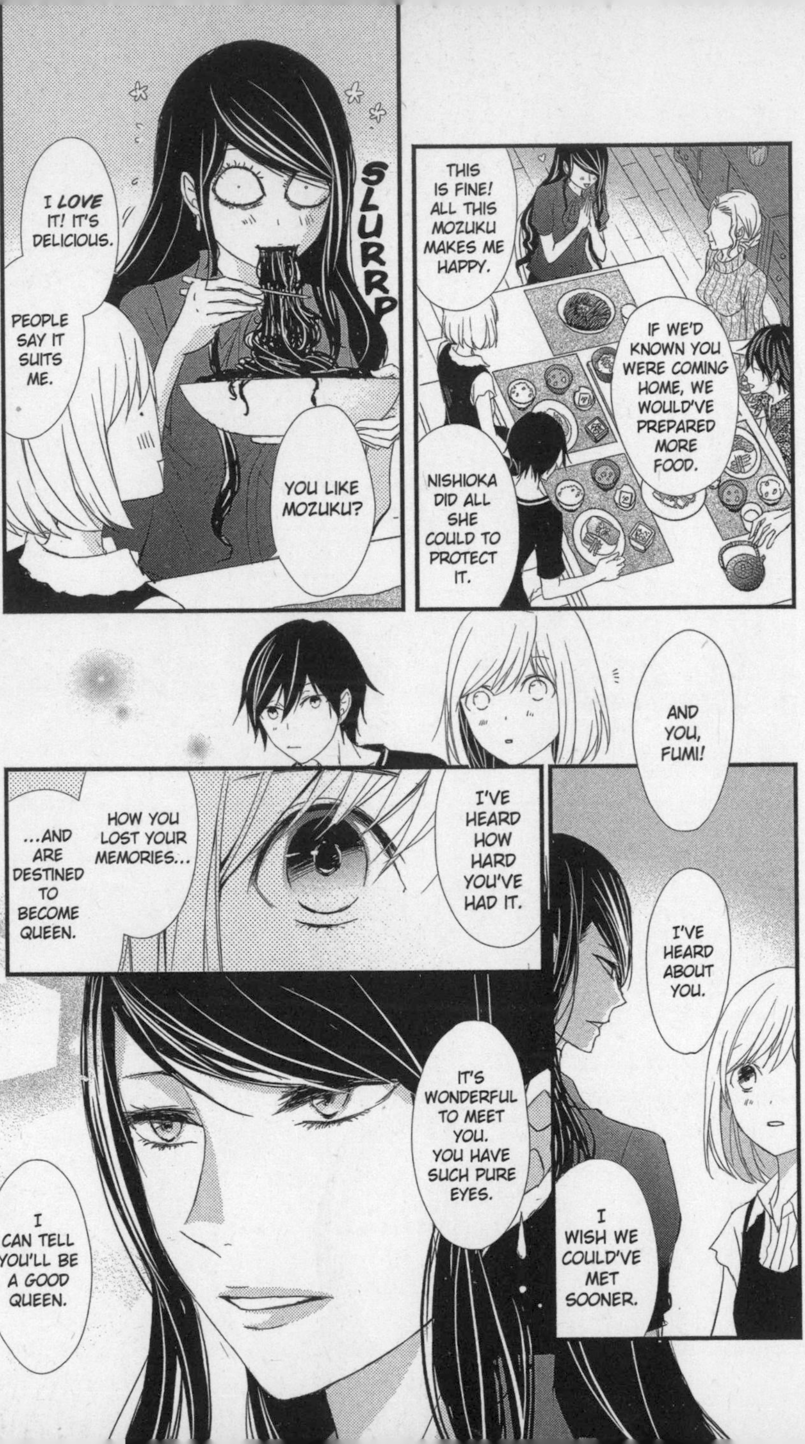
IF WE'D KNOWN YOU WERE COMING HOME, WE WOULD'VE PREPARED MORE FOOD.
THIS IS FINE! ALL THIS MOZUKU MAKES ME HAPPY.
NISHIOKA DID ALL SHE COULD TO PROTECT IT.
SLURRP
YOU LIKE MOZUKU?
I *LOVE* IT! IT'S DELICIOUS.
PEOPLE SAY IT SUITS ME.
AND YOU, FUMI!
I'VE HEARD ABOUT YOU.
I'VE HEARD HOW HARD YOU'VE HAD IT.
HOW YOU LOST YOUR MEMORIES...
...AND ARE DESTINED TO BECOME QUEEN.
I WISH WE COULD'VE MET SOONER.
IT'S WONDERFUL TO MEET YOU. YOU HAVE SUCH PURE EYES.
I CAN TELL YOU'LL BE A GOOD QUEEN.

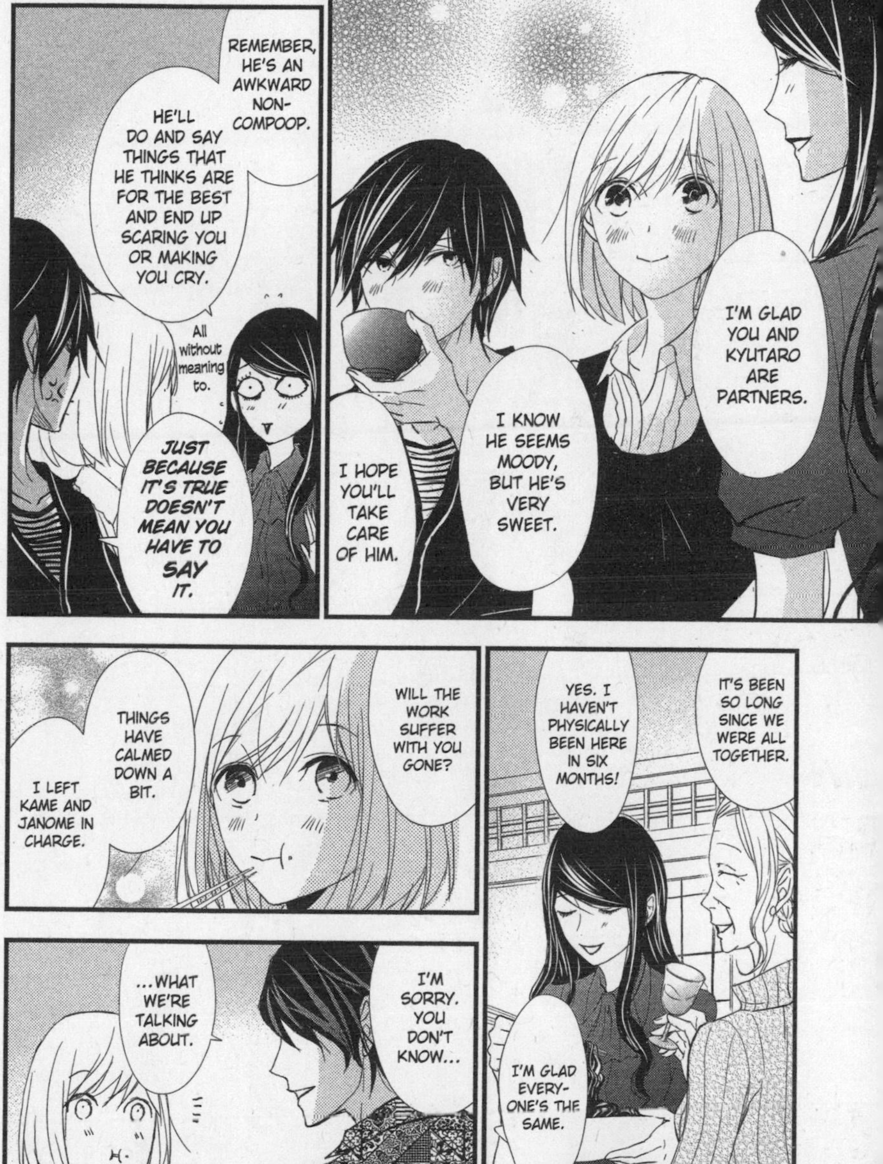
I'M GLAD YOU AND KYUTARO ARE PARTNERS.
I KNOW HE SEEMS MOODY, BUT HE'S VERY SWEET.
I HOPE YOU'LL TAKE CARE OF HIM.
REMEMBER, HE'S AN AWKWARD NON-COMPOOP.
HE'LL DO AND SAY THINGS THAT HE THINKS ARE FOR THE BEST AND END UP SCARING YOU OR MAKING YOU CRY.
All without meaning to.
JUST BECAUSE IT'S TRUE DOESN'T MEAN YOU HAVE TO SAY IT.
IT'S BEEN SO LONG SINCE WE WERE ALL TOGETHER.
YES. I HAVEN'T PHYSICALLY BEEN HERE IN SIX MONTHS!
I'M GLAD EVERY-ONE'S THE SAME.
WILL THE WORK SUFFER WITH YOU GONE?
THINGS HAVE CALMED DOWN A BIT.
I LEFT KAME AND JANOME IN CHARGE.
I'M SORRY. YOU DON'T KNOW...
...WHAT WE'RE TALKING ABOUT.

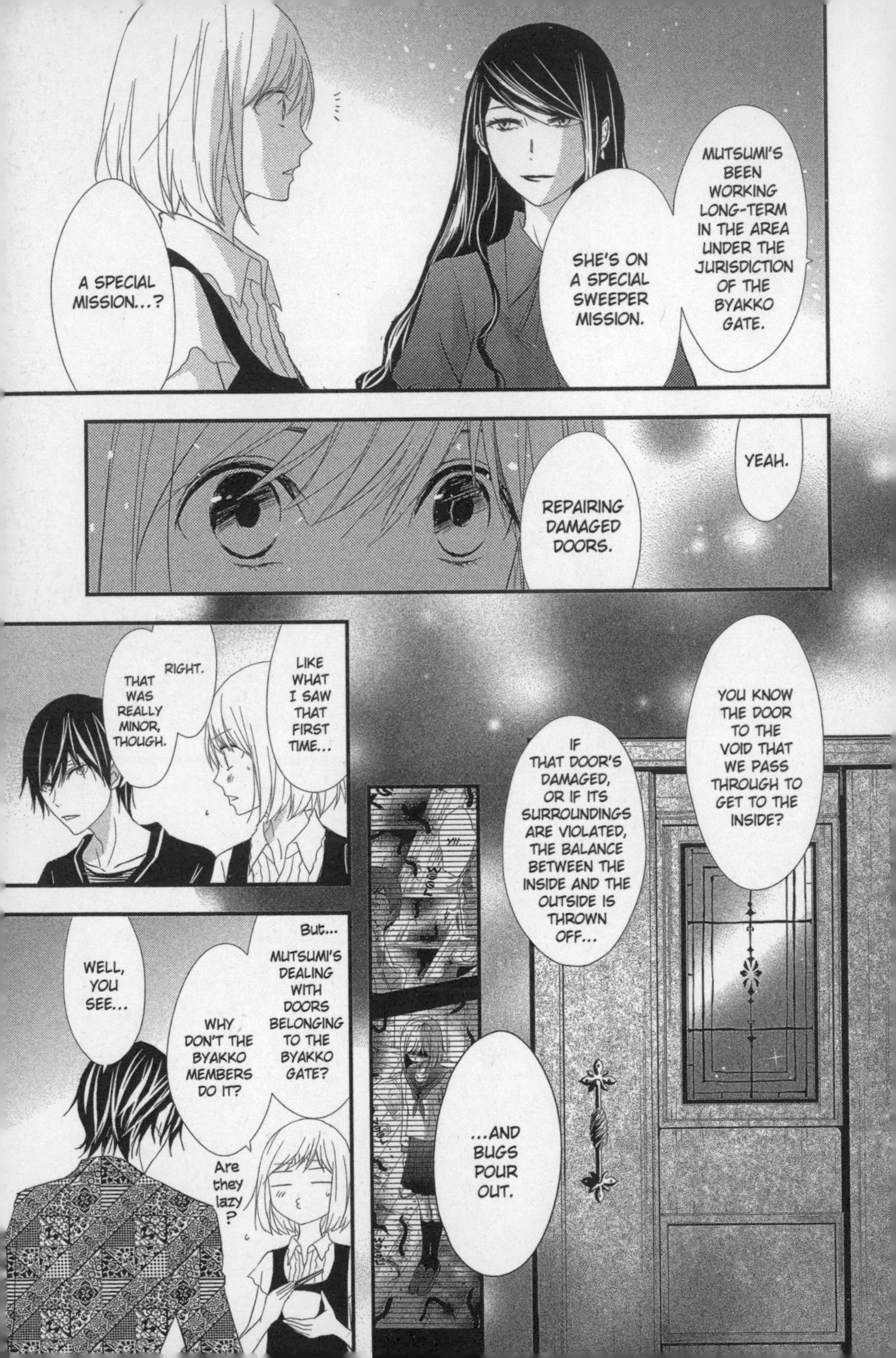
MUTSUMI'S BEEN WORKING LONG-TERM IN THE AREA UNDER THE JURISDICTION OF THE BYAKKO GATE.
SHE'S ON A SPECIAL SWEEPER MISSION.
A SPECIAL MISSION...?
YEAH.
REPAIRING DAMAGED DOORS.
YOU KNOW THE DOOR TO THE VOID THAT WE PASS THROUGH TO GET TO THE INSIDE?
IF THAT DOOR'S DAMAGED, OR IF ITS SURROUNDINGS ARE VIOLATED, THE BALANCE BETWEEN THE INSIDE AND THE OUTSIDE IS THROWN OFF...
...AND BUGS POUR OUT.
LIKE WHAT I SAW THAT FIRST TIME...
RIGHT. THAT WAS REALLY MINOR, THOUGH.
But... MUTSUMI'S DEALING WITH DOORS BELONGING TO THE BYAKKO GATE?
WHY DON'T THE BYAKKO MEMBERS DO IT?
Are they lazy?
WELL, YOU SEE...

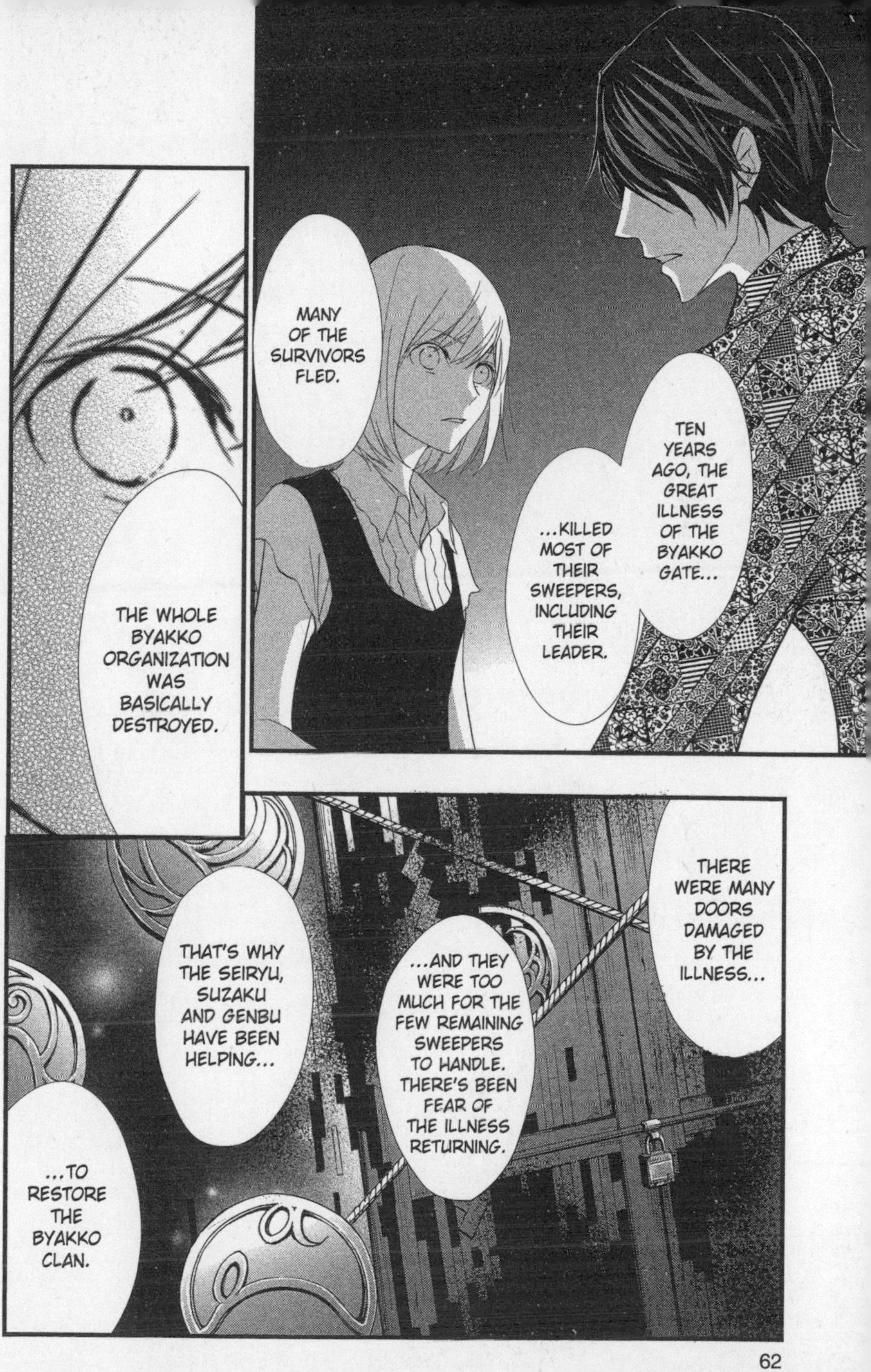
TEN YEARS AGO, THE GREAT ILLNESS OF THE BYAKKO GATE...
...KILLED MOST OF THEIR SWEEPERS, INCLUDING THEIR LEADER.
MANY OF THE SURVIVORS FLED.
THE WHOLE BYAKKO ORGANIZATION WAS BASICALLY DESTROYED.
THERE WERE MANY DOORS DAMAGED BY THE ILLNESS...
...AND THEY WERE TOO MUCH FOR THE FEW REMAINING SWEEPERS TO HANDLE. THERE'S BEEN FEAR OF THE ILLNESS RETURNING.
THAT'S WHY THE SEIRYU, SUZAKU AND GENBU HAVE BEEN HELPING...
...TO RESTORE THE BYAKKO CLAN.

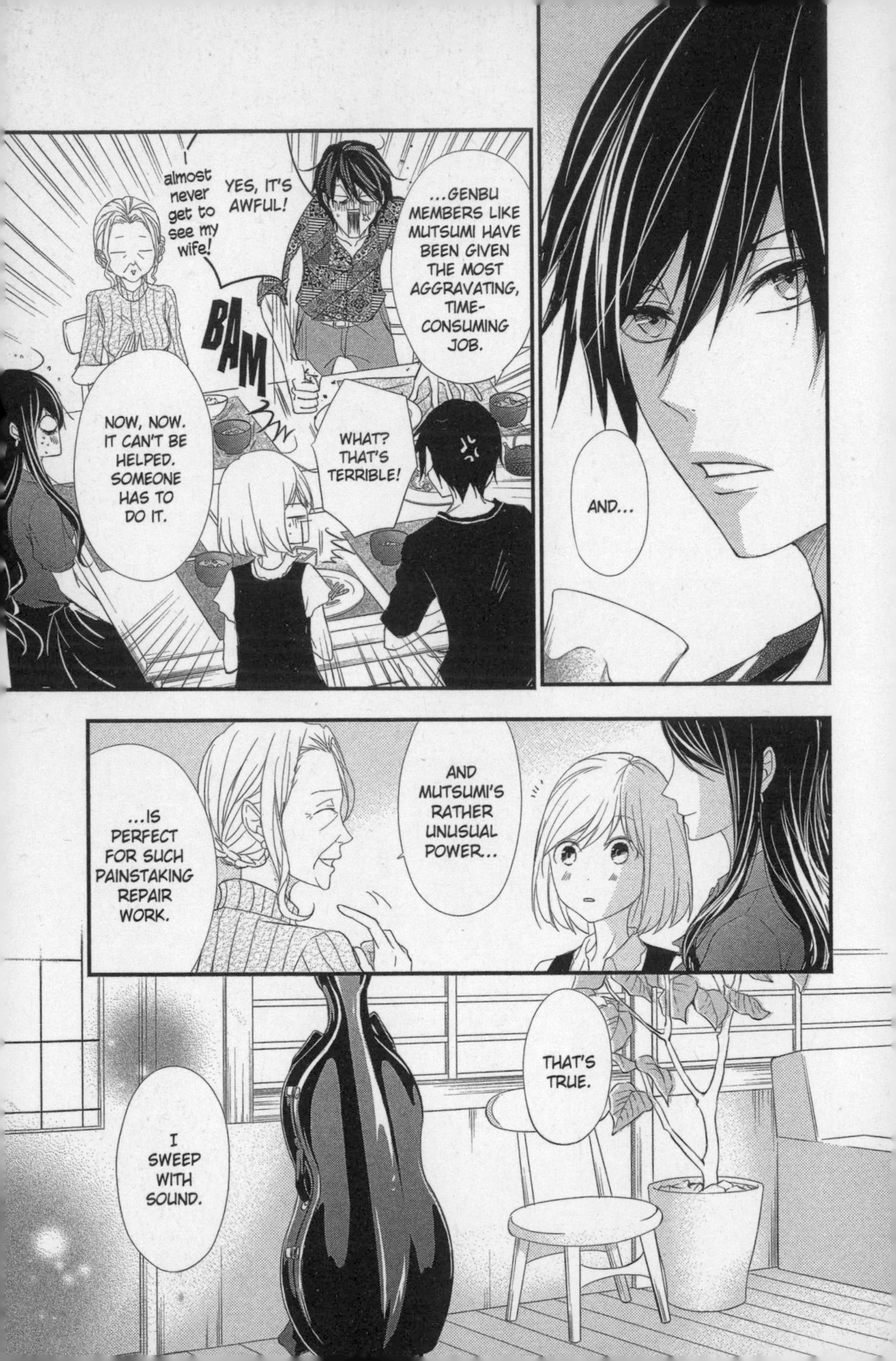
AND...
...GENBU MEMBERS LIKE MUTSUMI HAVE BEEN GIVEN THE MOST AGGRAVATING, TIME-CONSUMING JOB.
YES, IT'S AWFUL!
I almost never get to see my wife!
BAM
WHAT? THAT'S TERRIBLE!
NOW, NOW. IT CAN'T BE HELPED. SOMEONE HAS TO DO IT.
AND MUTSUMI'S RATHER UNUSUAL POWER...
...IS PERFECT FOR SUCH PAINSTAKING REPAIR WORK.
THAT'S TRUE.
I SWEEP WITH SOUND.

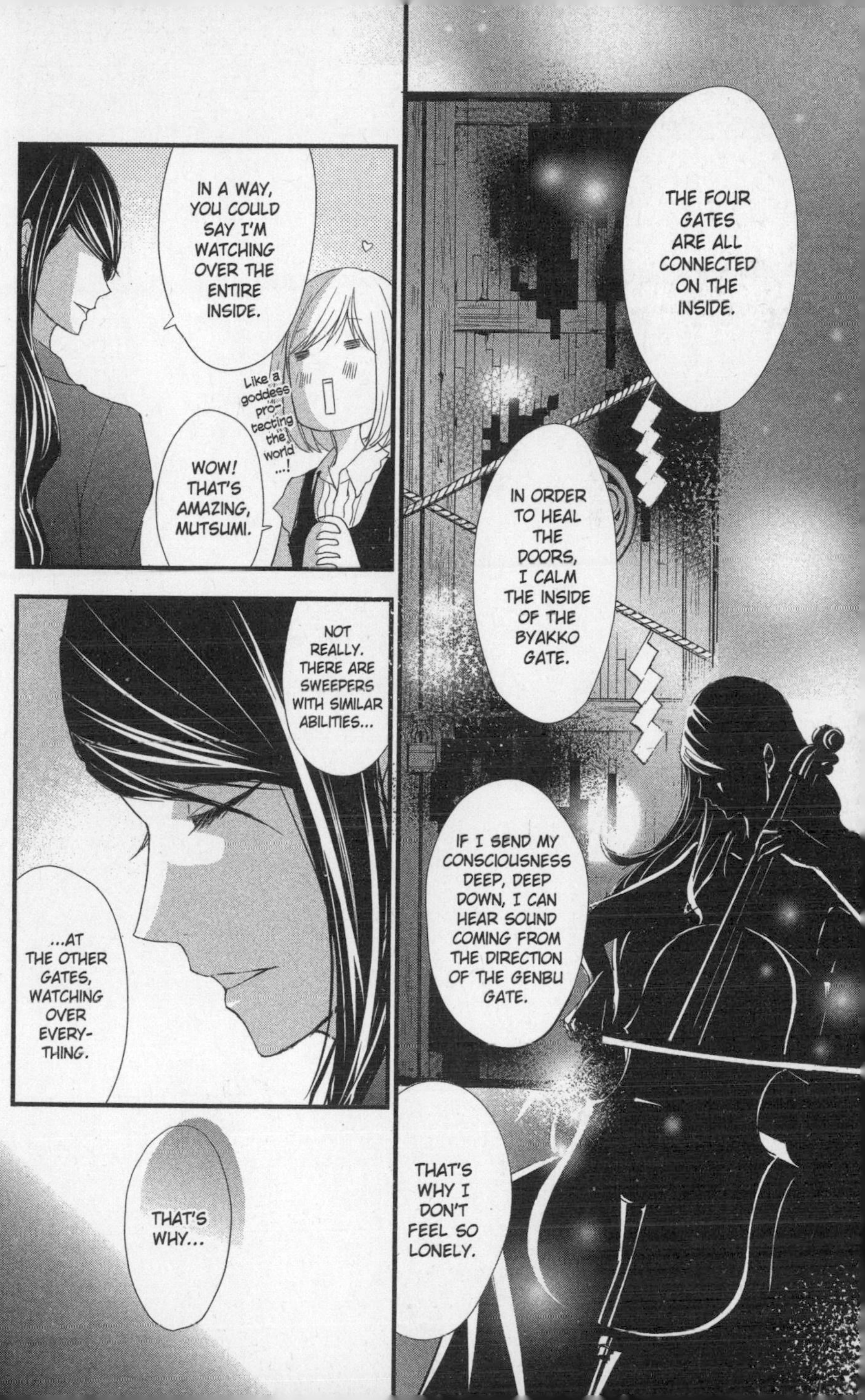
THE FOUR GATES ARE ALL CONNECTED ON THE INSIDE.
IN ORDER TO HEAL THE DOORS, I CALM THE INSIDE OF THE BYAKKO GATE.
IF I SEND MY CONSCIOUSNESS DEEP, DEEP DOWN, I CAN HEAR SOUND COMING FROM THE DIRECTION OF THE GENBU GATE.
THAT'S WHY I DON'T FEEL SO LONELY.
IN A WAY, YOU COULD SAY I'M WATCHING OVER THE ENTIRE INSIDE.
Like a goddess pro-tecting the world ...!
WOW! THAT'S AMAZING, MUTSUMI.
NOT REALLY. THERE ARE SWEEPERS WITH SIMILAR ABILITIES...
...AT THE OTHER GATES, WATCHING OVER EVERY-THING.
THAT'S WHY...

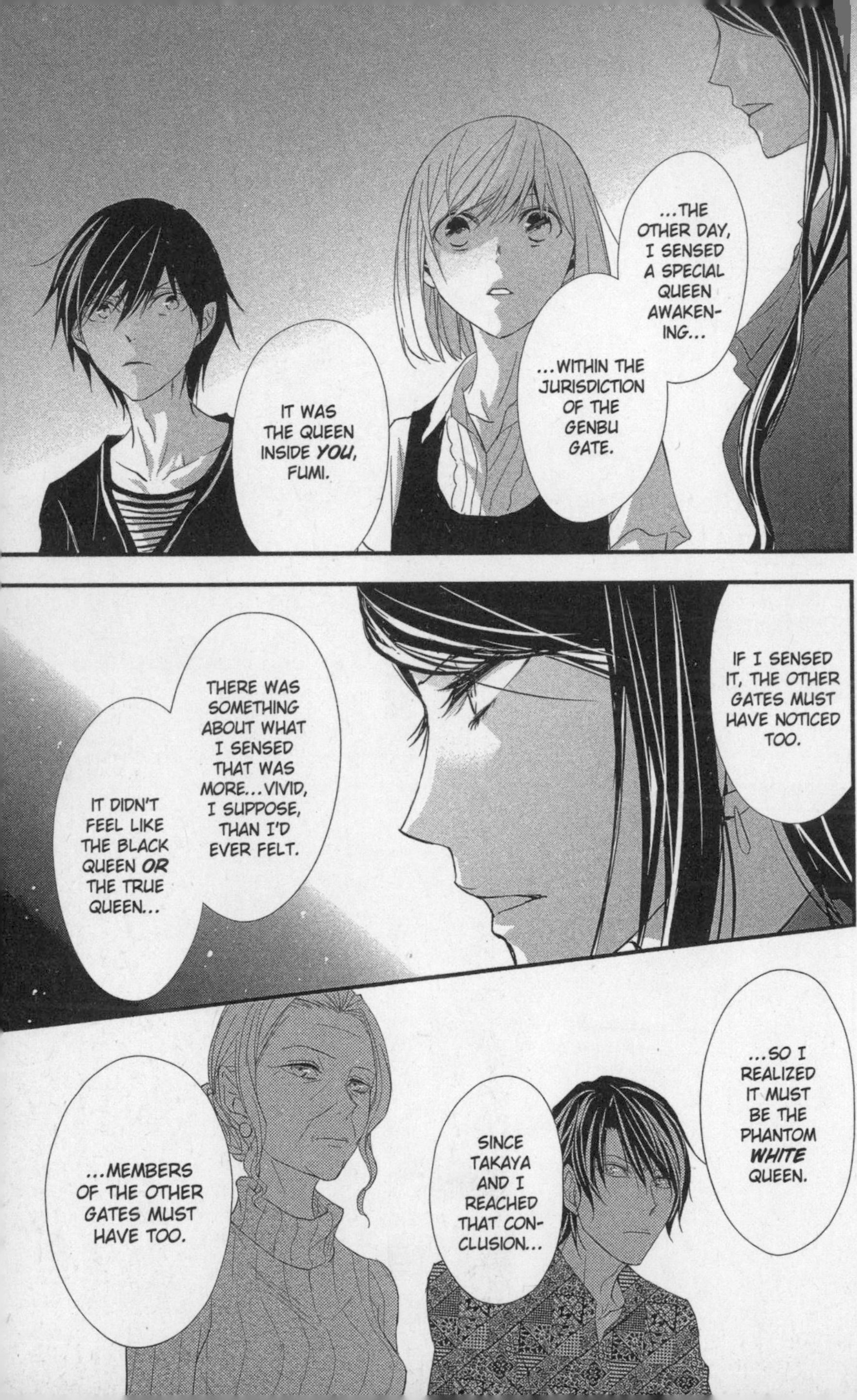
...THE OTHER DAY, I SENSED A SPECIAL QUEEN AWAKEN-ING...
...WITHIN THE JURISDICTION OF THE GENBU GATE.
IT WAS THE QUEEN INSIDE *YOU*, FUMI.
IF I SENSED IT, THE OTHER GATES MUST HAVE NOTICED TOO.
THERE WAS SOMETHING ABOUT WHAT I SENSED THAT WAS MORE...VIVID, I SUPPOSE, THAN I'D EVER FELT.
IT DIDN'T FEEL LIKE THE BLACK QUEEN *OR* THE TRUE QUEEN...
...SO I REALIZED IT MUST BE THE PHANTOM *WHITE* QUEEN.
SINCE TAKAYA AND I REACHED THAT CON-CLUSION...
...MEMBERS OF THE OTHER GATES MUST HAVE TOO.

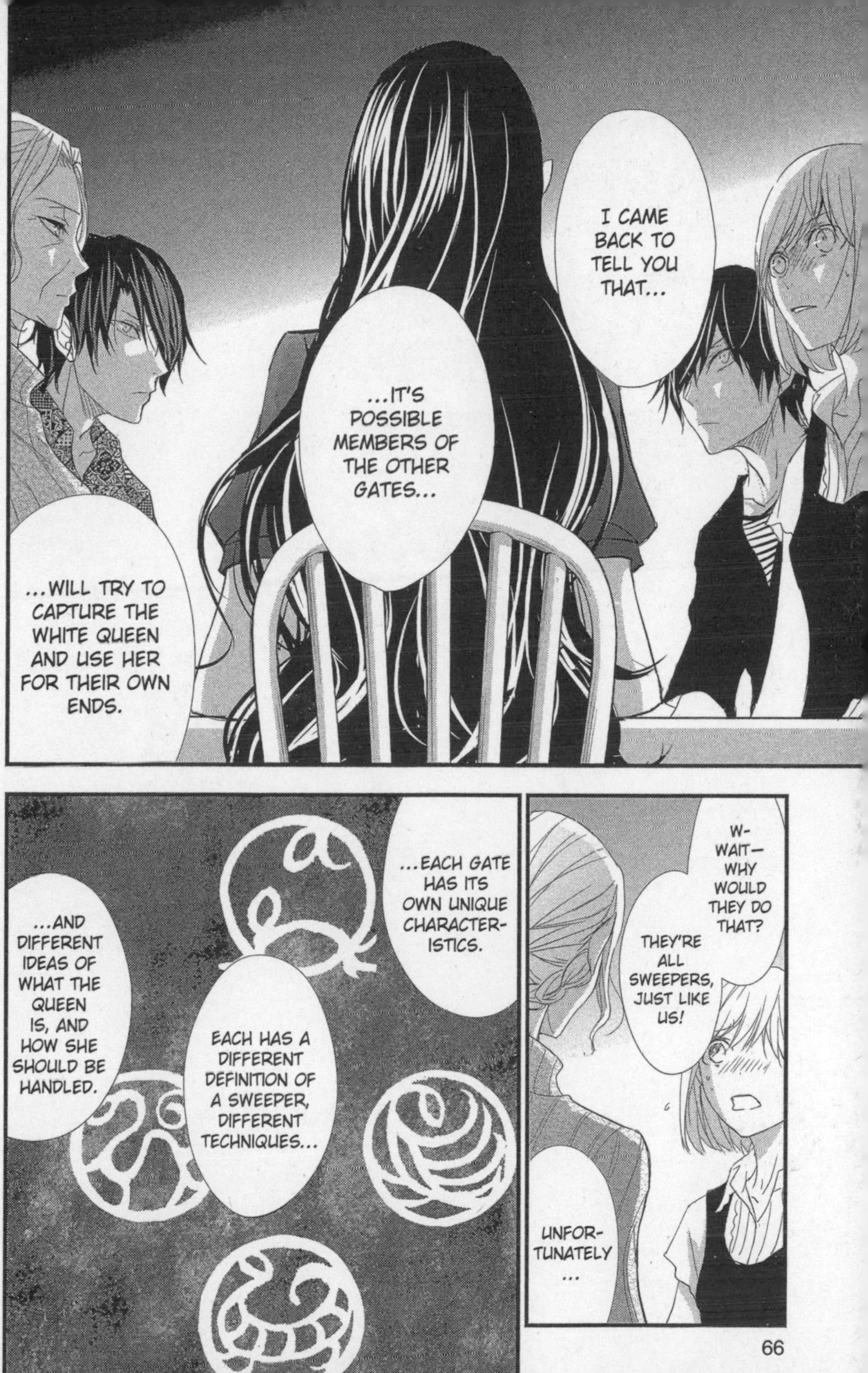
I CAME BACK TO TELL YOU THAT...
...IT'S POSSIBLE MEMBERS OF THE OTHER GATES...
...WILL TRY TO CAPTURE THE WHITE QUEEN AND USE HER FOR THEIR OWN ENDS.
W-WAIT—WHY WOULD THEY DO THAT?
THEY'RE ALL SWEEPERS, JUST LIKE US!
UNFORTUNATELY...
...EACH GATE HAS ITS OWN UNIQUE CHARACTERISTICS.
EACH HAS A DIFFERENT DEFINITION OF A SWEEPER, DIFFERENT TECHNIQUES...
...AND DIFFERENT IDEAS OF WHAT THE QUEEN IS, AND HOW SHE SHOULD BE HANDLED.

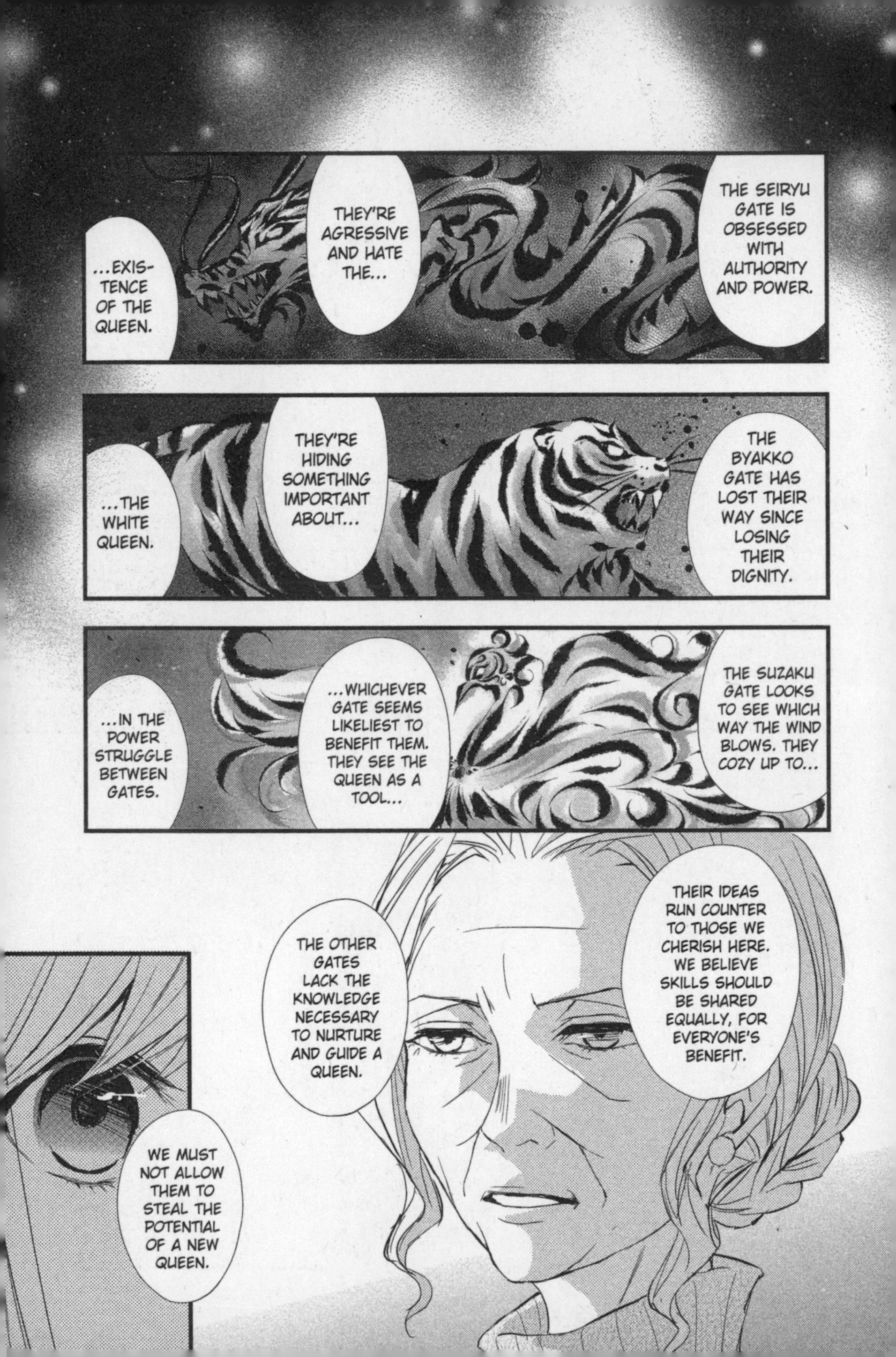
THE SEIRYU GATE IS OBSESSED WITH AUTHORITY AND POWER.
THEY'RE AGRESSIVE AND HATE THE...
...EXISTENCE OF THE QUEEN.
THE BYAKKO GATE HAS LOST THEIR WAY SINCE LOSING THEIR DIGNITY.
THEY'RE HIDING SOMETHING IMPORTANT ABOUT...
...THE WHITE QUEEN.
THE SUZAKU GATE LOOKS TO SEE WHICH WAY THE WIND BLOWS. THEY COZY UP TO...
...WHICHEVER OTHER GATE SEEMS LIKELIEST TO BENEFIT THEM. THEY SEE THE QUEEN AS A TOOL...
...IN THE POWER STRUGGLE BETWEEN GATES.
THEIR IDEAS RUN COUNTER TO THOSE WE CHERISH HERE. WE BELIEVE SKILLS SHOULD BE SHARED EQUALLY, FOR EVERYONE'S BENEFIT.
THE OTHER GATES LACK THE KNOWLEDGE NECESSARY TO NURTURE AND GUIDE A QUEEN.
WE MUST NOT ALLOW THEM TO STEAL THE POTENTIAL OF A NEW QUEEN.

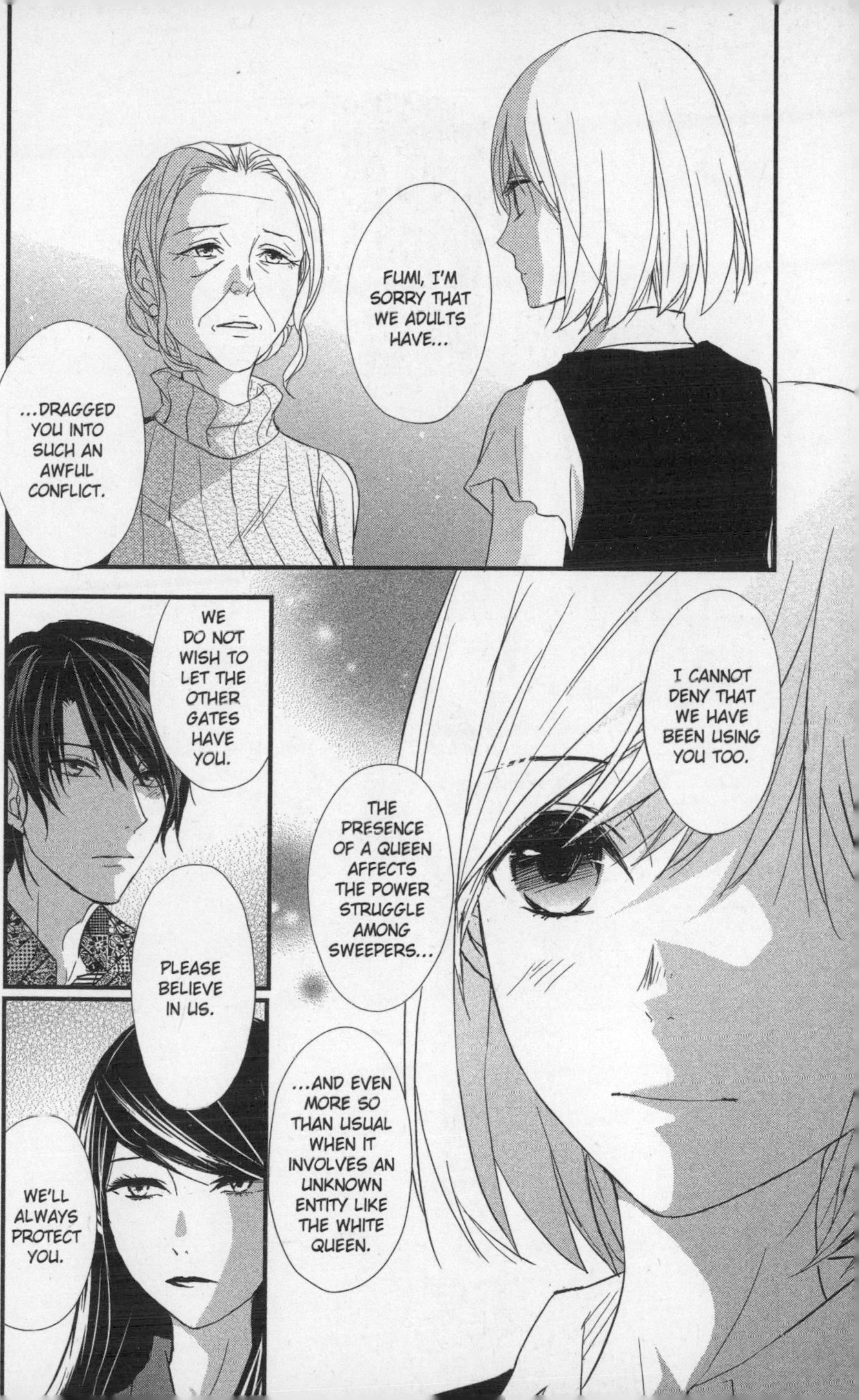
FUMI, I'M SORRY THAT WE ADULTS HAVE...
...DRAGGED YOU INTO SUCH AN AWFUL CONFLICT.
I CANNOT DENY THAT WE HAVE BEEN USING YOU TOO.
THE PRESENCE OF A QUEEN AFFECTS THE POWER STRUGGLE AMONG SWEEPERS...
...AND EVEN MORE SO THAN USUAL WHEN IT INVOLVES AN UNKNOWN ENTITY LIKE THE WHITE QUEEN.
WE DO NOT WISH TO LET THE OTHER GATES HAVE YOU.
PLEASE BELIEVE IN US.
WE'LL ALWAYS PROTECT YOU.

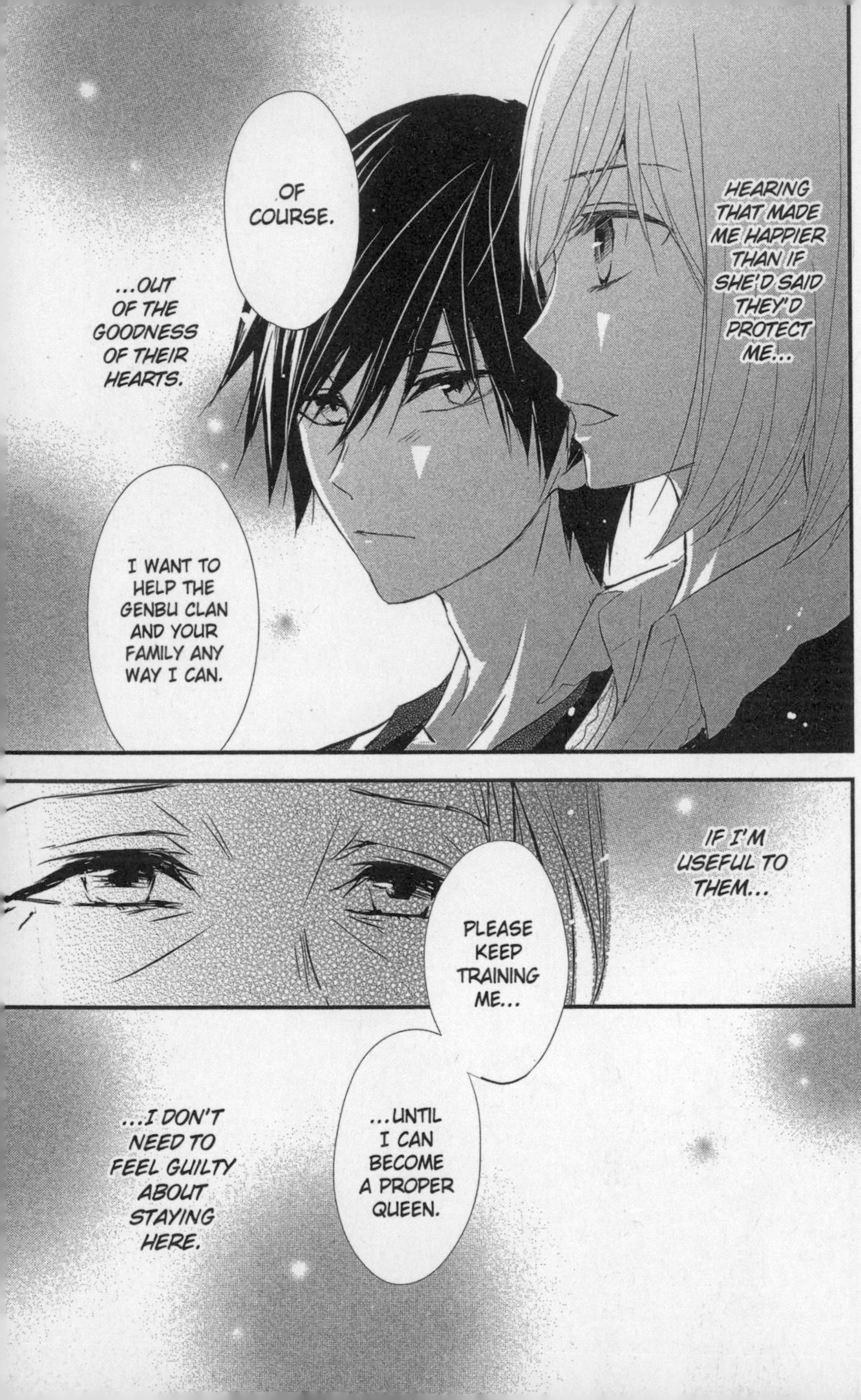
HEARING THAT MADE ME HAPPIER THAN IF SHE'D SAID THEY'D PROTECT ME...
OF COURSE.
...OUT OF THE GOODNESS OF THEIR HEARTS.
I WANT TO HELP THE GENBU CLAN AND YOUR FAMILY ANY WAY I CAN.
IF I'M USEFUL TO THEM...
PLEASE KEEP TRAINING ME...
...UNTIL I CAN BECOME A PROPER QUEEN.
...I DON'T NEED TO FEEL GUILTY ABOUT STAYING HERE.

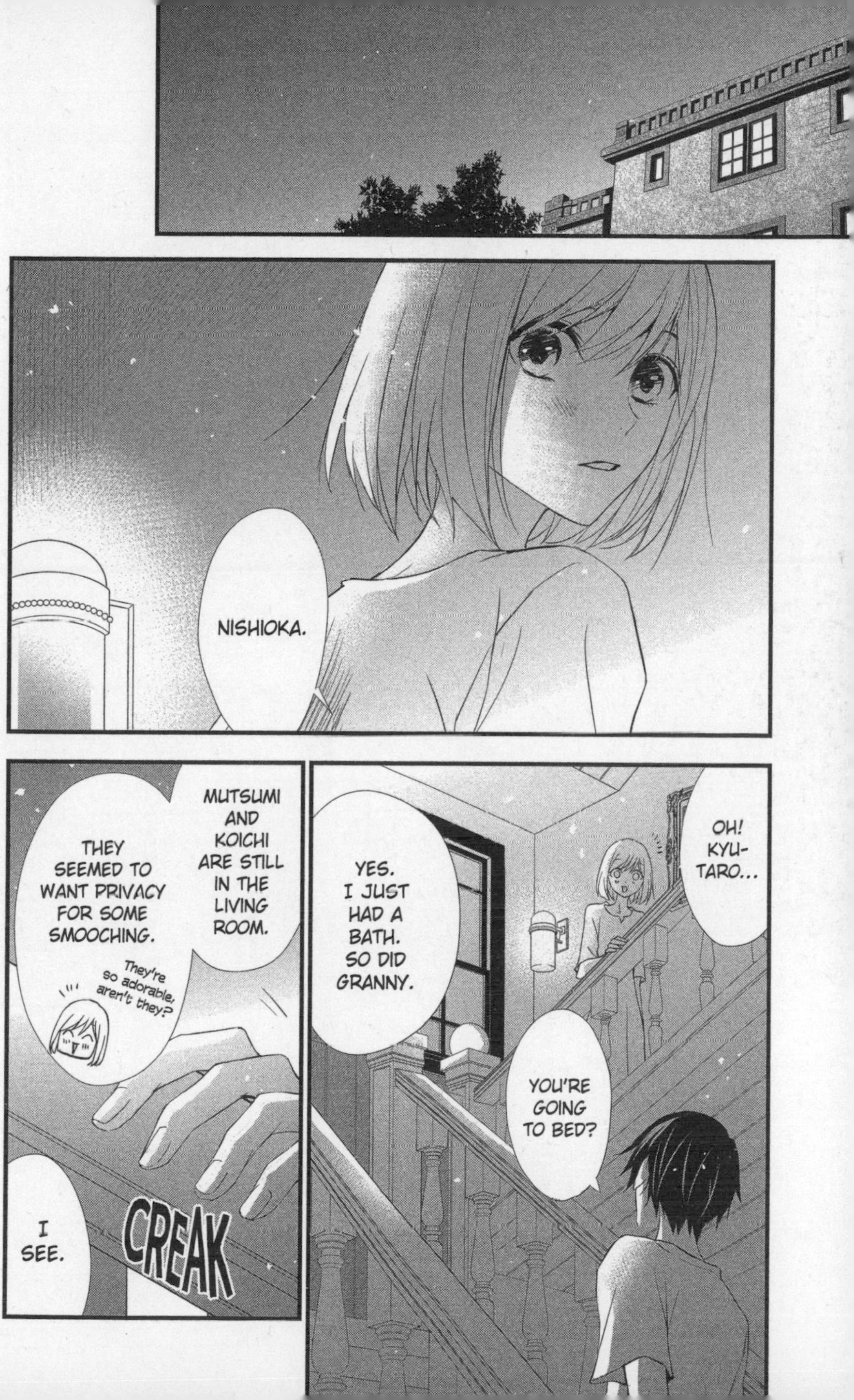
NISHIOKA.
OH! KYU-TARO...
YES. I JUST HAD A BATH. SO DID GRANNY.
YOU'RE GOING TO BED?
MUTSUMI AND KOICHI ARE STILL IN THE LIVING ROOM.
THEY SEEMED TO WANT PRIVACY FOR SOME SMOOCHING.
They're so adorable, aren't they?
CREAK
I SEE.

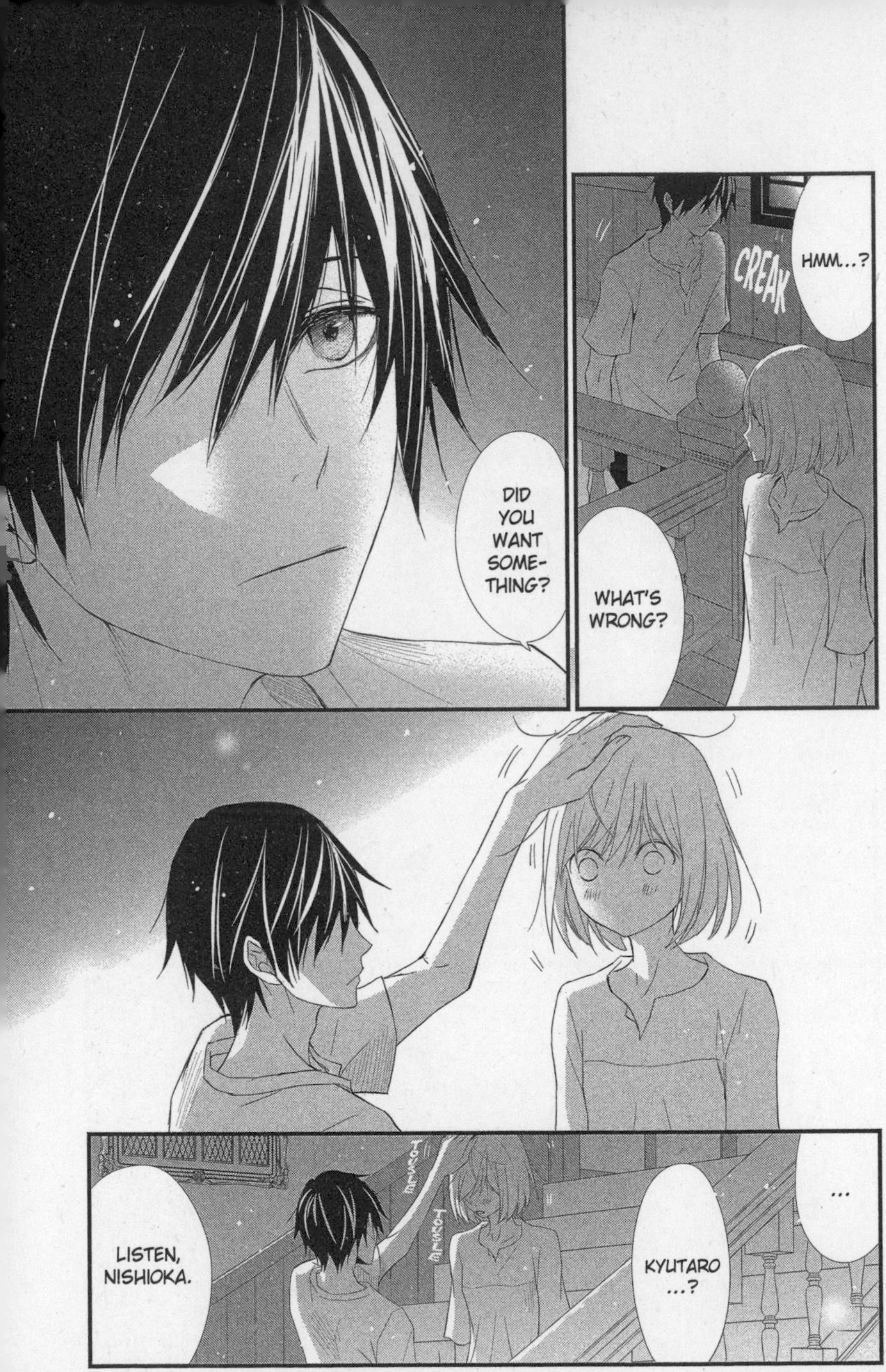
HMM...?
CREAK
WHAT'S WRONG?
DID YOU WANT SOMETHING?
...
KYUTARO ...?
TOUSLE
TOUSLE
LISTEN, NISHIOKA.

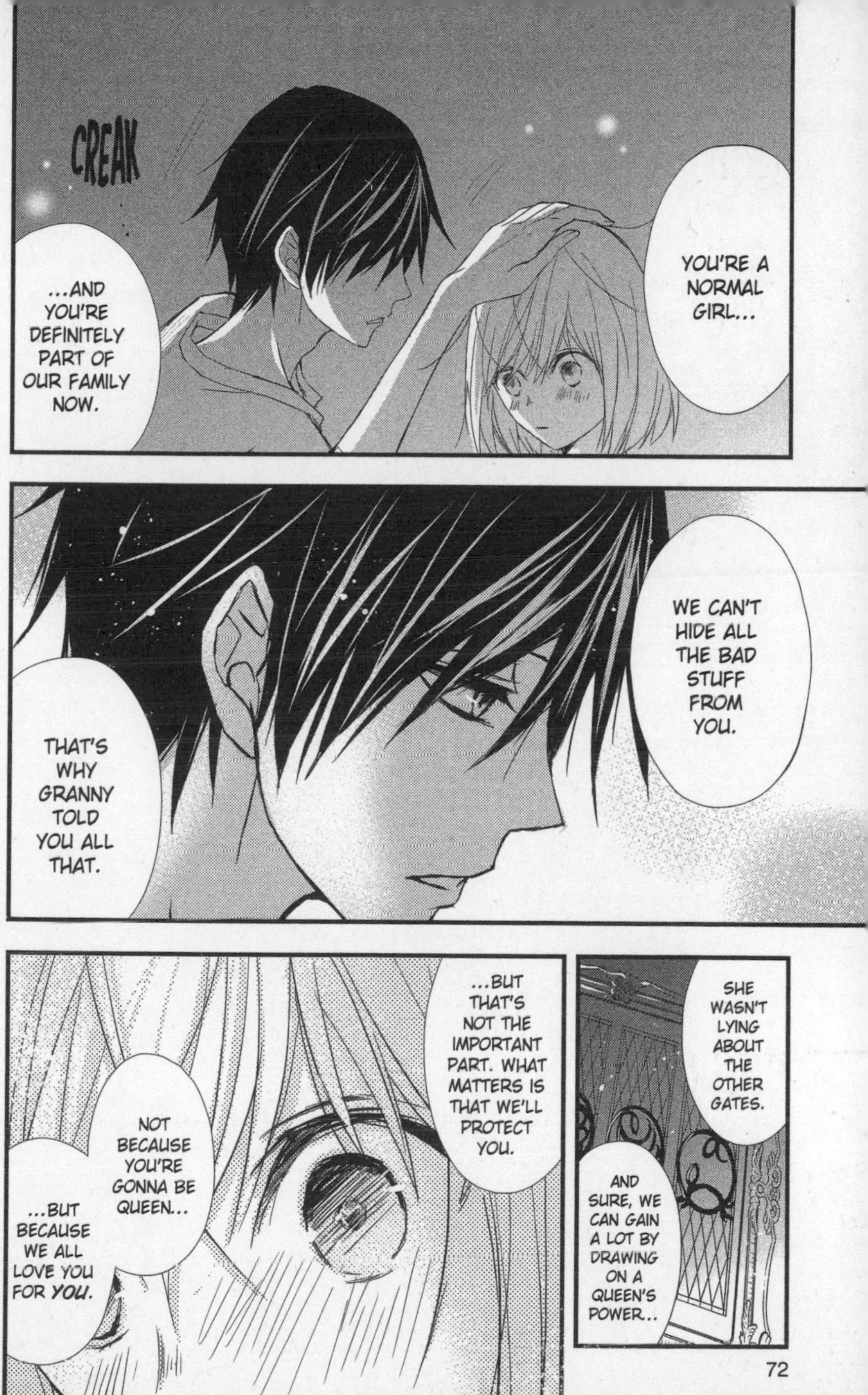
CREAK
YOU'RE A NORMAL GIRL...
...AND YOU'RE DEFINITELY PART OF OUR FAMILY NOW.
WE CAN'T HIDE ALL THE BAD STUFF FROM YOU.
THAT'S WHY GRANNY TOLD YOU ALL THAT.
SHE WASN'T LYING ABOUT THE OTHER GATES.
AND SURE, WE CAN GAIN A LOT BY DRAWING ON A QUEEN'S POWER...
...BUT THAT'S NOT THE IMPORTANT PART. WHAT MATTERS IS THAT WE'LL PROTECT YOU.
NOT BECAUSE YOU'RE GONNA BE QUEEN...
...BUT BECAUSE WE ALL LOVE YOU FOR *YOU*.

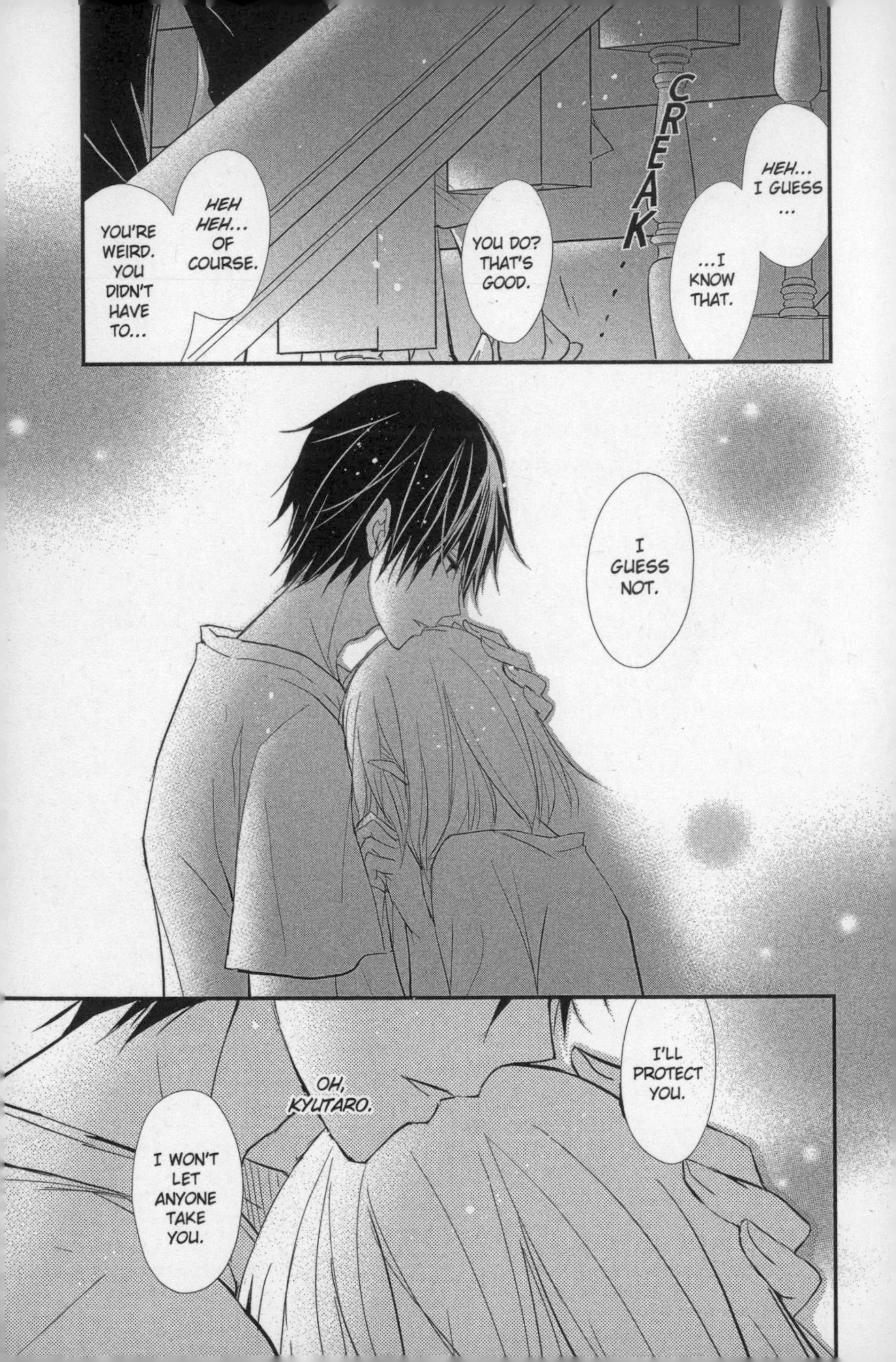
HEH... I GUESS ...
...I KNOW THAT.
CREAK
YOU DO? THAT'S GOOD.
HEH HEH... OF COURSE.
YOU'RE WEIRD. YOU DIDN'T HAVE TO...
I GUESS NOT.
I'LL PROTECT YOU.
OH, KYUTARO.
I WON'T LET ANYONE TAKE YOU.

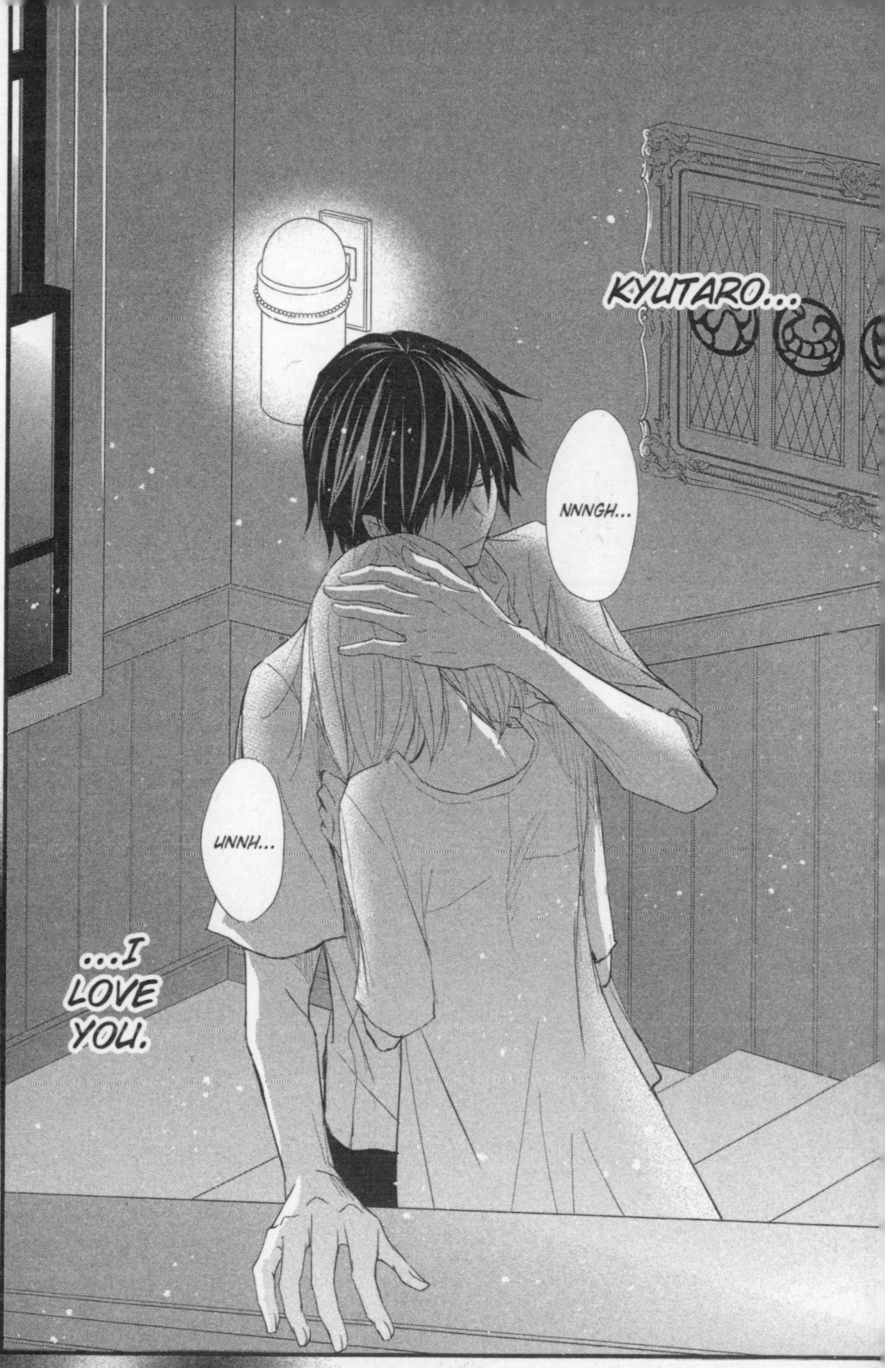
KYUTARO...
NNNGH...
UNNH...
...I LOVE YOU.

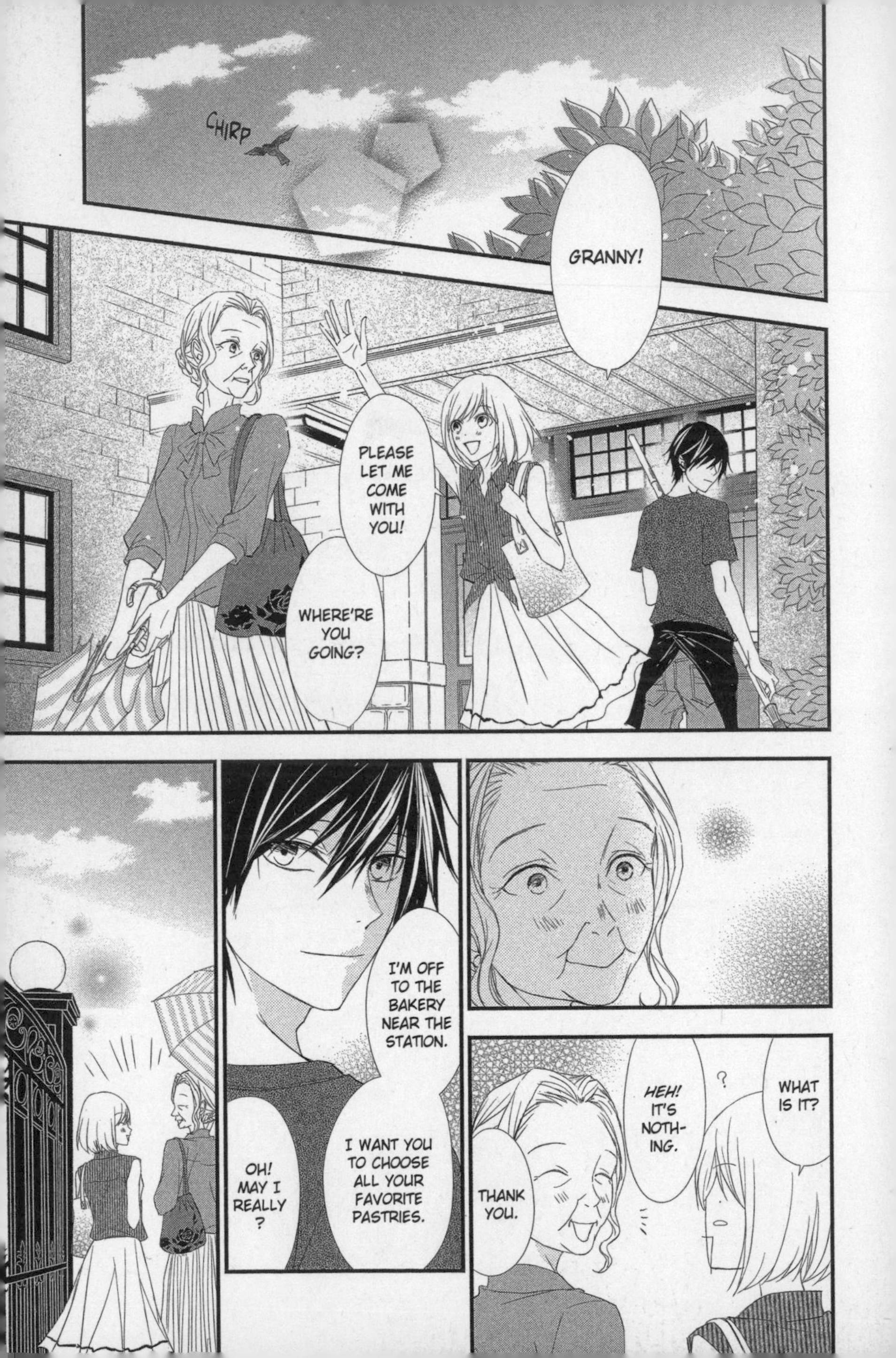
CHIRP
GRANNY!
PLEASE LET ME COME WITH YOU!
WHERE'RE YOU GOING?
WHAT IS IT?
?
HEH! IT'S NOTHING.
THANK YOU.
I'M OFF TO THE BAKERY NEAR THE STATION.
I WANT YOU TO CHOOSE ALL YOUR FAVORITE PASTRIES.
OH! MAY I REALLY?

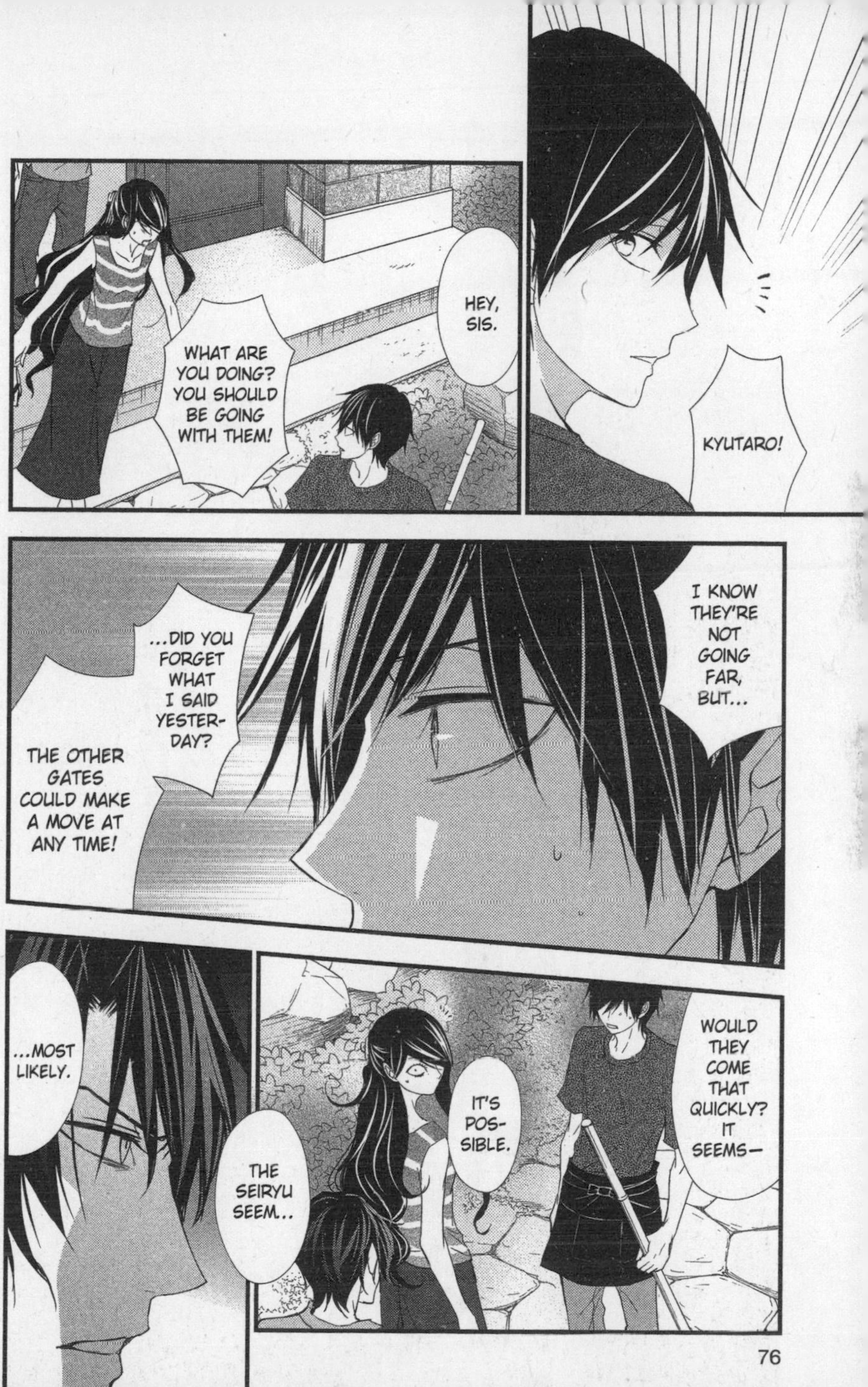
KYUTARO!
HEY, SIS.
WHAT ARE YOU DOING? YOU SHOULD BE GOING WITH THEM!
I KNOW THEY'RE NOT GOING FAR, BUT...
...DID YOU FORGET WHAT I SAID YESTER-DAY?
THE OTHER GATES COULD MAKE A MOVE AT ANY TIME!
WOULD THEY COME THAT QUICKLY? IT SEEMS—
IT'S POS-SIBLE.
THE SEIRYU SEEM...
...MOST LIKELY.

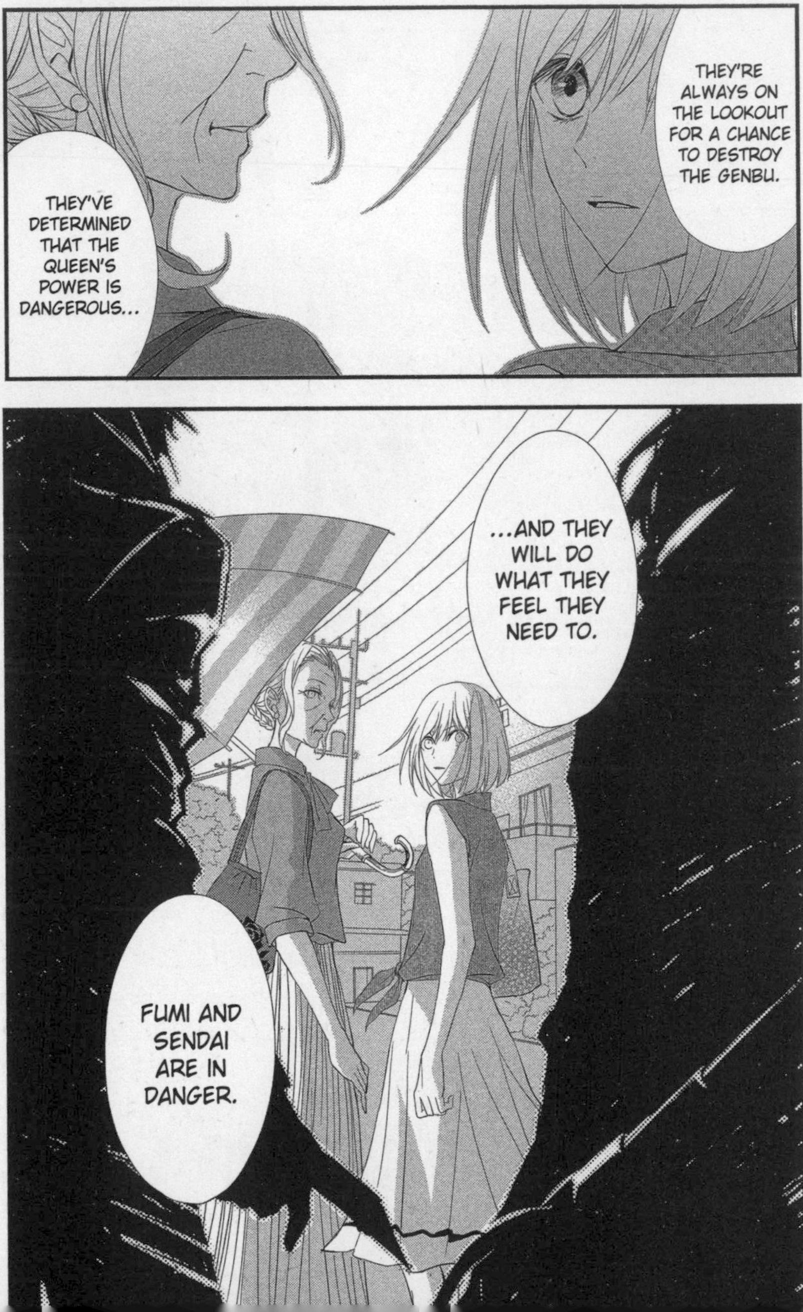
THEY'RE ALWAYS ON THE LOOKOUT FOR A CHANCE TO DESTROY THE GENBU.
THEY'VE DETERMINED THAT THE QUEEN'S POWER IS DANGEROUS...
...AND THEY WILL DO WHAT THEY FEEL THEY NEED TO.
FUMI AND SENDAI ARE IN DANGER.

MONTHLY BETSUCOMI SALE DATE NOTICE ON TWITTER

CHAPTER 13

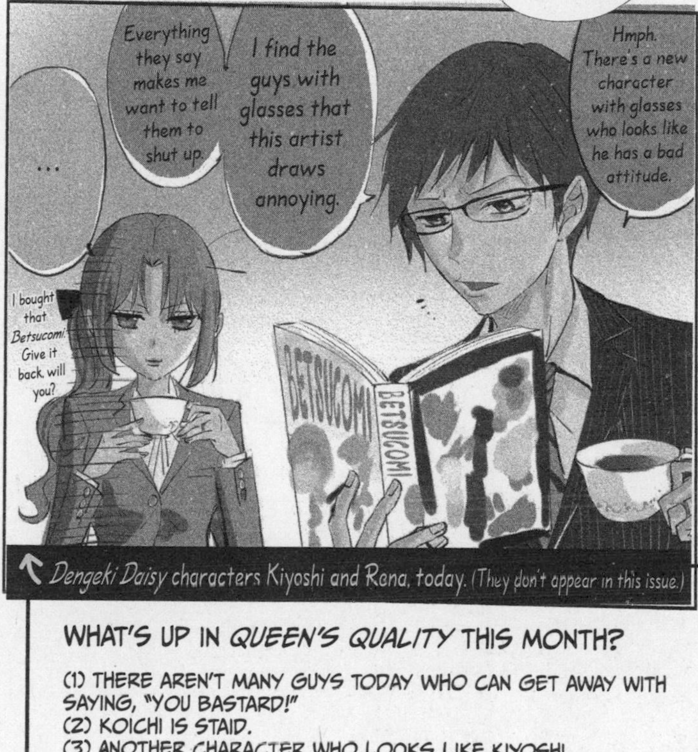

Hmph. There's a new character with glasses who looks like he has a bad attitude.
I find the guys with glasses that this artist draws annoying.
Everything they say makes me want to tell them to shut up.
...
I bought that Betsucomi. Give it back, will you?
BETSUCOMI
BETSUCOMI

↖ *Dengeki Daisy* characters Kiyoshi and Rena, today. (They don't appear in this issue.)

WHAT'S UP IN *QUEEN'S QUALITY* THIS MONTH?

(1) THERE AREN'T MANY GUYS TODAY WHO CAN GET AWAY WITH SAYING, "YOU BASTARD!"
(2) KOICHI IS STAID.
(3) ANOTHER CHARACTER WHO LOOKS LIKE KIYOSHI.

WE'LL HAVE A LOT MORE DARK SCENES IN THIS CHAPTER!

These two are characters from *Dengeki Daisy*, a previous series of mine. They don't appear in volume 3, but *Daisy* characters do sometimes pop up in the *Queequa* books. I often post drawings of them in my tweets.

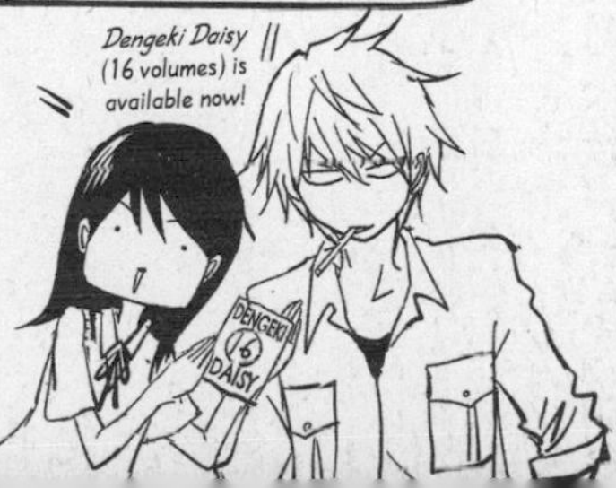

Dengeki Daisy (16 volumes) is available now!
DENGEKI 16 DAISY

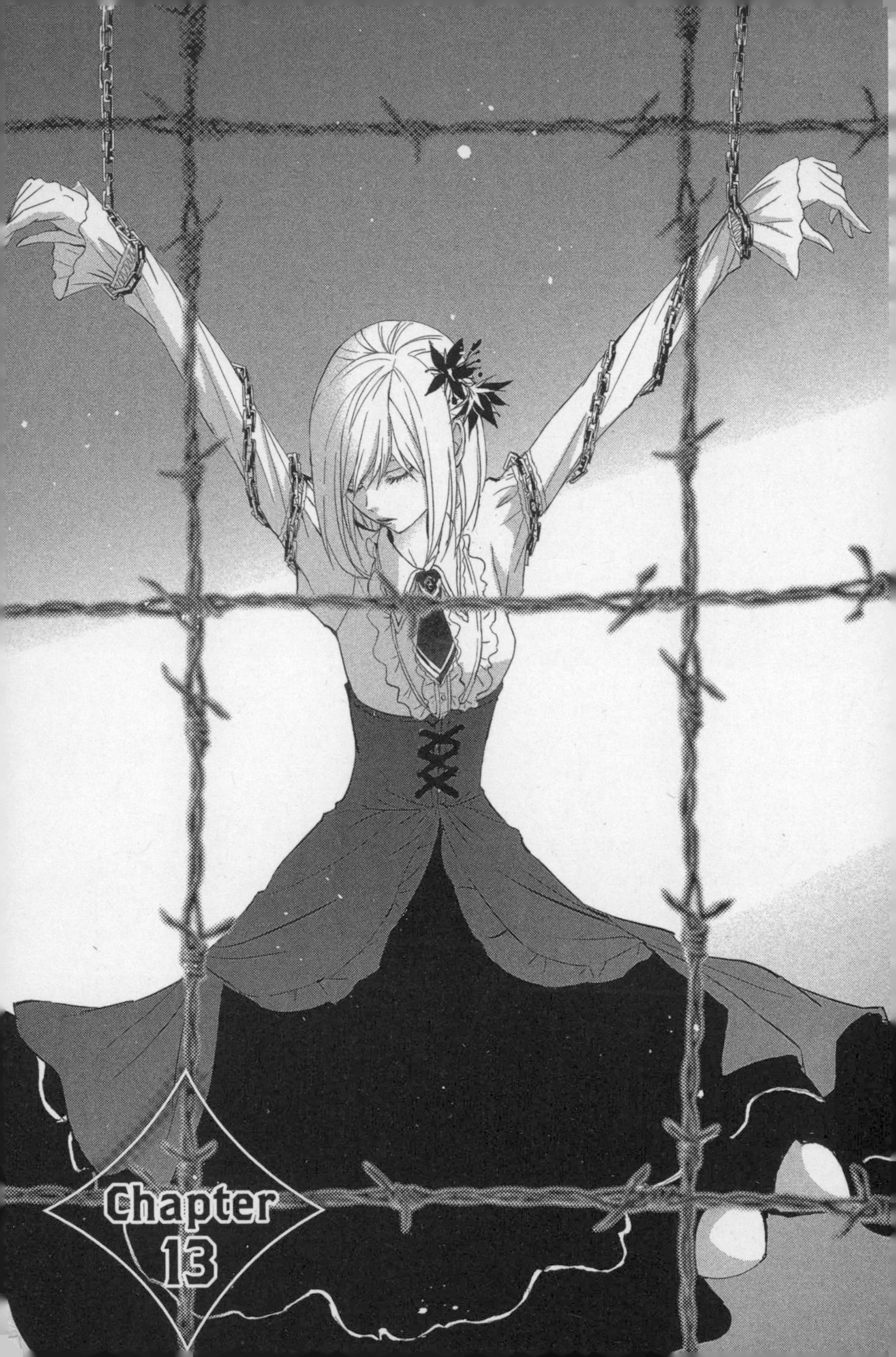
Chapter
13

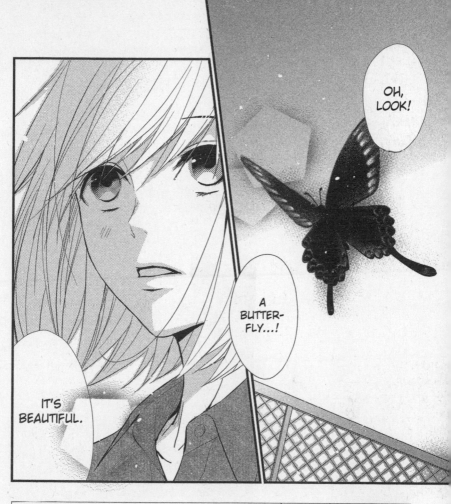

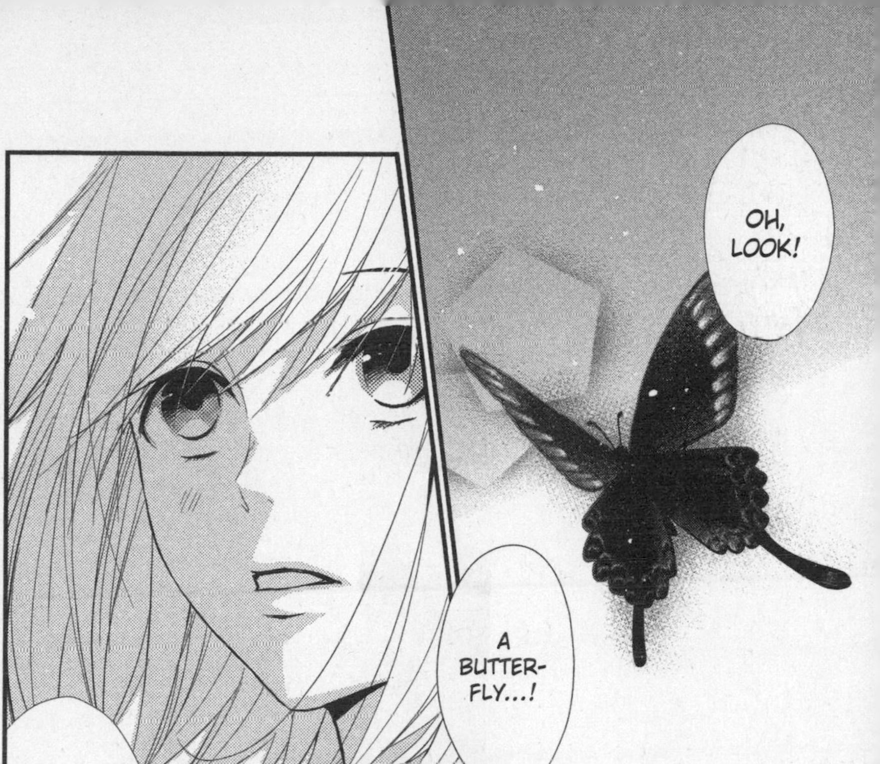
OH, LOOK!
A BUTTER-FLY...!
IT'S BEAUTIFUL.

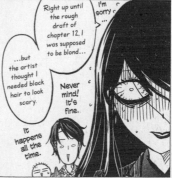

Finally getting to introduce Kyutaro's sister, Mutsumi, makes me awfully emotional. I had a tiny bit of trouble setting things up for her, and then the timing wasn't quite right to bring her in. But now you finally know what exactly Koichi's position in the Horikita family is. He's like the son-in-law who has to watch his step.

In the flashback scene in chapter 10 of QQ Sweeper volume 2, it was a younger Koichi and Mutsumi who hurried to little Kyutaro's side. Funnily, her hair was a different color then. I-I guess she colored it...

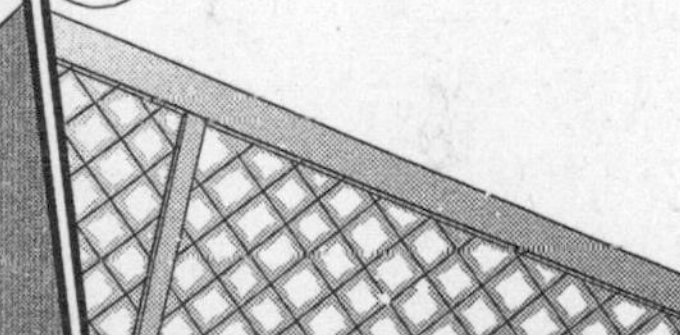
I'm sorry ...
Right up until the rough draft of chapter 12, I was supposed to be blond...
...but the artist thought I needed black hair to look scary.
Never mind! It's fine.
It happens all the time.

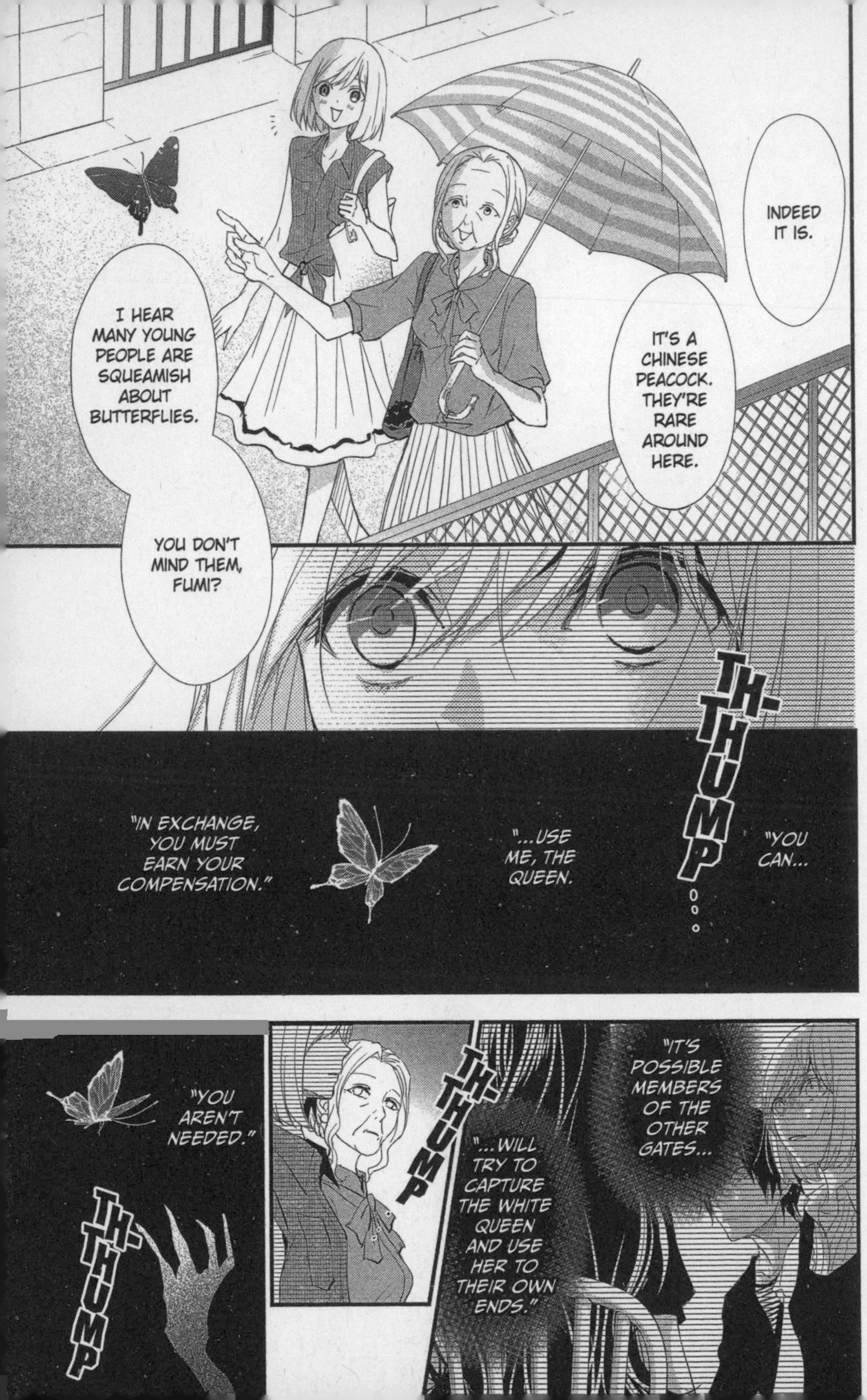
INDEED IT IS.
IT'S A CHINESE PEACOCK. THEY'RE RARE AROUND HERE.
I HEAR MANY YOUNG PEOPLE ARE SQUEAMISH ABOUT BUTTERFLIES.
YOU DON'T MIND THEM, FUMI?
TH-THUMP...
"YOU CAN...
"...USE ME, THE QUEEN.
"IN EXCHANGE, YOU MUST EARN YOUR COMPENSATION."
"IT'S POSSIBLE MEMBERS OF THE OTHER GATES...
"...WILL TRY TO CAPTURE THE WHITE QUEEN AND USE HER TO THEIR OWN ENDS."
TH-THUMP
"YOU AREN'T NEEDED."
TH-THUMP

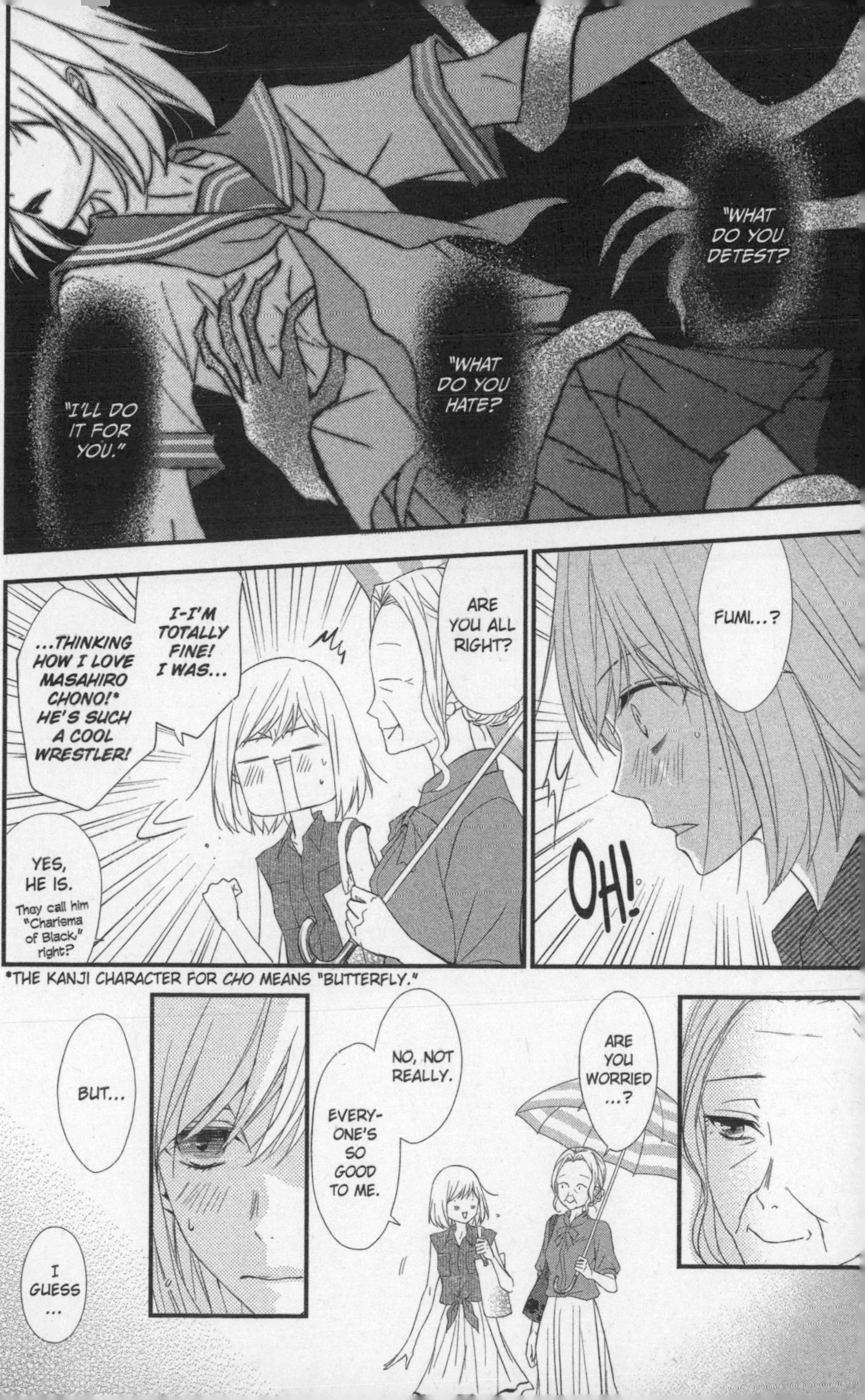
"WHAT DO YOU DETEST?
"WHAT DO YOU HATE?
"I'LL DO IT FOR YOU."
FUMI...?
OH!
ARE YOU ALL RIGHT?
I-I'M TOTALLY FINE! I WAS...
...THINKING HOW I LOVE MASAHIRO CHONO!* HE'S SUCH A COOL WRESTLER!
YES, HE IS. They call him "Charisma of Black," right?
ARE YOU WORRIED ...?
NO, NOT REALLY.
EVERY-ONE'S SO GOOD TO ME.
BUT...
I GUESS ...

*THE KANJI CHARACTER FOR *CHO* MEANS "BUTTERFLY."

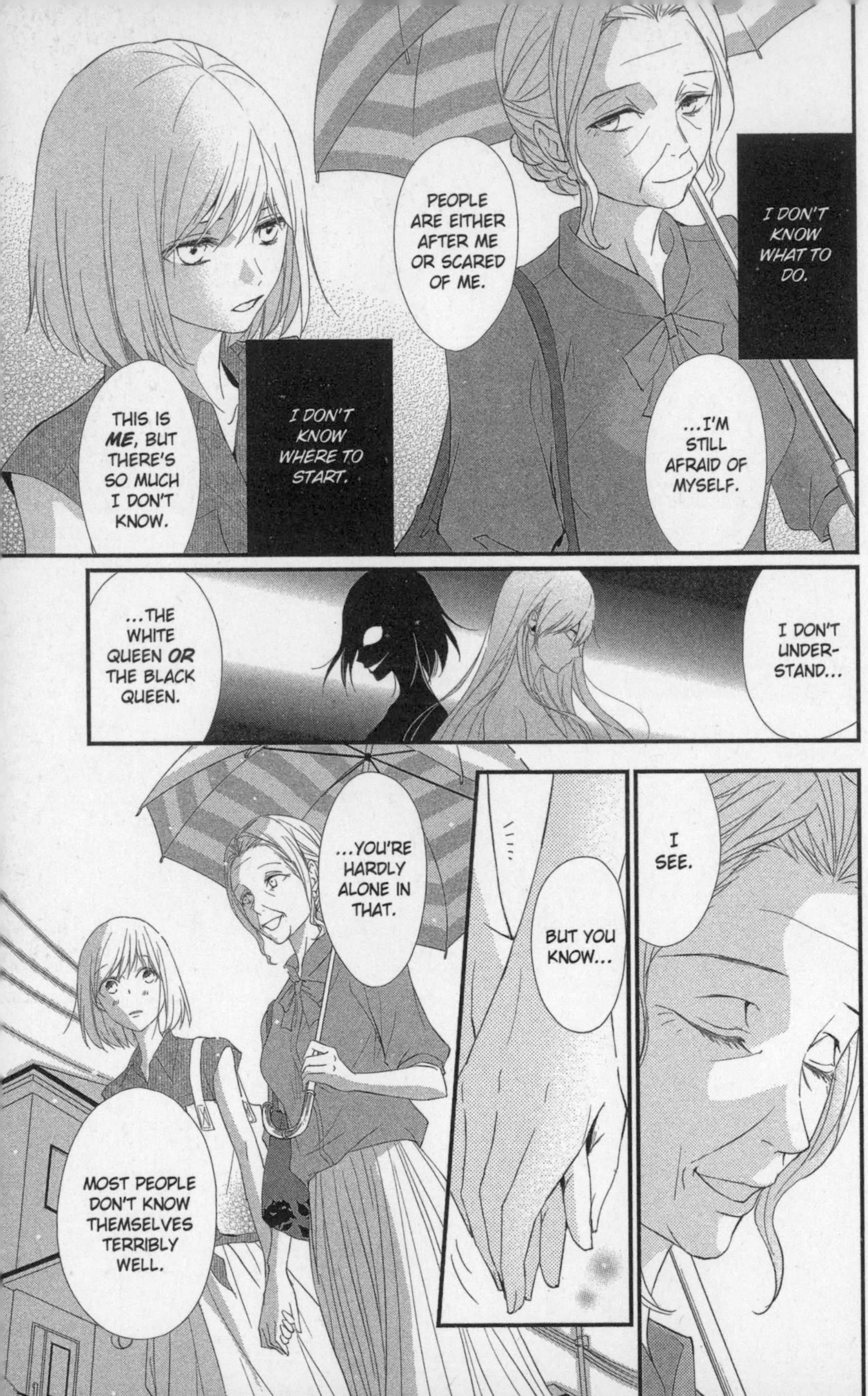
I DON'T KNOW WHAT TO DO.
PEOPLE ARE EITHER AFTER ME OR SCARED OF ME.
...I'M STILL AFRAID OF MYSELF.
I DON'T KNOW WHERE TO START.
THIS IS *ME*, BUT THERE'S SO MUCH I DON'T KNOW.
I DON'T UNDERSTAND...
...THE WHITE QUEEN *OR* THE BLACK QUEEN.
I SEE.
BUT YOU KNOW...
...YOU'RE HARDLY ALONE IN THAT.
MOST PEOPLE DON'T KNOW THEMSELVES TERRIBLY WELL.

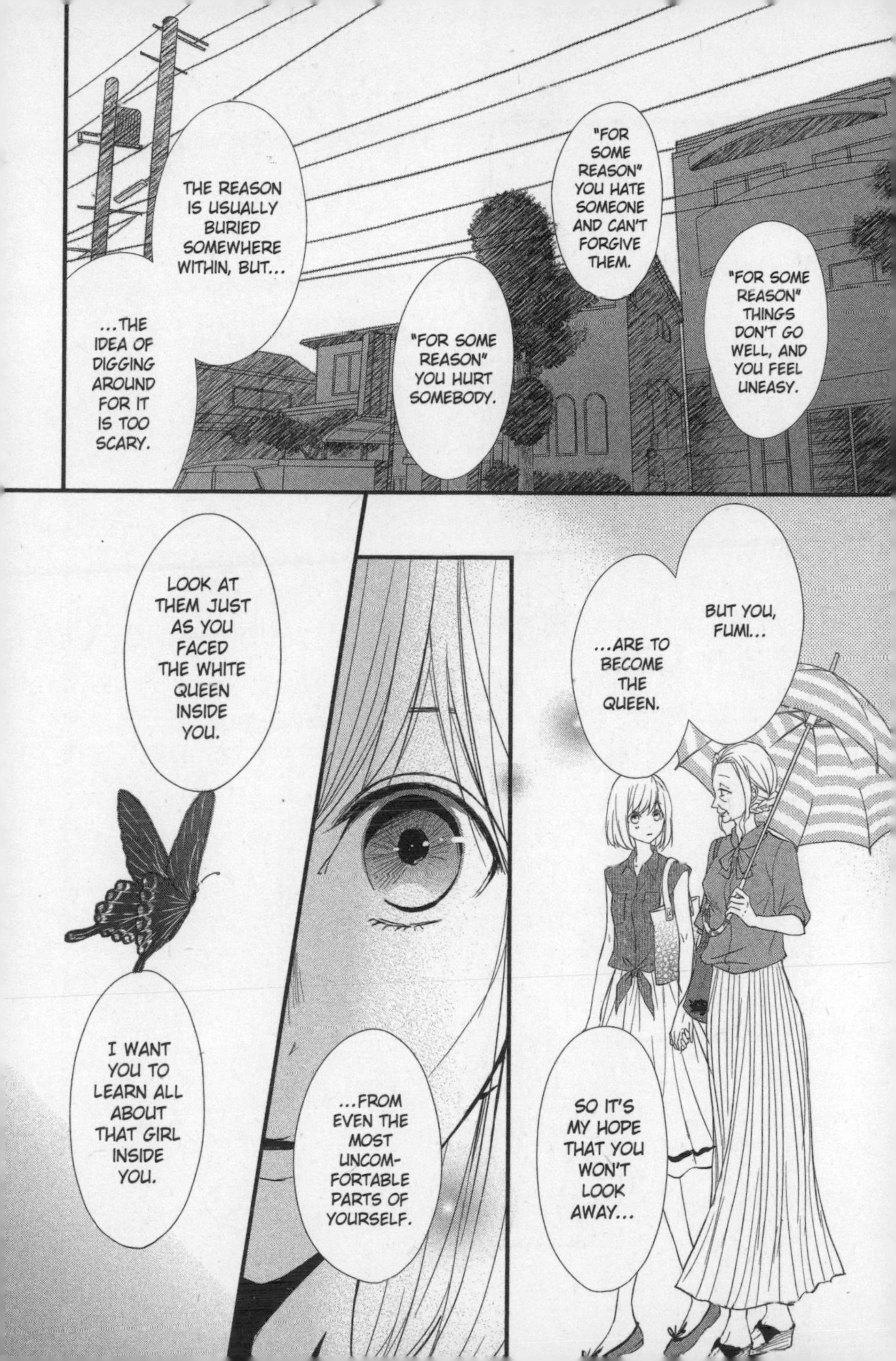
"FOR SOME REASON" THINGS DON'T GO WELL, AND YOU FEEL UNEASY.
"FOR SOME REASON" YOU HATE SOMEONE AND CAN'T FORGIVE THEM.
"FOR SOME REASON" YOU HURT SOMEBODY.
THE REASON IS USUALLY BURIED SOMEWHERE WITHIN, BUT...
...THE IDEA OF DIGGING AROUND FOR IT IS TOO SCARY.
BUT YOU, FUMI...
...ARE TO BECOME THE QUEEN.
SO IT'S MY HOPE THAT YOU WON'T LOOK AWAY...
...FROM EVEN THE MOST UNCOM-FORTABLE PARTS OF YOURSELF.
LOOK AT THEM JUST AS YOU FACED THE WHITE QUEEN INSIDE YOU.
I WANT YOU TO LEARN ALL ABOUT THAT GIRL INSIDE YOU.

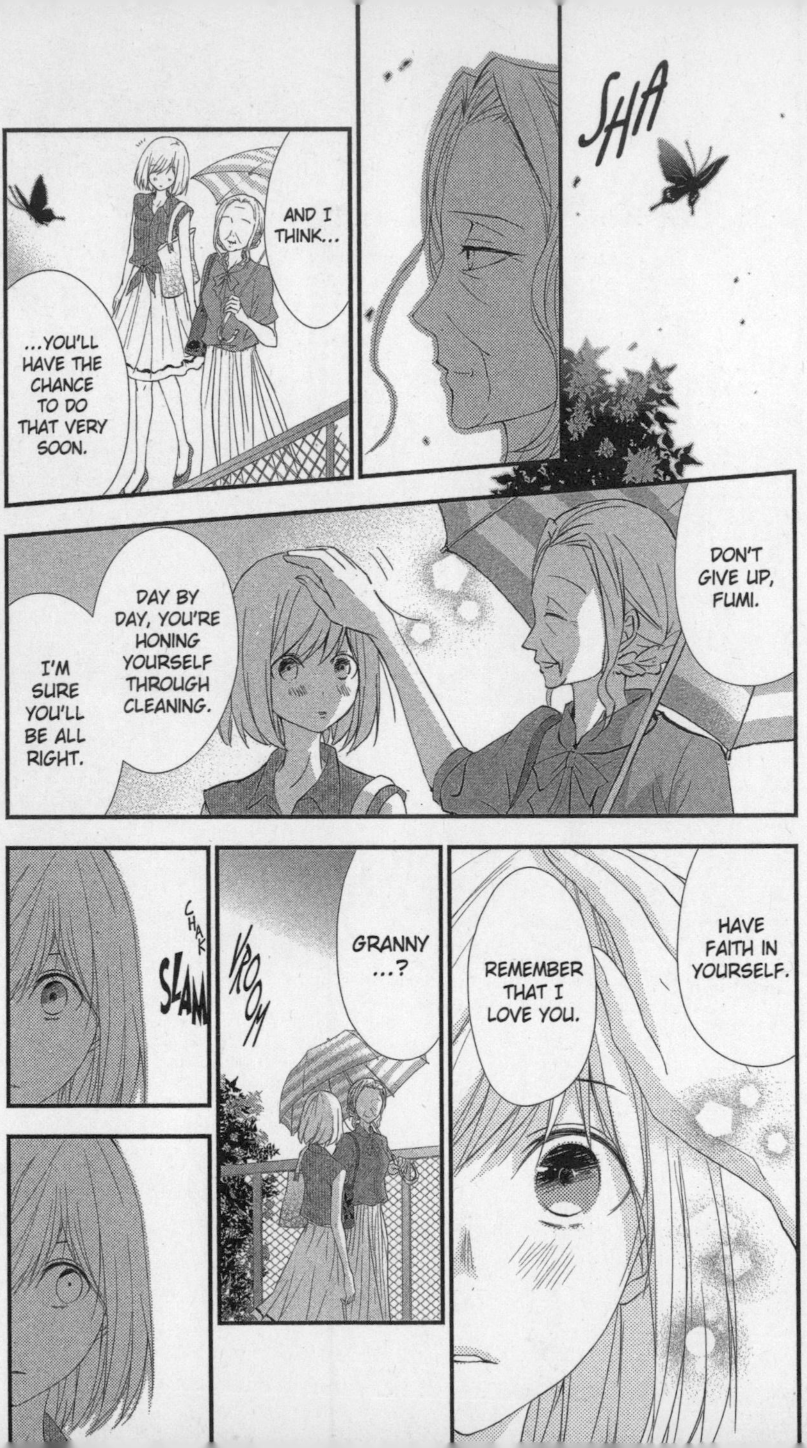
SHIA
AND I THINK...
...YOU'LL HAVE THE CHANCE TO DO THAT VERY SOON.
DON'T GIVE UP, FUMI.
DAY BY DAY, YOU'RE HONING YOURSELF THROUGH CLEANING.
I'M SURE YOU'LL BE ALL RIGHT.
HAVE FAITH IN YOURSELF.
REMEMBER THAT I LOVE YOU.
GRANNY ...?
VROOM
CHAK
SLAM

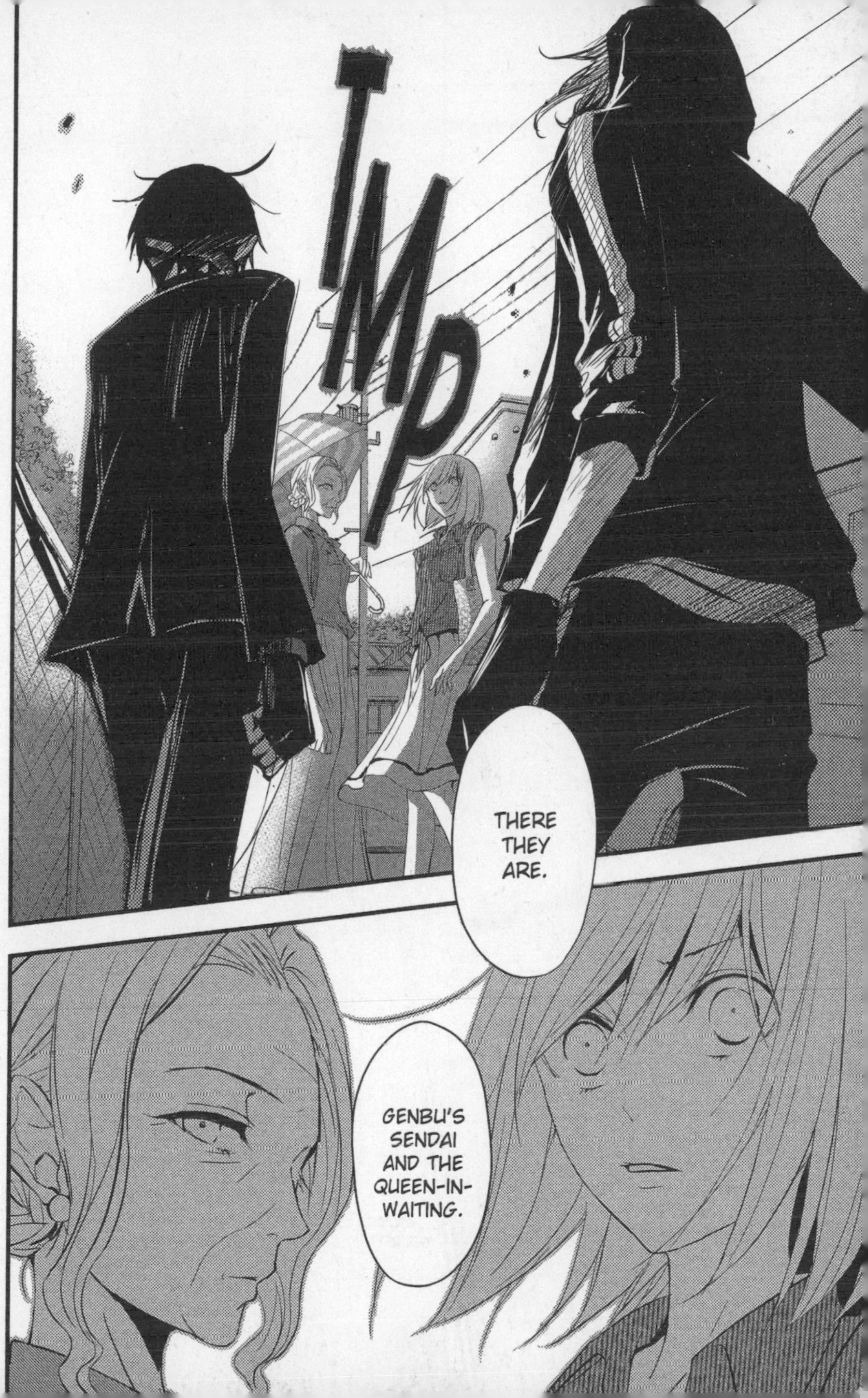
IMP
THERE THEY ARE.
GENBU'S SENDAI AND THE QUEEN-IN-WAITING.

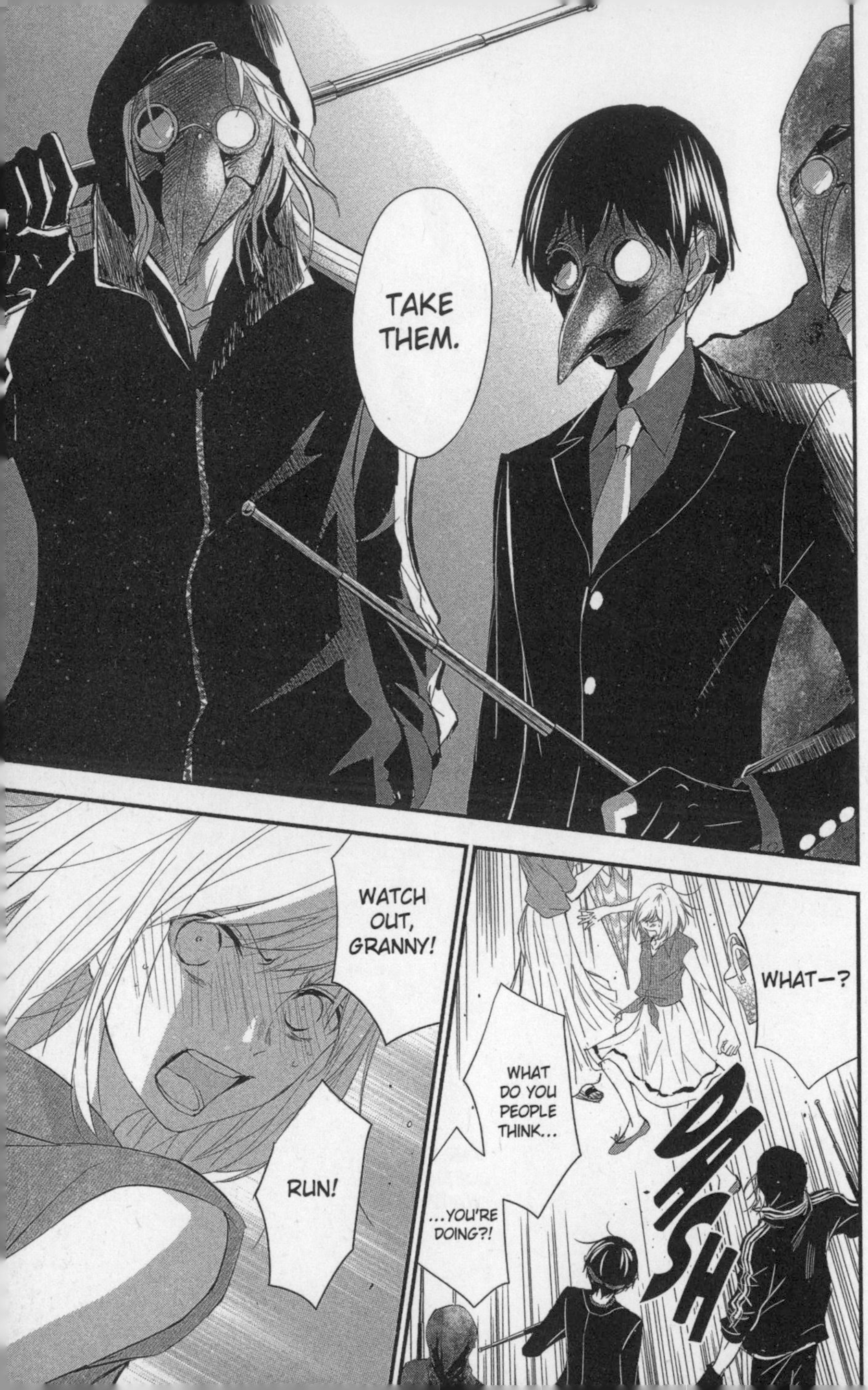
TAKE THEM.
WHAT—?
WHAT DO YOU PEOPLE THINK...
...YOU'RE DOING?!
DASH
WATCH OUT, GRANNY!
RUN!

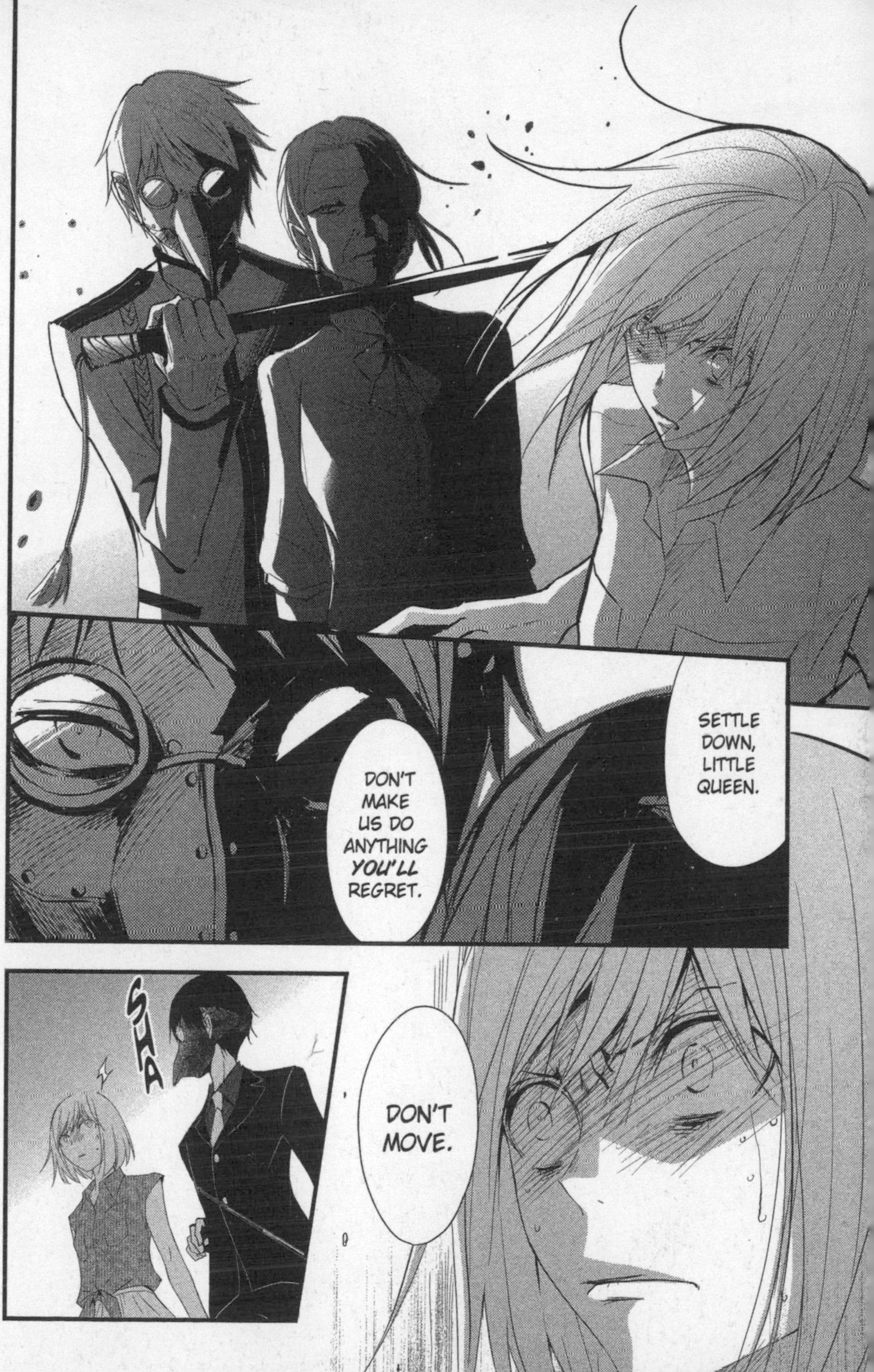
SETTLE DOWN, LITTLE QUEEN.
DON'T MAKE US DO ANYTHING *YOU'LL* REGRET.
DON'T MOVE.
SHA

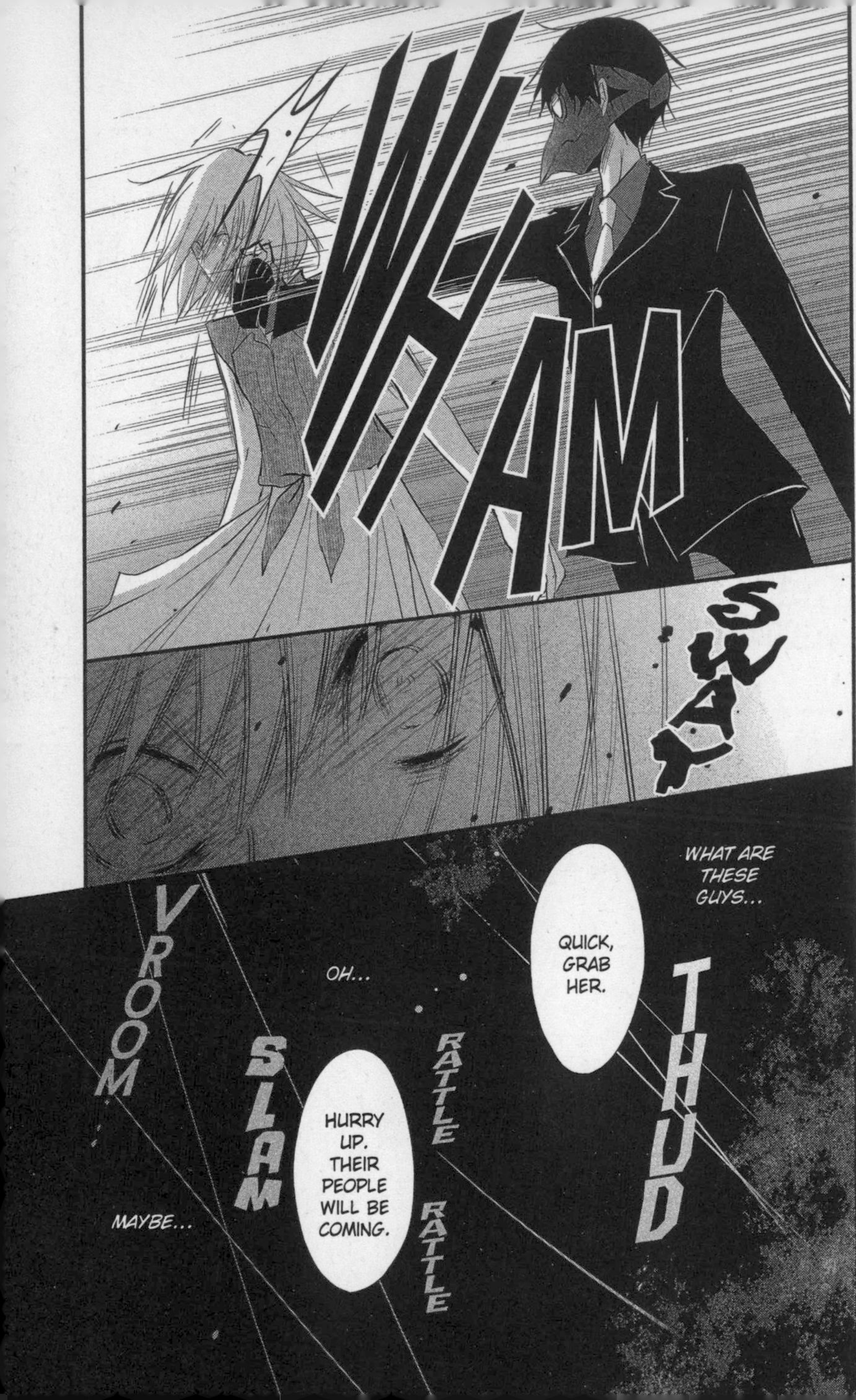
WHAM
SWAY
WHAT ARE THESE GUYS...
QUICK, GRAB HER.
THUD
OH...
RATTLE RATTLE
HURRY UP. THEIR PEOPLE WILL BE COMING.
SLAM
VROOM
MAYBE...

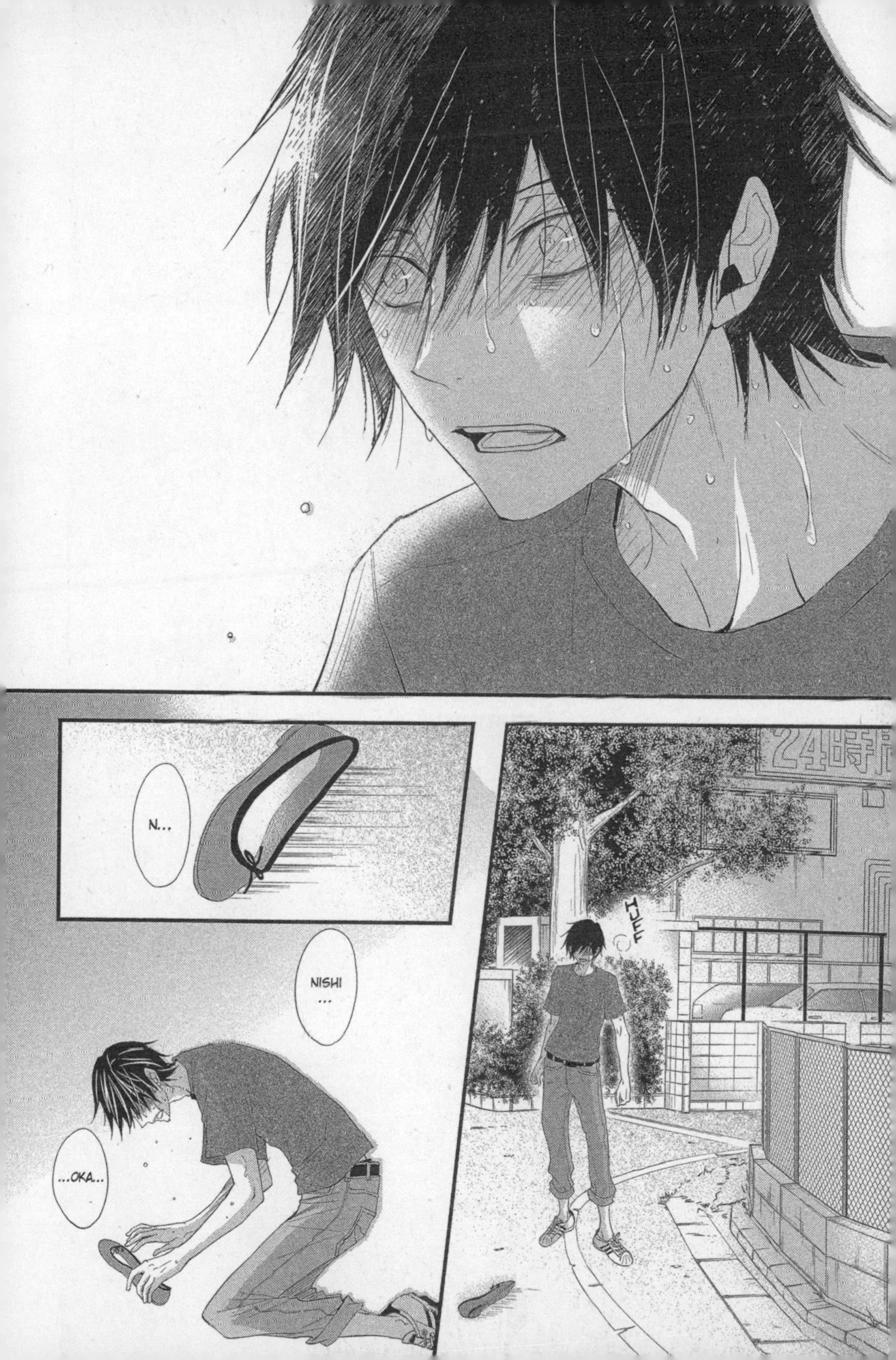
HUFF
N...
NISHI ...
...OKA...

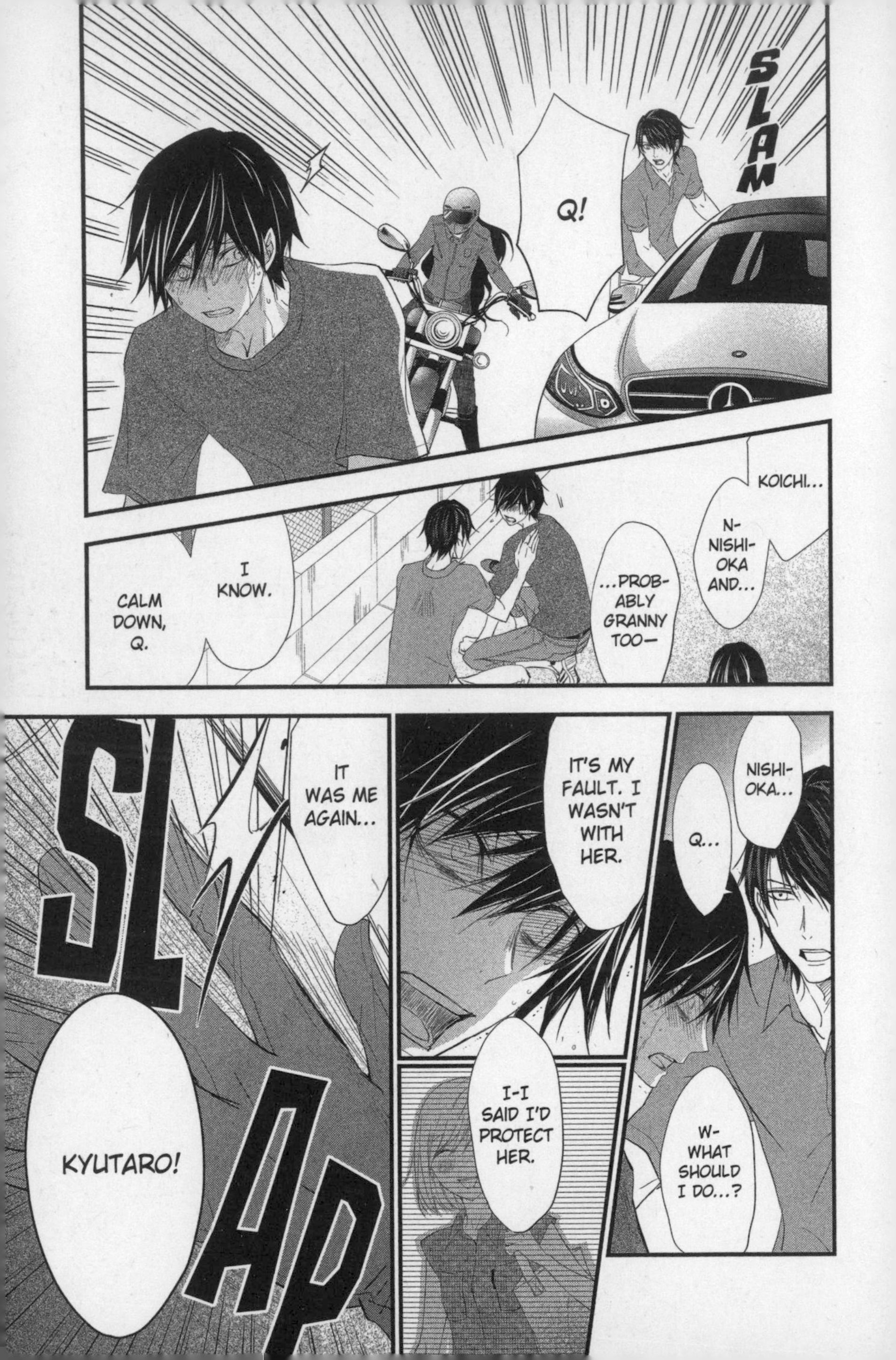
SLAM
Q!
KOICHI...
N-NISHIOKA AND...
...PROBABLY GRANNY TOO—
I KNOW.
CALM DOWN, Q.
NISHIOKA...
Q...
W-WHAT SHOULD I DO...?
IT'S MY FAULT. I WASN'T WITH HER.
I-I SAID I'D PROTECT HER.
IT WAS ME AGAIN...
SLAP
KYUTARO!

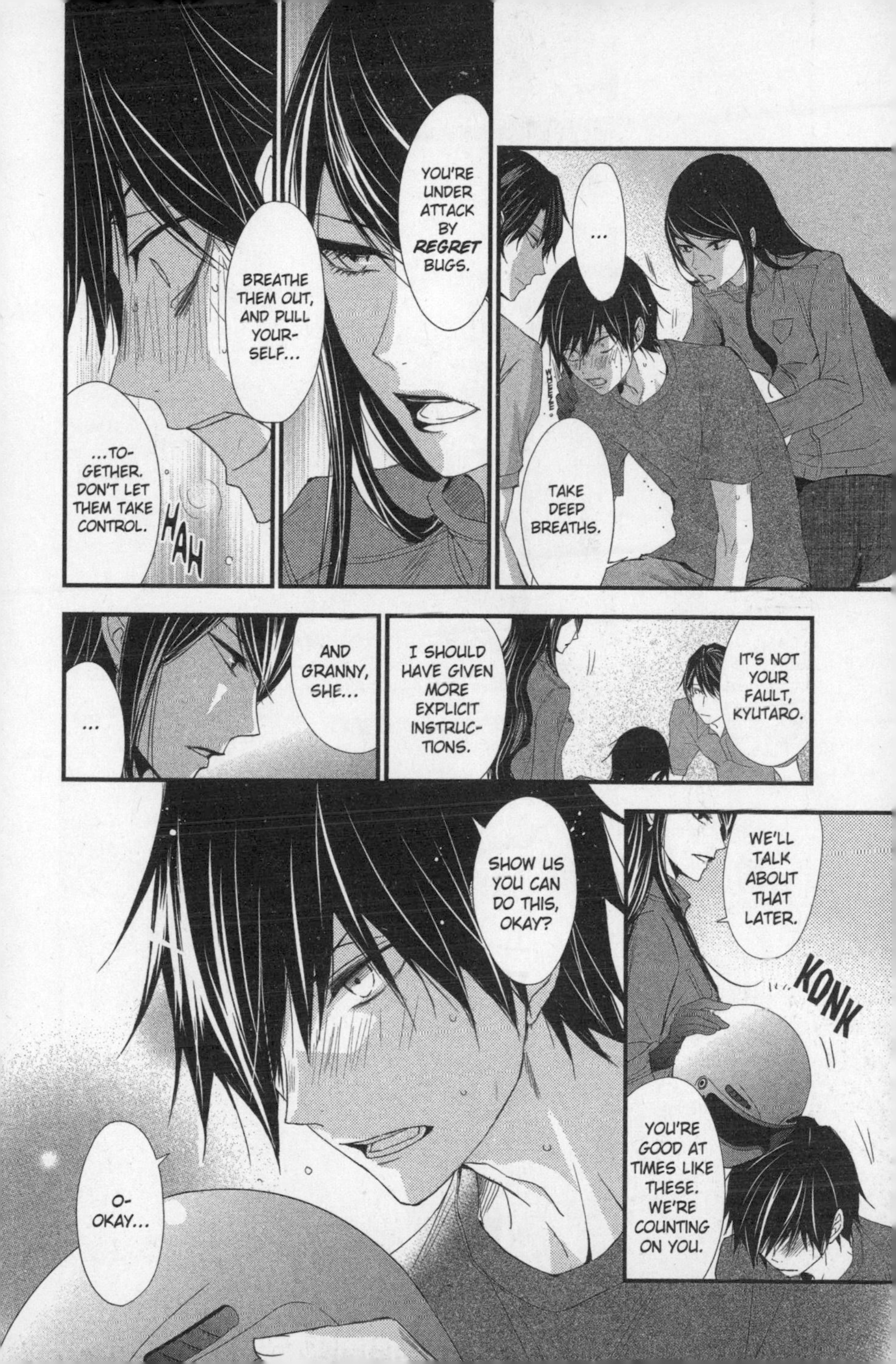
...
WHEEZE
TAKE DEEP BREATHS.
YOU'RE UNDER ATTACK BY REGRET BUGS.
BREATHE THEM OUT, AND PULL YOUR-SELF...
...TO-GETHER. DON'T LET THEM TAKE CONTROL.
HAH
IT'S NOT YOUR FAULT, KYUTARO.
I SHOULD HAVE GIVEN MORE EXPLICIT INSTRUC-TIONS.
AND GRANNY, SHE...
...
WE'LL TALK ABOUT THAT LATER.
KONK
YOU'RE GOOD AT TIMES LIKE THESE. WE'RE COUNTING ON YOU.
SHOW US YOU CAN DO THIS, OKAY?
O-OKAY...

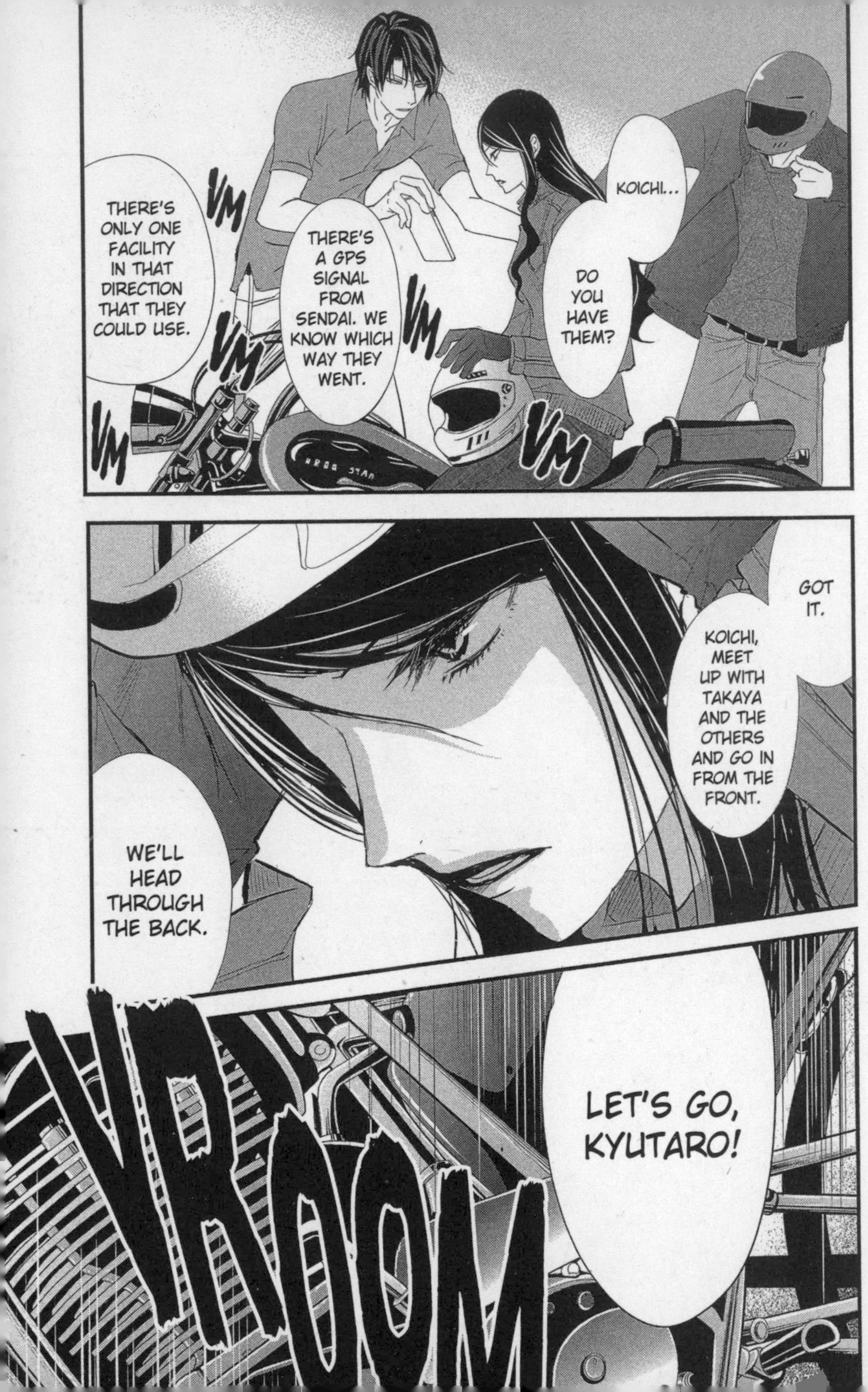
KOICHI...
DO YOU HAVE THEM?
VM
VM
THERE'S A GPS SIGNAL FROM SENDAI. WE KNOW WHICH WAY THEY WENT.
THERE'S ONLY ONE FACILITY IN THAT DIRECTION THAT THEY COULD USE.
VM
VM
VM
GOT IT.
KOICHI, MEET UP WITH TAKAYA AND THE OTHERS AND GO IN FROM THE FRONT.
WE'LL HEAD THROUGH THE BACK.
LET'S GO, KYUTARO!
VROOOM

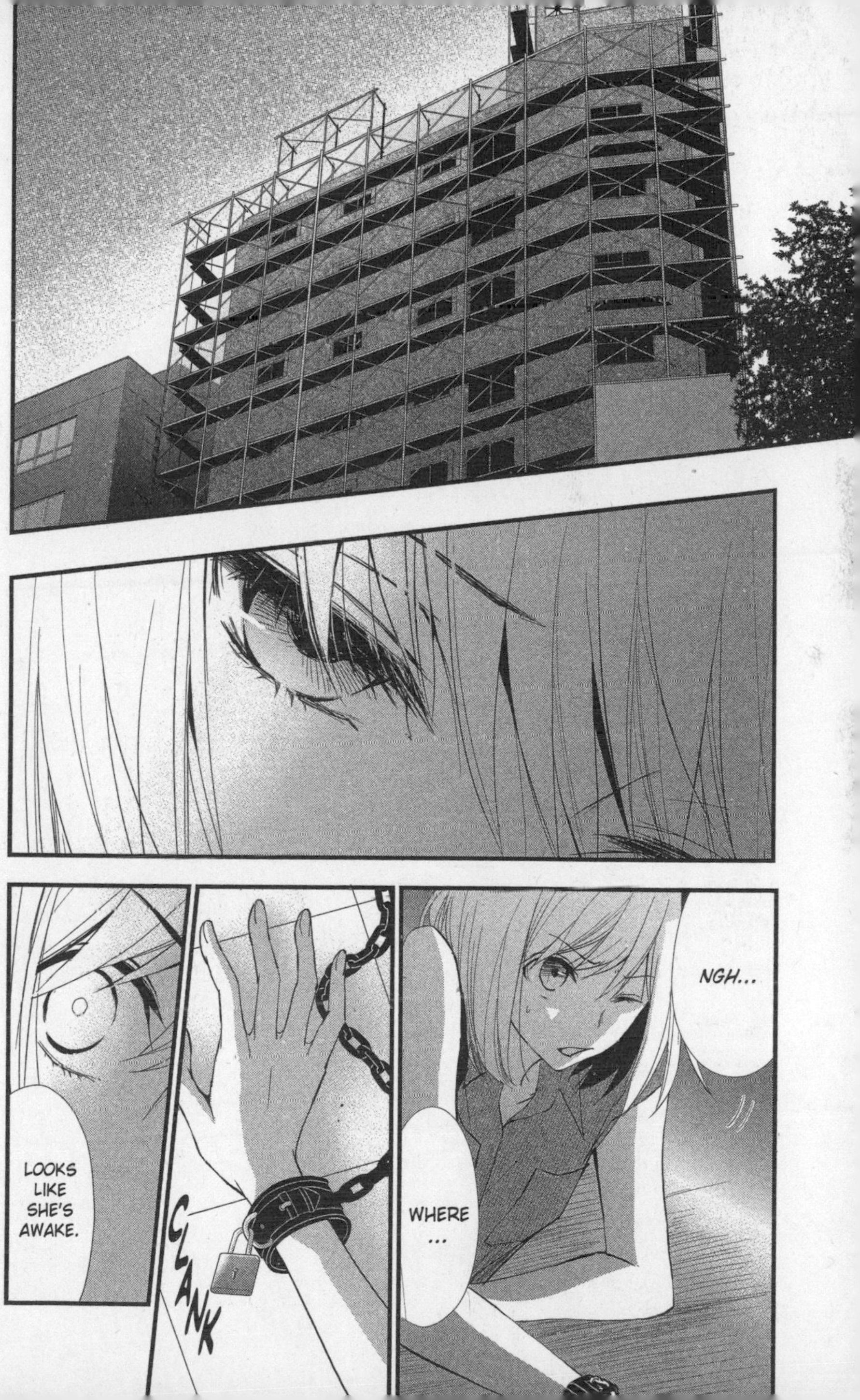
NGH...
WHERE ...
CLANK
LOOKS LIKE SHE'S AWAKE.

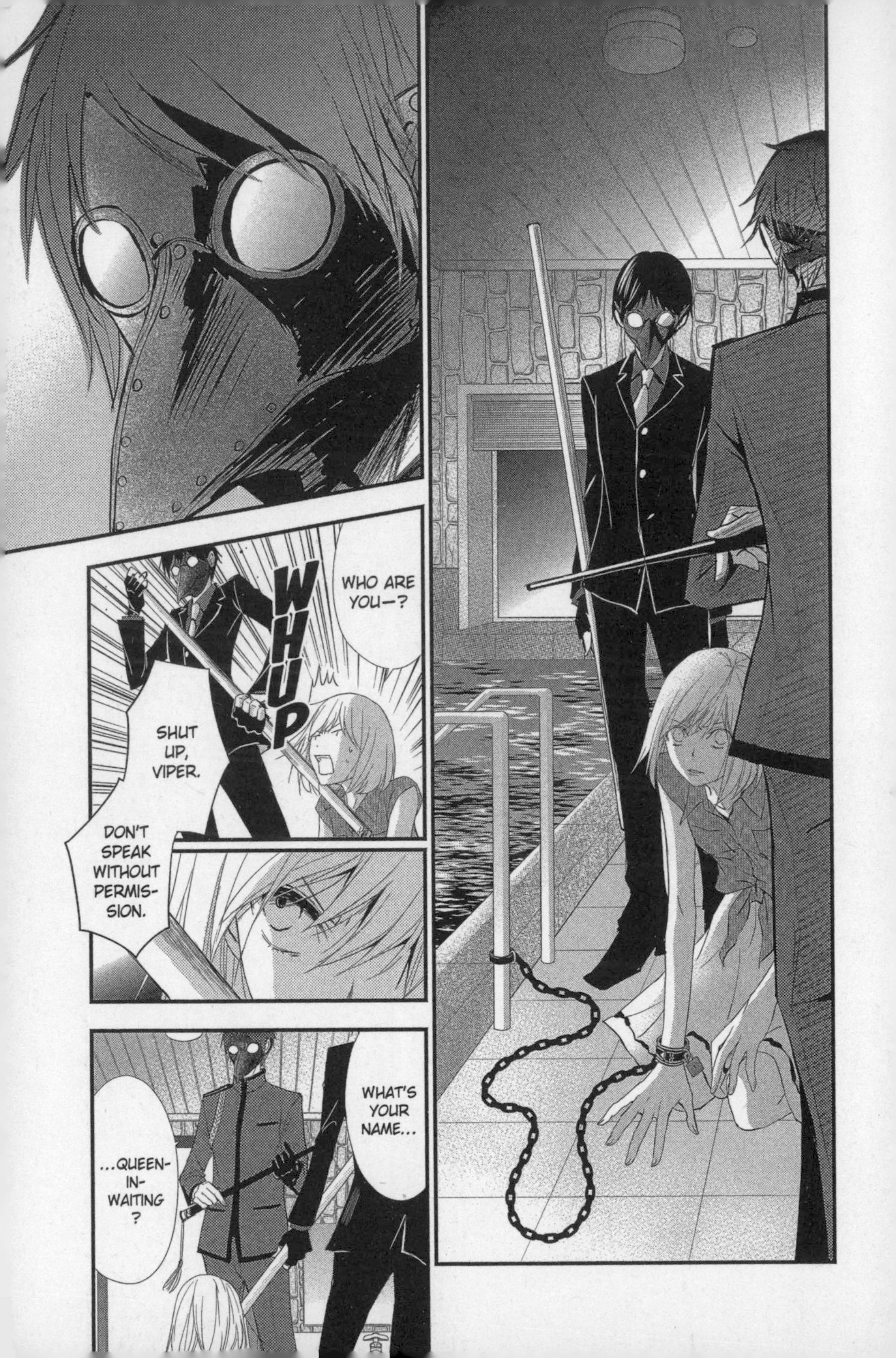
WHO ARE YOU—?
WHUP
SHUT UP, VIPER.
DON'T SPEAK WITHOUT PERMIS-SION.
WHAT'S YOUR NAME...
...QUEEN-IN-WAITING?

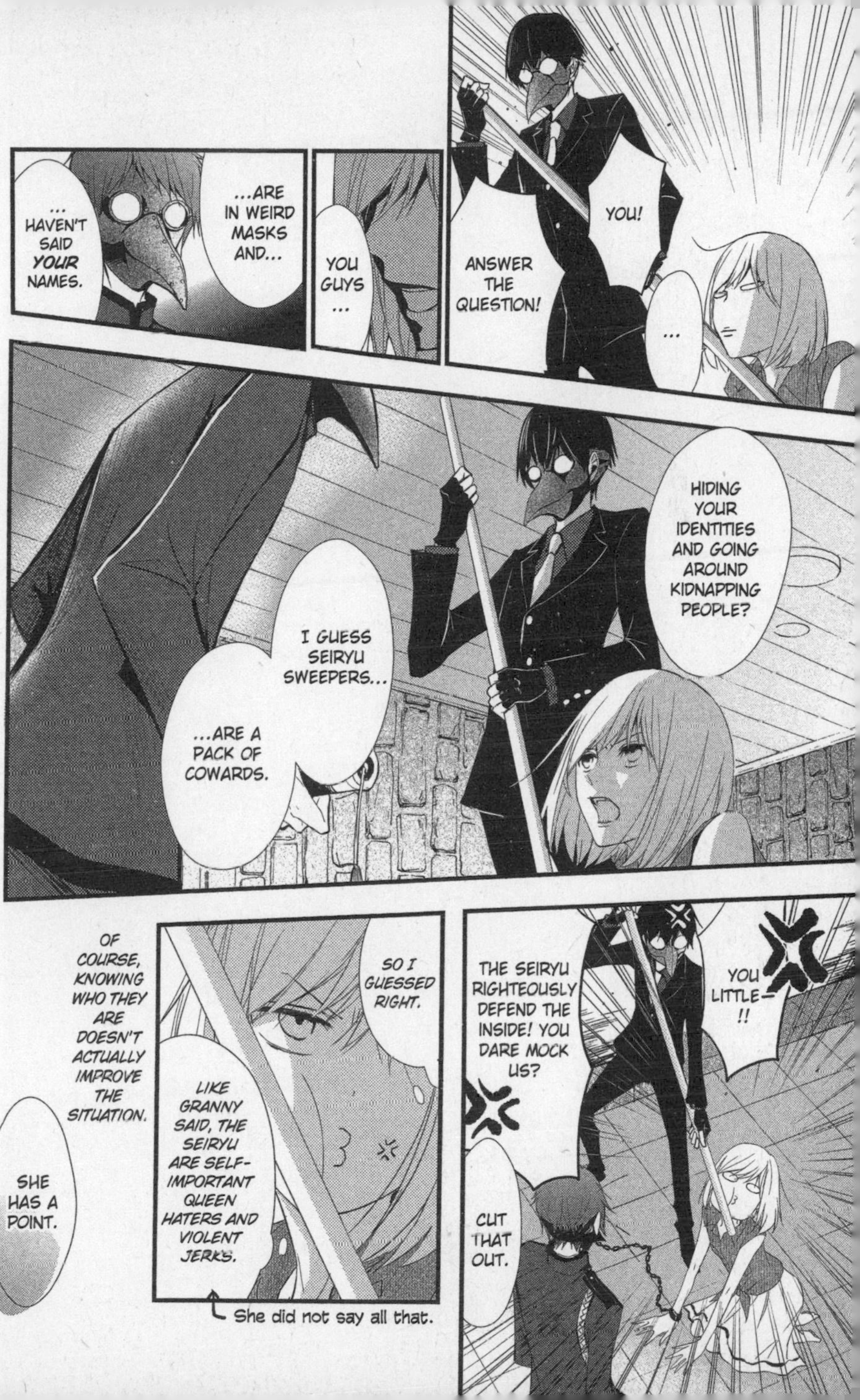
YOU!
ANSWER THE QUESTION!
...
YOU GUYS ...
...ARE IN WEIRD MASKS AND...
... HAVEN'T SAID YOUR NAMES.
HIDING YOUR IDENTITIES AND GOING AROUND KIDNAPPING PEOPLE?
I GUESS SEIRYU SWEEPERS...
...ARE A PACK OF COWARDS.
YOU LITTLE— !!
THE SEIRYU RIGHTEOUSLY DEFEND THE INSIDE! YOU DARE MOCK US?
CUT THAT OUT.
SO I GUESSED RIGHT.
LIKE GRANNY SAID, THE SEIRYU ARE SELF-IMPORTANT QUEEN HATERS AND VIOLENT JERKS.
She did not say all that.
OF COURSE, KNOWING WHO THEY ARE DOESN'T ACTUALLY IMPROVE THE SITUATION.
SHE HAS A POINT.

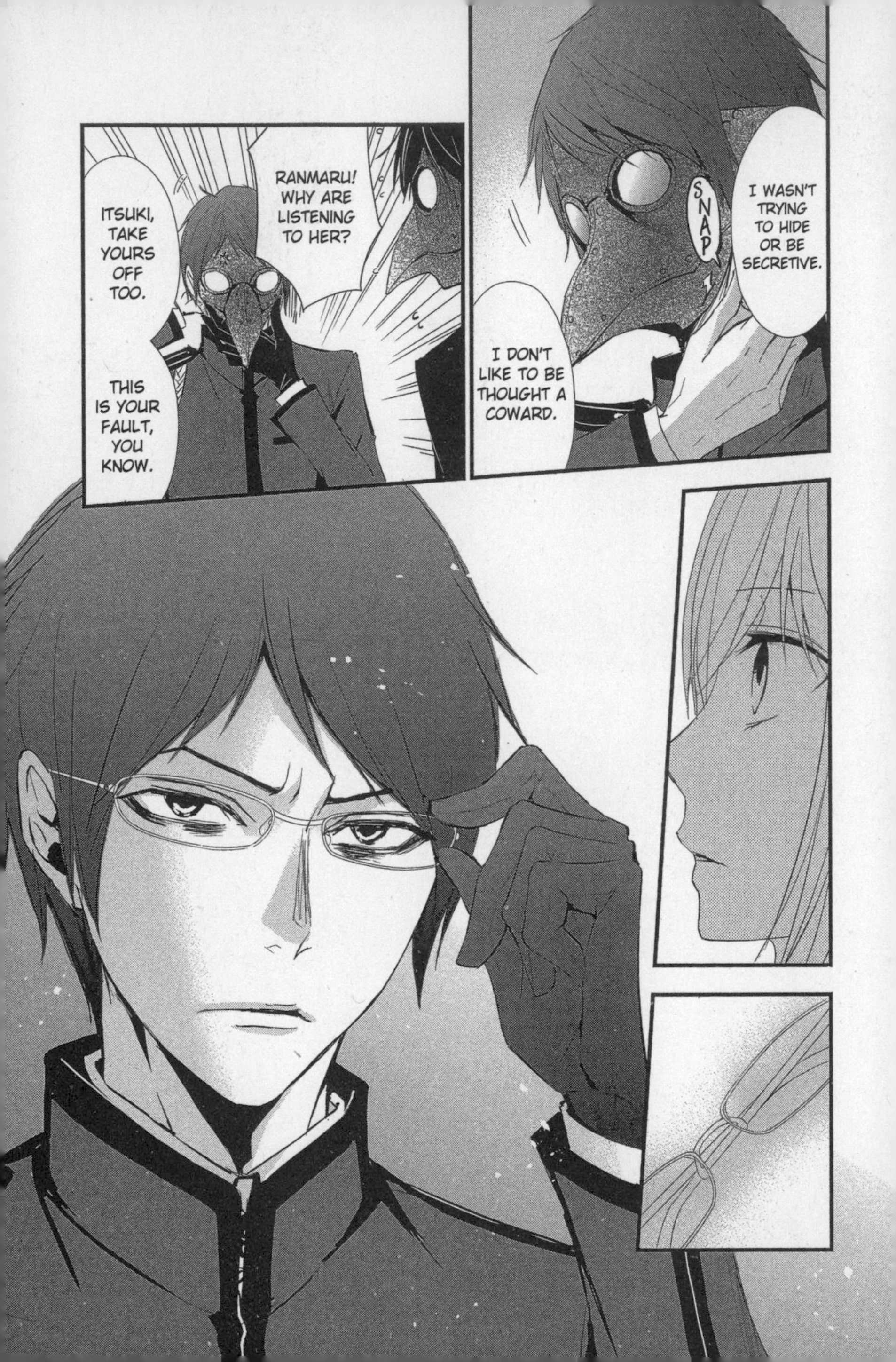
I WASN'T TRYING TO HIDE OR BE SECRETIVE.
SNAP
I DON'T LIKE TO BE THOUGHT A COWARD.
RANMARU! WHY ARE LISTENING TO HER?
ITSUKI, TAKE YOURS OFF TOO.
THIS IS YOUR FAULT, YOU KNOW.

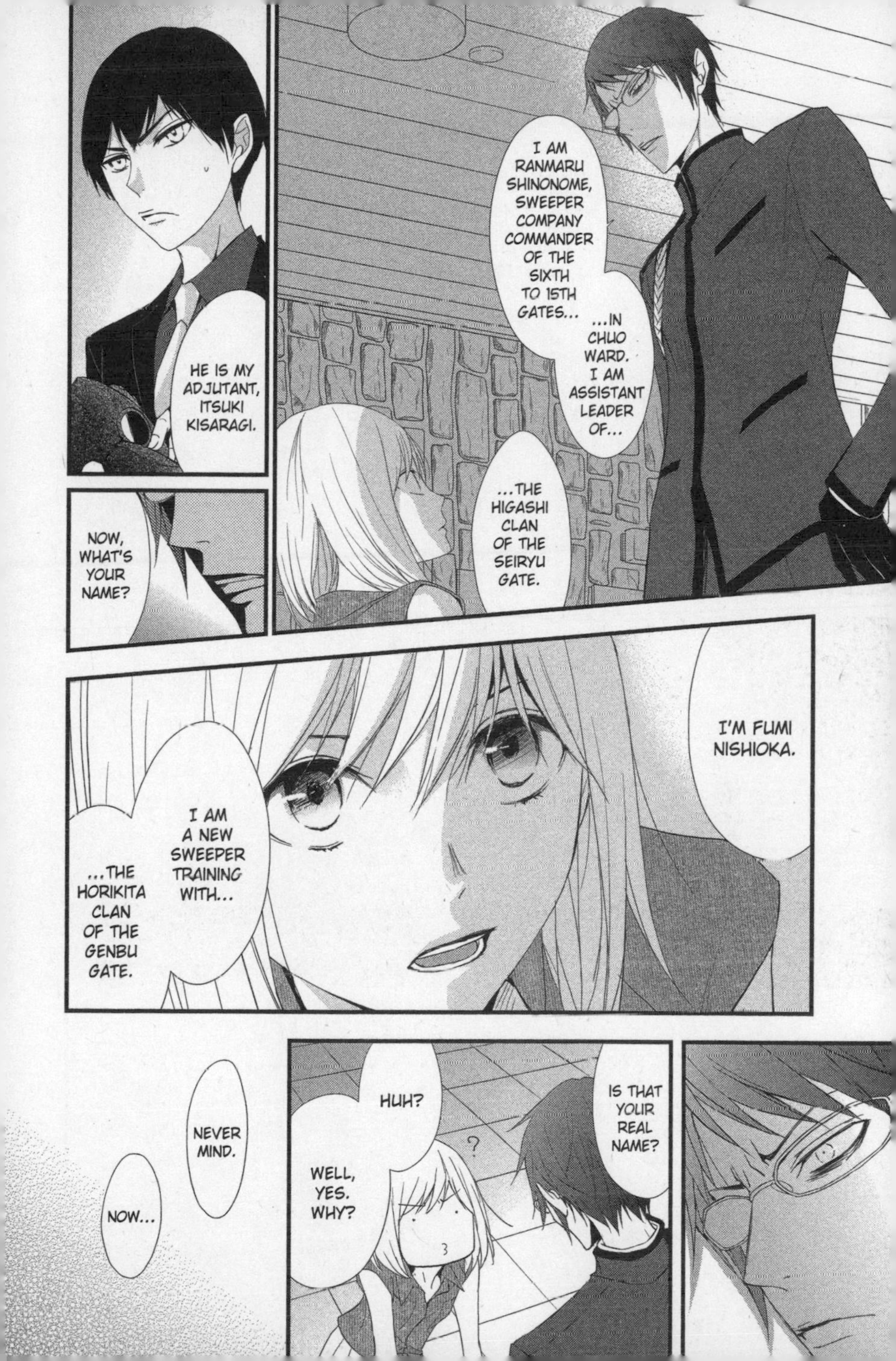
I AM RANMARU SHINONOME, SWEEPER COMPANY COMMANDER OF THE SIXTH TO 15TH GATES...
...IN CHUO WARD. I AM ASSISTANT LEADER OF...
...THE HIGASHI CLAN OF THE SEIRYU GATE.
HE IS MY ADJUTANT, ITSUKI KISARAGI.
NOW, WHAT'S YOUR NAME?
I'M FUMI NISHIOKA.
I AM A NEW SWEEPER TRAINING WITH...
...THE HORIKITA CLAN OF THE GENBU GATE.
IS THAT YOUR REAL NAME?
HUH?
WELL, YES. WHY?
NEVER MIND.
NOW...

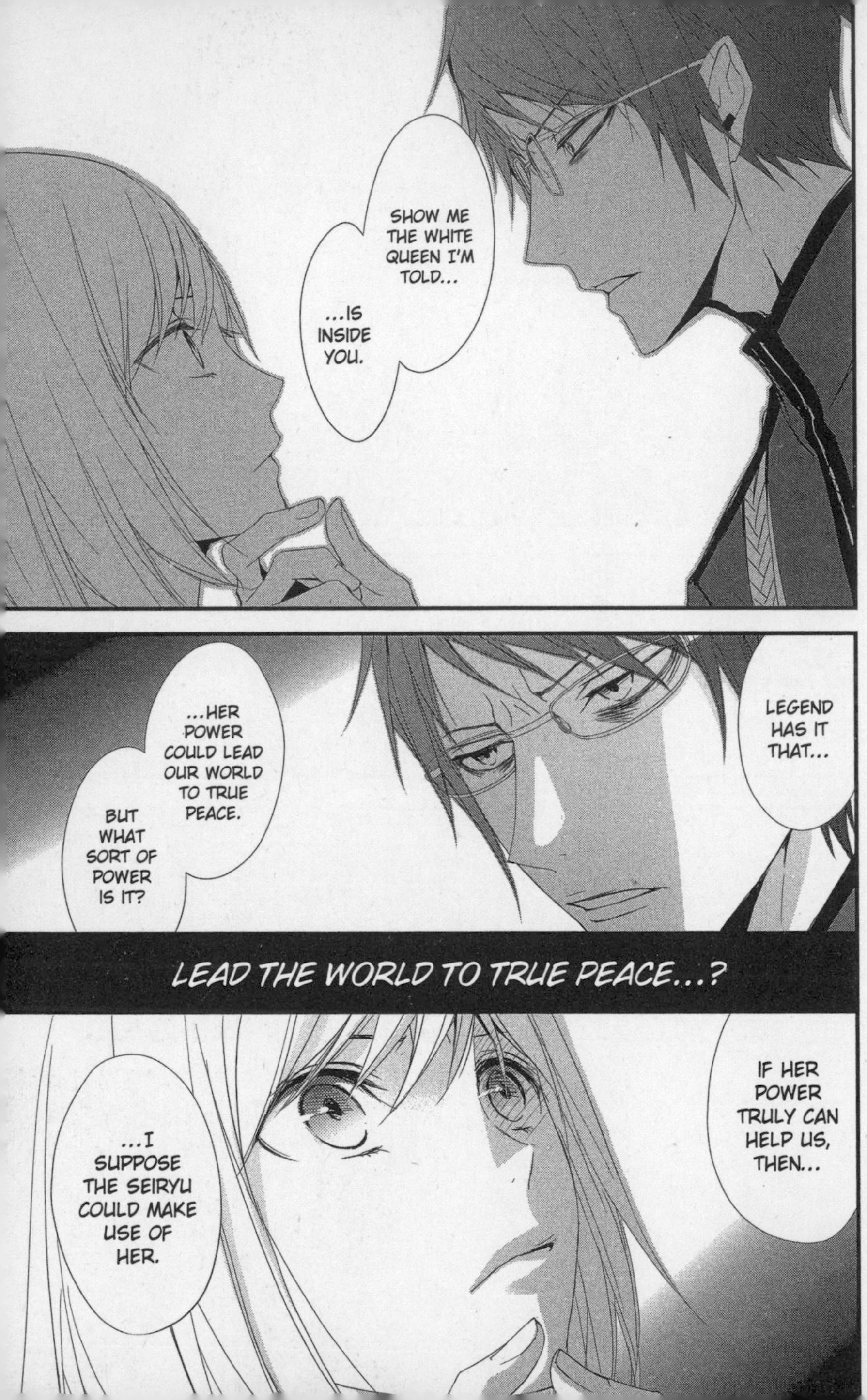
SHOW ME THE WHITE QUEEN I'M TOLD...
...IS INSIDE YOU.
LEGEND HAS IT THAT...
...HER POWER COULD LEAD OUR WORLD TO TRUE PEACE.
BUT WHAT SORT OF POWER IS IT?
LEAD THE WORLD TO TRUE PEACE...?
IF HER POWER TRULY CAN HELP US, THEN...
...I SUPPOSE THE SEIRYU COULD MAKE USE OF HER.

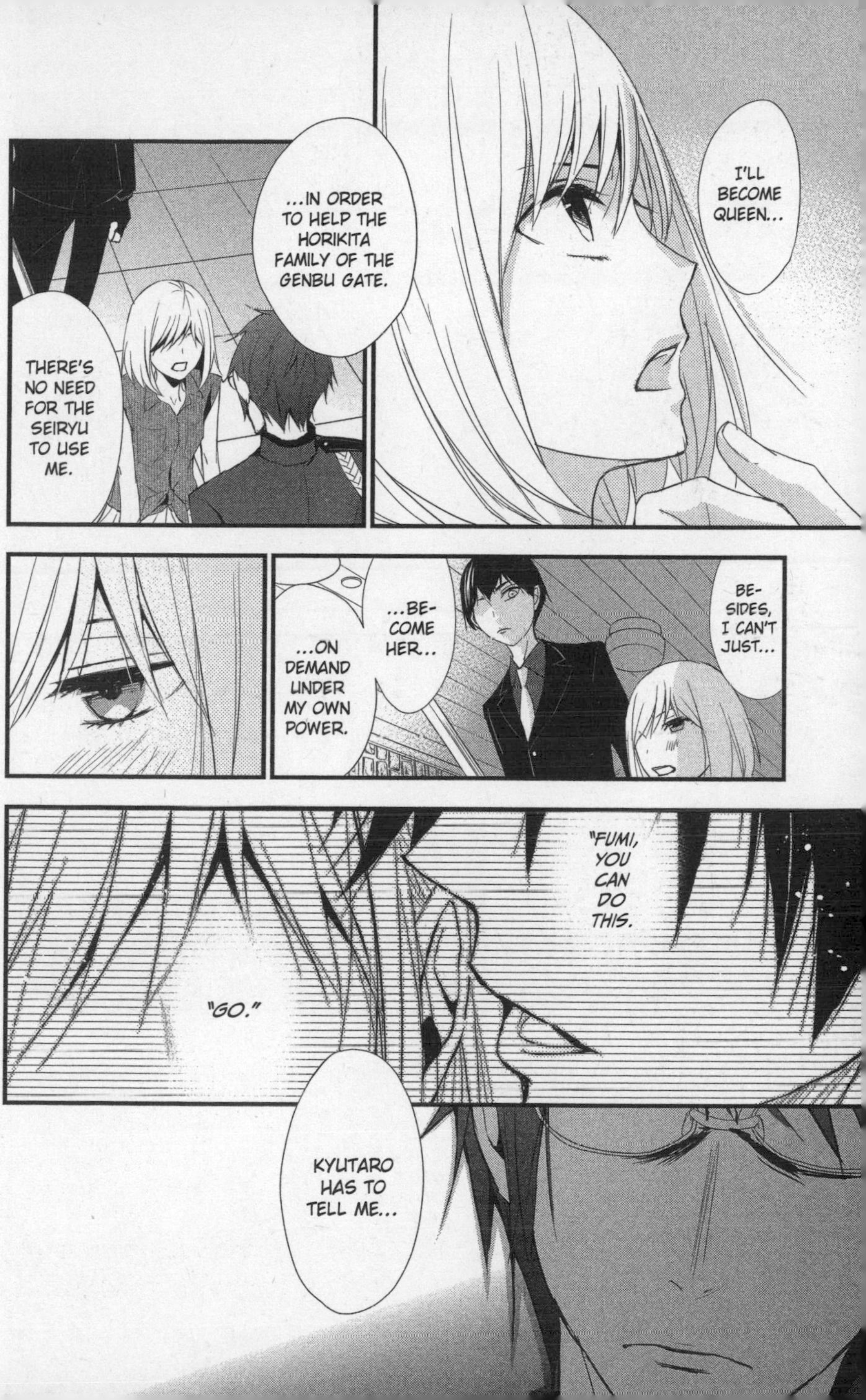
I'LL BECOME QUEEN...
...IN ORDER TO HELP THE HORIKITA FAMILY OF THE GENBU GATE.
THERE'S NO NEED FOR THE SEIRYU TO USE ME.
BE-SIDES, I CAN'T JUST...
...BE-COME HER...
...ON DEMAND UNDER MY OWN POWER.
"FUMI, YOU CAN DO THIS.
"GO."
KYUTARO HAS TO TELL ME...

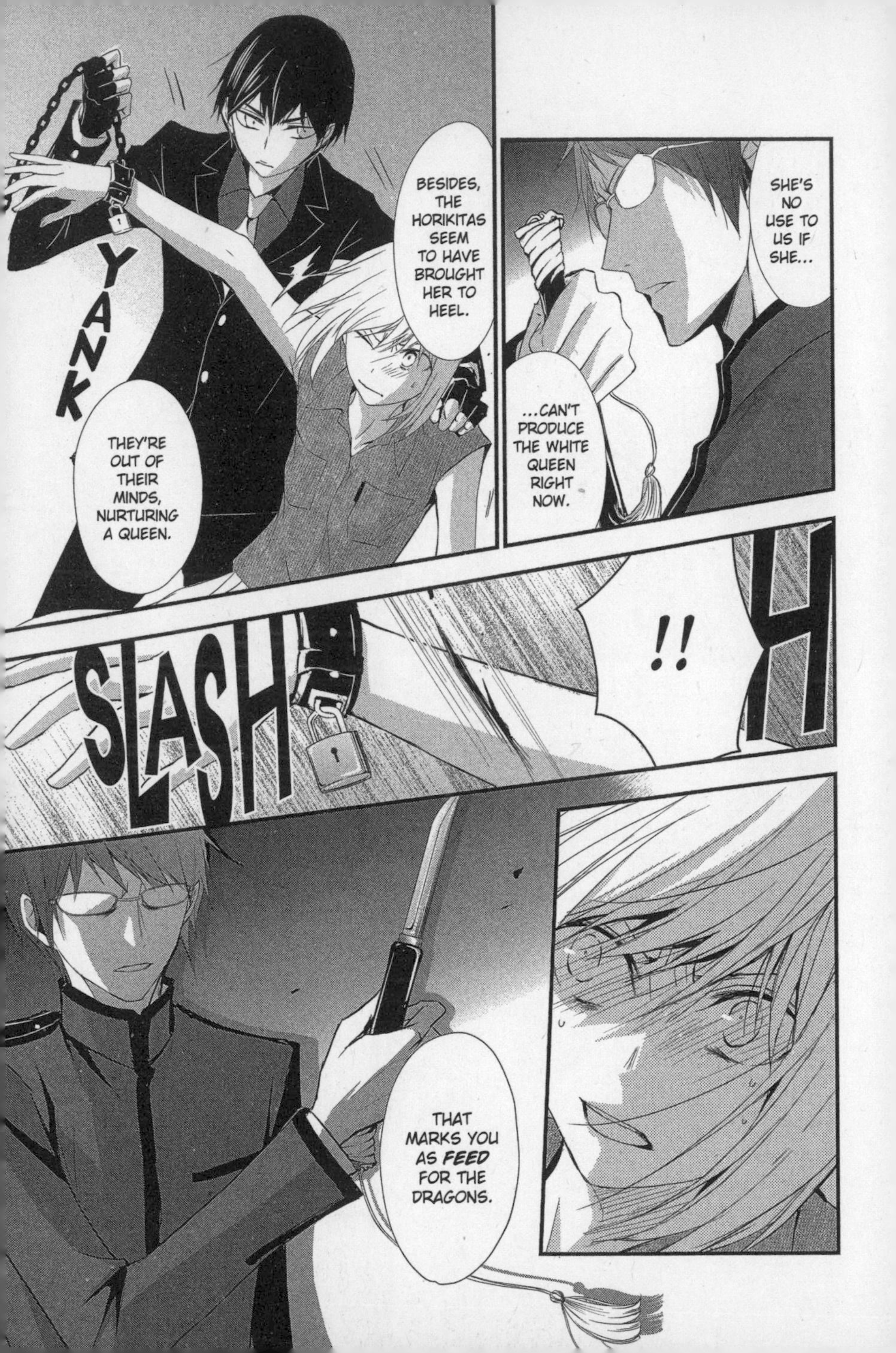
SHE'S NO USE TO US IF SHE...
...CAN'T PRODUCE THE WHITE QUEEN RIGHT NOW.
BESIDES, THE HORIKITAS SEEM TO HAVE BROUGHT HER TO HEEL.
YANK
THEY'RE OUT OF THEIR MINDS, NURTURING A QUEEN.
!!
SLASH
THAT MARKS YOU AS *FEED* FOR THE DRAGONS.

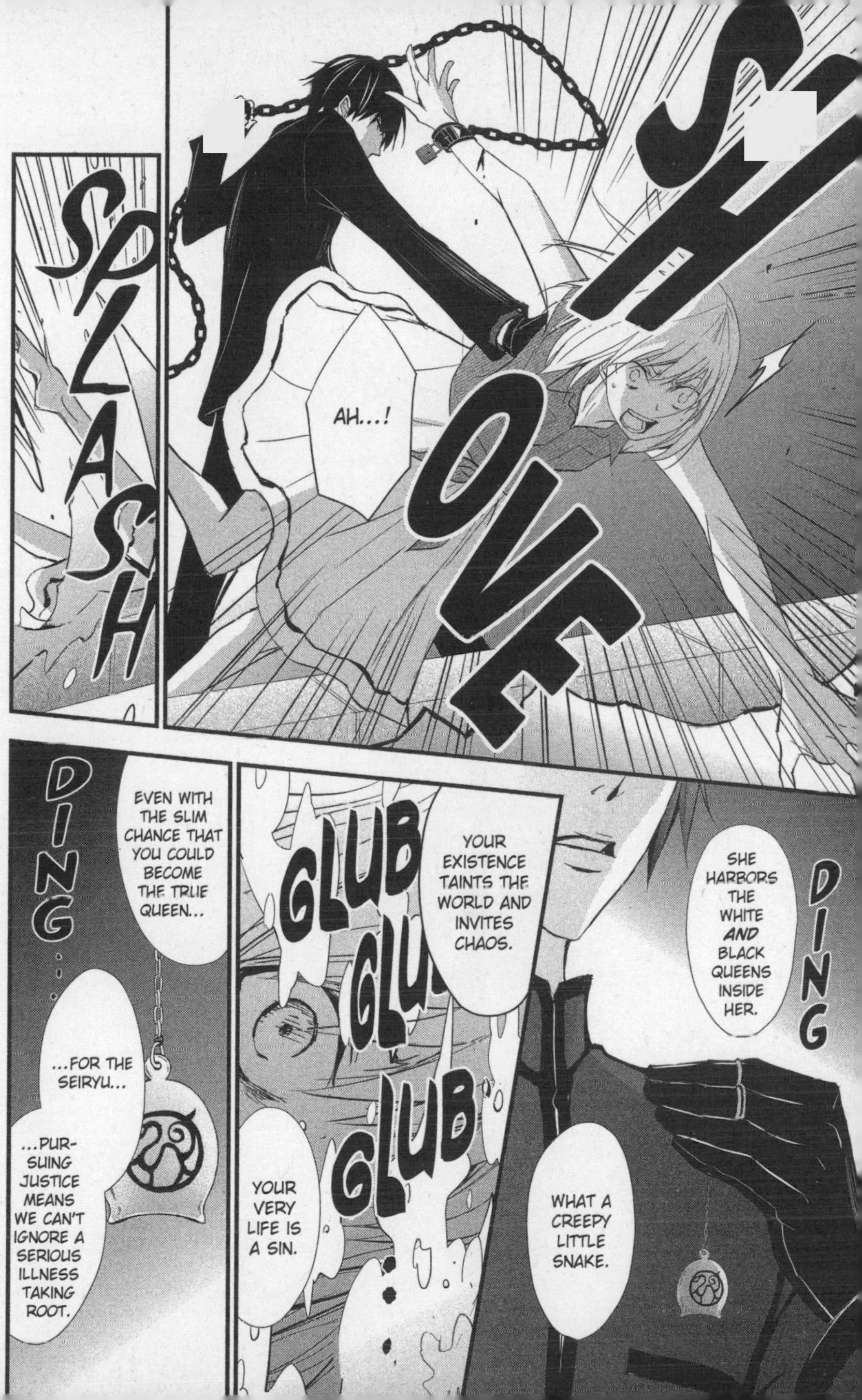
SHOVE
AH...!
SPLASH
DING
SHE HARBORS THE WHITE AND BLACK QUEENS INSIDE HER.
WHAT A CREEPY LITTLE SNAKE.
GLUB GLUB
YOUR EXISTENCE TAINTS THE WORLD AND INVITES CHAOS.
GLUB GLUB
YOUR VERY LIFE IS A SIN.
DING...
EVEN WITH THE SLIM CHANCE THAT YOU COULD BECOME THE TRUE QUEEN...
...FOR THE SEIRYU...
...PUR-SUING JUSTICE MEANS WE CAN'T IGNORE A SERIOUS ILLNESS TAKING ROOT.

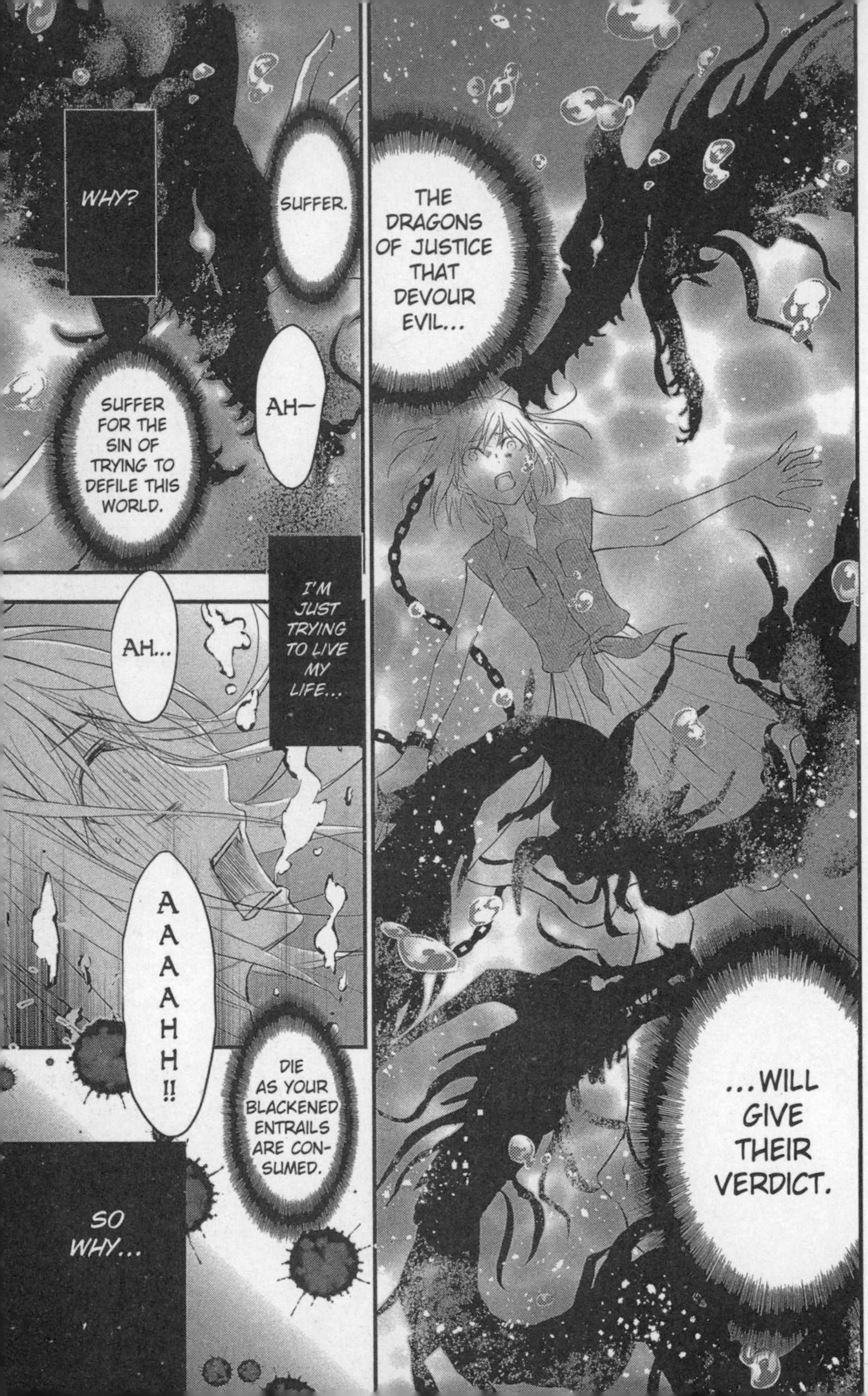
THE DRAGONS OF JUSTICE THAT DEVOUR EVIL...
...WILL GIVE THEIR VERDICT.
SUFFER.
WHY?
AH—
SUFFER FOR THE SIN OF TRYING TO DEFILE THIS WORLD.
I'M JUST TRYING TO LIVE MY LIFE...
AH...
AAAAAH!!
DIE AS YOUR BLACKENED ENTRAILS ARE CONSUMED.
SO WHY...

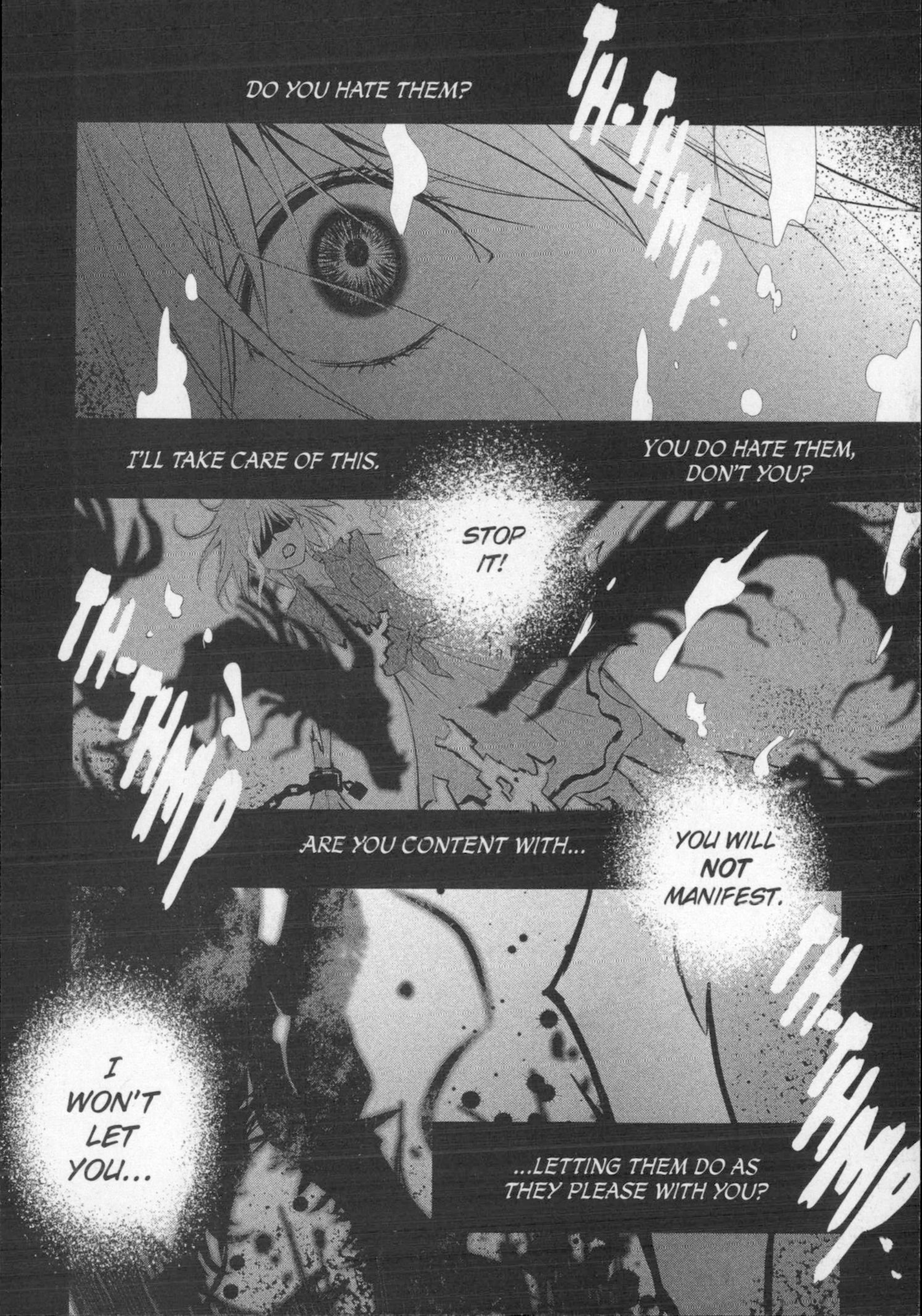
TH-THMP
DO YOU HATE THEM?
YOU DO HATE THEM, DON'T YOU?
I'LL TAKE CARE OF THIS.
STOP IT!
TH-THMP
YOU WILL NOT MANIFEST.
ARE YOU CONTENT WITH...
TH-THMP
...LETTING THEM DO AS THEY PLEASE WITH YOU?
I WON'T LET YOU...

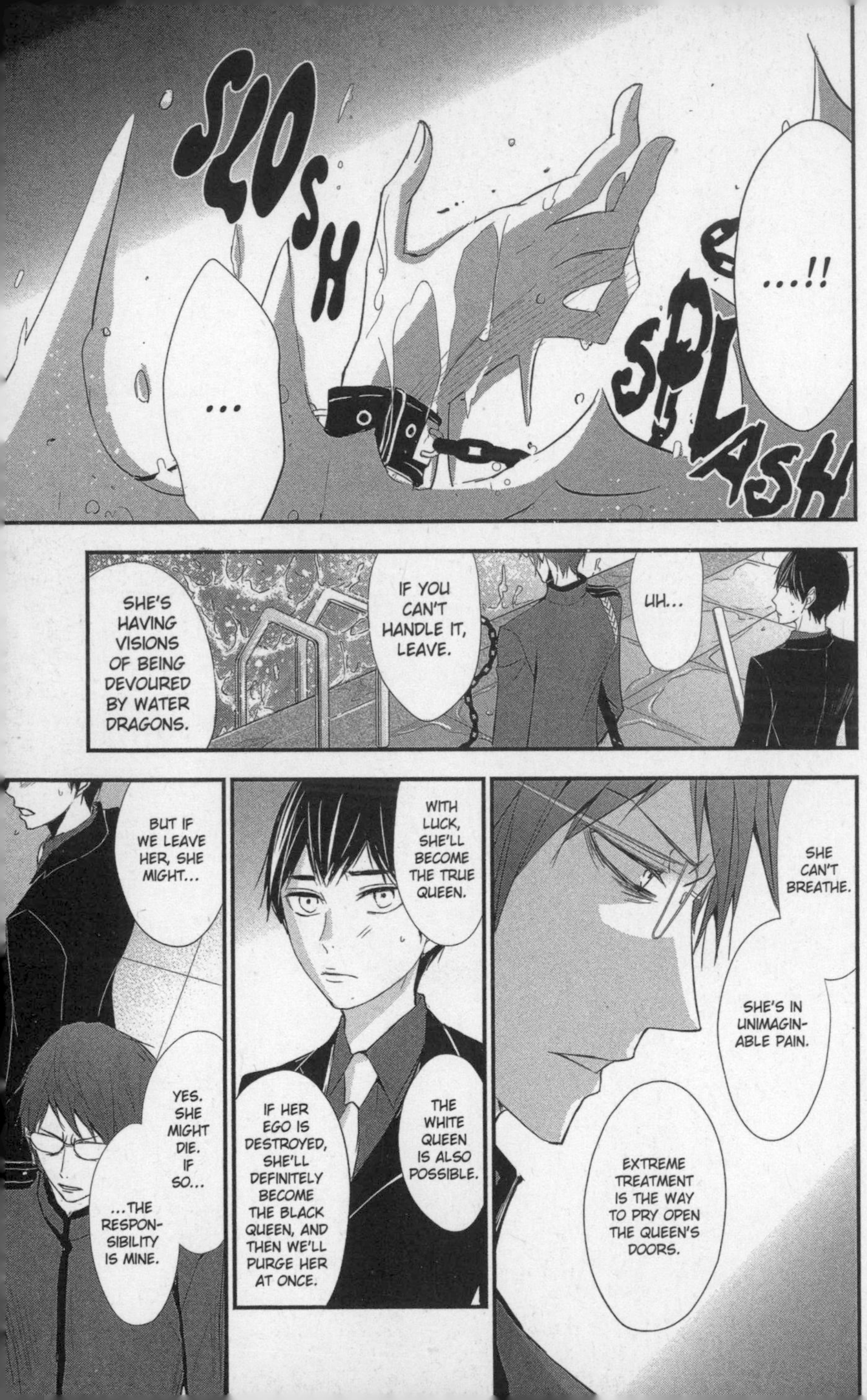
...!!
SPLASH
SLOSH
...
UH...
IF YOU CAN'T HANDLE IT, LEAVE.
SHE'S HAVING VISIONS OF BEING DEVOURED BY WATER DRAGONS.
SHE CAN'T BREATHE.
SHE'S IN UNIMAGIN-ABLE PAIN.
EXTREME TREATMENT IS THE WAY TO PRY OPEN THE QUEEN'S DOORS.
WITH LUCK, SHE'LL BECOME THE TRUE QUEEN.
THE WHITE QUEEN IS ALSO POSSIBLE.
IF HER EGO IS DESTROYED, SHE'LL DEFINITELY BECOME THE BLACK QUEEN, AND THEN WE'LL PURGE HER AT ONCE.
BUT IF WE LEAVE HER, SHE MIGHT...
YES. SHE MIGHT DIE. IF SO...
...THE RESPON-SIBILITY IS MINE.

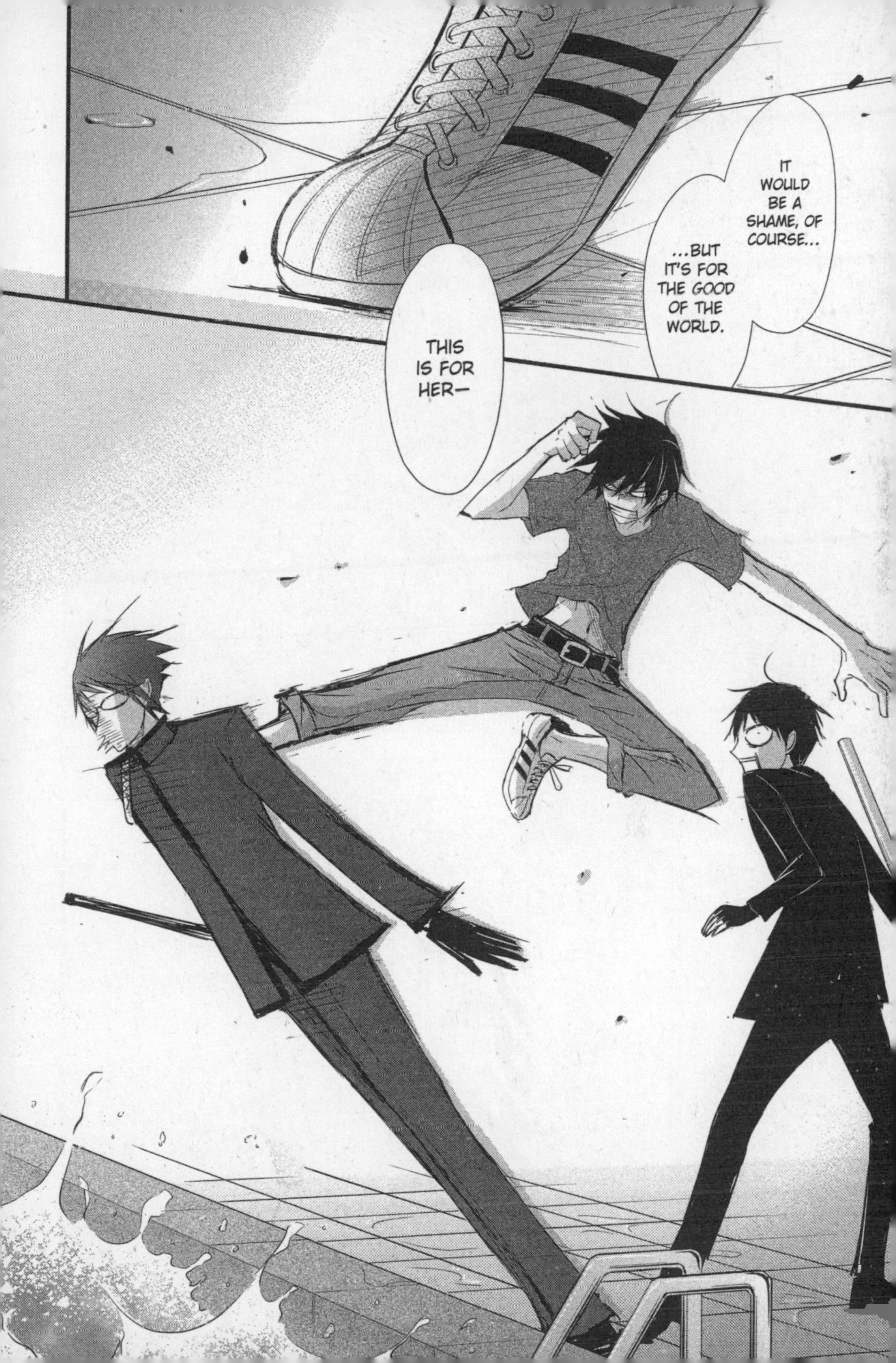
IT WOULD BE A SHAME, OF COURSE...
...BUT IT'S FOR THE GOOD OF THE WORLD.
THIS IS FOR HER—

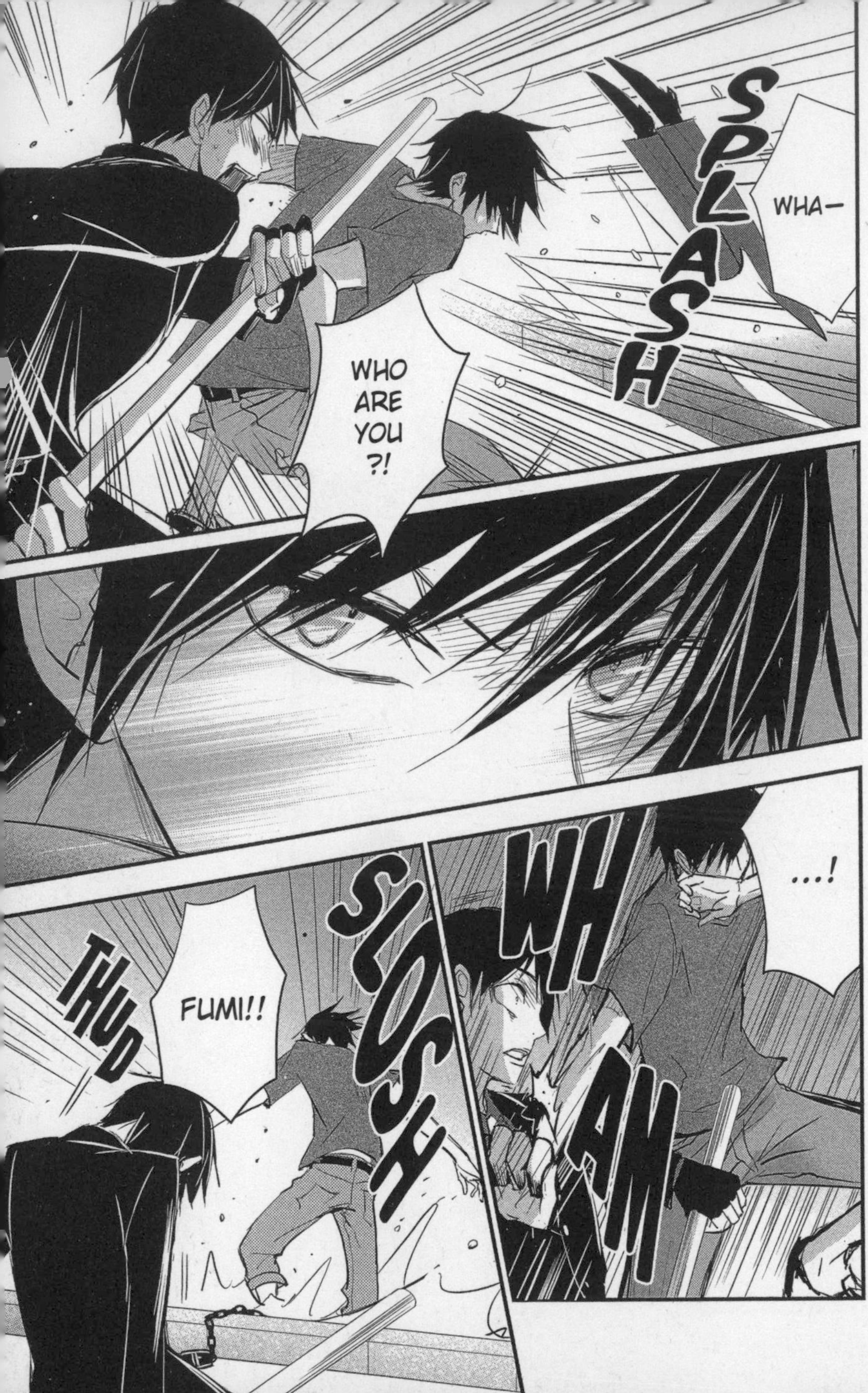
WHA—
SPLASH
WHO ARE YOU?!
...!
WHAM
SLOSH
FUMI!!
THUD

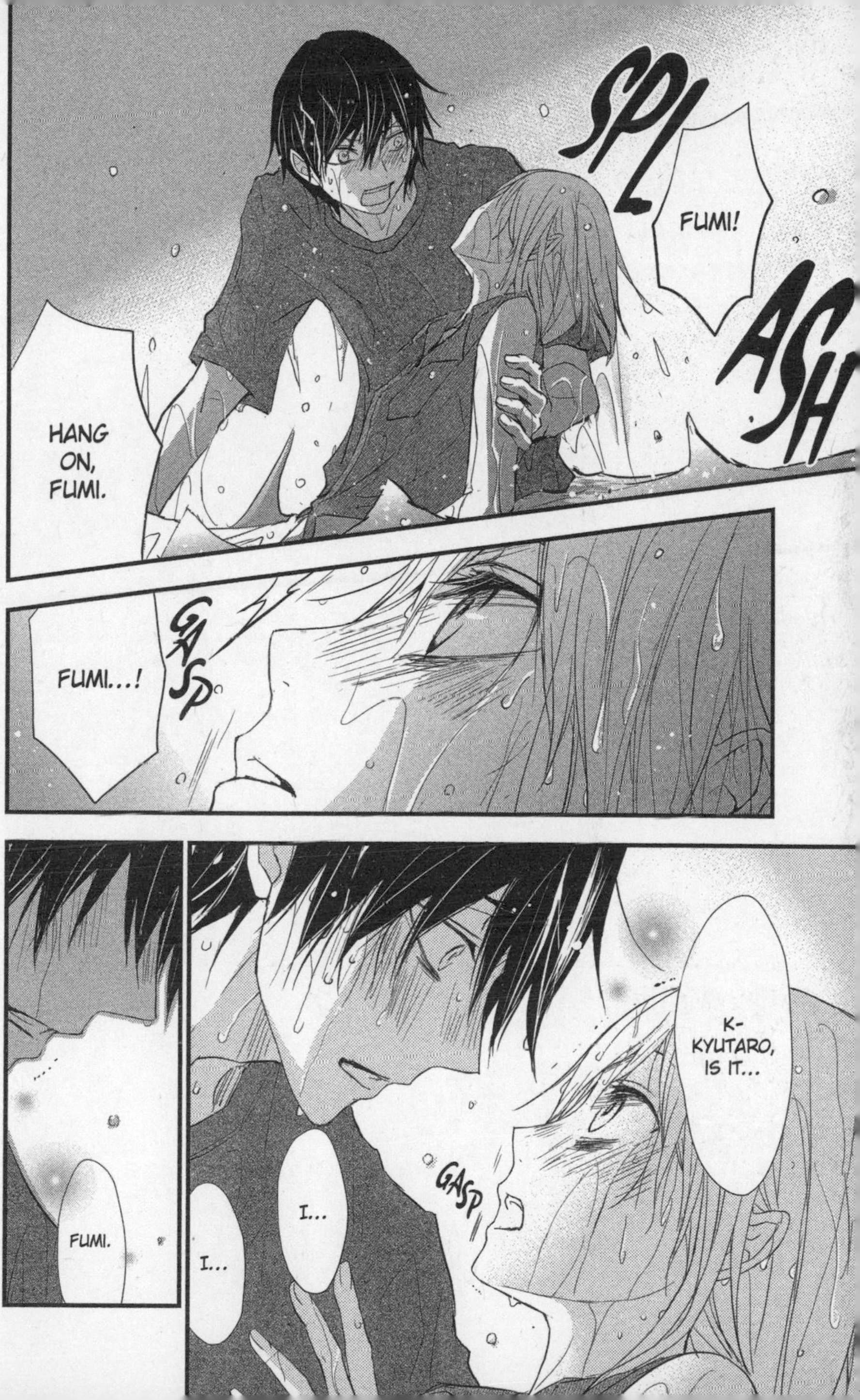
SPLASH
FUMI!
HANG ON, FUMI.
GASP
FUMI...!
K-KYUTARO, IS IT...
GASP
I...
I...
FUMI.

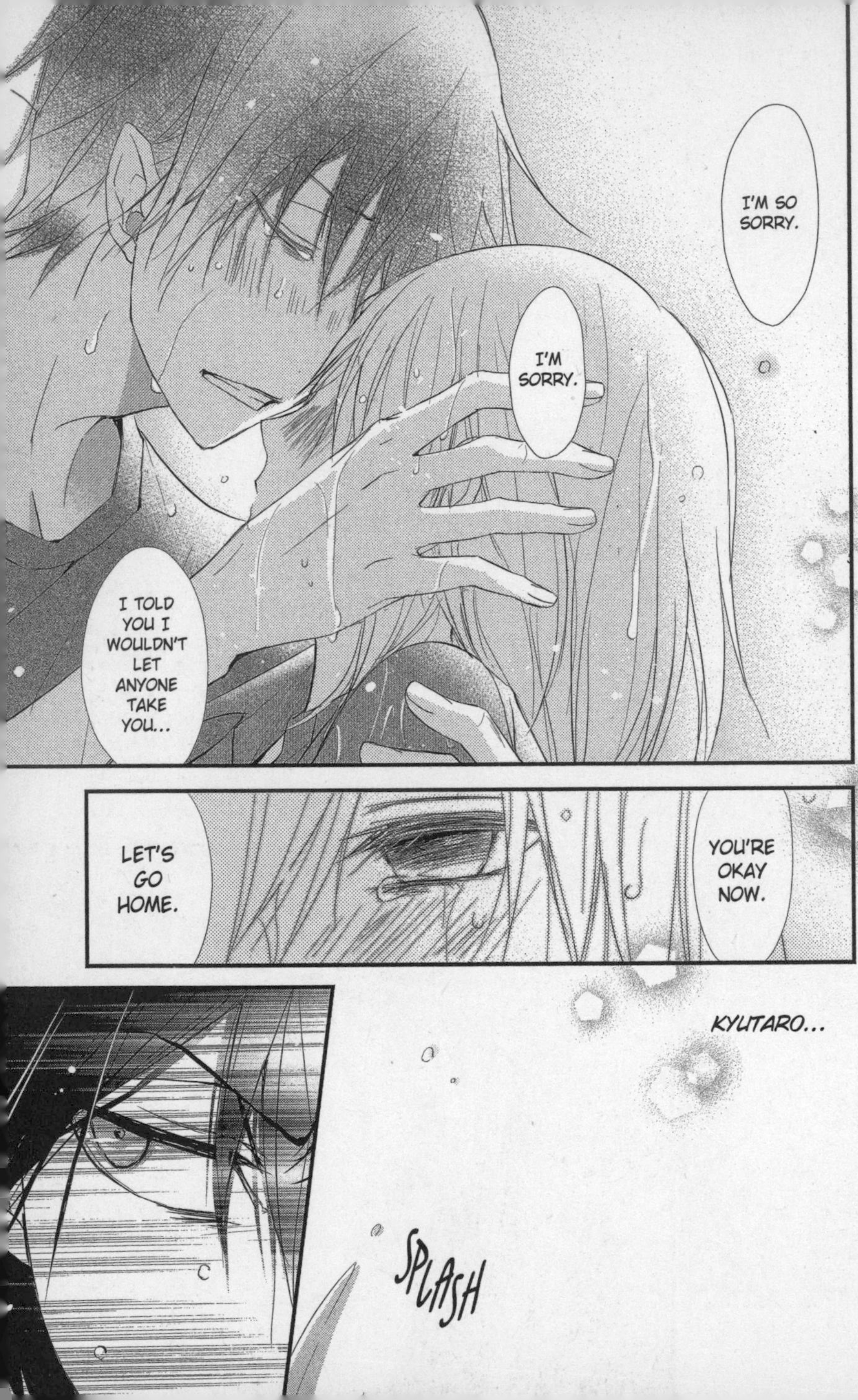
I'M SO SORRY.
I'M SORRY.
I TOLD YOU I WOULDN'T LET ANYONE TAKE YOU...
YOU'RE OKAY NOW.
LET'S GO HOME.
KYUTARO...
SPLASH

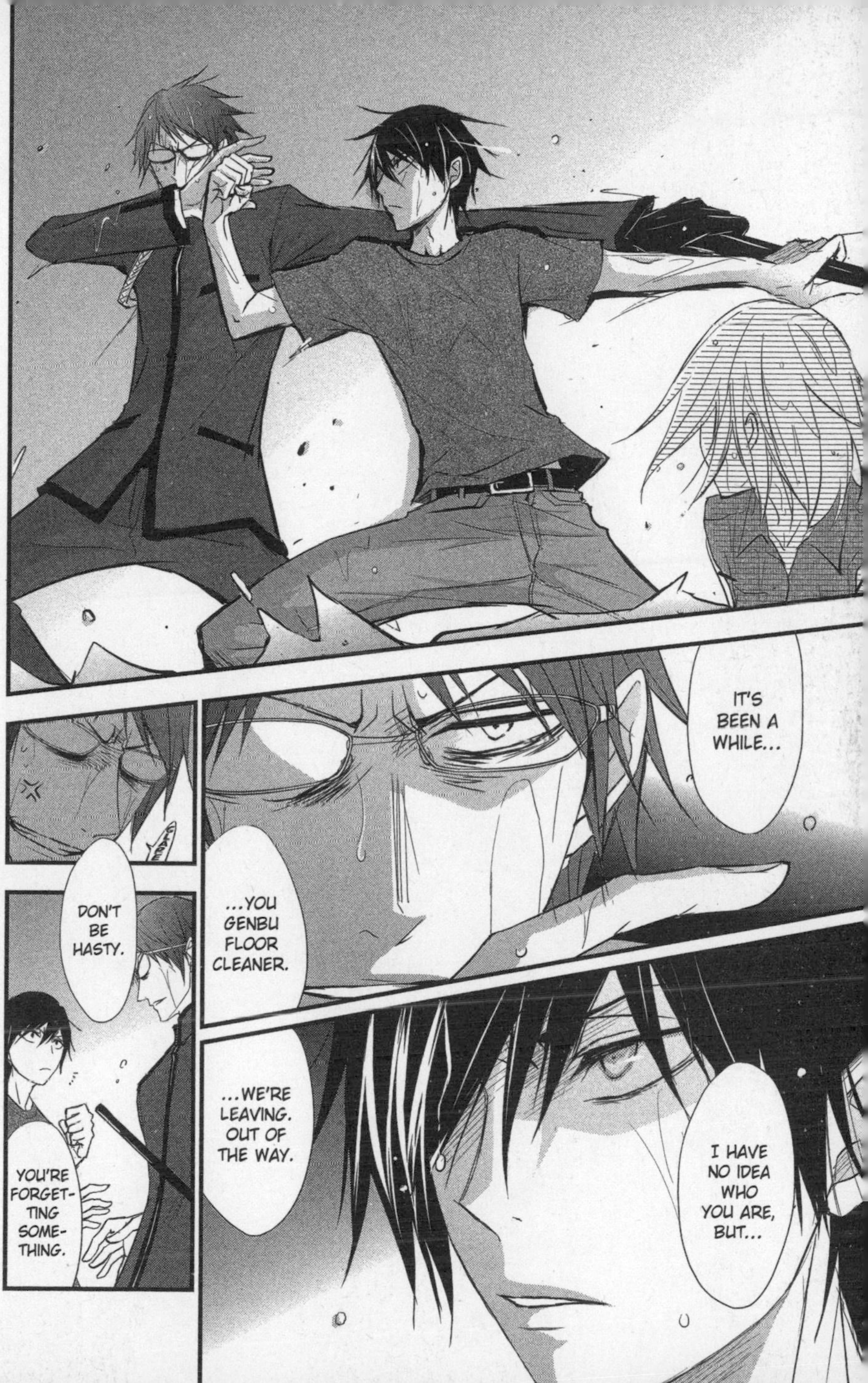
IT'S BEEN A WHILE...
...YOU GENBU FLOOR CLEANER.
I HAVE NO IDEA WHO YOU ARE, BUT...
...WE'RE LEAVING. OUT OF THE WAY.
DON'T BE HASTY.
YOU'RE FORGET-TING SOME-THING.

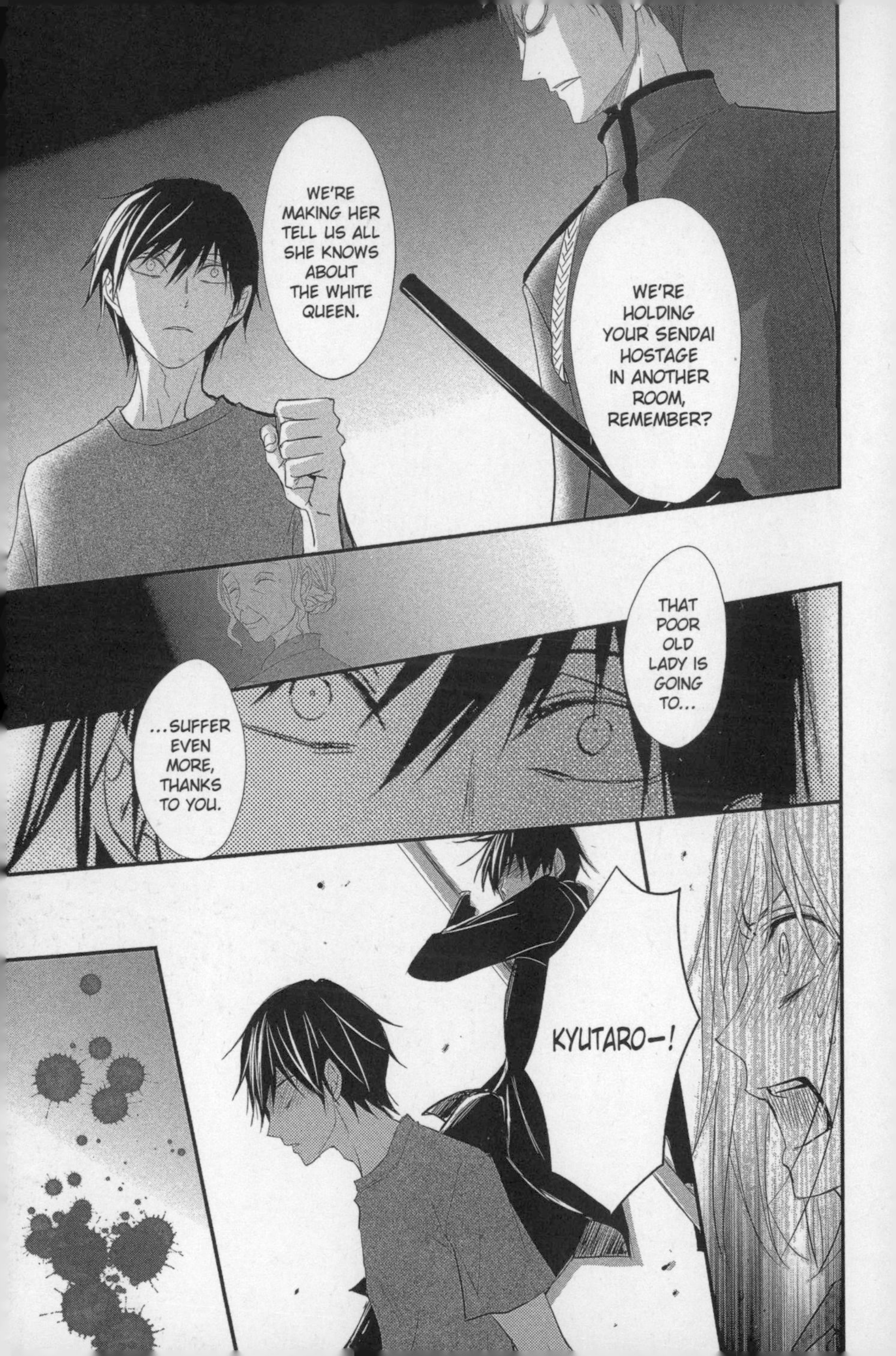
WE'RE HOLDING YOUR SENDAI HOSTAGE IN ANOTHER ROOM, REMEMBER?
WE'RE MAKING HER TELL US ALL SHE KNOWS ABOUT THE WHITE QUEEN.
THAT POOR OLD LADY IS GOING TO...
...SUFFER EVEN MORE, THANKS TO YOU.
KYUTARO—!

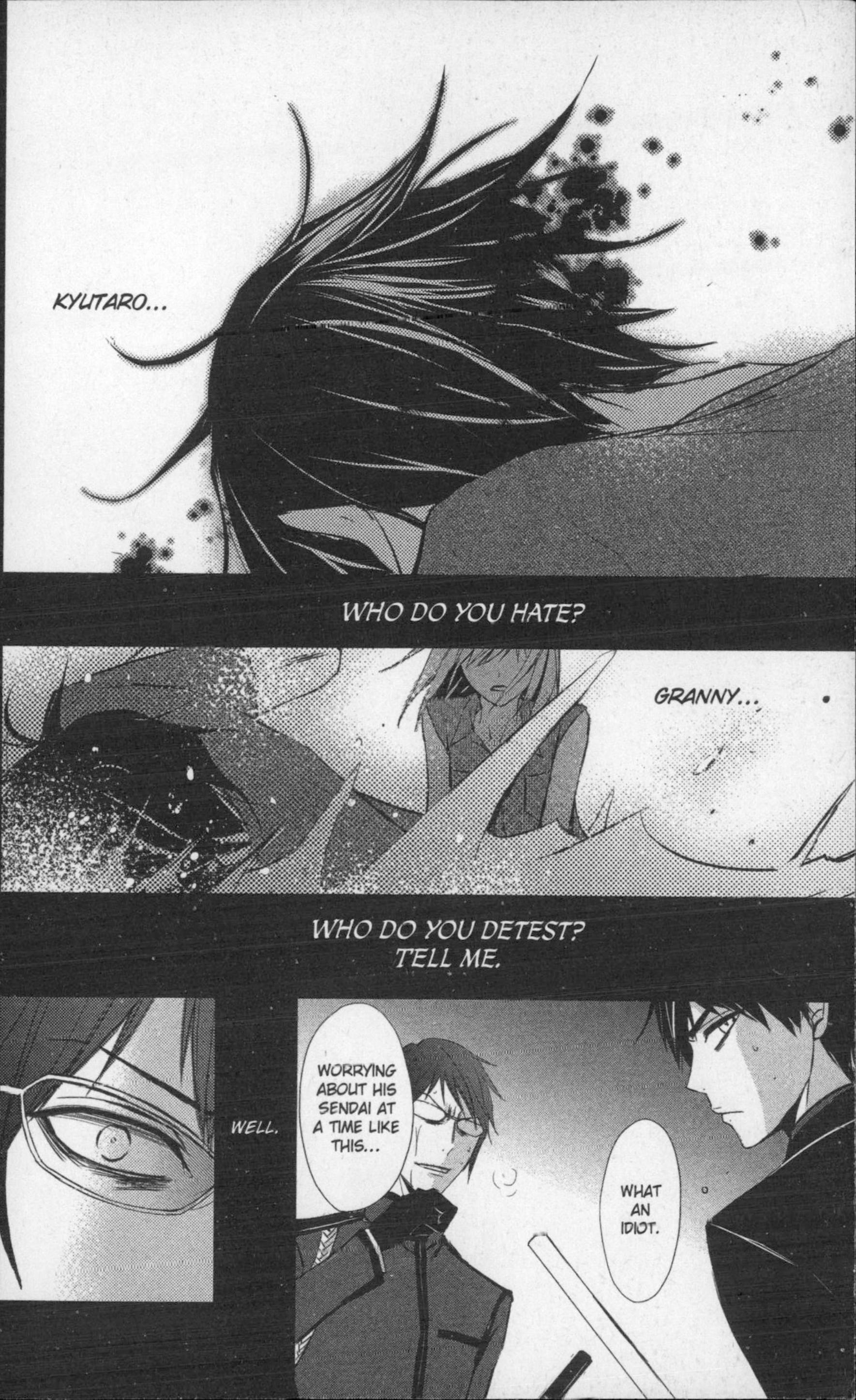
KYUTARO...
WHO DO YOU HATE?
GRANNY...
WHO DO YOU DETEST? TELL ME.
WORRYING ABOUT HIS SENDAI AT A TIME LIKE THIS...
WHAT AN IDIOT.
WELL.

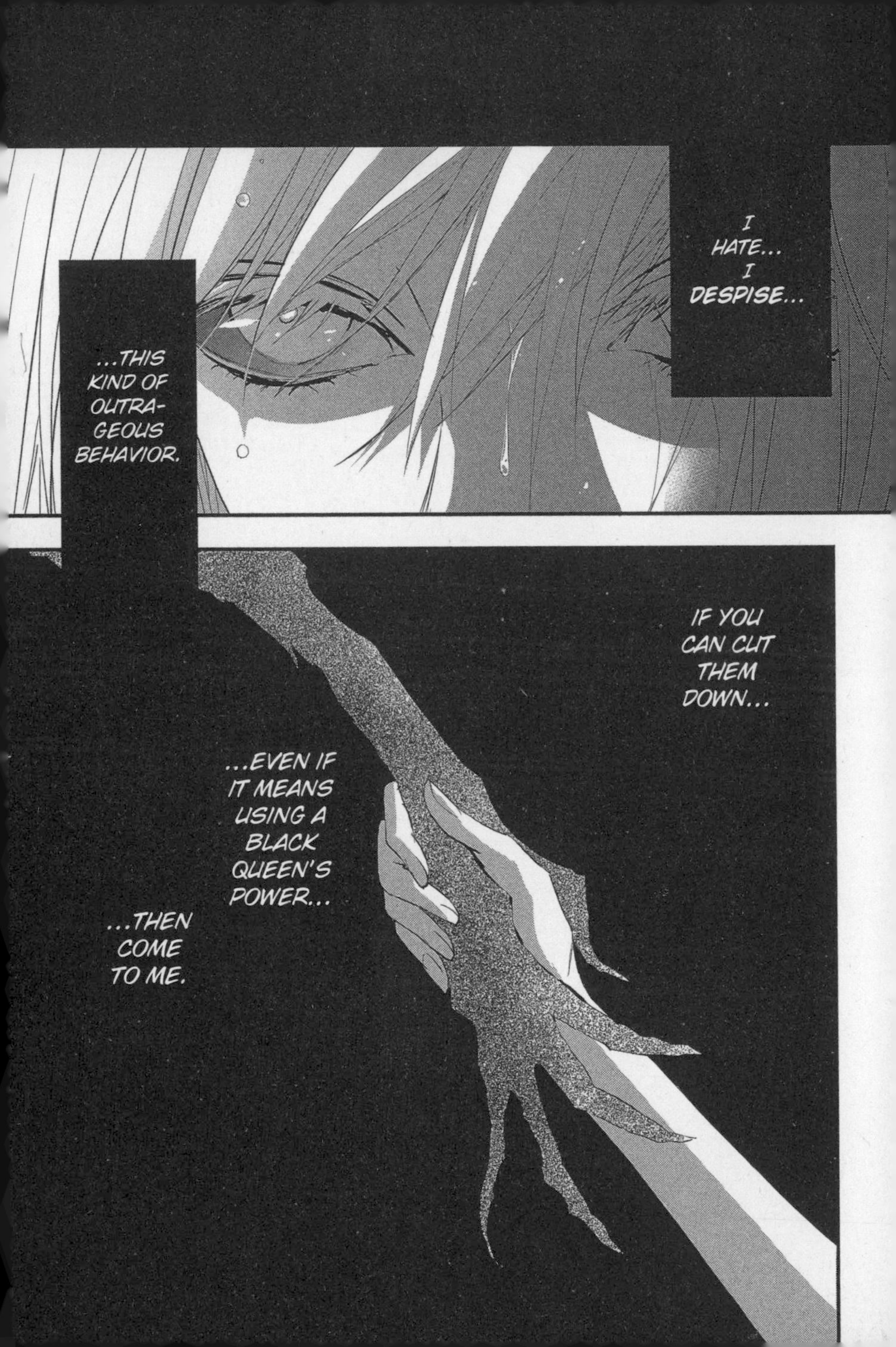
I HATE... I DESPISE...
...THIS KIND OF OUTRAGEOUS BEHAVIOR.
IF YOU CAN CUT THEM DOWN...
...EVEN IF IT MEANS USING A BLACK QUEEN'S POWER...
...THEN COME TO ME.

MONTHLY BETSUCOMI SALE DATE NOTICE ON TWITTER

CHAPTER 14

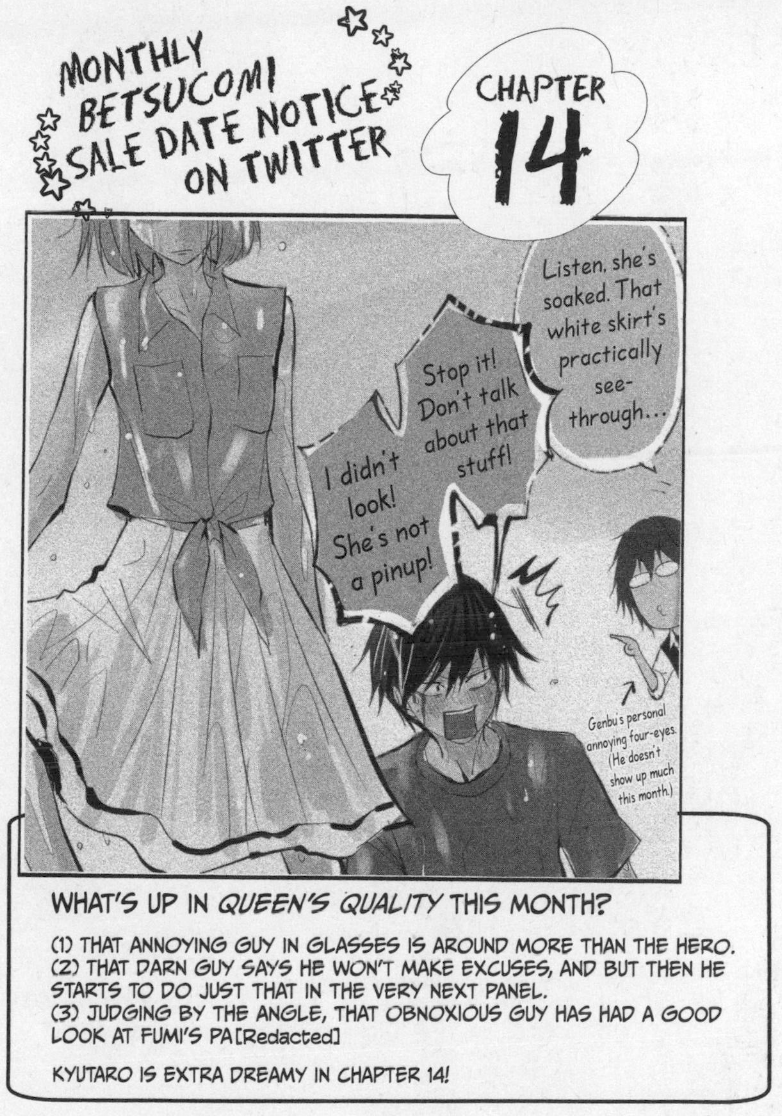
Listen, she's soaked. That white skirt's practically see-through...
Stop it! Don't talk about that stuff!
I didn't look! She's not a pinup!
Genbu's personal annoying four-eyes. (He doesn't show up much this month.)

WHAT'S UP IN *QUEEN'S QUALITY* THIS MONTH?

(1) THAT ANNOYING GUY IN GLASSES IS AROUND MORE THAN THE HERO.
(2) THAT DARN GUY SAYS HE WON'T MAKE EXCUSES, AND BUT THEN HE STARTS TO DO JUST THAT IN THE VERY NEXT PANEL.
(3) JUDGING BY THE ANGLE, THAT OBNOXIOUS GUY HAS HAD A GOOD LOOK AT FUMI'S PA[Redacted]

KYUTARO IS EXTRA DREAMY IN CHAPTER 14!

Chapter 14

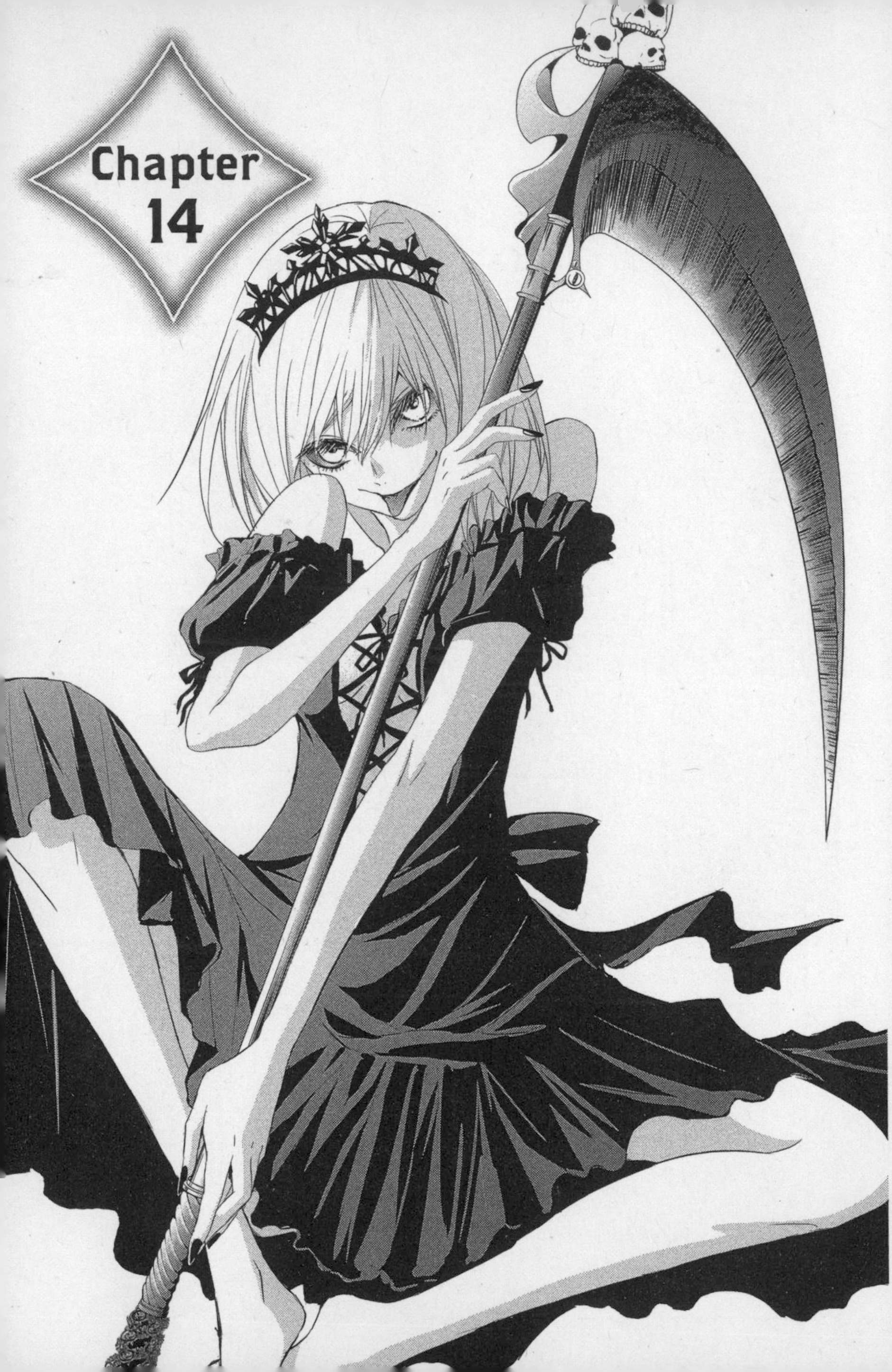

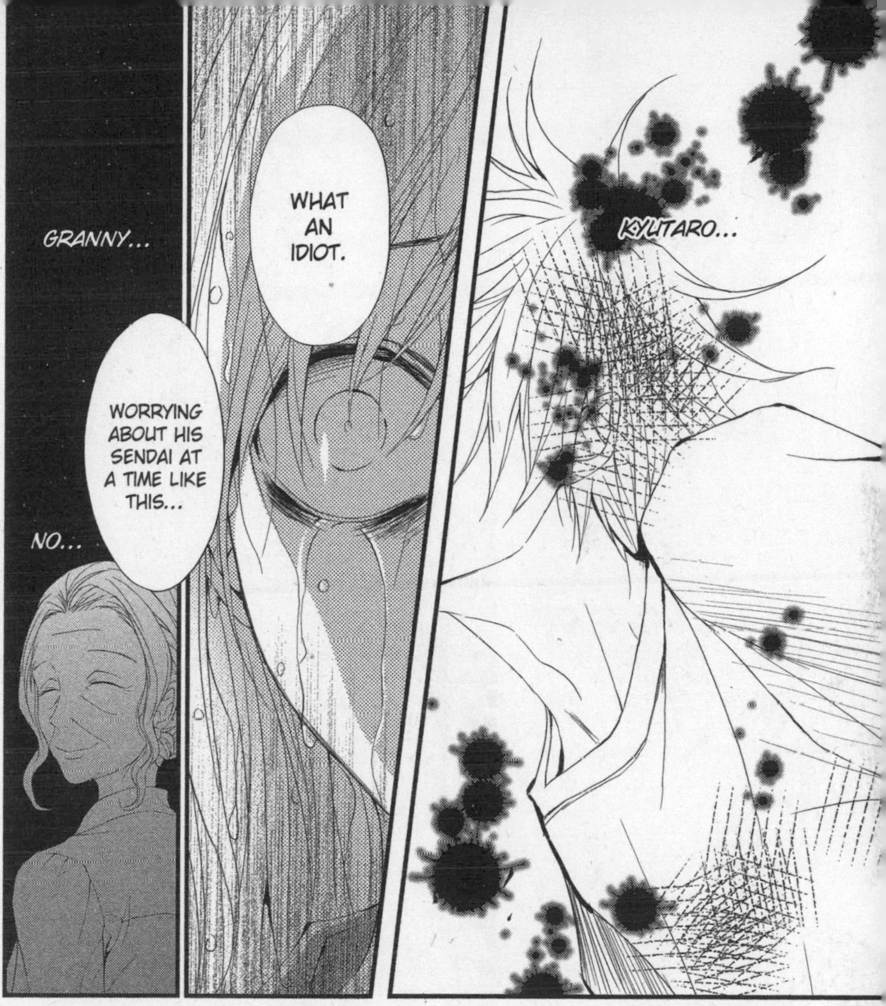
KYUTARO...
WHAT AN IDIOT.
WORRYING ABOUT HIS SENDAI AT A TIME LIKE THIS...
GRANNY...
NO...

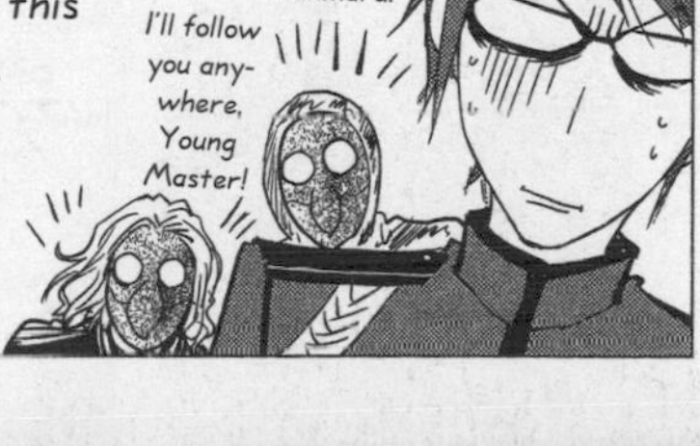
The very picture of an intellectual gangster.
Young Master Ranmaru!
I'll follow you anywhere, Young Master!

Oh, look, another glasses-wearing character with a bad attitude. It's not like I have issues with glasses, but...
Or maybe I do, because I can't ever seem to draw them right! I have to admit I gave this guy the most awful kind of introduction, but I kinda like him. He's easy to draw (glasses notwithstanding).
Things won't be easy for you, Ranmaru, but hang in there.

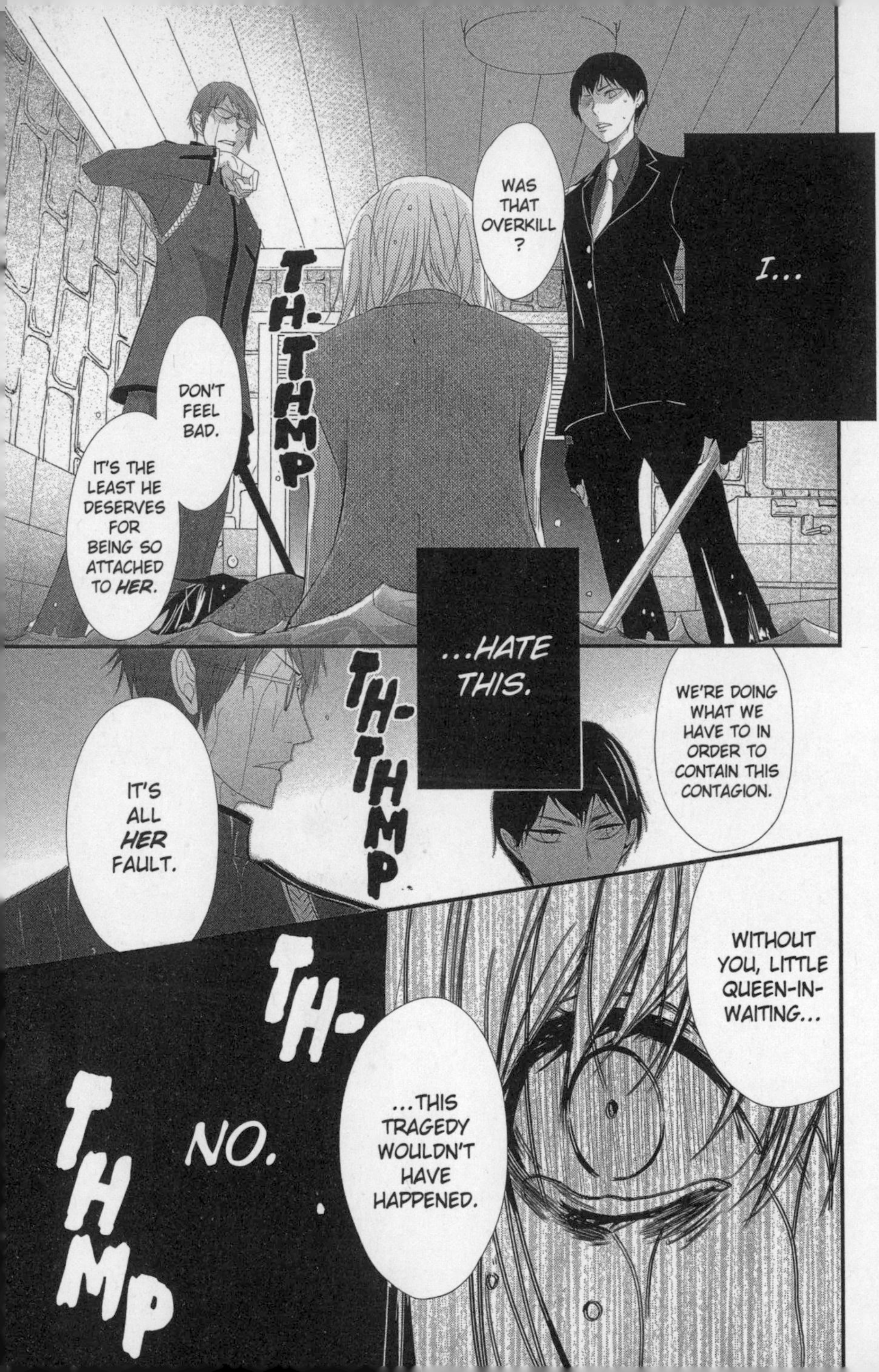
I...
WAS THAT OVERKILL?
TH-THMP
DON'T FEEL BAD.
IT'S THE LEAST HE DESERVES FOR BEING SO ATTACHED TO *HER*.
...HATE THIS.
WE'RE DOING WHAT WE HAVE TO IN ORDER TO CONTAIN THIS CONTAGION.
TH-THMP
IT'S ALL *HER* FAULT.
WITHOUT YOU, LITTLE QUEEN-IN-WAITING...
...THIS TRAGEDY WOULDN'T HAVE HAPPENED.
NO.
TH-THMP

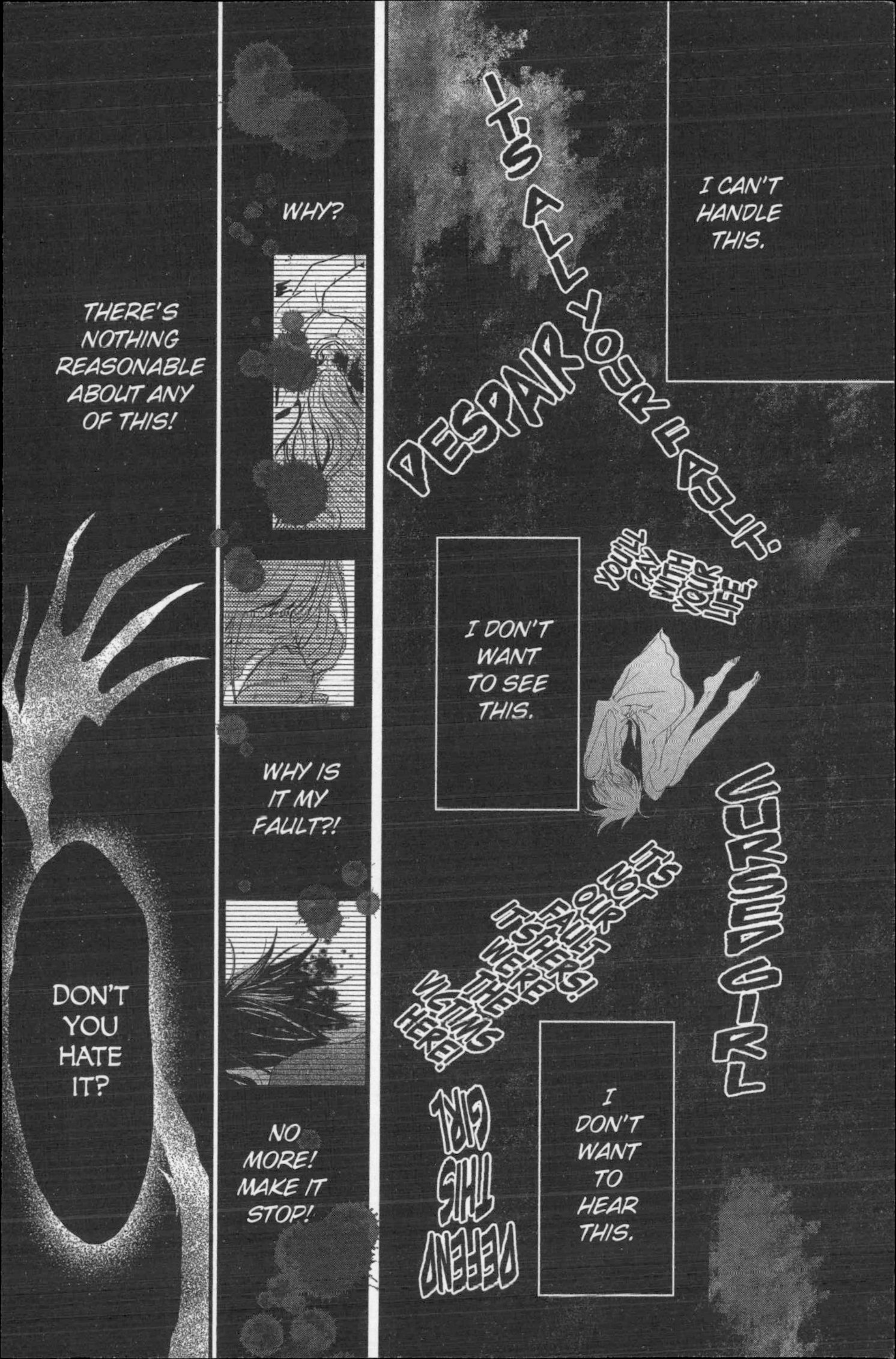
I CAN'T HANDLE THIS.
IT'S ALL YOUR FAULT.
DESPAIR
YOU'LL PAY WITH YOUR LIFE.
I DON'T WANT TO SEE THIS.
IT'S NOT OUR FAULT. IT'S HERS! WE'RE THE VICTIMS HERE!
DEFEND THIS GIRL
I DON'T WANT TO HEAR THIS.
WHY?
WHY IS IT MY FAULT?!
NO MORE! MAKE IT STOP!
THERE'S NOTHING REASONABLE ABOUT ANY OF THIS!
DON'T YOU HATE IT?

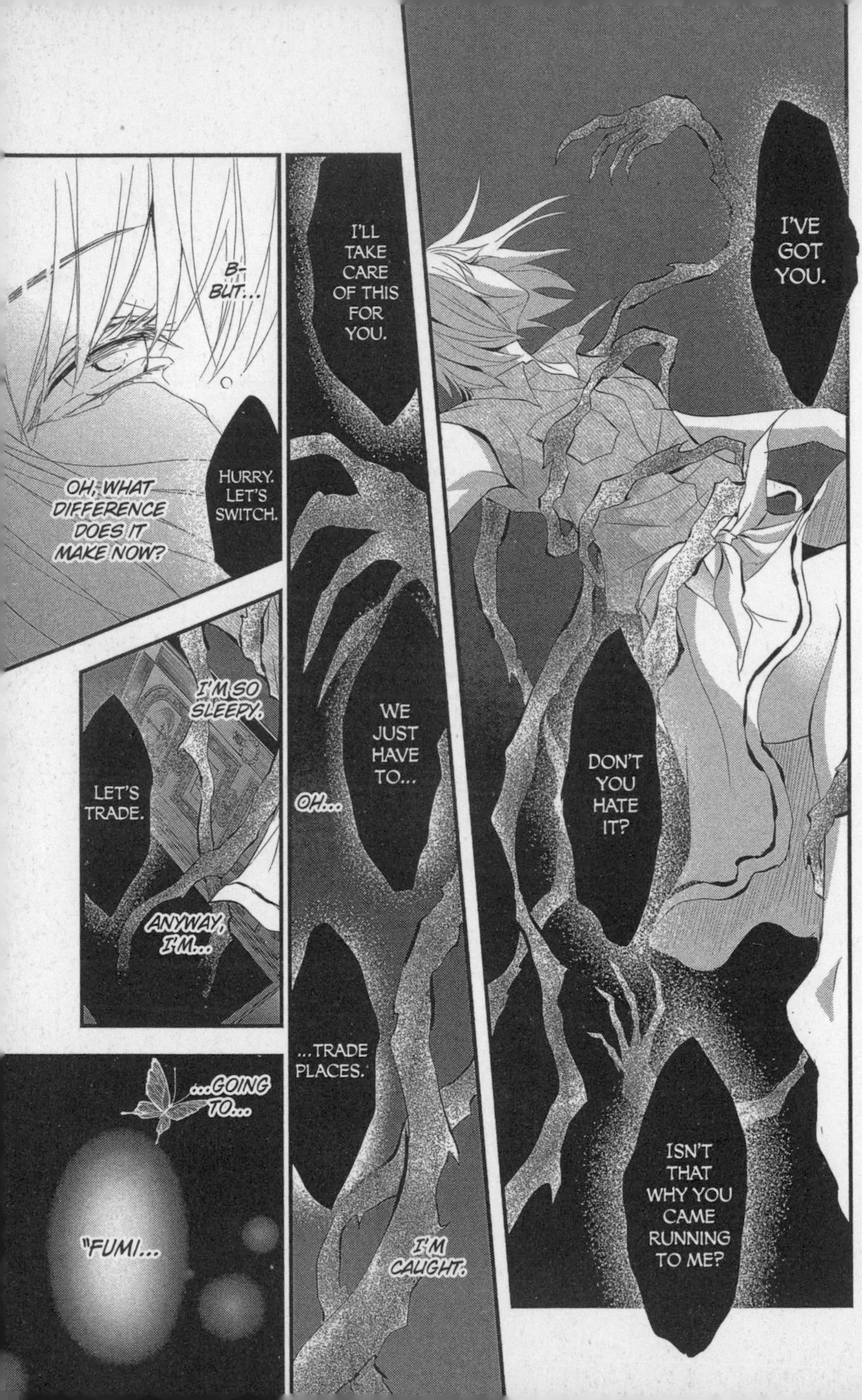
I'VE GOT YOU.
DON'T YOU HATE IT?
ISN'T THAT WHY YOU CAME RUNNING TO ME?
I'LL TAKE CARE OF THIS FOR YOU.
WE JUST HAVE TO...
OH...
...TRADE PLACES.
I'M CAUGHT.
B-BUT...
HURRY. LET'S SWITCH.
OH, WHAT DIFFERENCE DOES IT MAKE NOW?
I'M SO SLEEPY.
LET'S TRADE.
ANYWAY, I'M...
...GOING TO...
"FUMI...

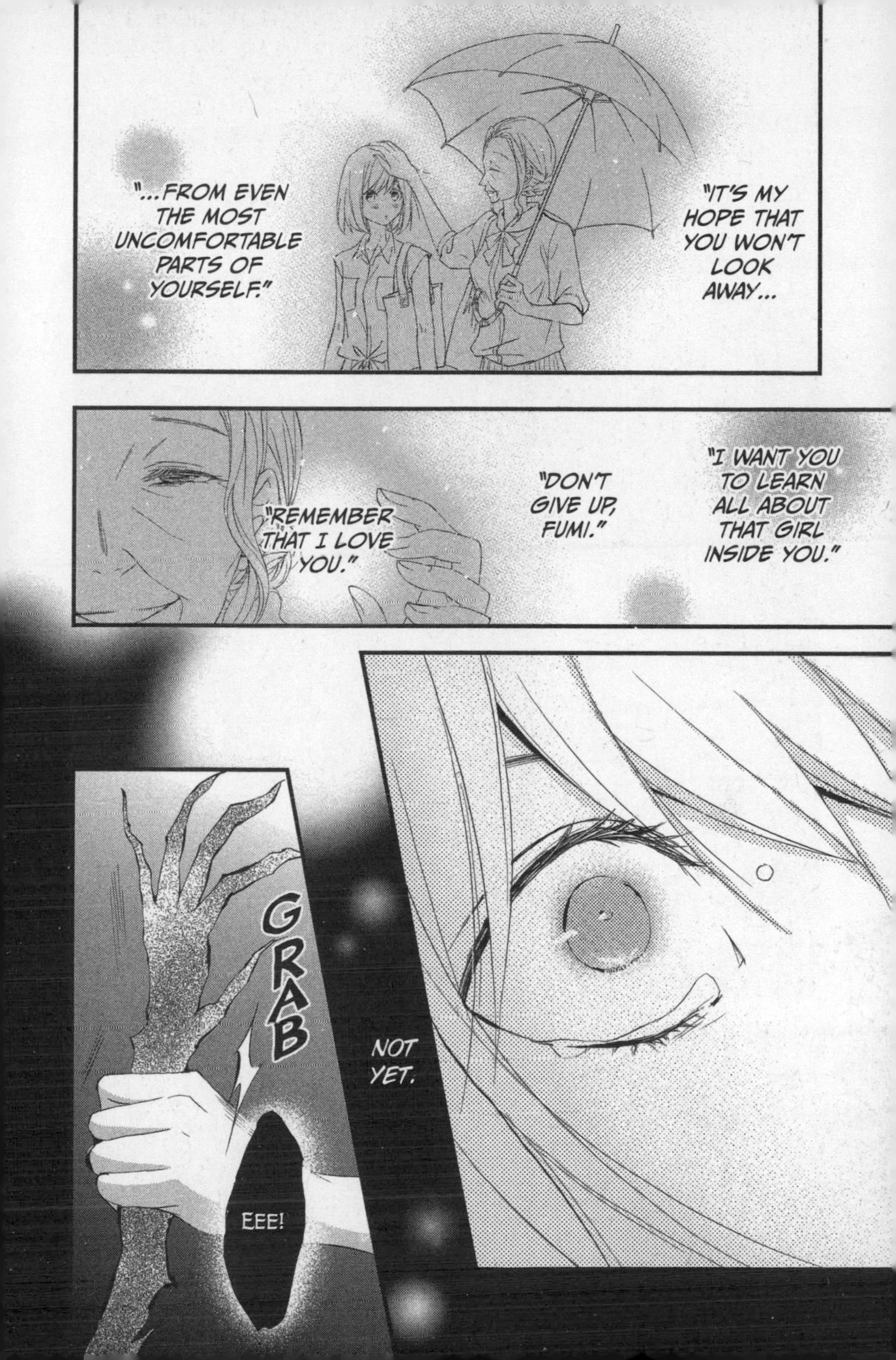
"IT'S MY HOPE THAT YOU WON'T LOOK AWAY...
"...FROM EVEN THE MOST UNCOMFORTABLE PARTS OF YOURSELF."
"I WANT YOU TO LEARN ALL ABOUT THAT GIRL INSIDE YOU."
"DON'T GIVE UP, FUMI."
"REMEMBER THAT I LOVE YOU."
NOT YET.
GRAB
EEE!

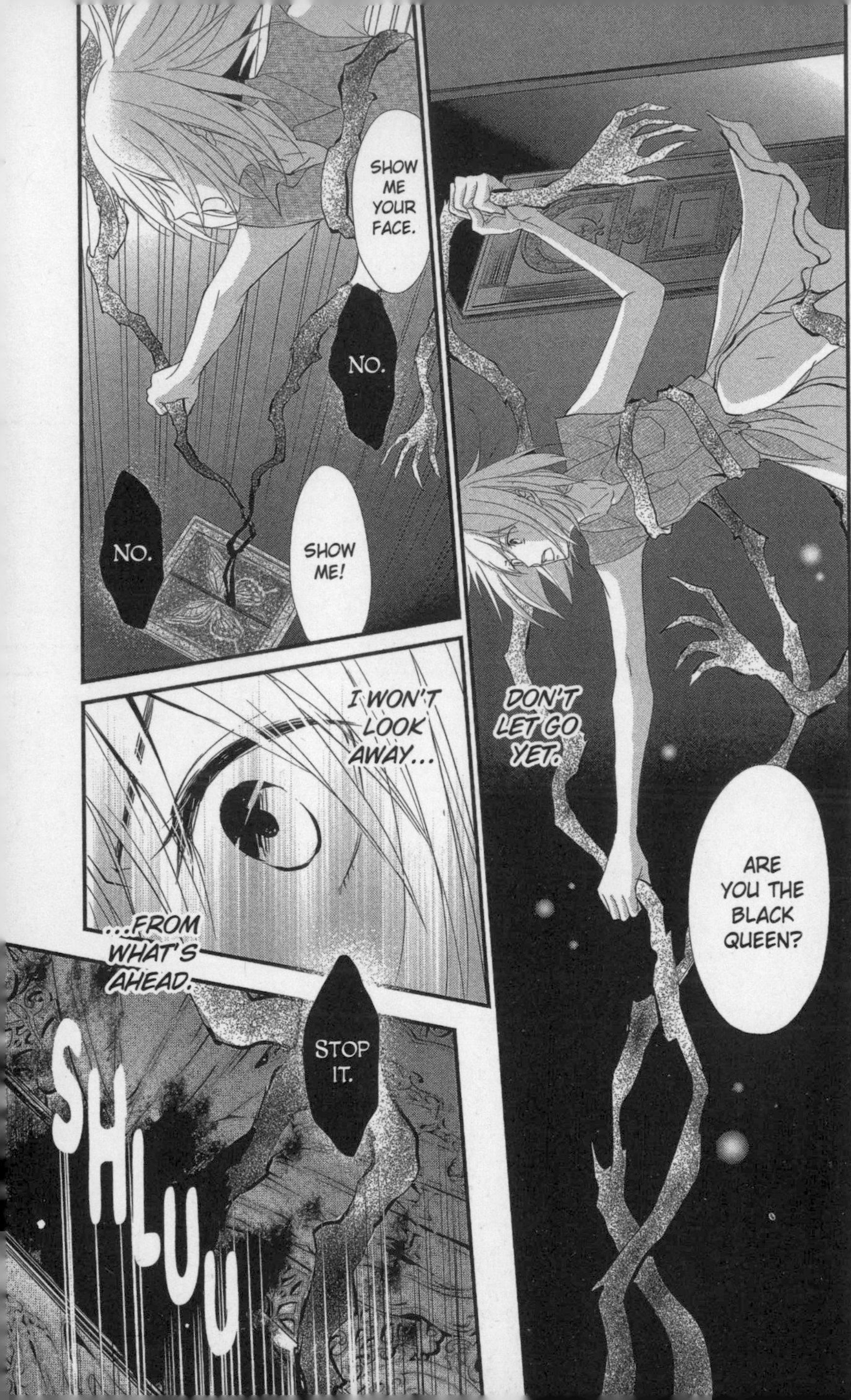
DON'T LET GO YET.
ARE YOU THE BLACK QUEEN?
SHOW ME YOUR FACE.
NO.
SHOW ME!
NO.
I WON'T LOOK AWAY...
...FROM WHAT'S AHEAD.
STOP IT.
SHLUU

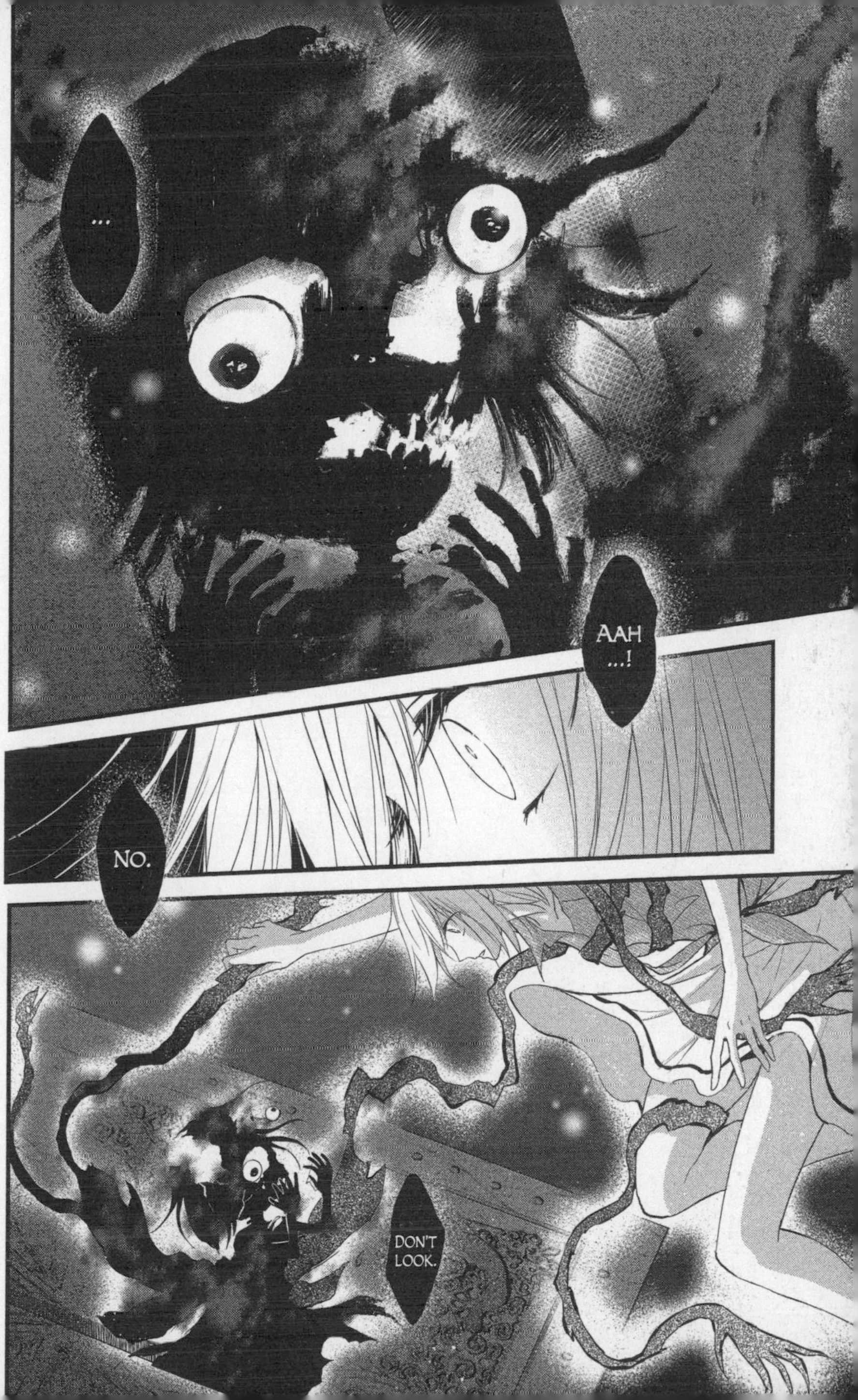
...
AAH ...!
NO.
DON'T LOOK.

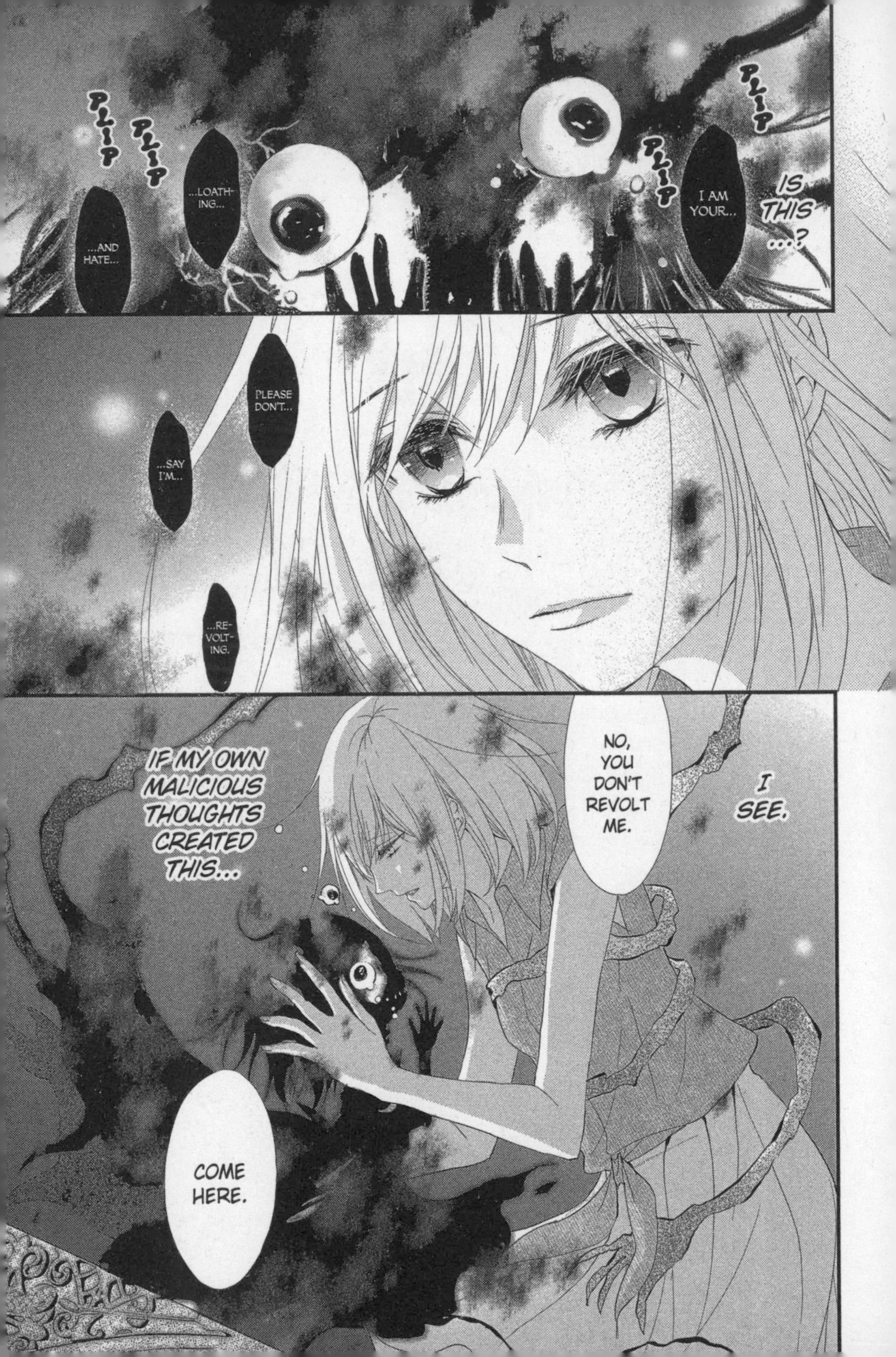
IS THIS ...?
PLIP
PLIP
I AM YOUR...
...LOATHING...
PLIP
PLIP
...AND HATE...
PLEASE DON'T...
...SAY I'M...
...REVOLTING.
I SEE.
NO, YOU DON'T REVOLT ME.
IF MY OWN MALICIOUS THOUGHTS CREATED THIS...
COME HERE.

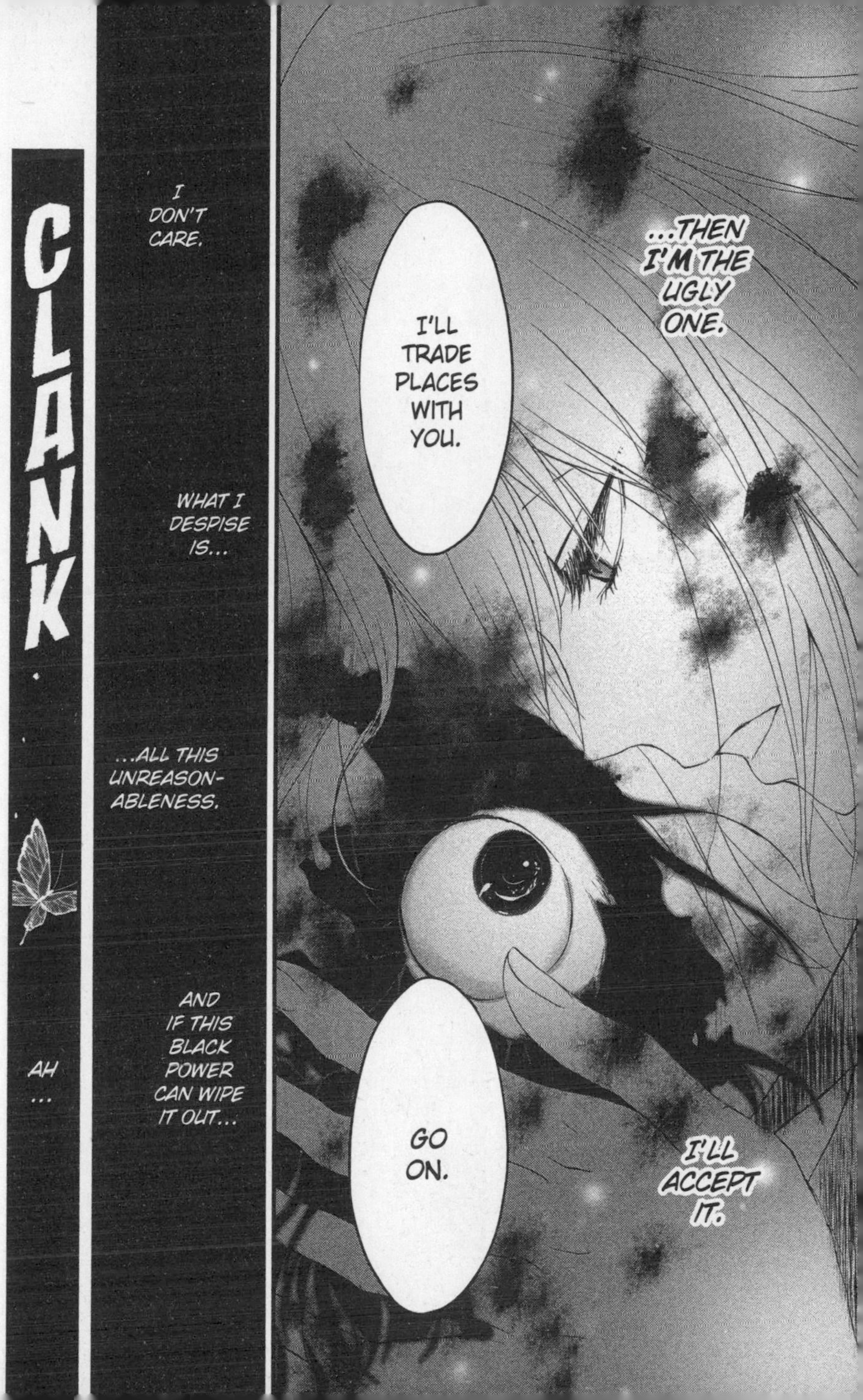
...THEN I'M THE UGLY ONE.
I'LL TRADE PLACES WITH YOU.
I'LL ACCEPT IT.
GO ON.
I DON'T CARE.
WHAT I DESPISE IS...
...ALL THIS UNREASON-ABLENESS.
AND IF THIS BLACK POWER CAN WIPE IT OUT...
CLANK
AH...

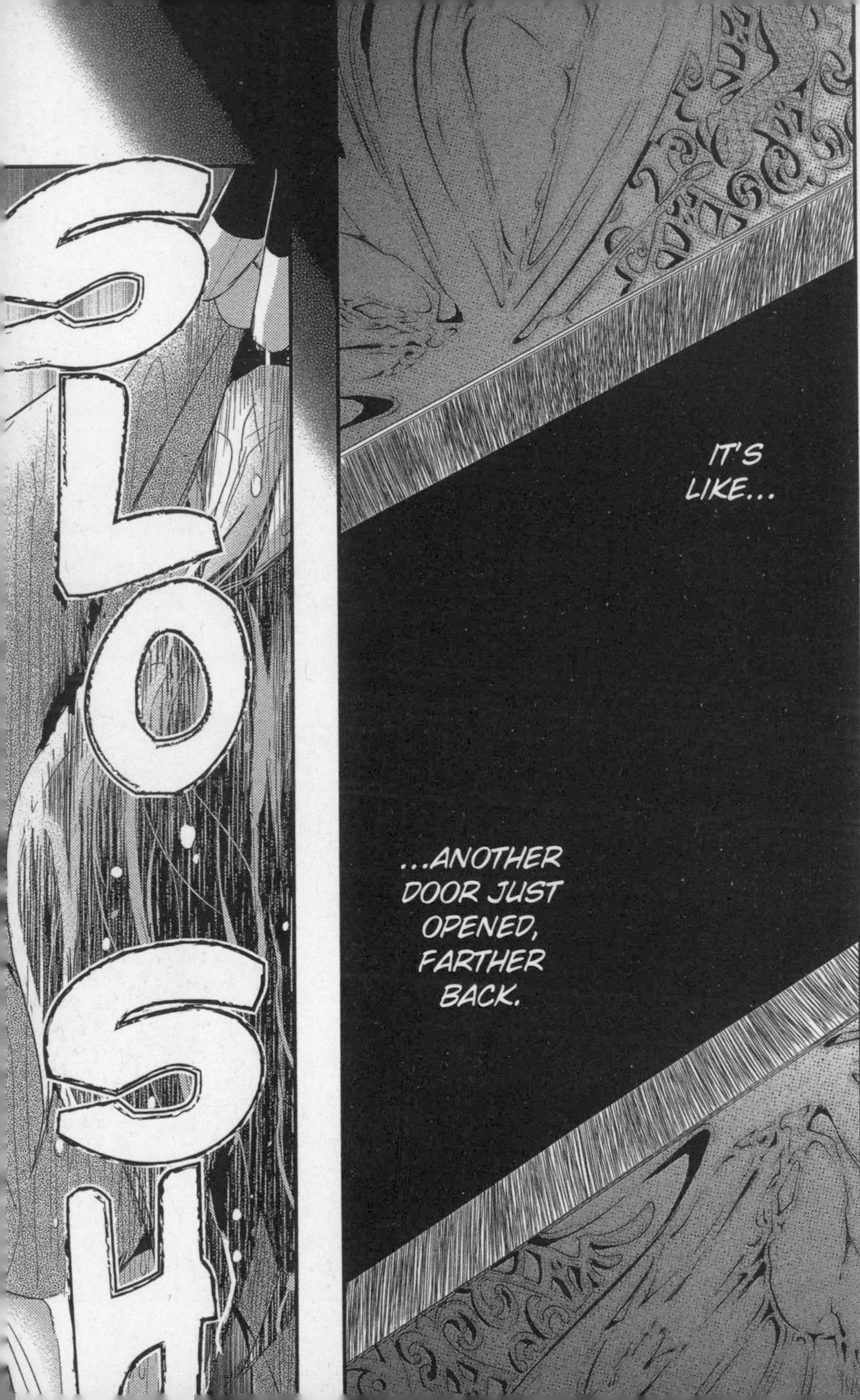
IT'S LIKE...
...ANOTHER DOOR JUST OPENED, FARTHER BACK.
SLOSH

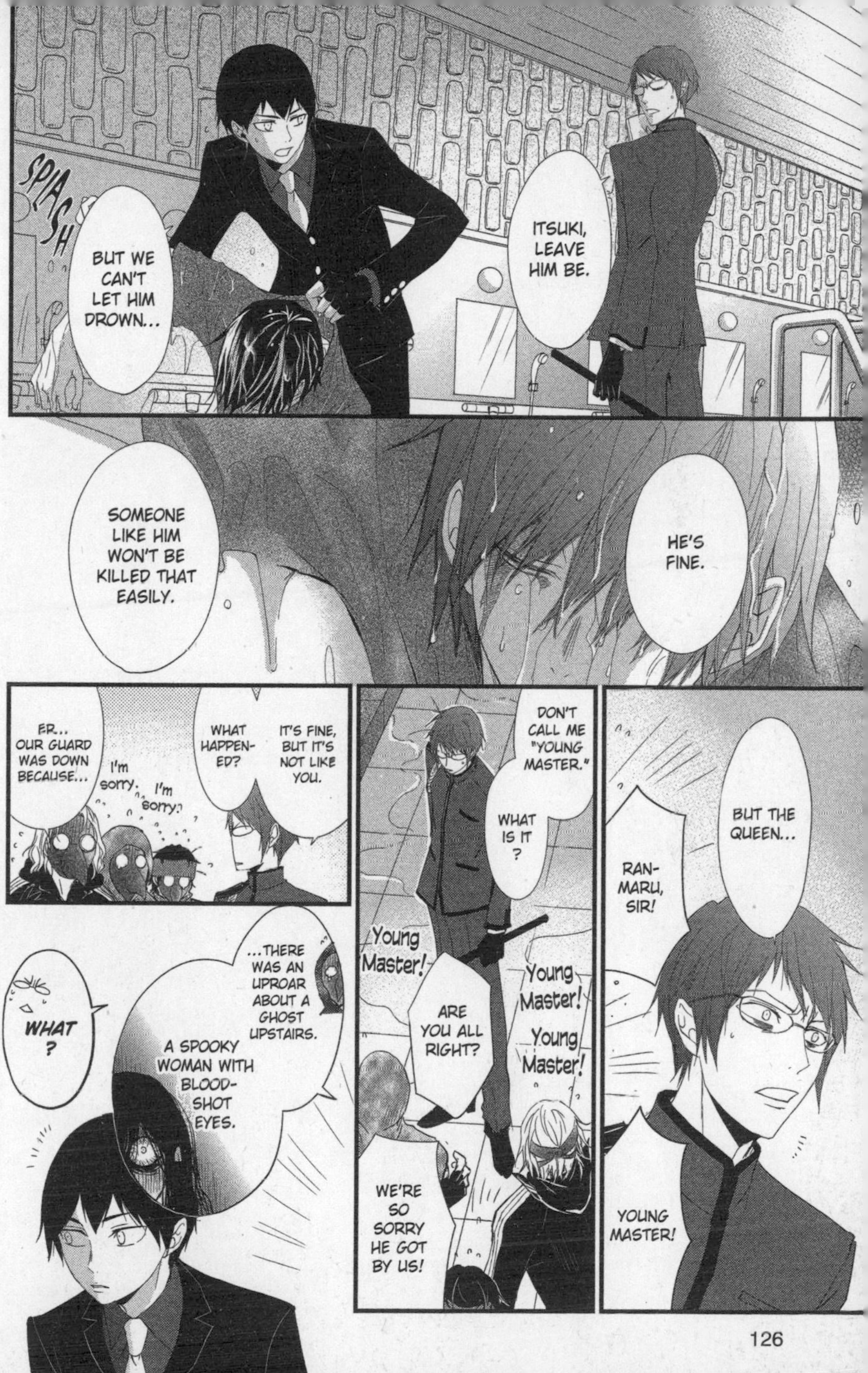
ITSUKI, LEAVE HIM BE.
SPLASH
BUT WE CAN'T LET HIM DROWN...
HE'S FINE.
SOMEONE LIKE HIM WON'T BE KILLED THAT EASILY.
BUT THE QUEEN...
RAN-MARU, SIR!
YOUNG MASTER!
DON'T CALL ME "YOUNG MASTER."
WHAT IS IT ?
Young Master!
Young Master!
Young Master!
ARE YOU ALL RIGHT?
WE'RE SO SORRY HE GOT BY US!
IT'S FINE, BUT IT'S NOT LIKE YOU.
WHAT HAPPEN-ED?
ER... OUR GUARD WAS DOWN BECAUSE...
I'm sorry.
I'm sorry.
...THERE WAS AN UPROAR ABOUT A GHOST UPSTAIRS.
A SPOOKY WOMAN WITH BLOOD-SHOT EYES.
WHAT ?

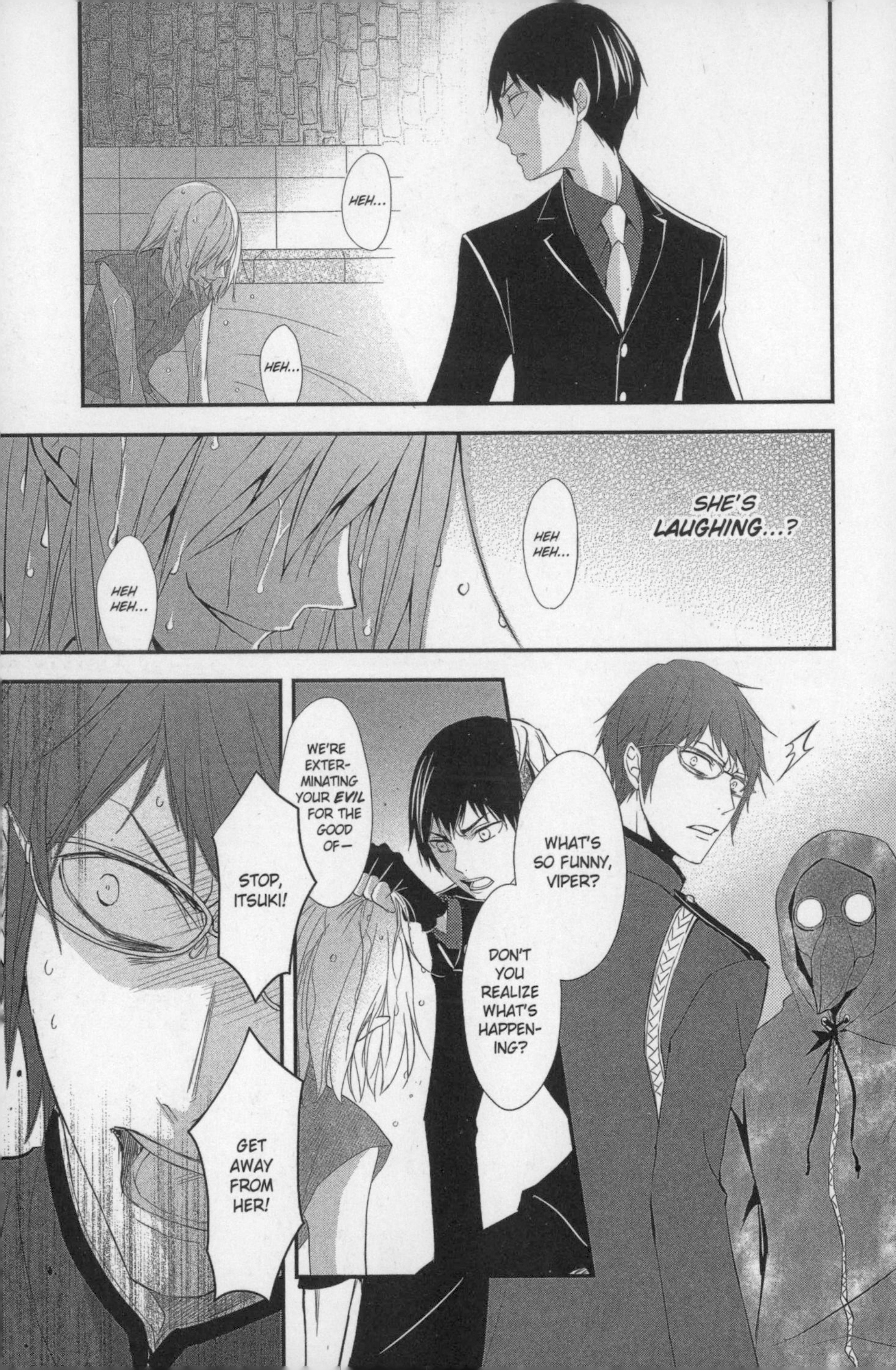
HEH...
HEH...
SHE'S LAUGHING...?
HEH HEH...
HEH HEH...
WHAT'S SO FUNNY, VIPER?
DON'T YOU REALIZE WHAT'S HAPPEN-ING?
WE'RE EXTER-MINATING YOUR *EVIL* FOR THE GOOD OF—
STOP, ITSUKI!
GET AWAY FROM HER!

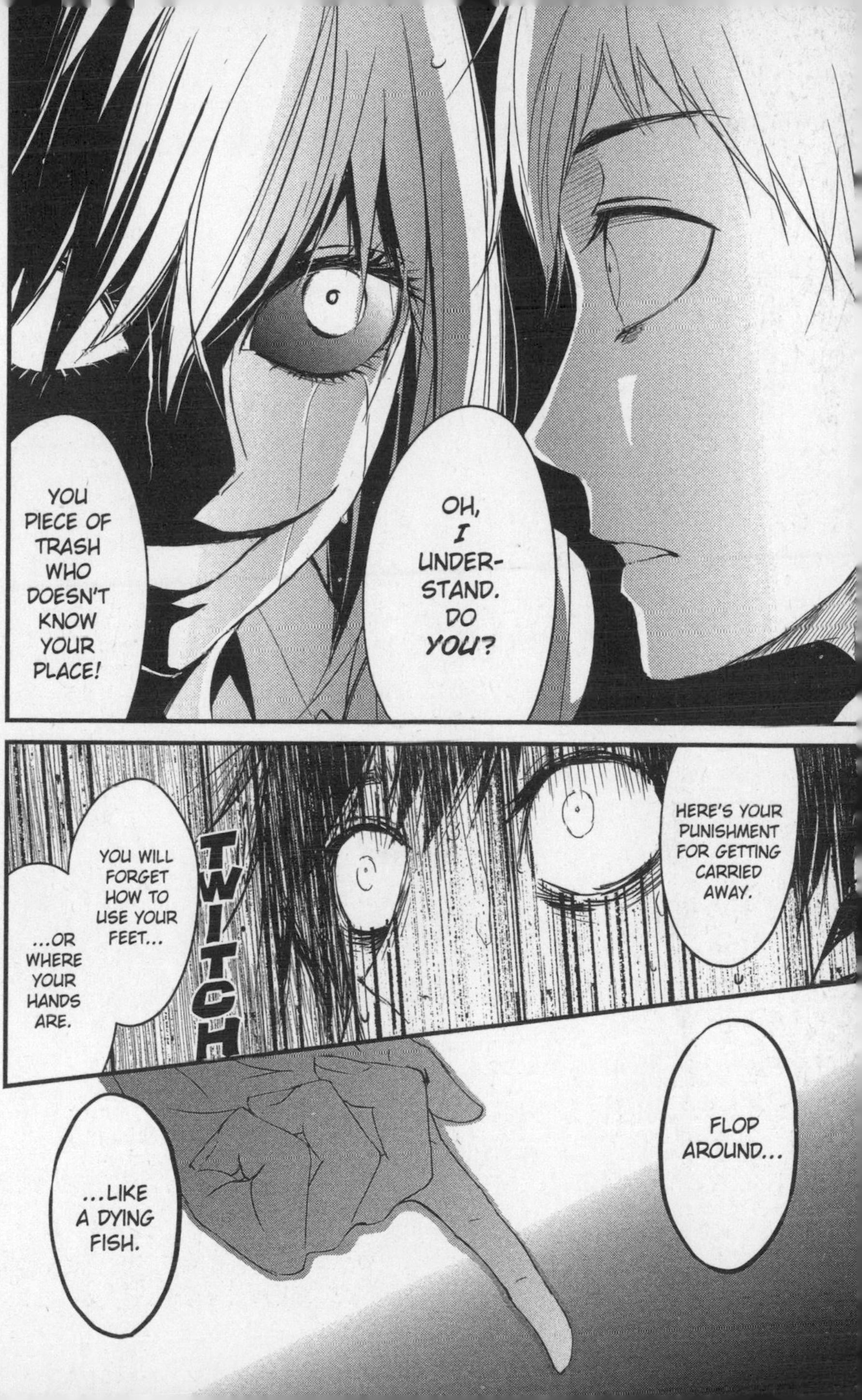
OH, I UNDERSTAND. DO YOU?
YOU PIECE OF TRASH WHO DOESN'T KNOW YOUR PLACE!
HERE'S YOUR PUNISHMENT FOR GETTING CARRIED AWAY.
TWITCH
YOU WILL FORGET HOW TO USE YOUR FEET...
...OR WHERE YOUR HANDS ARE.
FLOP AROUND...
...LIKE A DYING FISH.

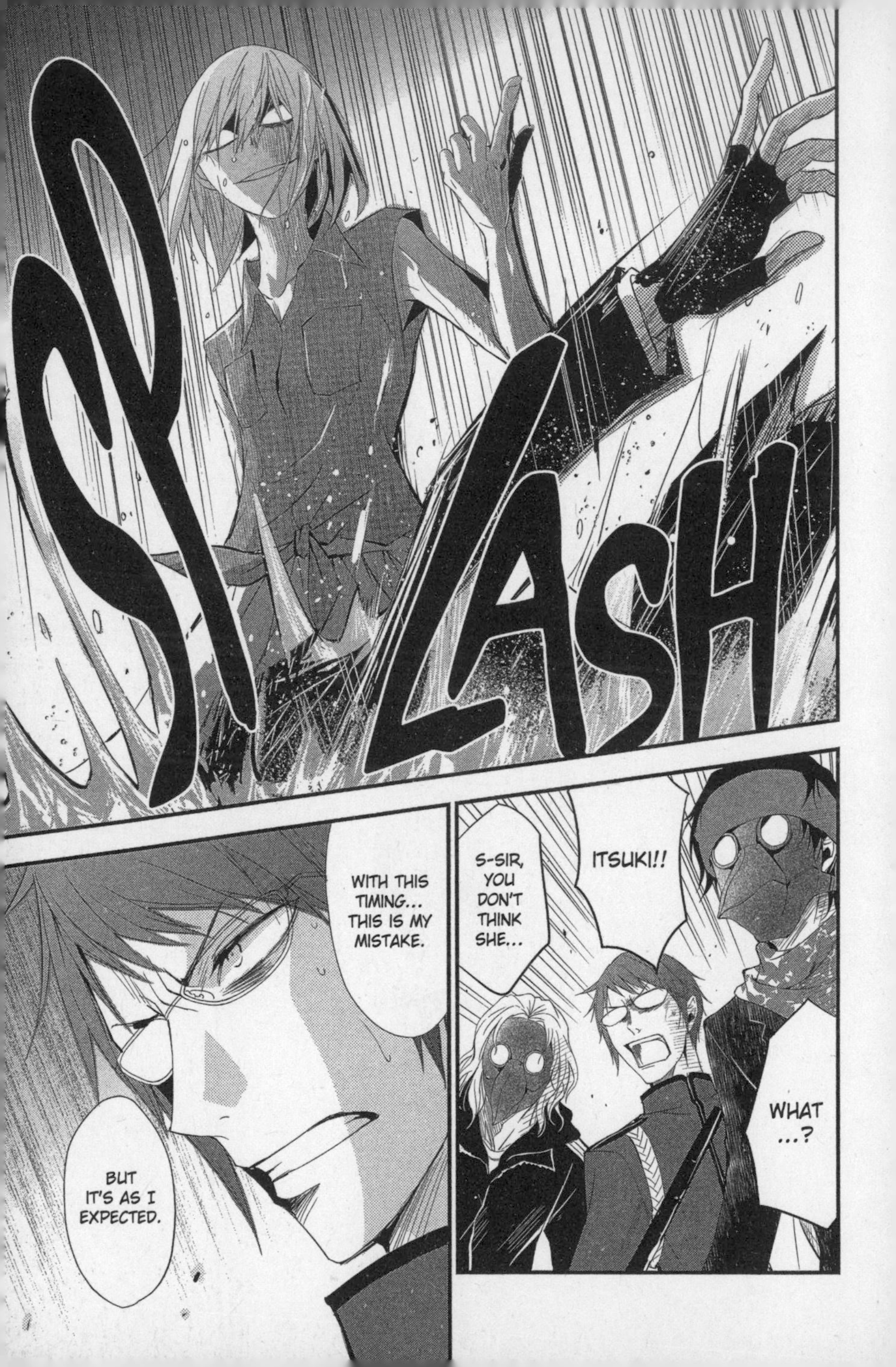
SLASH
ITSUKI!!
S-SIR, YOU DON'T THINK SHE...
WHAT ...?
WITH THIS TIMING... THIS IS MY MISTAKE.
BUT IT'S AS I EXPECTED.

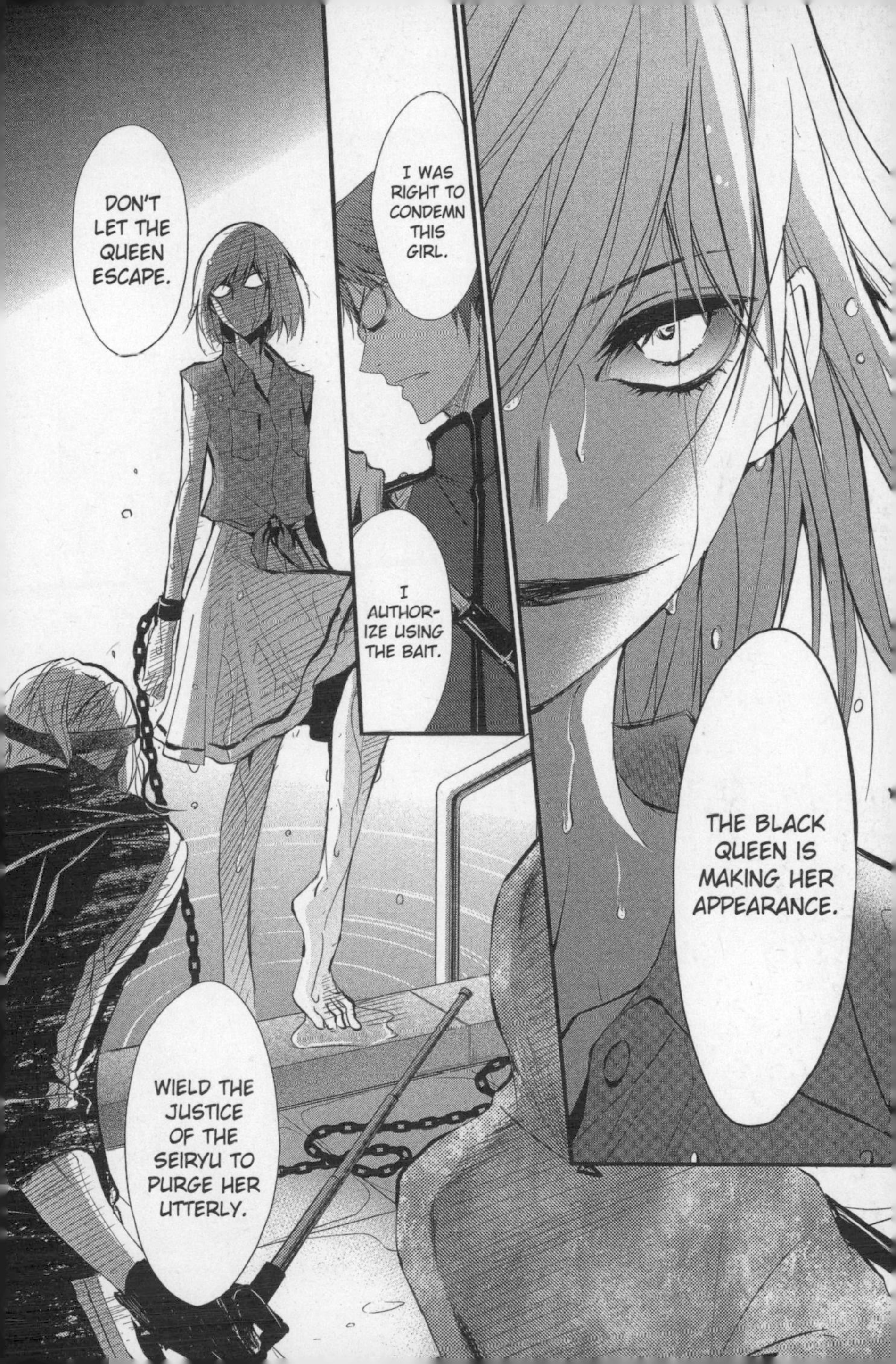
THE BLACK QUEEN IS MAKING HER APPEARANCE.
I WAS RIGHT TO CONDEMN THIS GIRL.
I AUTHOR-IZE USING THE BAIT.
DON'T LET THE QUEEN ESCAPE.
WIELD THE JUSTICE OF THE SEIRYU TO PURGE HER UTTERLY.

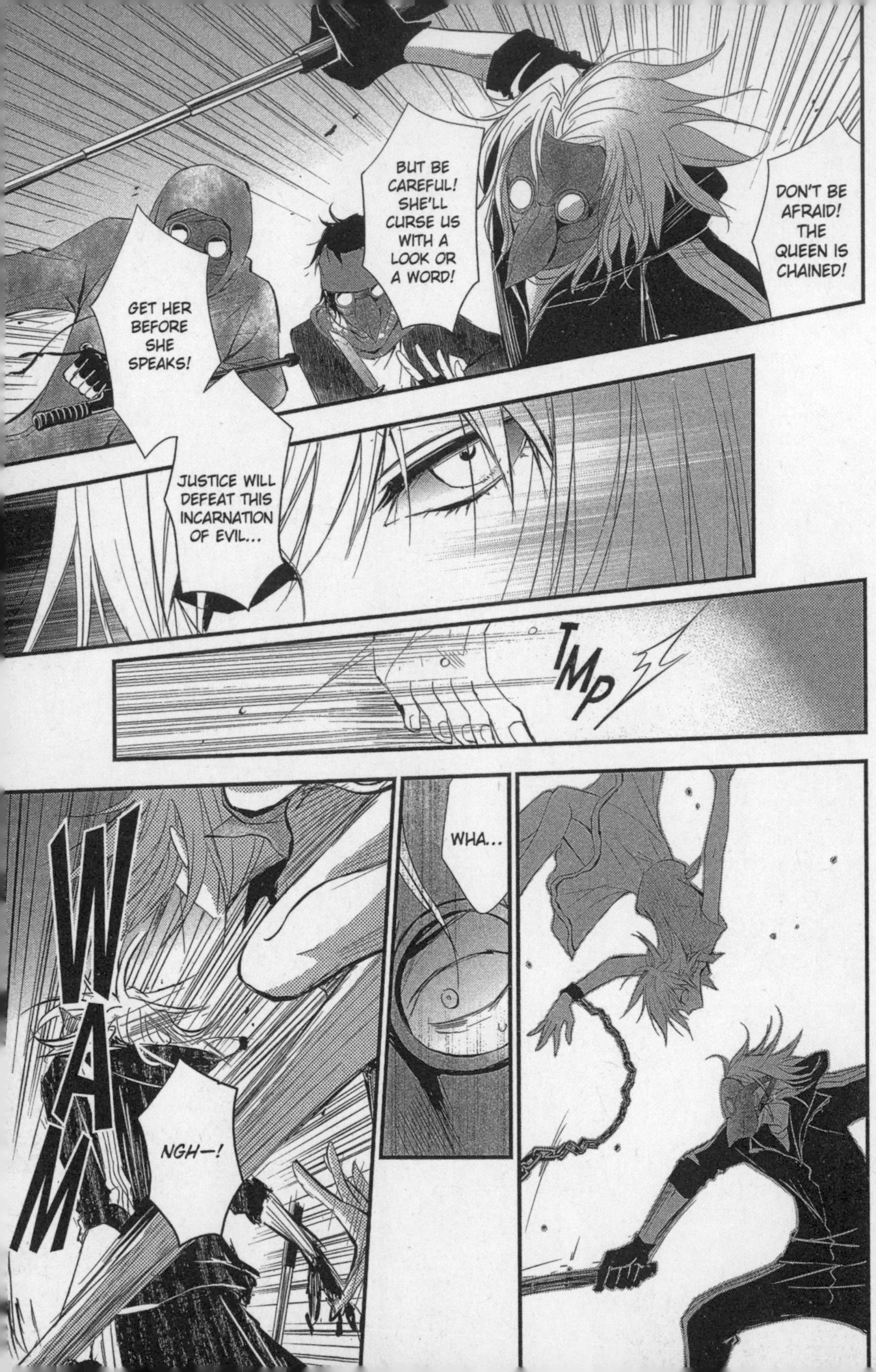
DON'T BE AFRAID! THE QUEEN IS CHAINED!
BUT BE CAREFUL! SHE'LL CURSE US WITH A LOOK OR A WORD!
GET HER BEFORE SHE SPEAKS!
JUSTICE WILL DEFEAT THIS INCARNATION OF EVIL...
TMP
WHA...
WAM
NGH—!

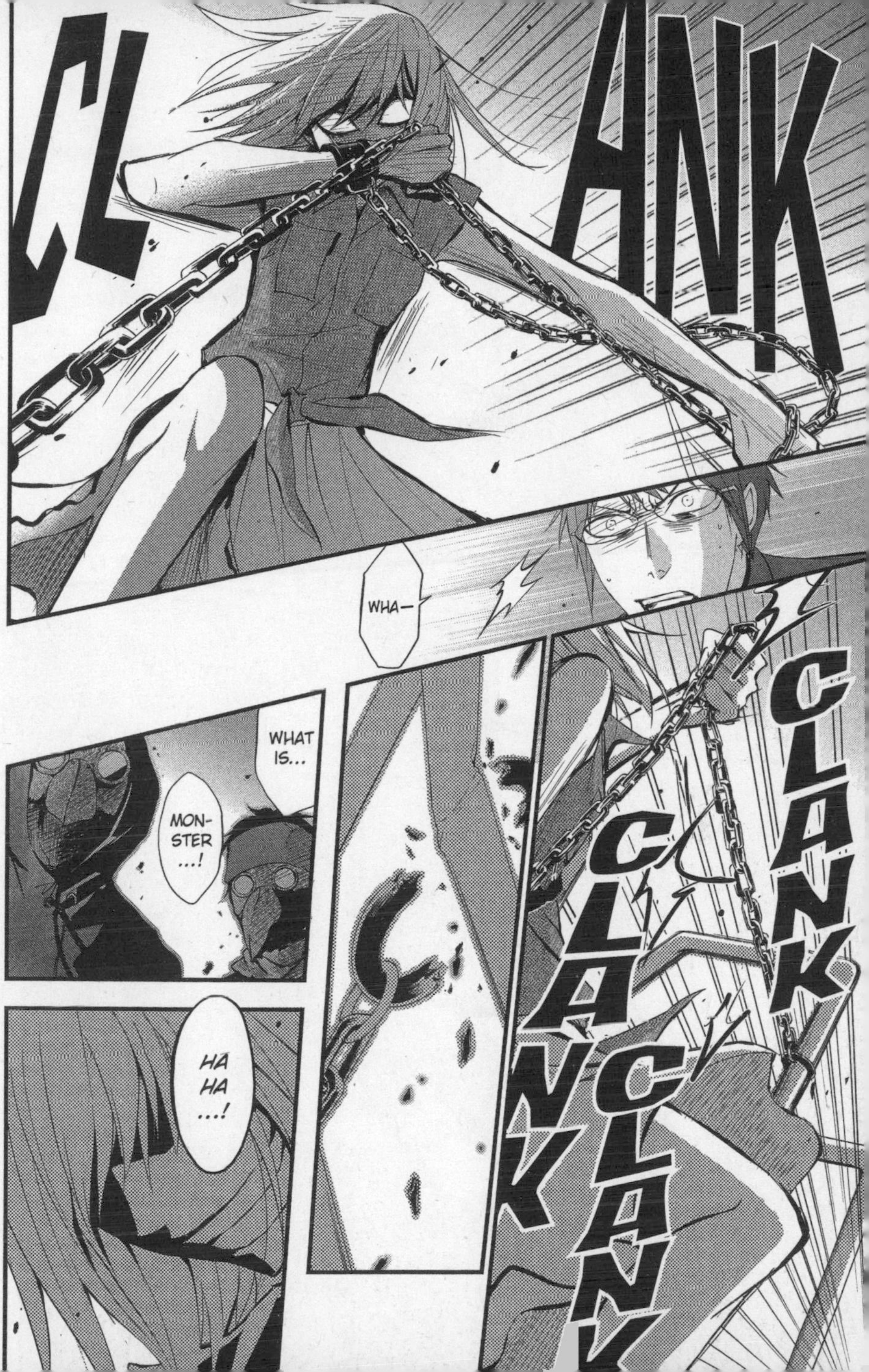
CLANK
WHA—
CLANK
CLANK
CLANK
WHAT IS...
MONSTER...!
HA HA...!

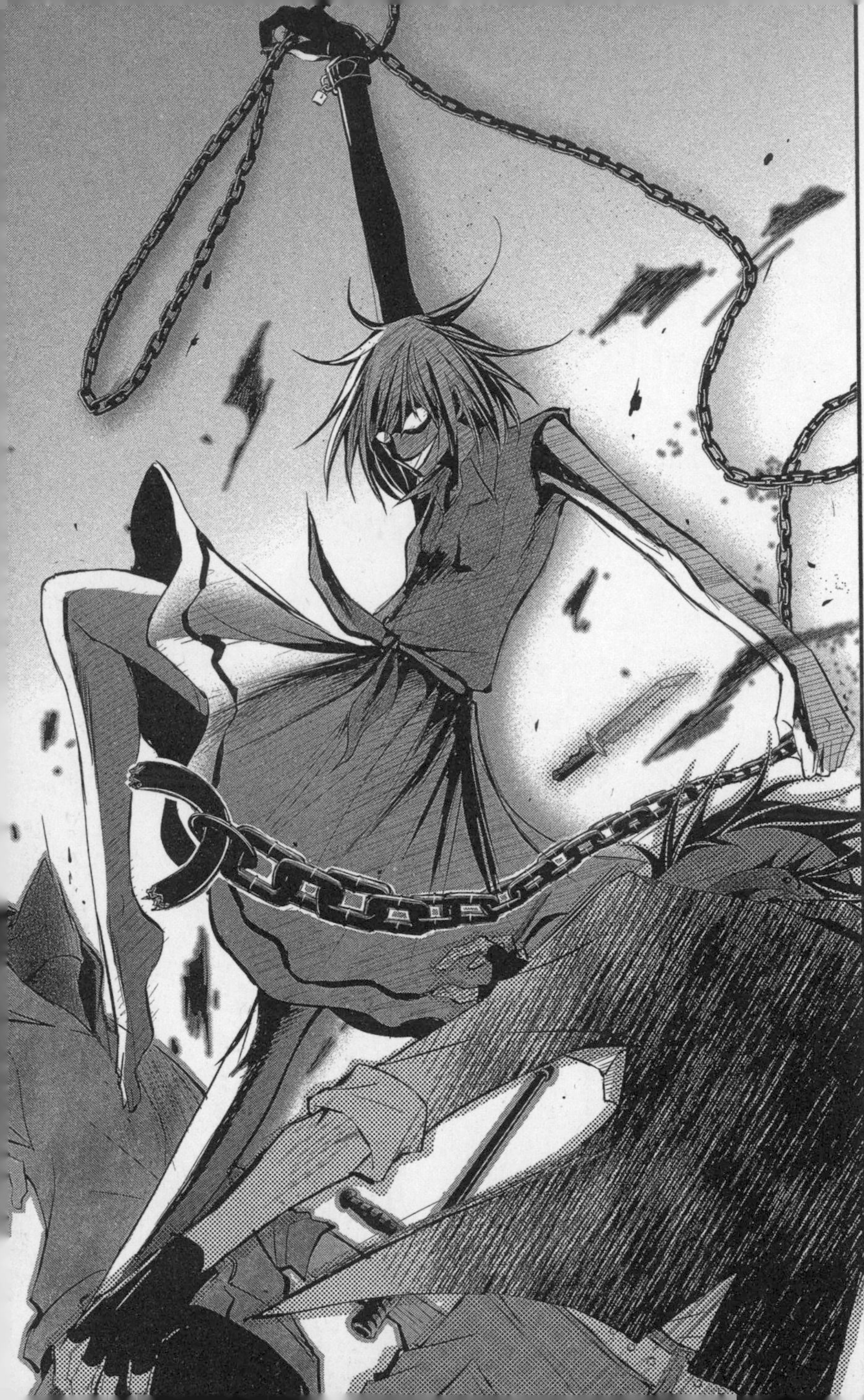

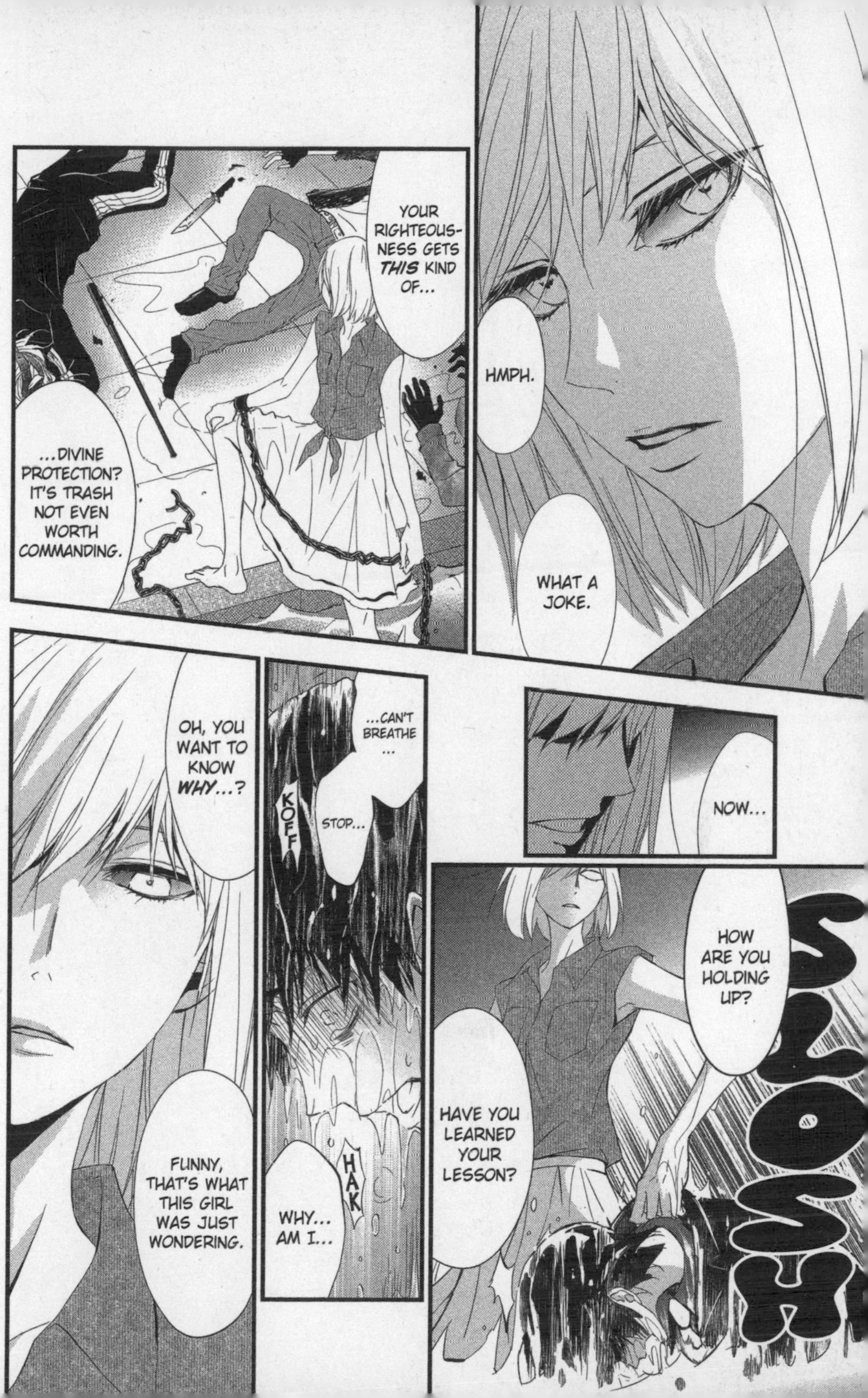
HMPH.
WHAT A JOKE.
YOUR RIGHTEOUSNESS GETS *THIS* KIND OF...
...DIVINE PROTECTION? IT'S TRASH NOT EVEN WORTH COMMANDING.
NOW...
HOW ARE YOU HOLDING UP?
HAVE YOU LEARNED YOUR LESSON?
...CAN'T BREATHE...
KOFF
STOP...
HAK
WHY... AM I...
OH, YOU WANT TO KNOW *WHY*...?
FUNNY, THAT'S WHAT THIS GIRL WAS JUST WONDERING.

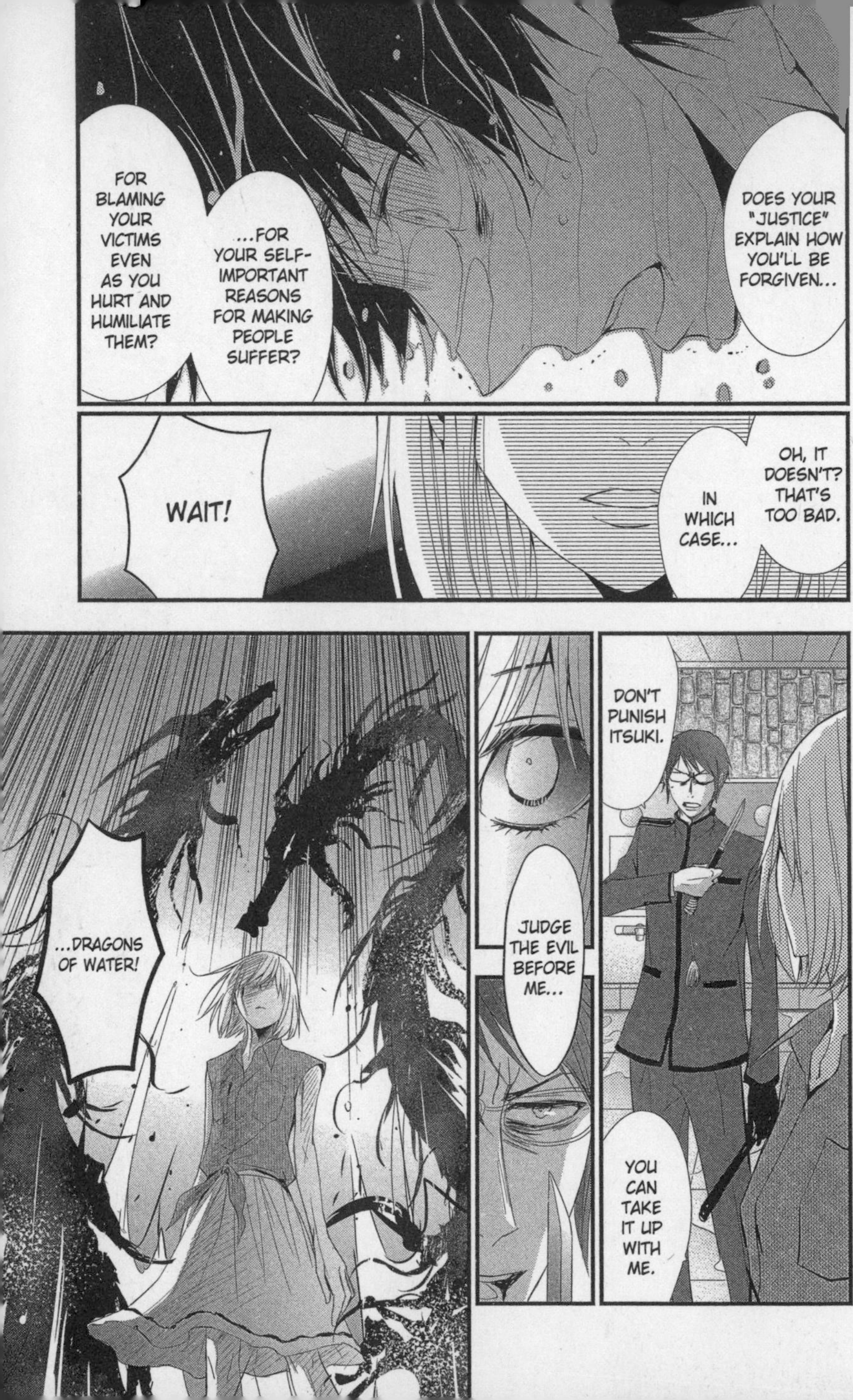
DOES YOUR "JUSTICE" EXPLAIN HOW YOU'LL BE FORGIVEN...
...FOR YOUR SELF-IMPORTANT REASONS FOR MAKING PEOPLE SUFFER?
FOR BLAMING YOUR VICTIMS EVEN AS YOU HURT AND HUMILIATE THEM?
OH, IT DOESN'T? THAT'S TOO BAD.
IN WHICH CASE...
WAIT!
DON'T PUNISH ITSUKI.
YOU CAN TAKE IT UP WITH ME.
JUDGE THE EVIL BEFORE ME...
...DRAGONS OF WATER!

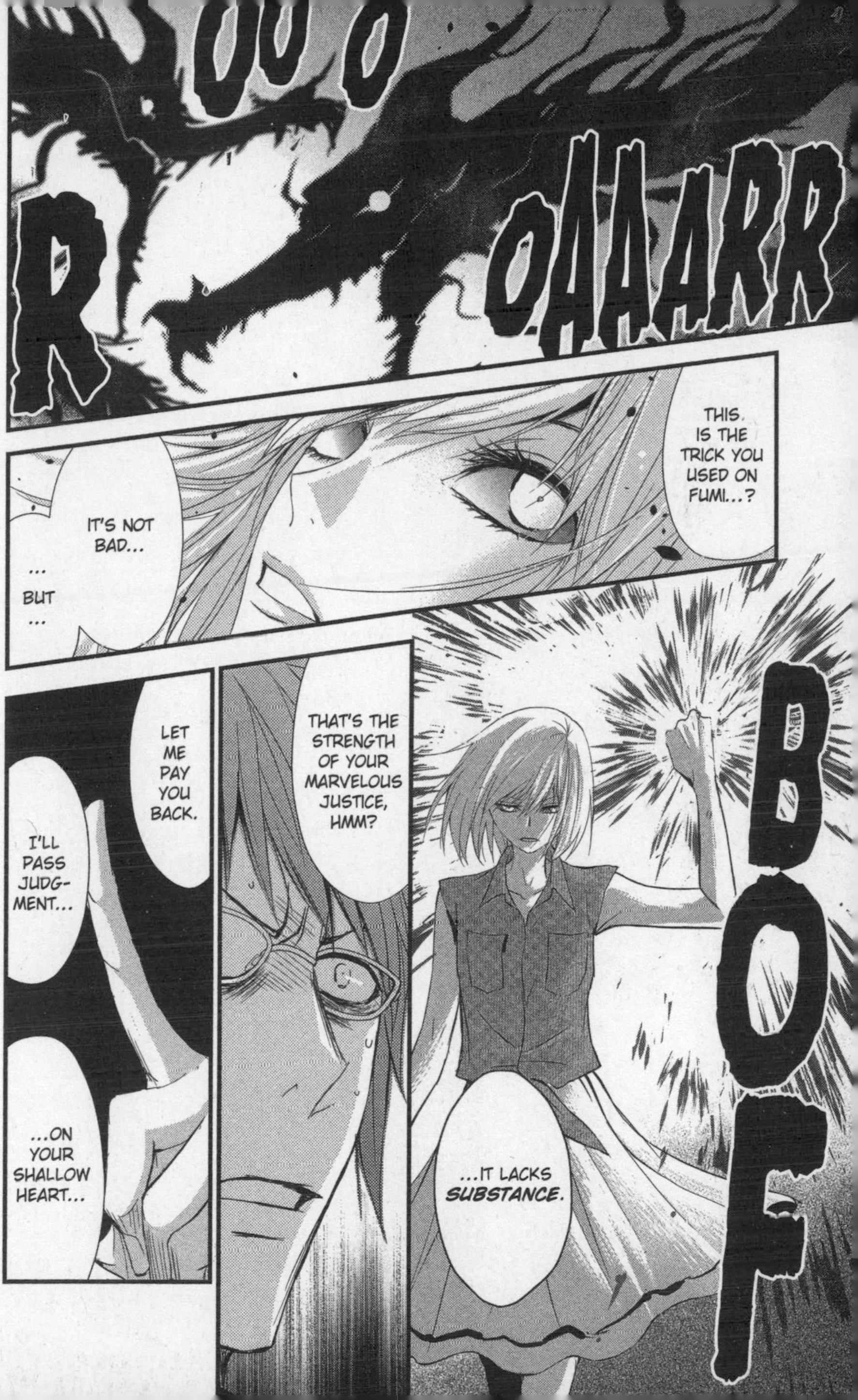
ROOOOAAARR
THIS. IS THE TRICK YOU USED ON FUMI...?
IT'S NOT BAD... ... BUT ...
BOF
...IT LACKS **SUBSTANCE**.
THAT'S THE STRENGTH OF YOUR MARVELOUS JUSTICE, HMM?
LET ME PAY YOU BACK.
I'LL PASS JUDG-MENT...
...ON YOUR SHALLOW HEART...

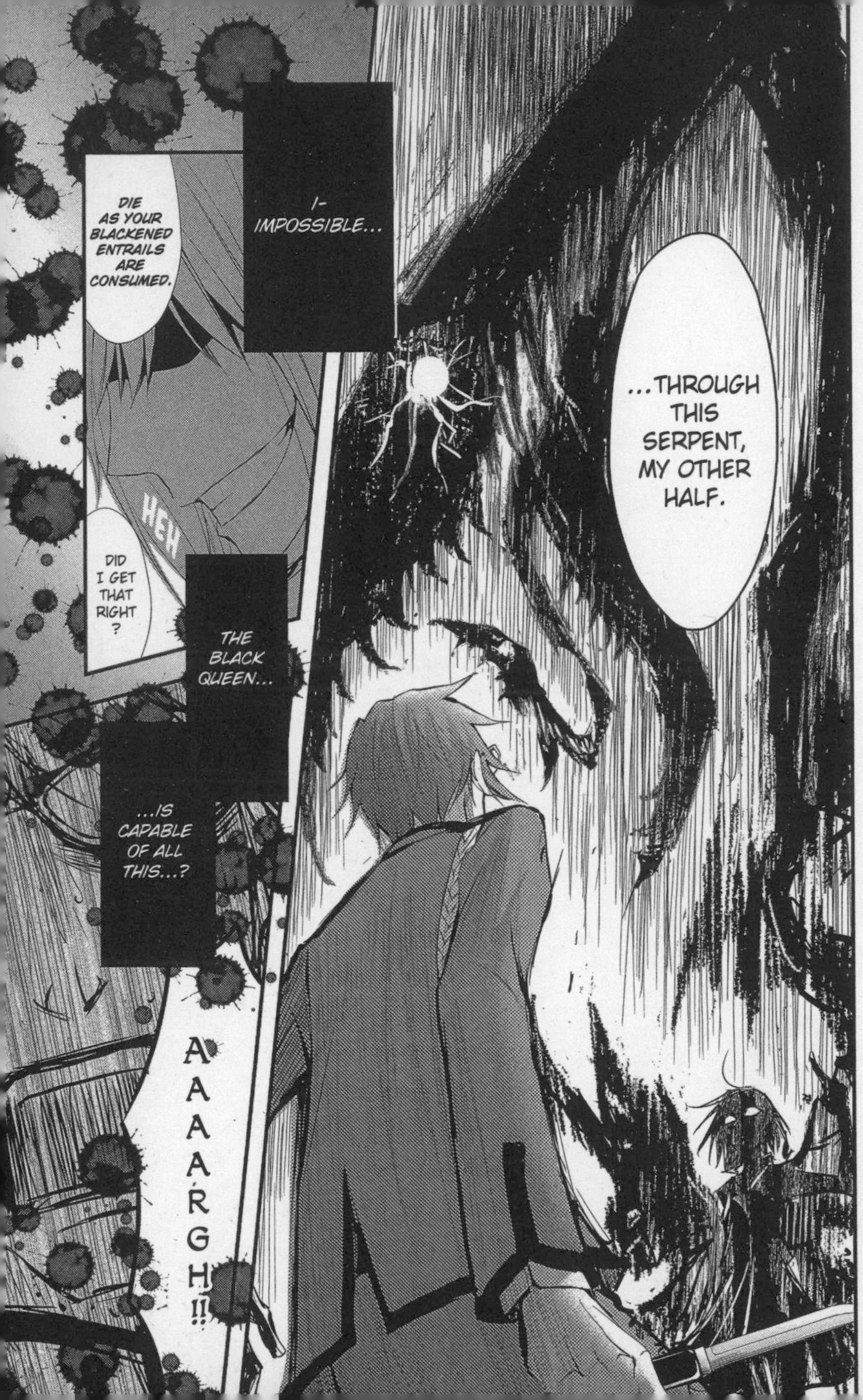
...THROUGH THIS SERPENT, MY OTHER HALF.
I- IMPOSSIBLE...
DIE AS YOUR BLACKENED ENTRAILS ARE CONSUMED.
HEH
DID I GET THAT RIGHT?
THE BLACK QUEEN...
...IS CAPABLE OF ALL THIS...?
AAAARGH!!

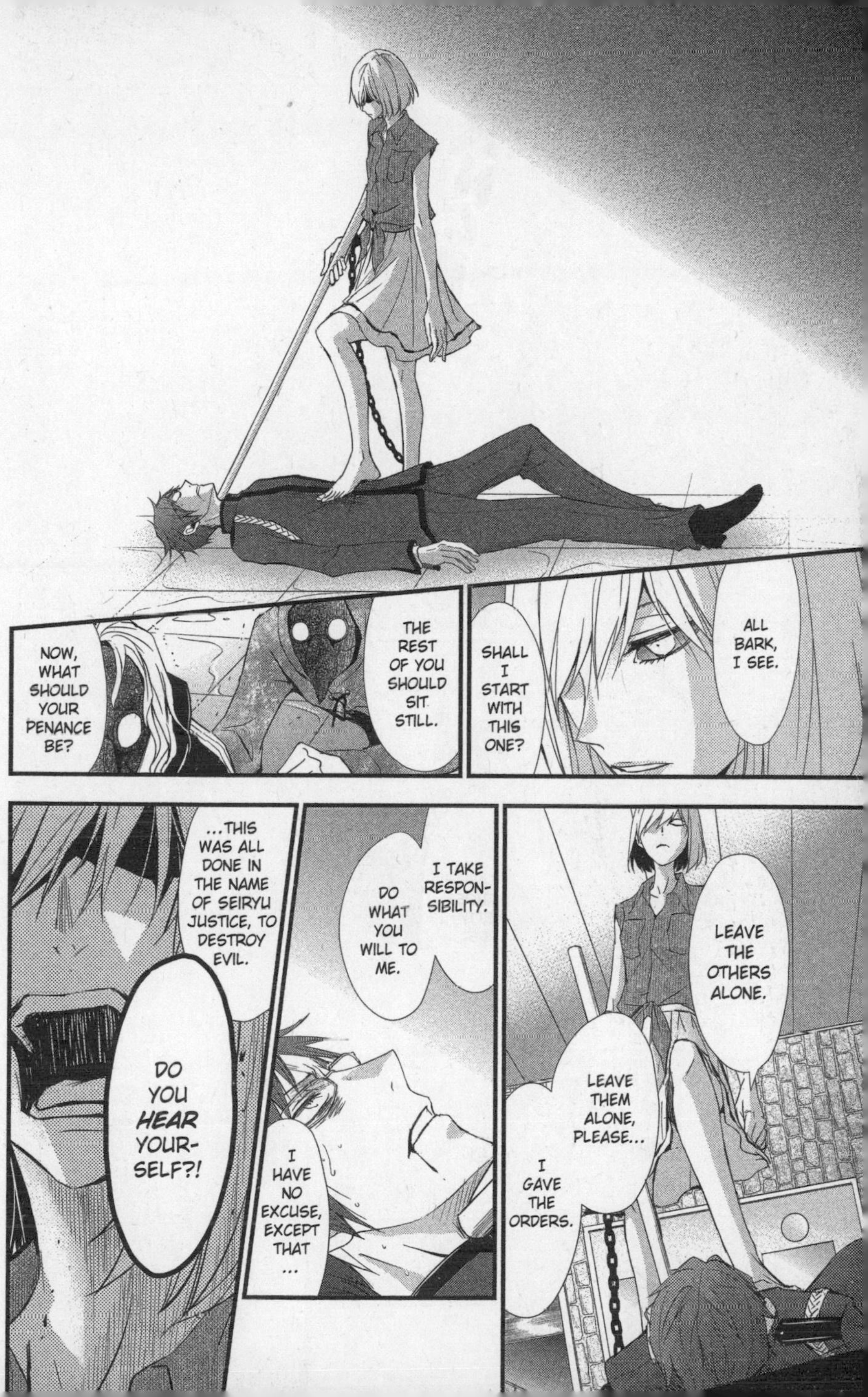
ALL BARK, I SEE.
SHALL I START WITH THIS ONE?
THE REST OF YOU SHOULD SIT STILL.
NOW, WHAT SHOULD YOUR PENANCE BE?
LEAVE THE OTHERS ALONE.
LEAVE THEM ALONE, PLEASE...
I GAVE THE ORDERS.
I TAKE RESPONSIBILITY.
DO WHAT YOU WILL TO ME.
I HAVE NO EXCUSE, EXCEPT THAT ...
...THIS WAS ALL DONE IN THE NAME OF SEIRYU JUSTICE, TO DESTROY EVIL.
DO YOU ***HEAR*** YOURSELF?!

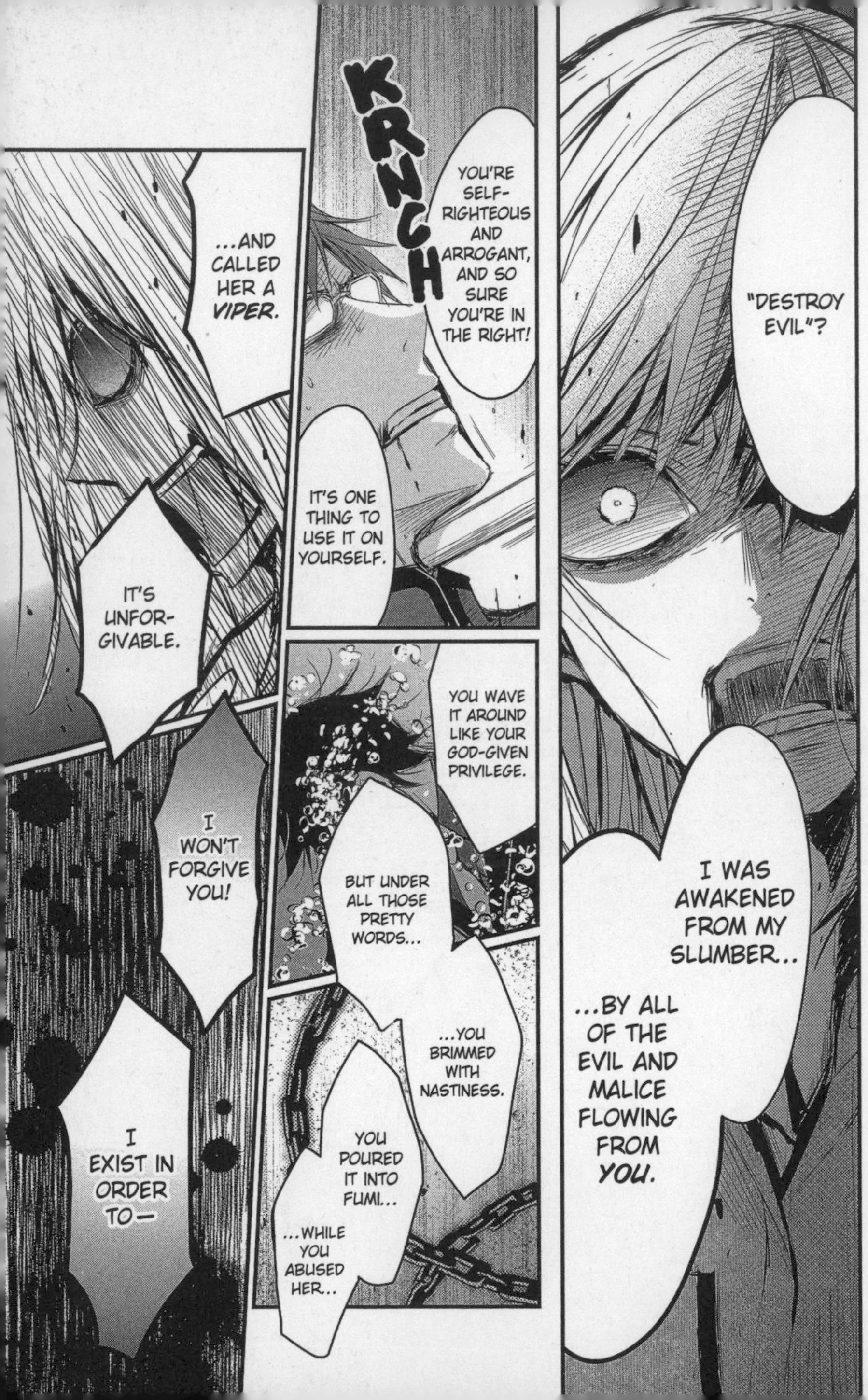
"DESTROY EVIL"?
I WAS AWAKENED FROM MY SLUMBER...
...BY ALL OF THE EVIL AND MALICE FLOWING FROM *YOU*.
YOU'RE SELF-RIGHTEOUS AND ARROGANT, AND SO SURE YOU'RE IN THE RIGHT!
KRNCH
IT'S ONE THING TO USE IT ON YOURSELF.
YOU WAVE IT AROUND LIKE YOUR GOD-GIVEN PRIVILEGE.
BUT UNDER ALL THOSE PRETTY WORDS...
...YOU BRIMMED WITH NASTINESS.
YOU POURED IT INTO FUMI...
...WHILE YOU ABUSED HER...
...AND CALLED HER A *VIPER*.
IT'S UNFORGIVABLE.
I WON'T FORGIVE YOU!
I EXIST IN ORDER TO—

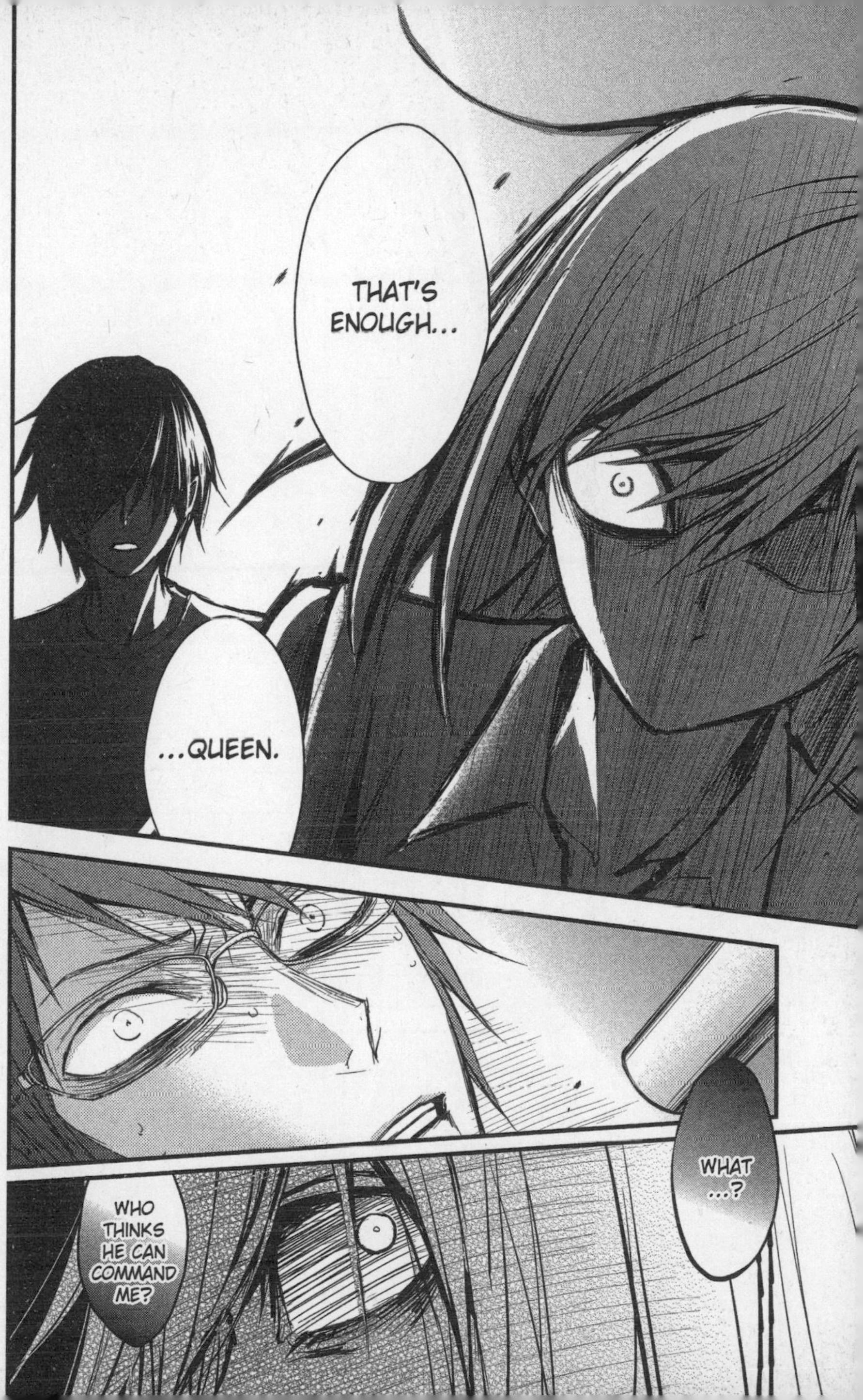
THAT'S ENOUGH...
...QUEEN.
WHAT ...?
WHO THINKS HE CAN COMMAND ME?

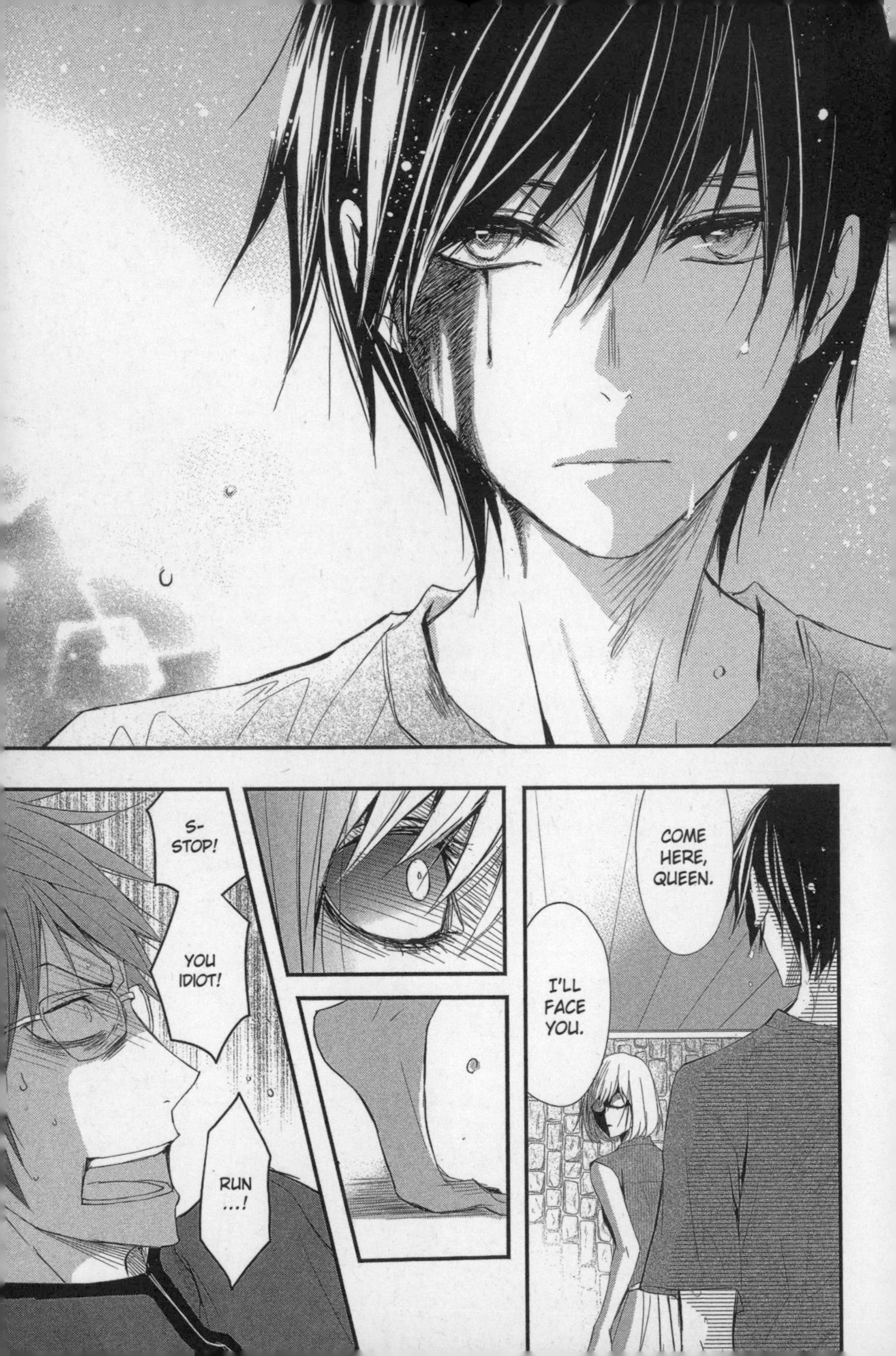
COME HERE, QUEEN.
I'LL FACE YOU.
S-STOP!
YOU IDIOT!
RUN ...!

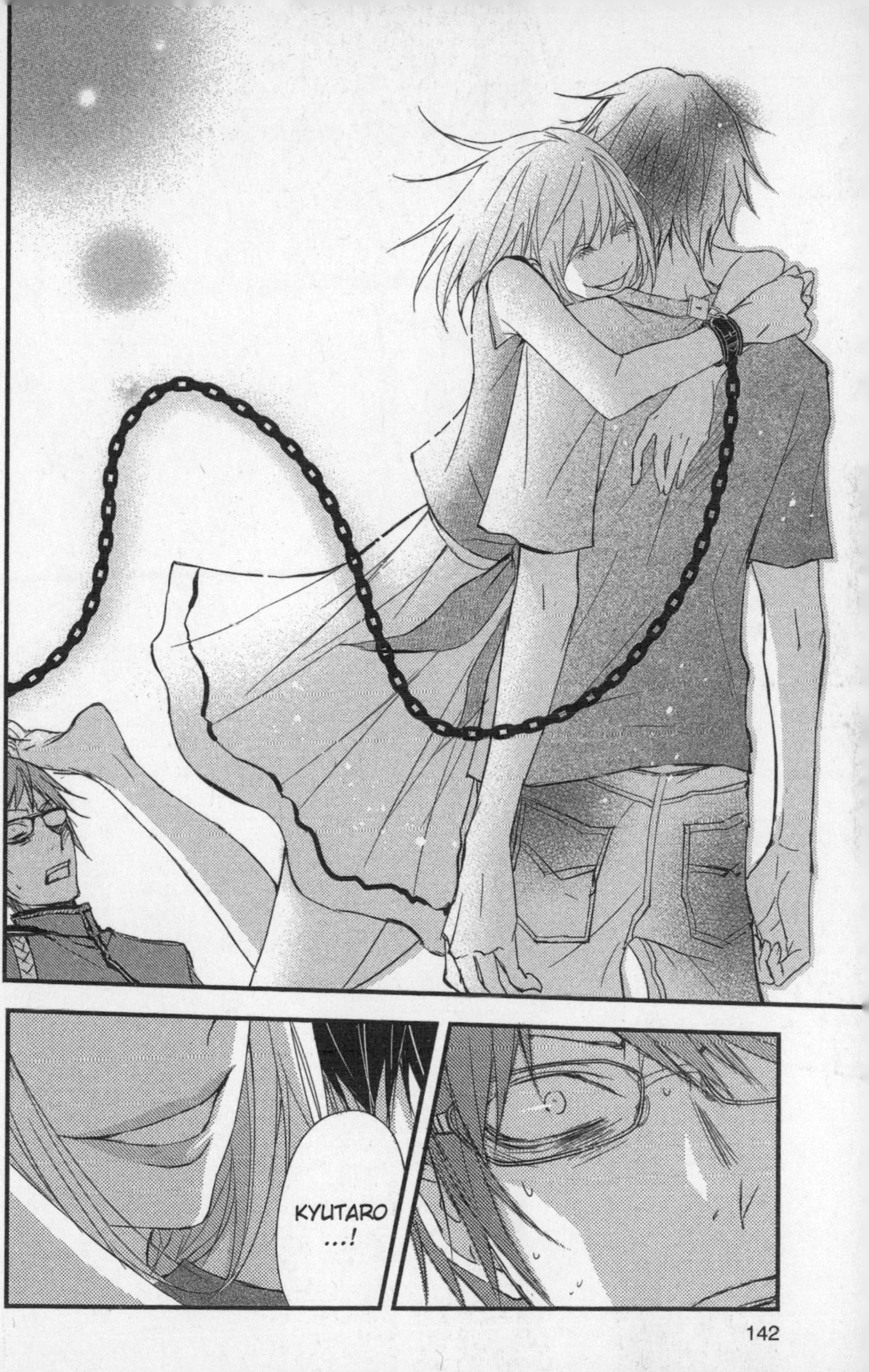
KYUTARO ...!

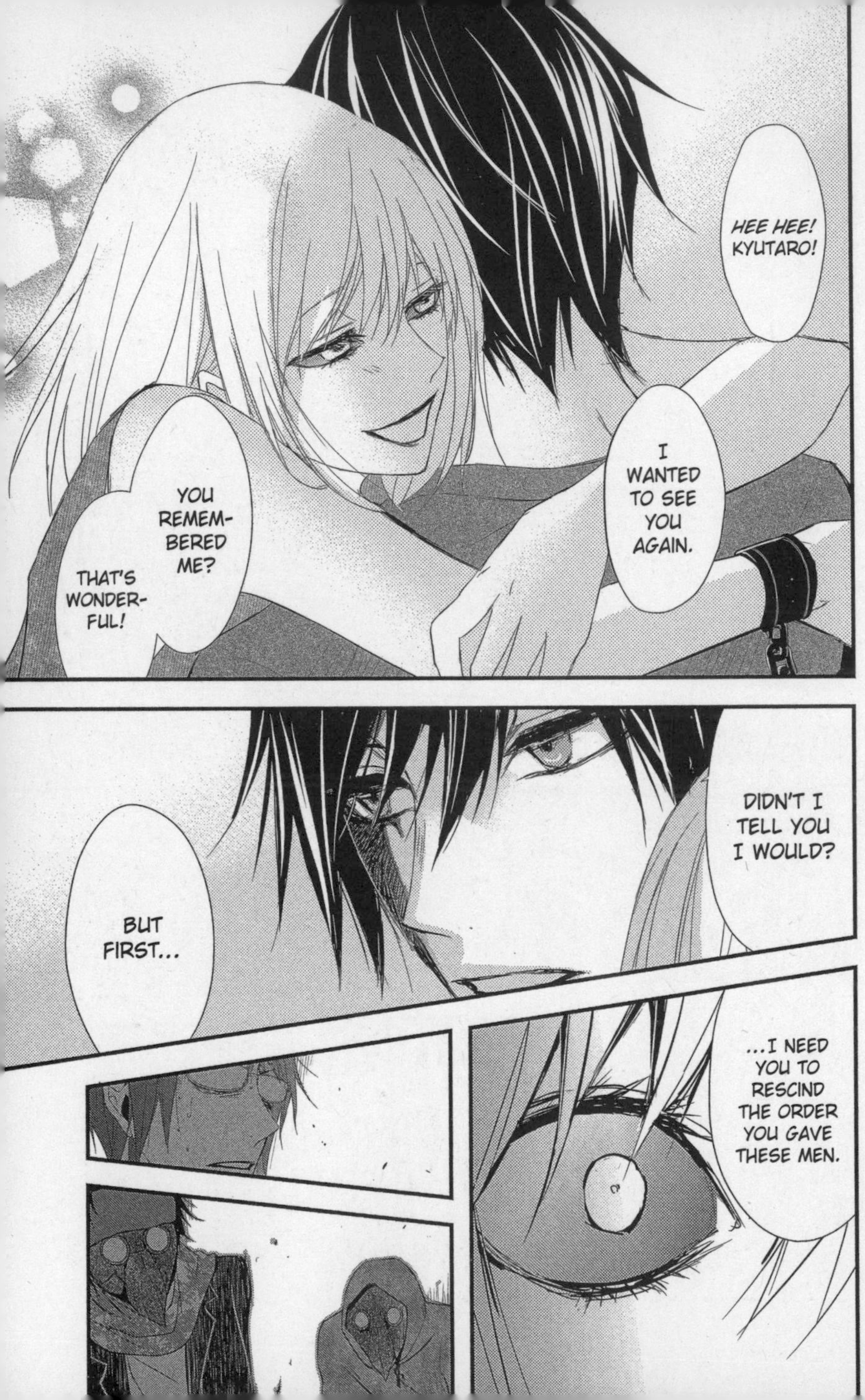
HEE HEE! KYUTARO!
I WANTED TO SEE YOU AGAIN.
YOU REMEM-BERED ME?
THAT'S WONDER-FUL!
DIDN'T I TELL YOU I WOULD?
BUT FIRST...
...I NEED YOU TO RESCIND THE ORDER YOU GAVE THESE MEN.

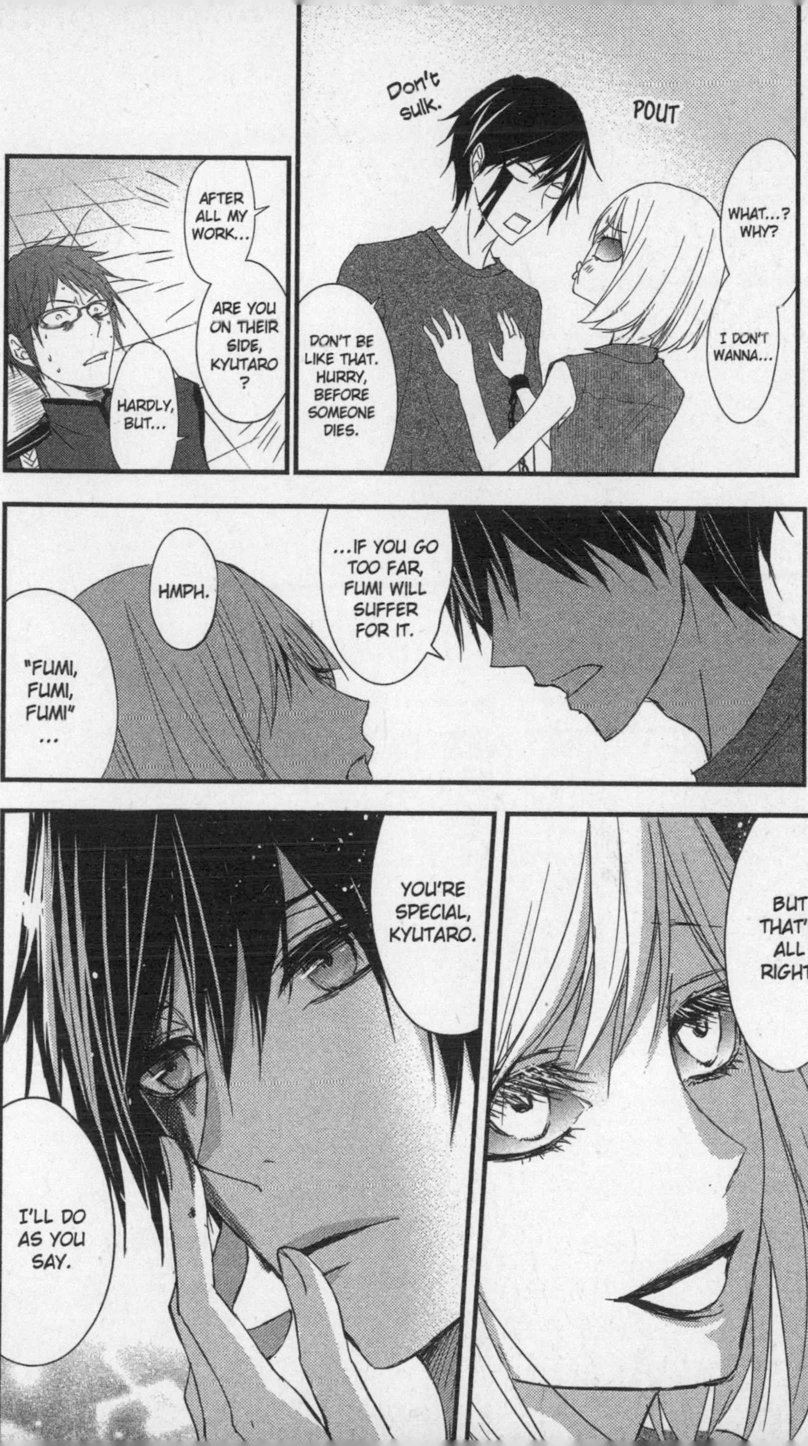
POUT
WHAT...? WHY?
Don't sulk.
I DON'T WANNA...
DON'T BE LIKE THAT. HURRY, BEFORE SOMEONE DIES.
AFTER ALL MY WORK...
ARE YOU ON THEIR SIDE, KYUTARO?
HARDLY, BUT...
...IF YOU GO TOO FAR, FUMI WILL SUFFER FOR IT.
HMPH.
"FUMI, FUMI, FUMI"...
BUT THAT'S ALL RIGHT.
YOU'RE SPECIAL, KYUTARO.
I'LL DO AS YOU SAY.

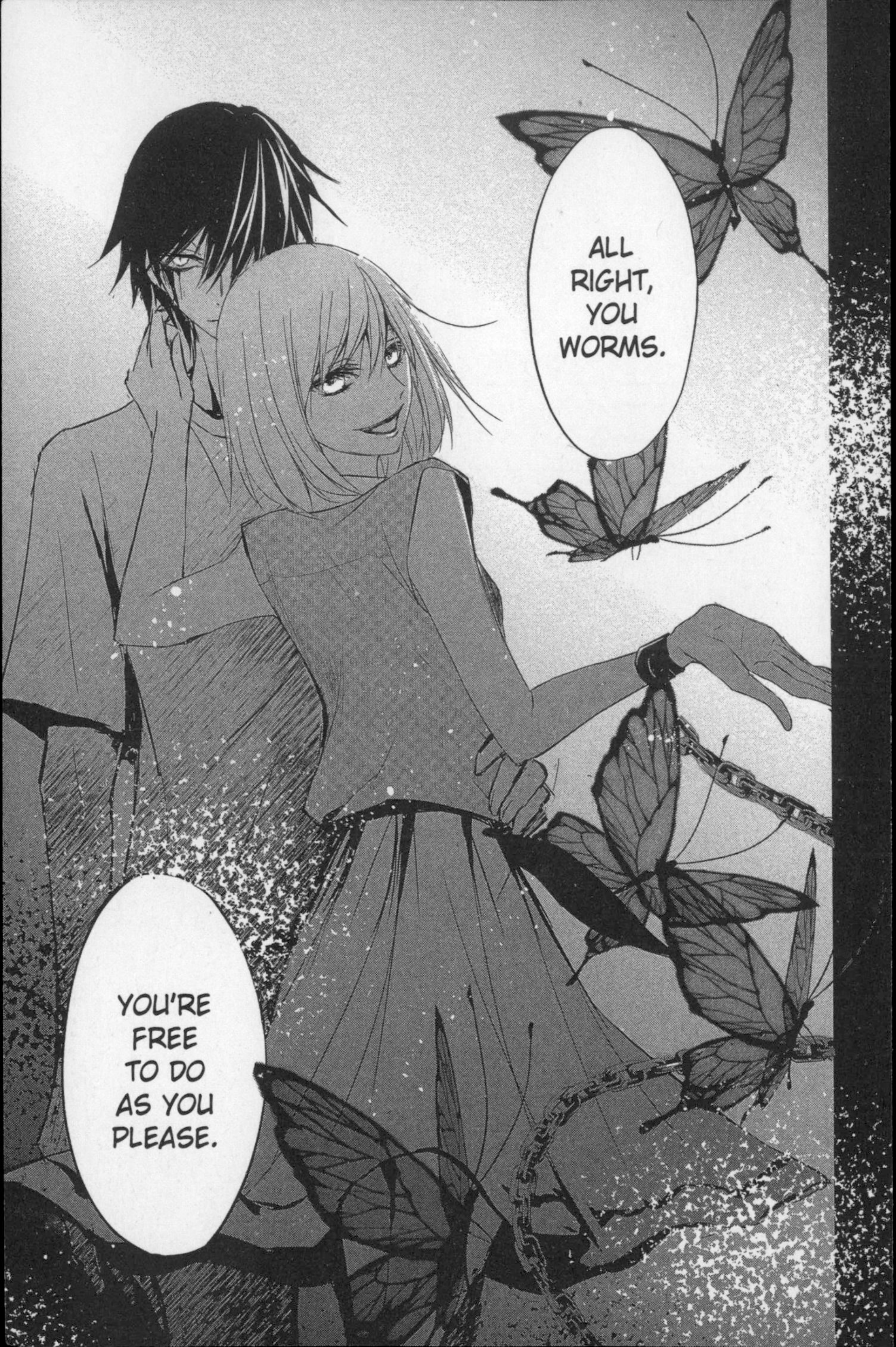
ALL RIGHT, YOU WORMS.
YOU'RE FREE TO DO AS YOU PLEASE.

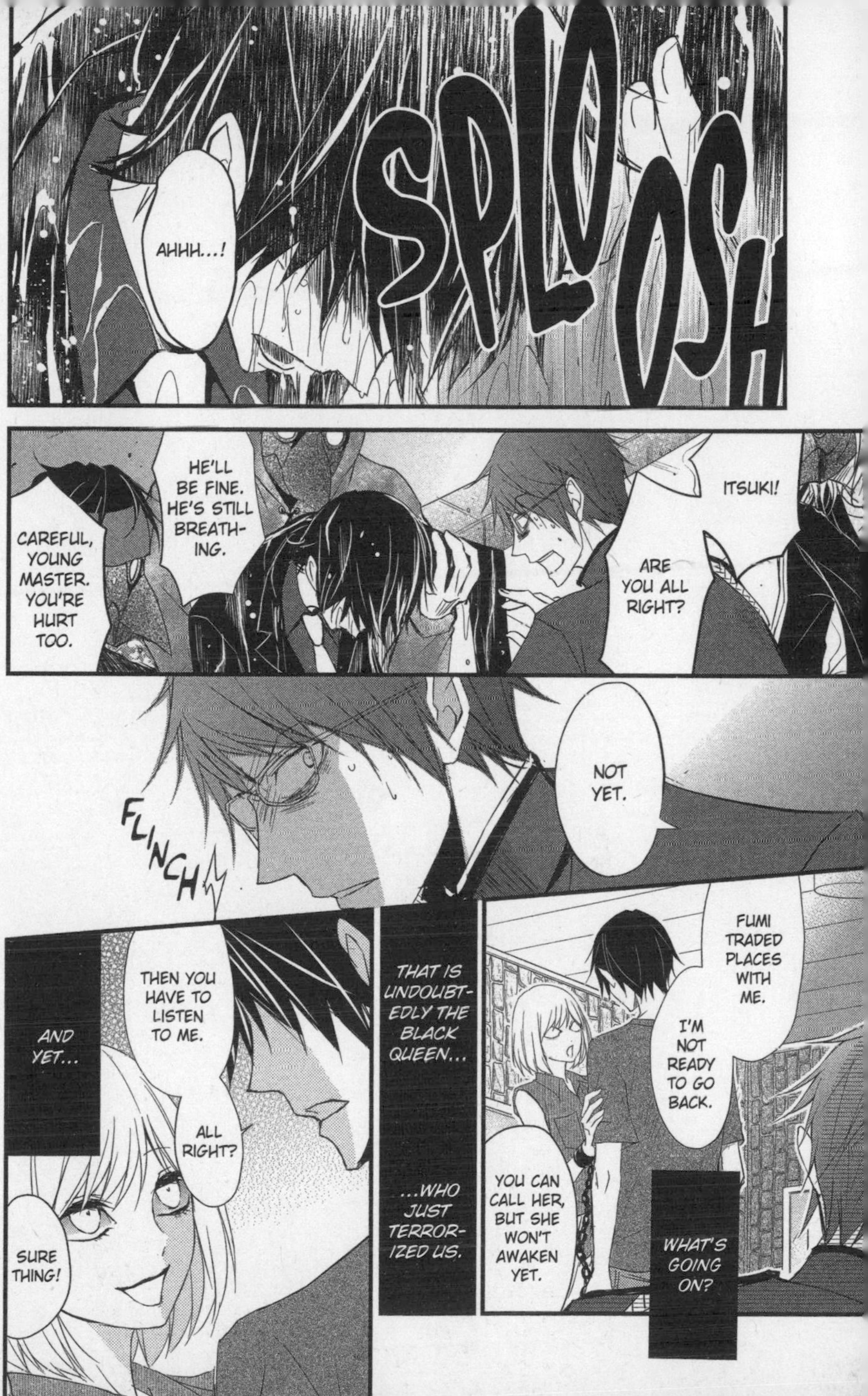
SPLOOSH
AHHH...!
ITSUKI!
ARE YOU ALL RIGHT?
HE'LL BE FINE. HE'S STILL BREATH-ING.
CAREFUL, YOUNG MASTER. YOU'RE HURT TOO.
NOT YET.
FLINCH
FUMI TRADED PLACES WITH ME.
I'M NOT READY TO GO BACK.
YOU CAN CALL HER, BUT SHE WON'T AWAKEN YET.
WHAT'S GOING ON?
THAT IS UNDOUBT-EDLY THE BLACK QUEEN...
...WHO JUST TERROR-IZED US.
THEN YOU HAVE TO LISTEN TO ME.
AND YET...
ALL RIGHT?
SURE THING!

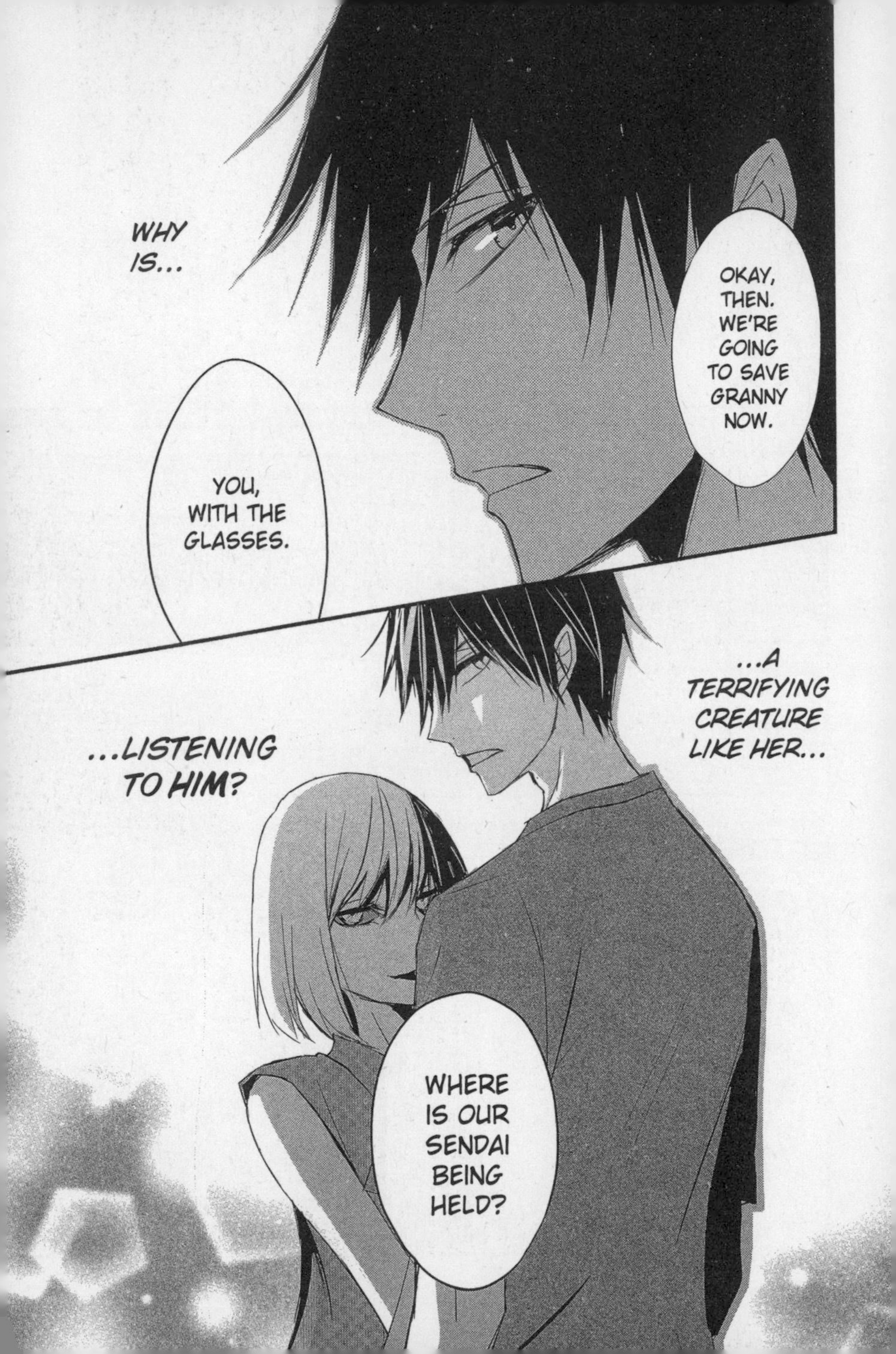
OKAY, THEN. WE'RE GOING TO SAVE GRANNY NOW.
YOU, WITH THE GLASSES.
WHY IS...
...A TERRIFYING CREATURE LIKE HER...
...LISTENING TO HIM?
WHERE IS OUR SENDAI BEING HELD?

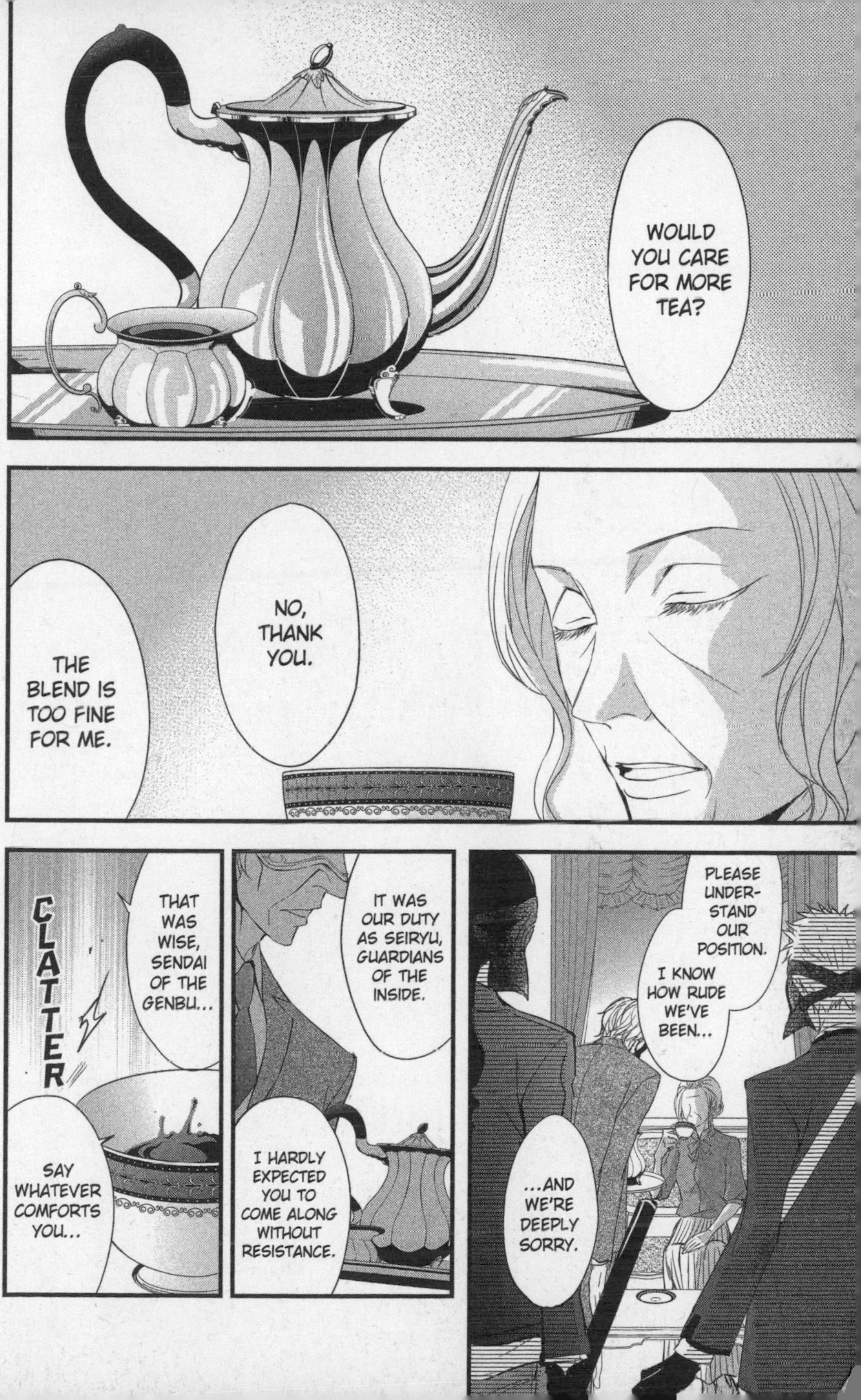
WOULD YOU CARE FOR MORE TEA?
NO, THANK YOU.
THE BLEND IS TOO FINE FOR ME.
PLEASE UNDER-STAND OUR POSITION.
I KNOW HOW RUDE WE'VE BEEN...
...AND WE'RE DEEPLY SORRY.
IT WAS OUR DUTY AS SEIRYU, GUARDIANS OF THE INSIDE.
I HARDLY EXPECTED YOU TO COME ALONG WITHOUT RESISTANCE.
THAT WAS WISE, SENDAI OF THE GENBU...
CLATTER
SAY WHATEVER COMFORTS YOU...

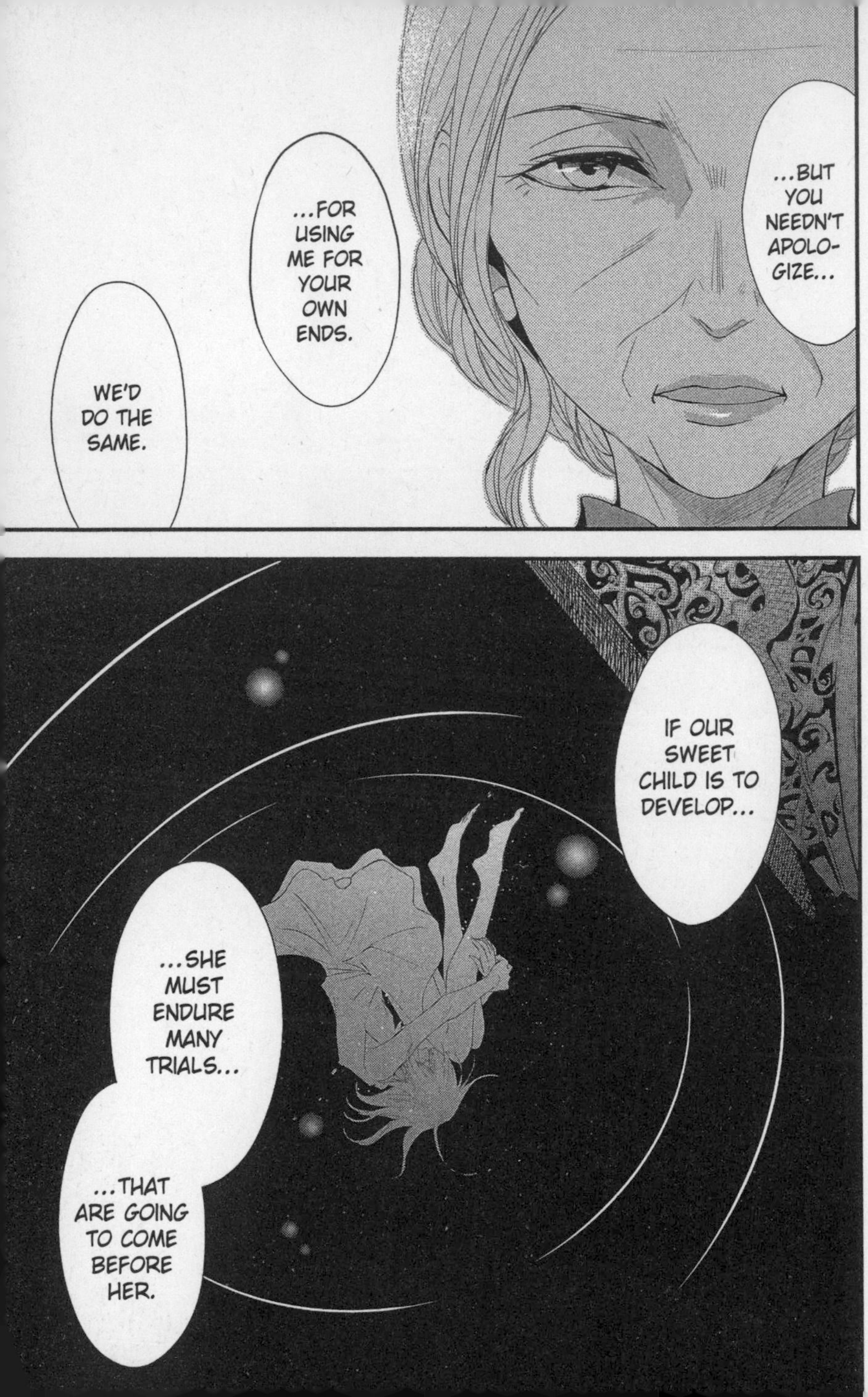
...BUT YOU NEEDN'T APOLO-GIZE...
...FOR USING ME FOR YOUR OWN ENDS.
WE'D DO THE SAME.
IF OUR SWEET CHILD IS TO DEVELOP...
...SHE MUST ENDURE MANY TRIALS...
...THAT ARE GOING TO COME BEFORE HER.

MONTHLY BETSUCOMI SALE DATE NOTICE ON TWITTER

CHAPTER 15

Mmm
Yes, right there. Ah...
That's perfect!
Kyuturu needs more training.
Does he have to react to every vaguely erotic sound he hears?
She's just breathing hard! Don't blush!
Cut him some slack, Takaya. Remember the distant past, when our only hope for a little excitement was stumbling across even a hint of an erotic moment.
That's just how young people react.

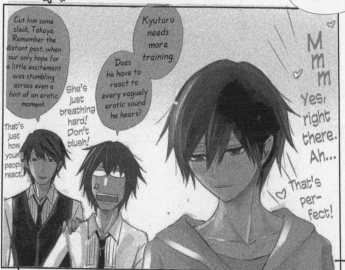

WHAT'S UP IN *QUEEN'S QUALITY* THIS MONTH?

(1) THERE ARE SO MANY...!!! (AUTHOR'S INNER VOICE)
(2) I THOUGHT SOMEONE WAS UNCONSCIOUSLY SHOWING ME RESPECT, BUT IT TURNS OUT IT WAS JUNKO KOSHINO.
(3) OH, WHAT'S UP WITH KOICHI...?

THE TRUTH IS, THERE'S NOTHING EROTIC IN CHAPTER 15!

And that's *Queequa* volume 3 up to chapter 15!
There are so many pages in this volume that there's no space for an afterword, but I hope you've enjoyed it.
If you did, I hope to see you again in volume 4!

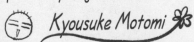

Kyousuke Motomi

Chapter 15

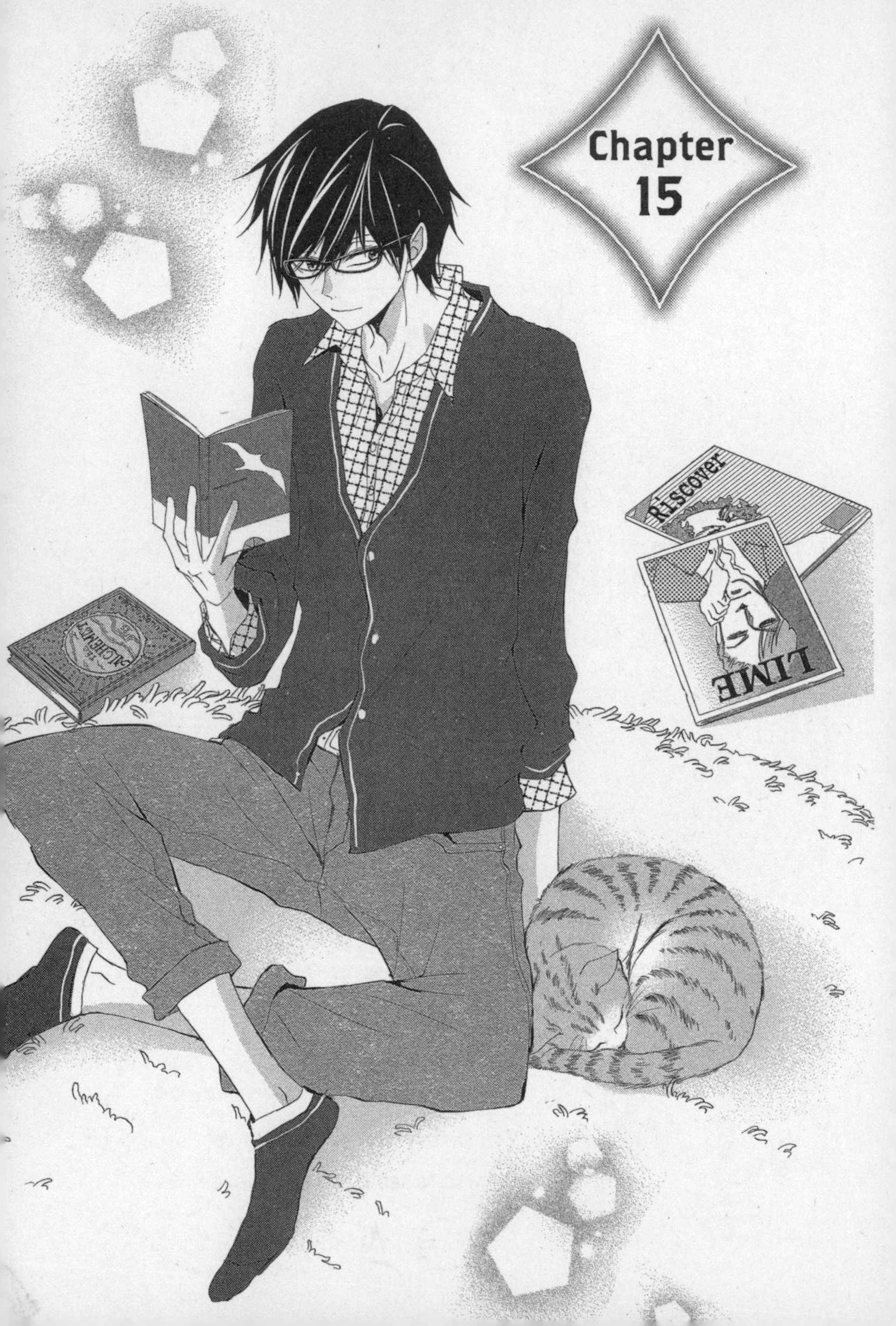

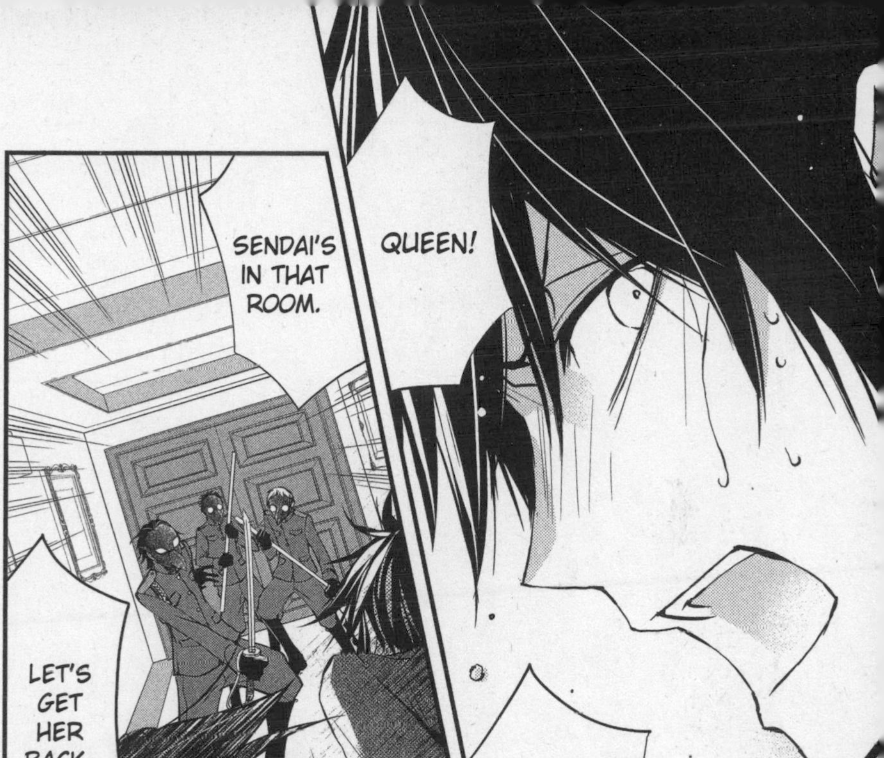
QUEEN!
HERE! I'VE FOUND HER!
SENDAI'S IN THAT ROOM.
LET'S GET HER BACK.

Pokémon Go was launched right around when I was drawing this section, and I got really into it. It was the first game I played on my smartphone, and it was also my introduction to Pokémon. They're so cute! I'm thoroughly hooked.
The Pokémon Venonat turns up around my home fairly often. When I was drawing the Black Queen I kept laughing, because I thought Venonat resembled her in the moment in chapter 14 where she's saying, "What…? Why? I don't wanna…"
But when I looked at the scene again later, I didn't see much resemblance. Sometimes I hallucinate a little when I'm working.

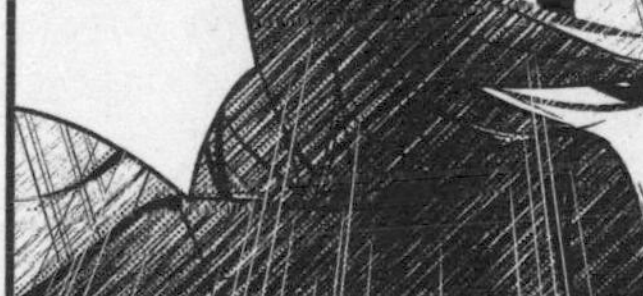
I wish we could choose the caps to go with the guys' tracksuits.

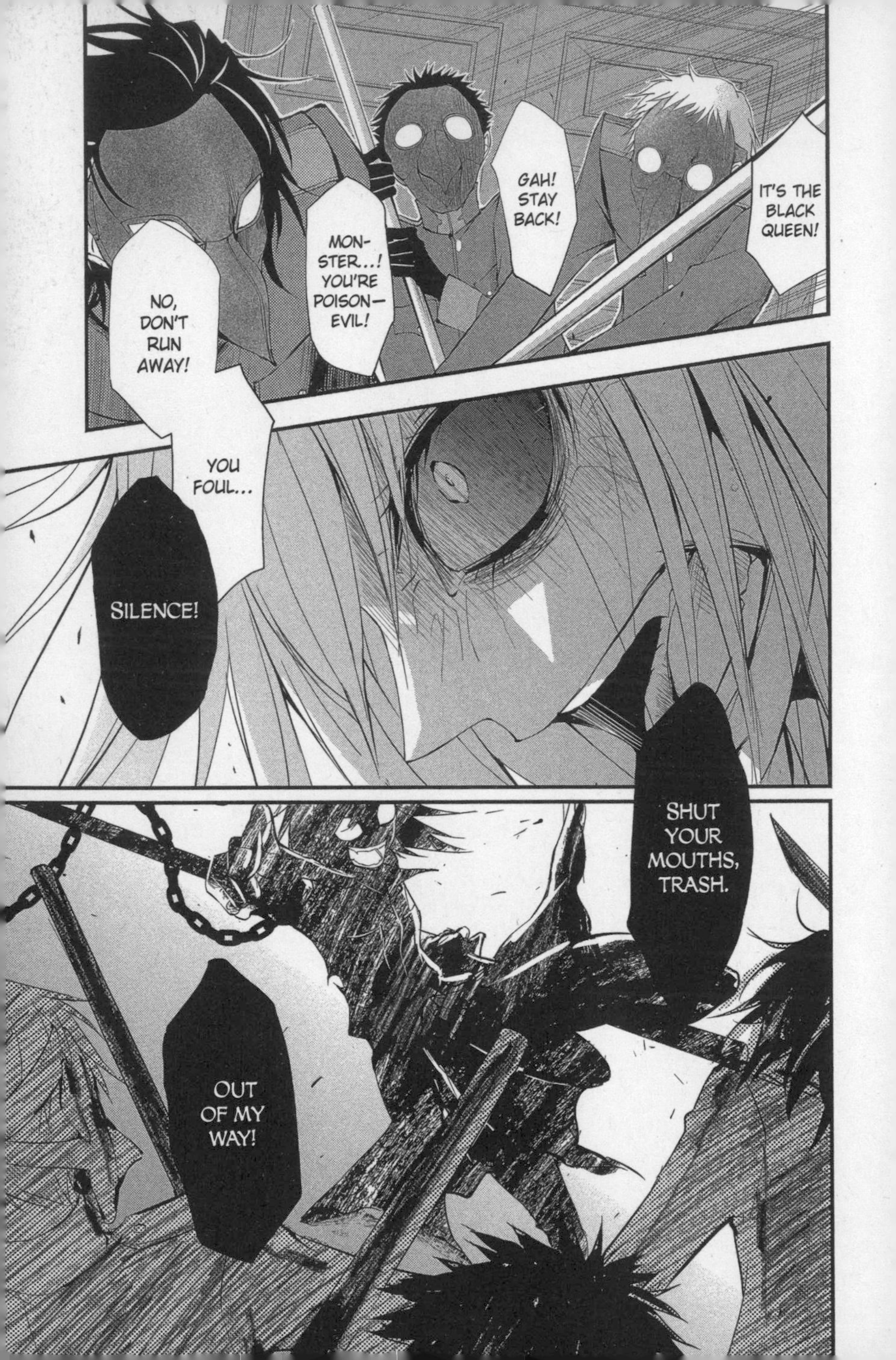
IT'S THE BLACK QUEEN!
GAH! STAY BACK!
MON-STER...! YOU'RE POISON—EVIL!
NO, DON'T RUN AWAY!
YOU FOUL...
SILENCE!
SHUT YOUR MOUTHS, TRASH.
OUT OF MY WAY!

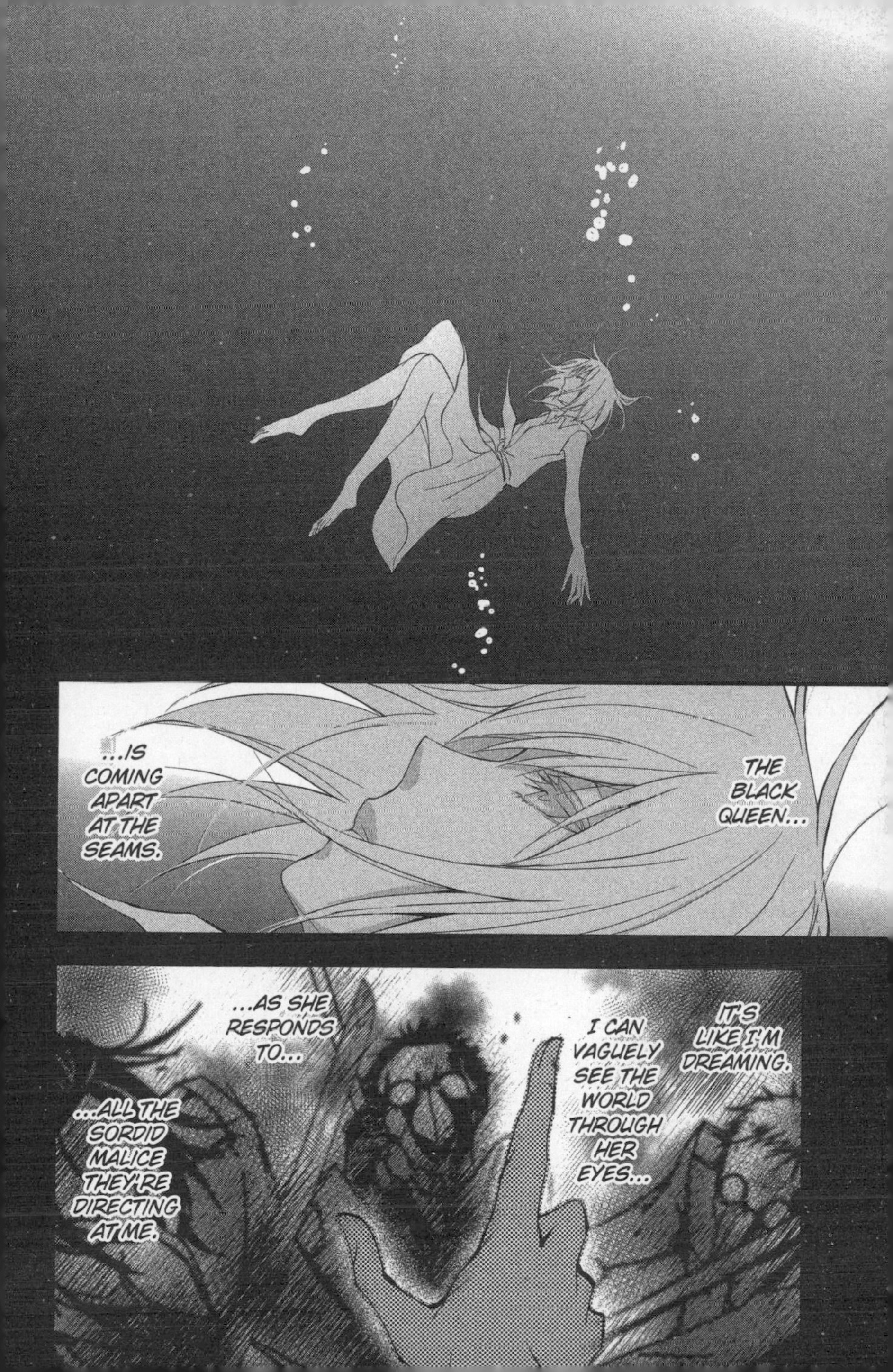
THE BLACK QUEEN...
...IS COMING APART AT THE SEAMS.
IT'S LIKE I'M DREAMING.
I CAN VAGUELY SEE THE WORLD THROUGH HER EYES...
...AS SHE RESPONDS TO...
...ALL THE SORDID MALICE THEY'RE DIRECTING AT ME.

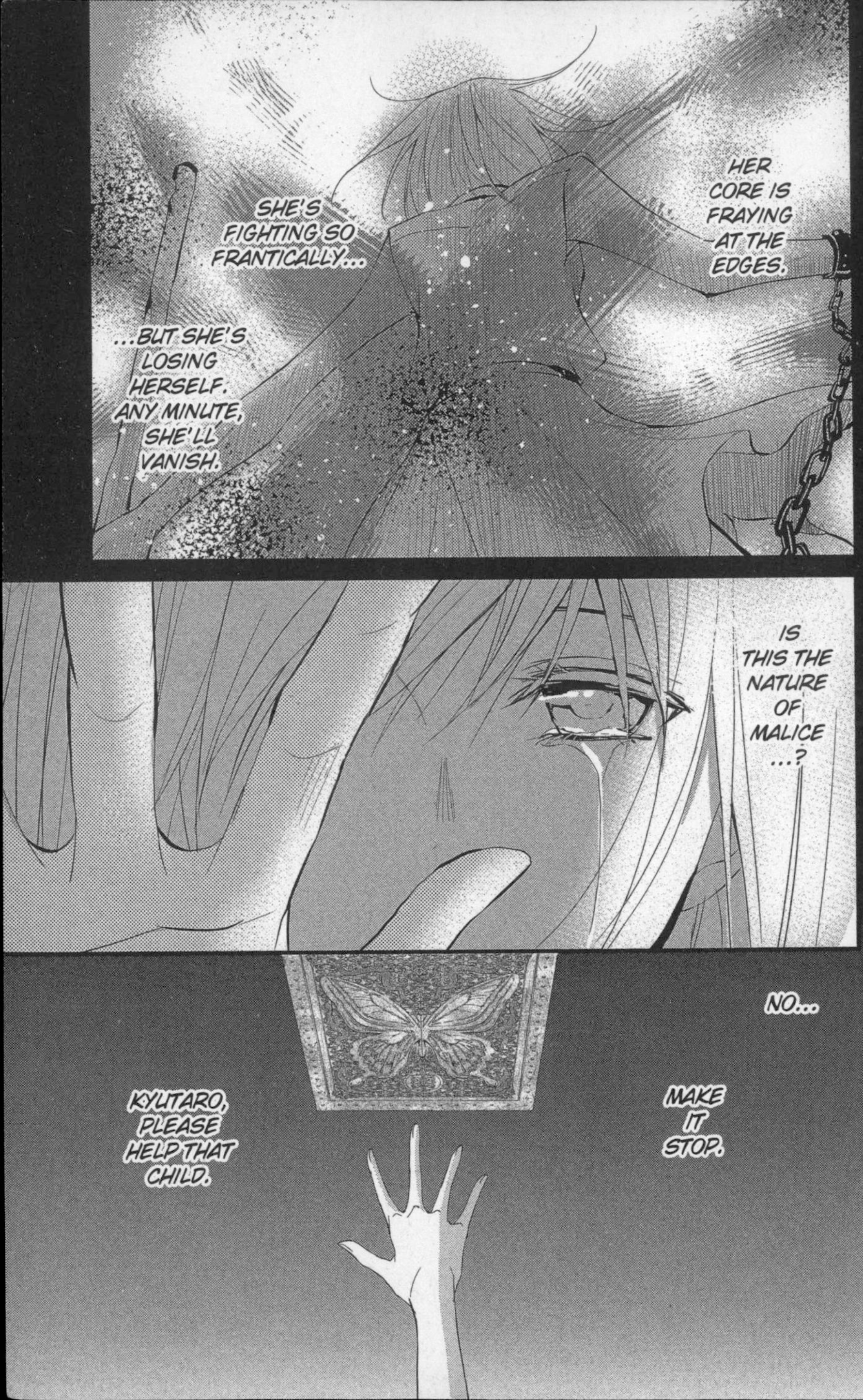
HER CORE IS FRAYING AT THE EDGES.
SHE'S FIGHTING SO FRANTICALLY...
...BUT SHE'S LOSING HERSELF. ANY MINUTE, SHE'LL VANISH.
IS THIS THE NATURE OF MALICE...?
NO...
MAKE IT STOP.
KYUTARO, PLEASE HELP THAT CHILD.

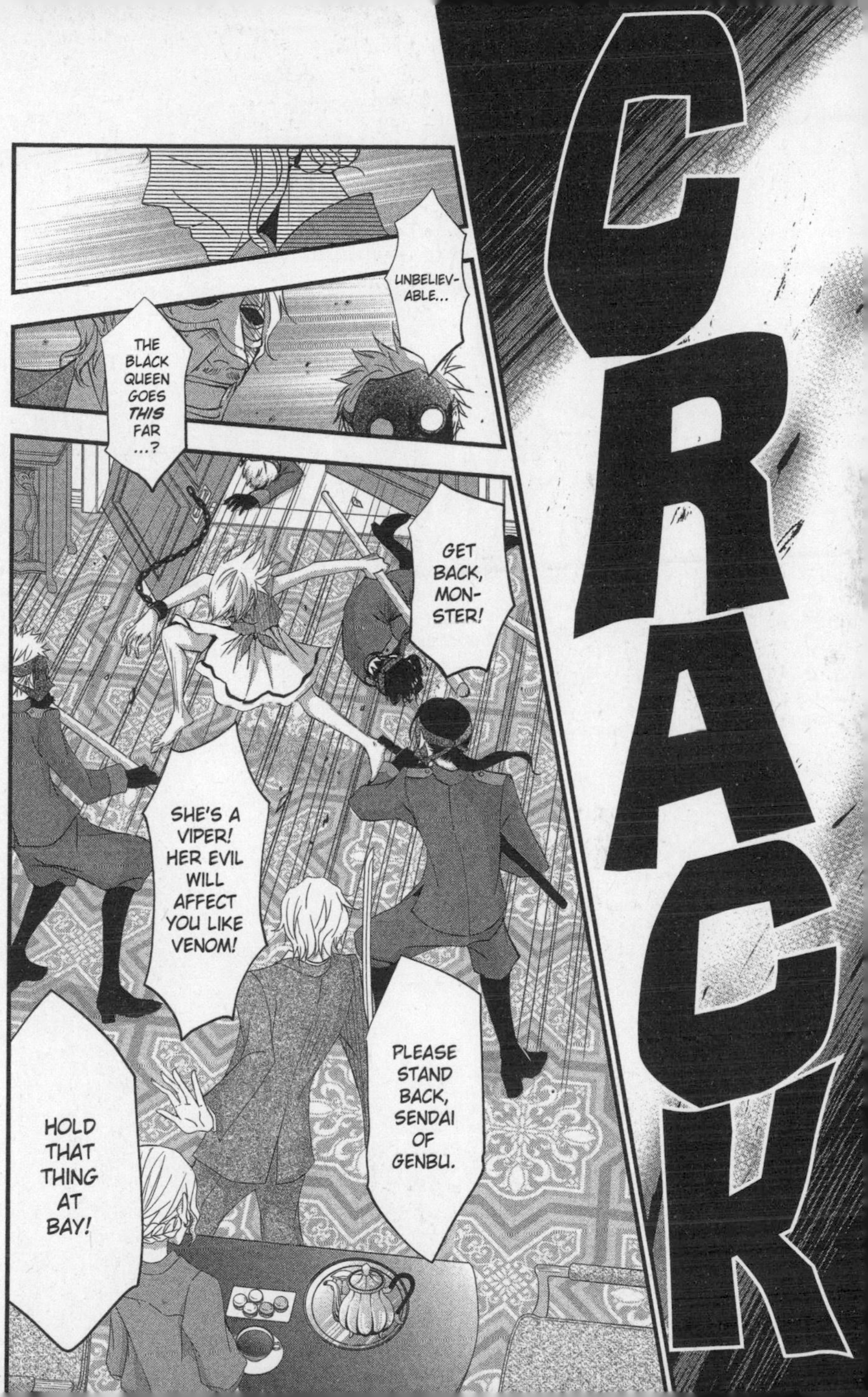
CRACK
UNBELIEVABLE...
THE BLACK QUEEN GOES *THIS* FAR ...?
GET BACK, MONSTER!
SHE'S A VIPER! HER EVIL WILL AFFECT YOU LIKE VENOM!
PLEASE STAND BACK, SENDAI OF GENBU.
HOLD THAT THING AT BAY!

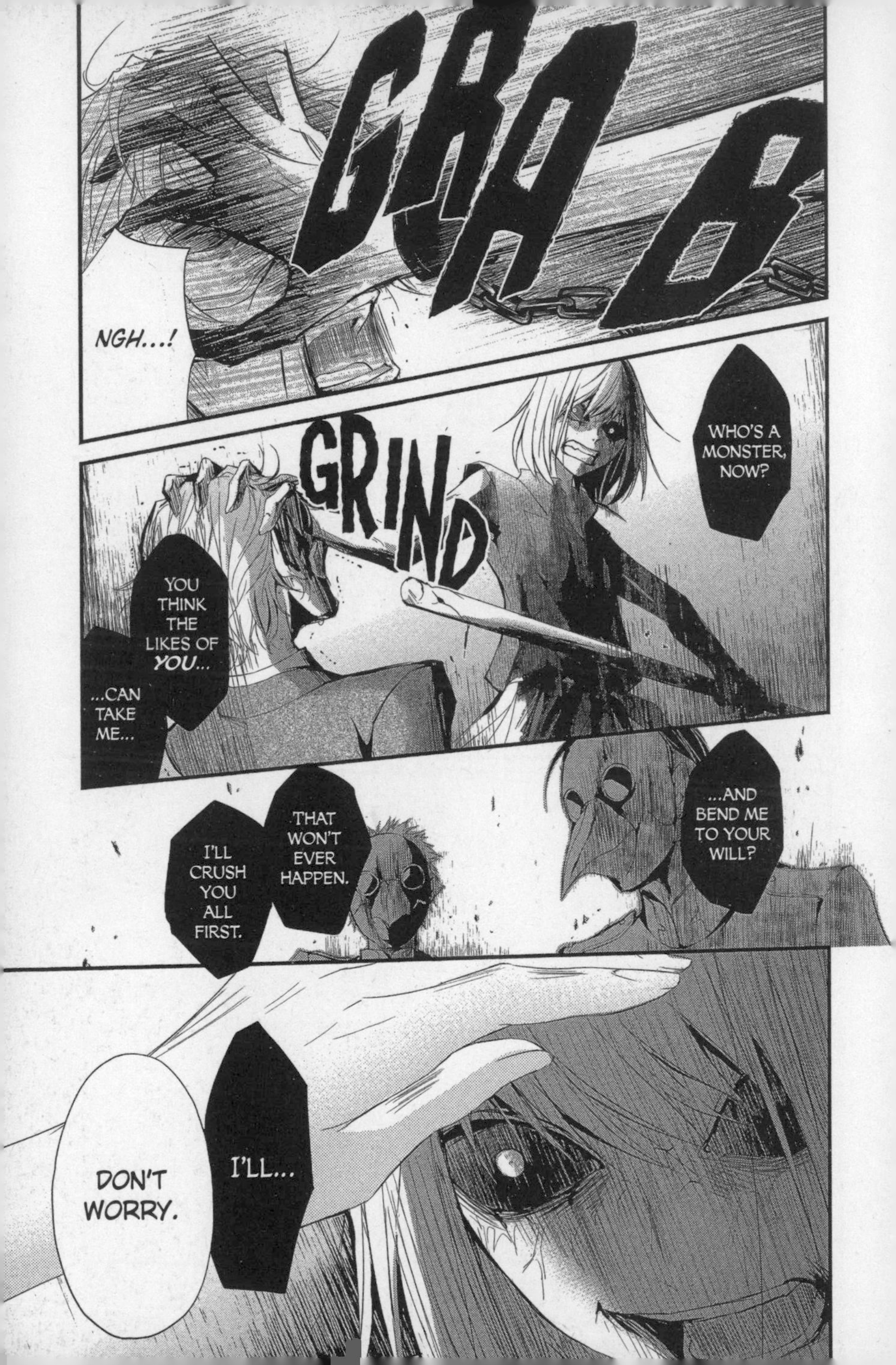
GRAB
NGH...!
WHO'S A MONSTER, NOW?
GRIND
YOU THINK THE LIKES OF *YOU*...
...CAN TAKE ME...
...AND BEND ME TO YOUR WILL?
THAT WON'T EVER HAPPEN.
I'LL CRUSH YOU ALL FIRST.
I'LL...
DON'T WORRY.

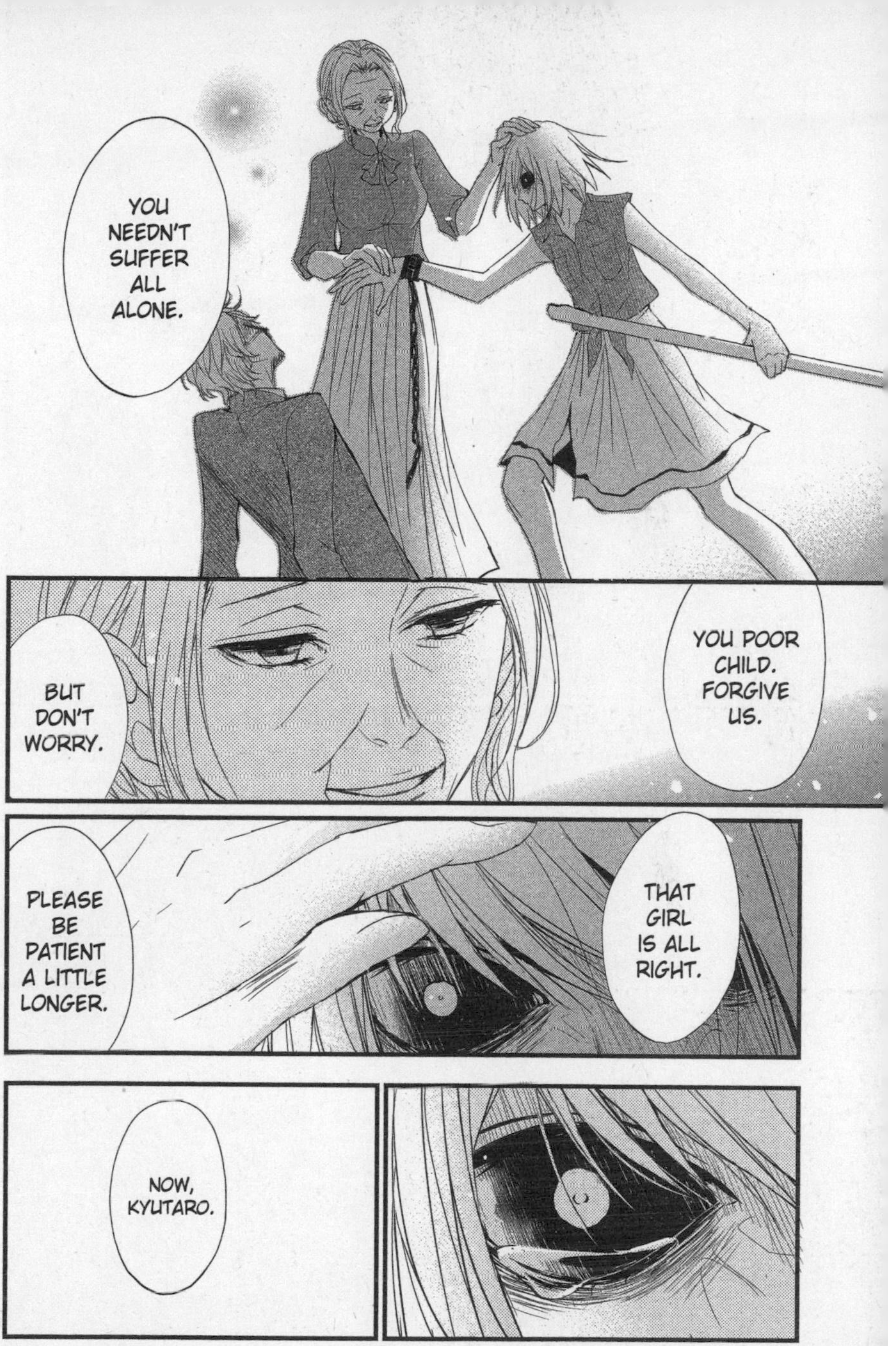
YOU NEEDN'T SUFFER ALL ALONE.
YOU POOR CHILD. FORGIVE US.
BUT DON'T WORRY.
THAT GIRL IS ALL RIGHT.
PLEASE BE PATIENT A LITTLE LONGER.
NOW, KYUTARO.

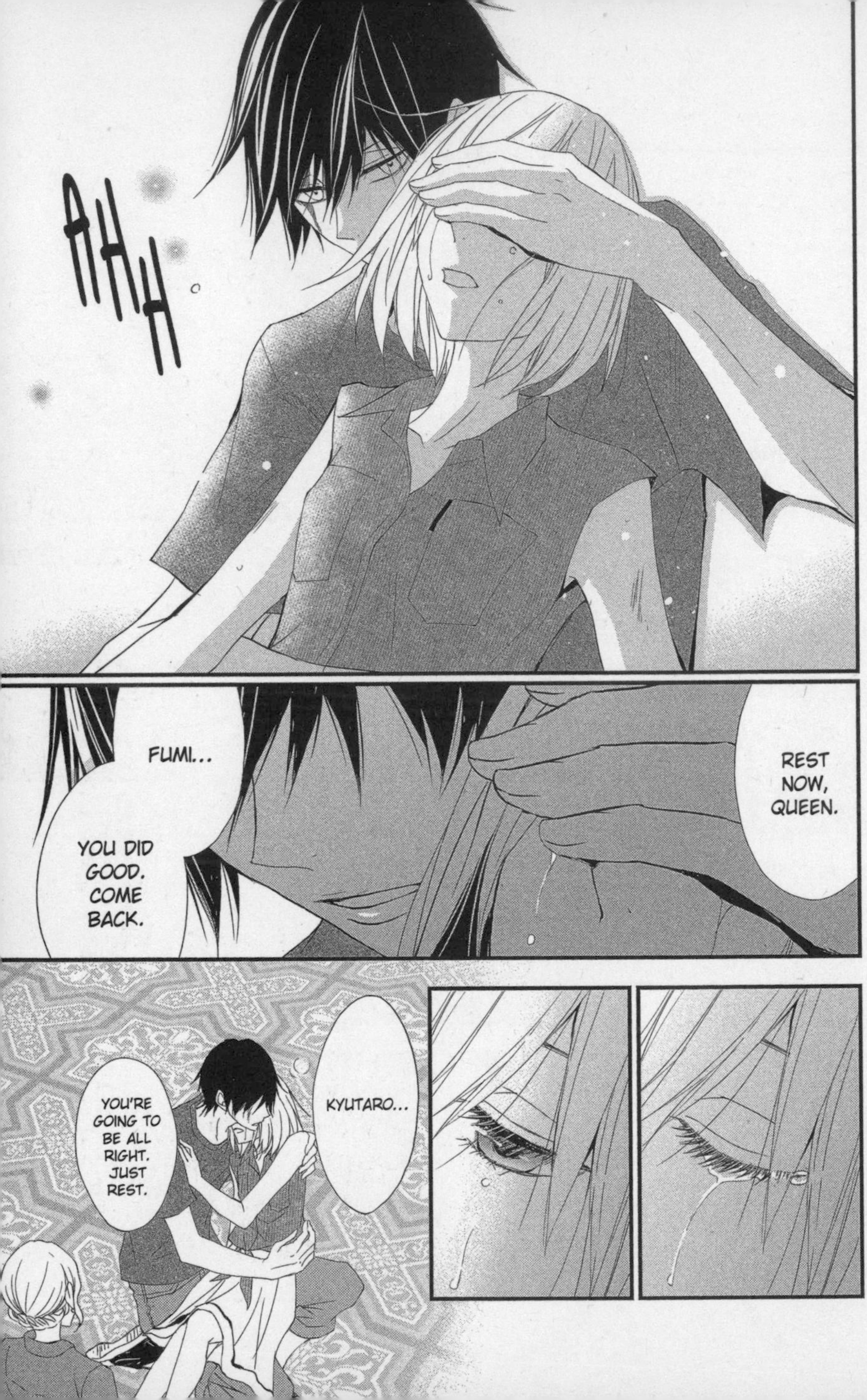
AHHH
REST NOW, QUEEN.
FUMI...
YOU DID GOOD. COME BACK.
KYUTARO...
YOU'RE GOING TO BE ALL RIGHT. JUST REST.

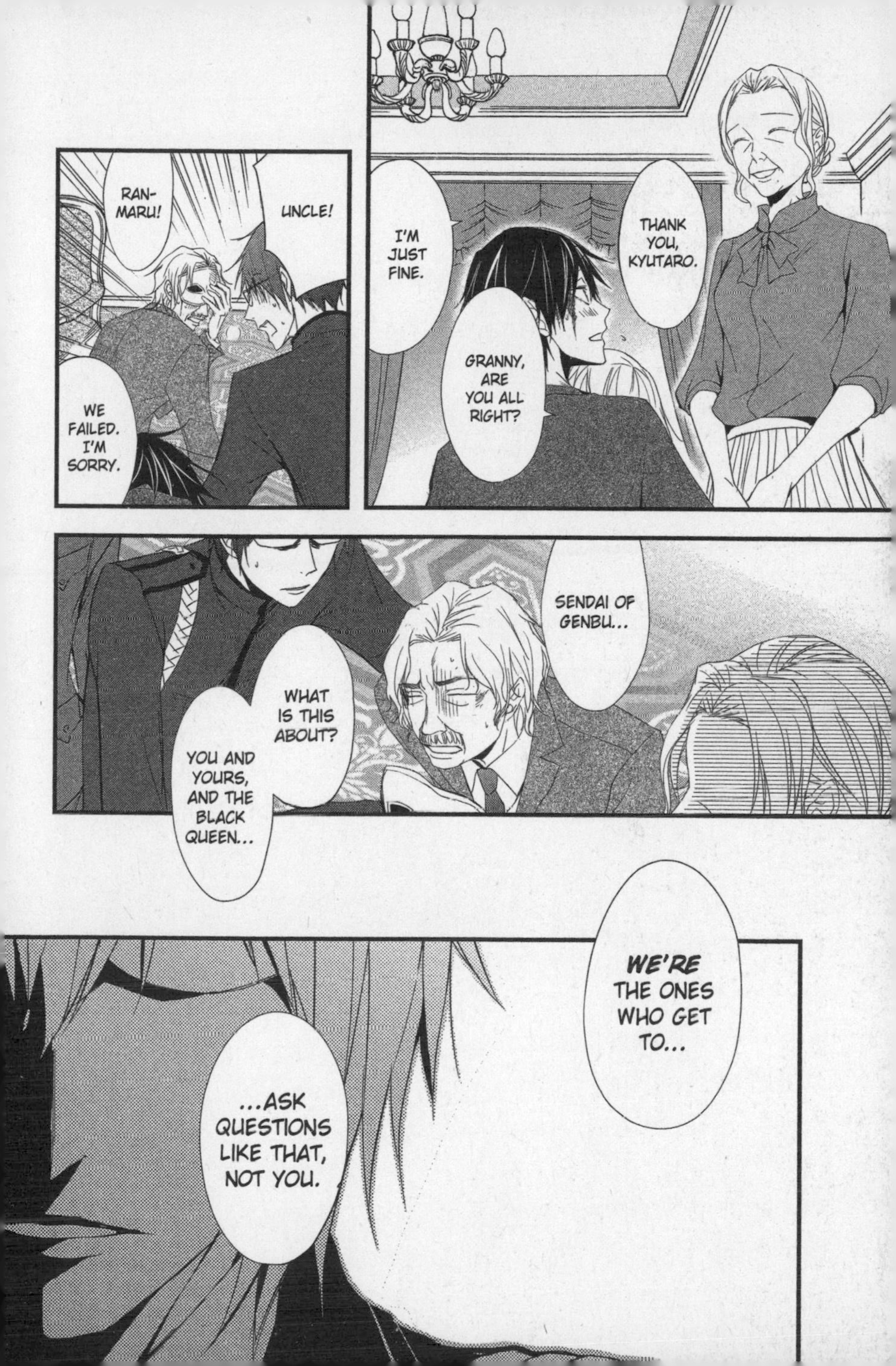
THANK YOU, KYUTARO.
I'M JUST FINE.
GRANNY, ARE YOU ALL RIGHT?
UNCLE!
RAN-MARU!
WE FAILED. I'M SORRY.
SENDAI OF GENBU...
WHAT IS THIS ABOUT?
YOU AND YOURS, AND THE BLACK QUEEN...
WE'RE THE ONES WHO GET TO...
...ASK QUESTIONS LIKE THAT, NOT YOU.

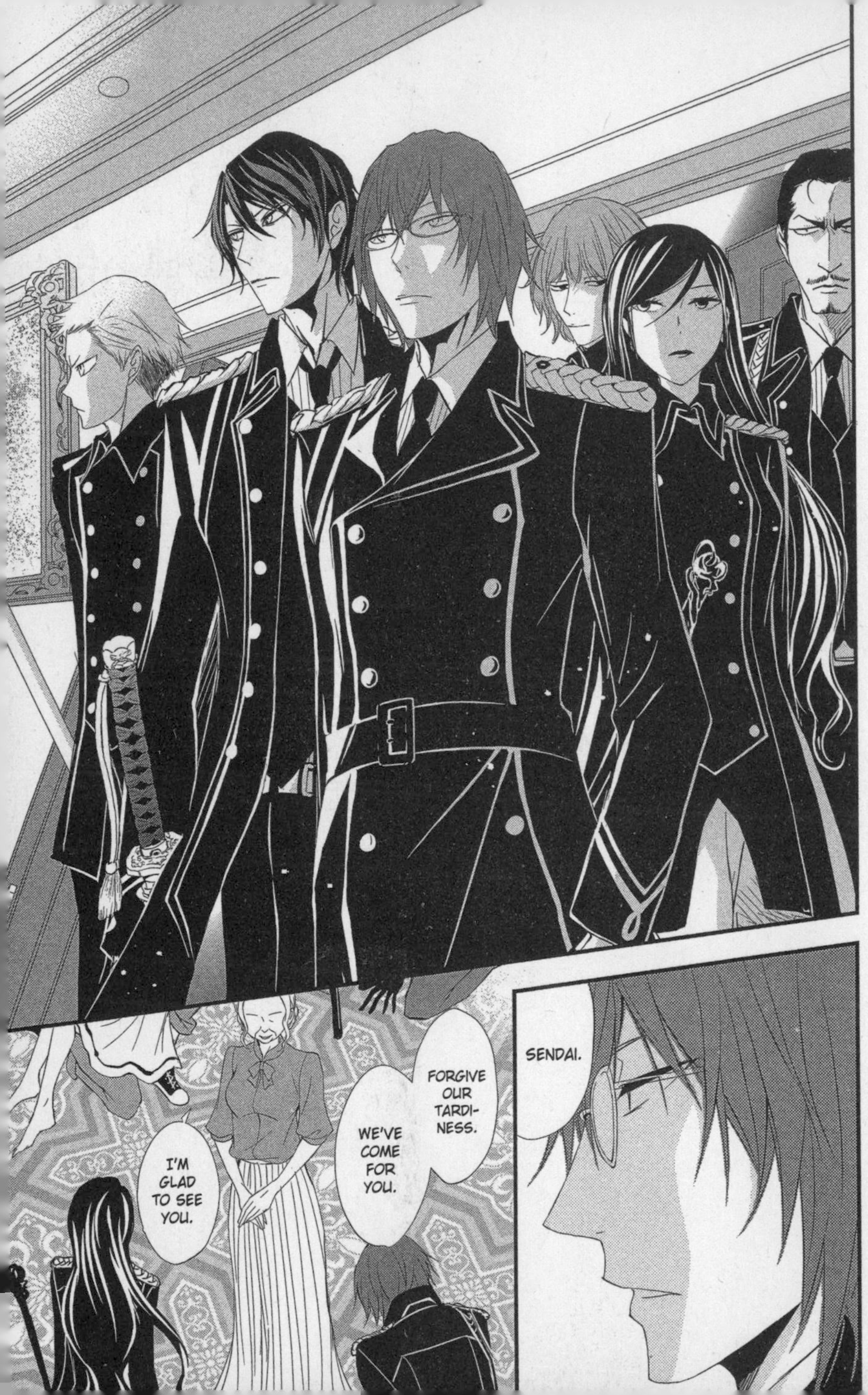
SENDAI.
FORGIVE OUR TARDI-NESS.
WE'VE COME FOR YOU.
I'M GLAD TO SEE YOU.

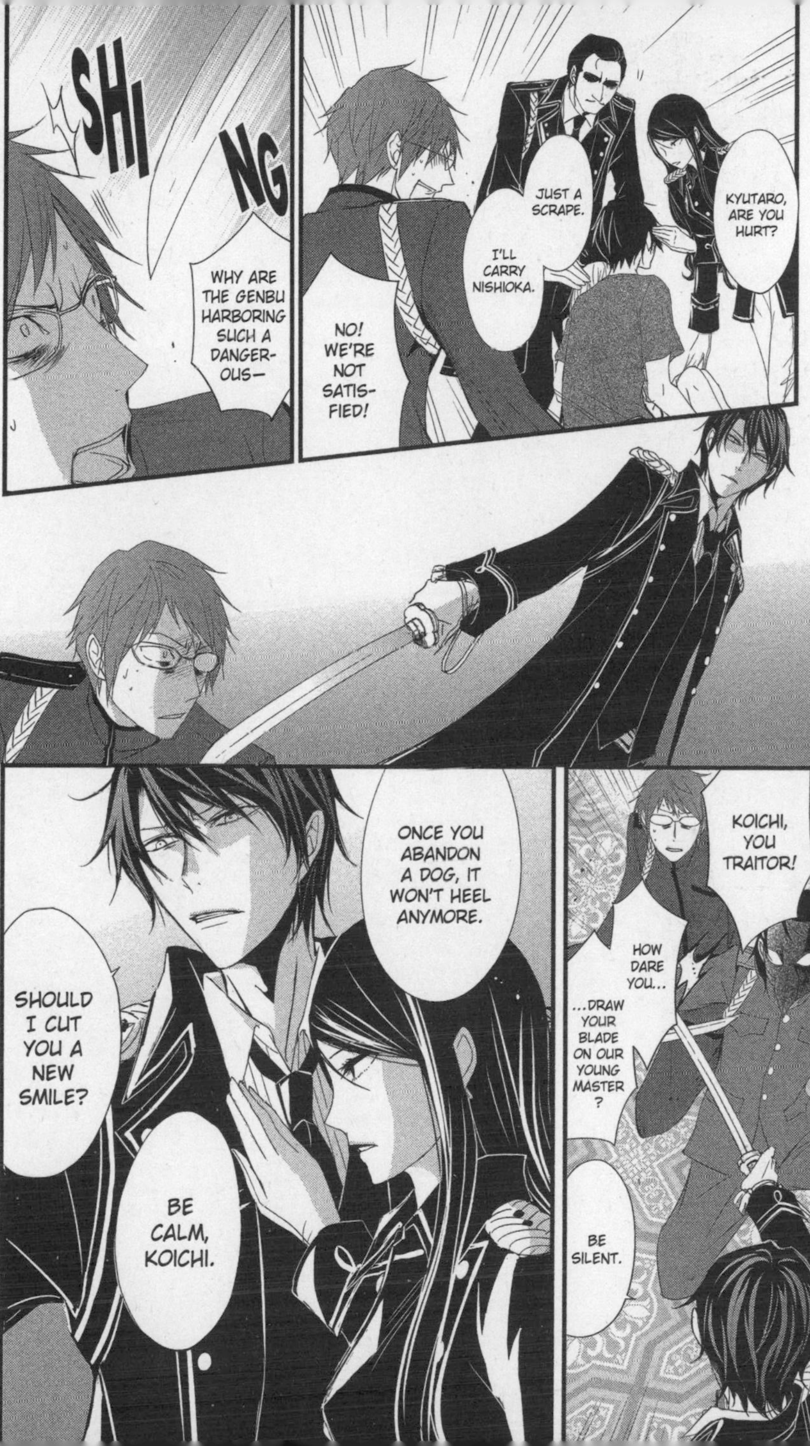
KYUTARO, ARE YOU HURT?
JUST A SCRAPE.
I'LL CARRY NISHIOKA.
NO! WE'RE NOT SATISFIED!
SHING
WHY ARE THE GENBU HARBORING SUCH A DANGEROUS—
KOICHI, YOU TRAITOR!
HOW DARE YOU...
...DRAW YOUR BLADE ON OUR YOUNG MASTER?
BE SILENT.
ONCE YOU ABANDON A DOG, IT WON'T HEEL ANYMORE.
SHOULD I CUT YOU A NEW SMILE?
BE CALM, KOICHI.

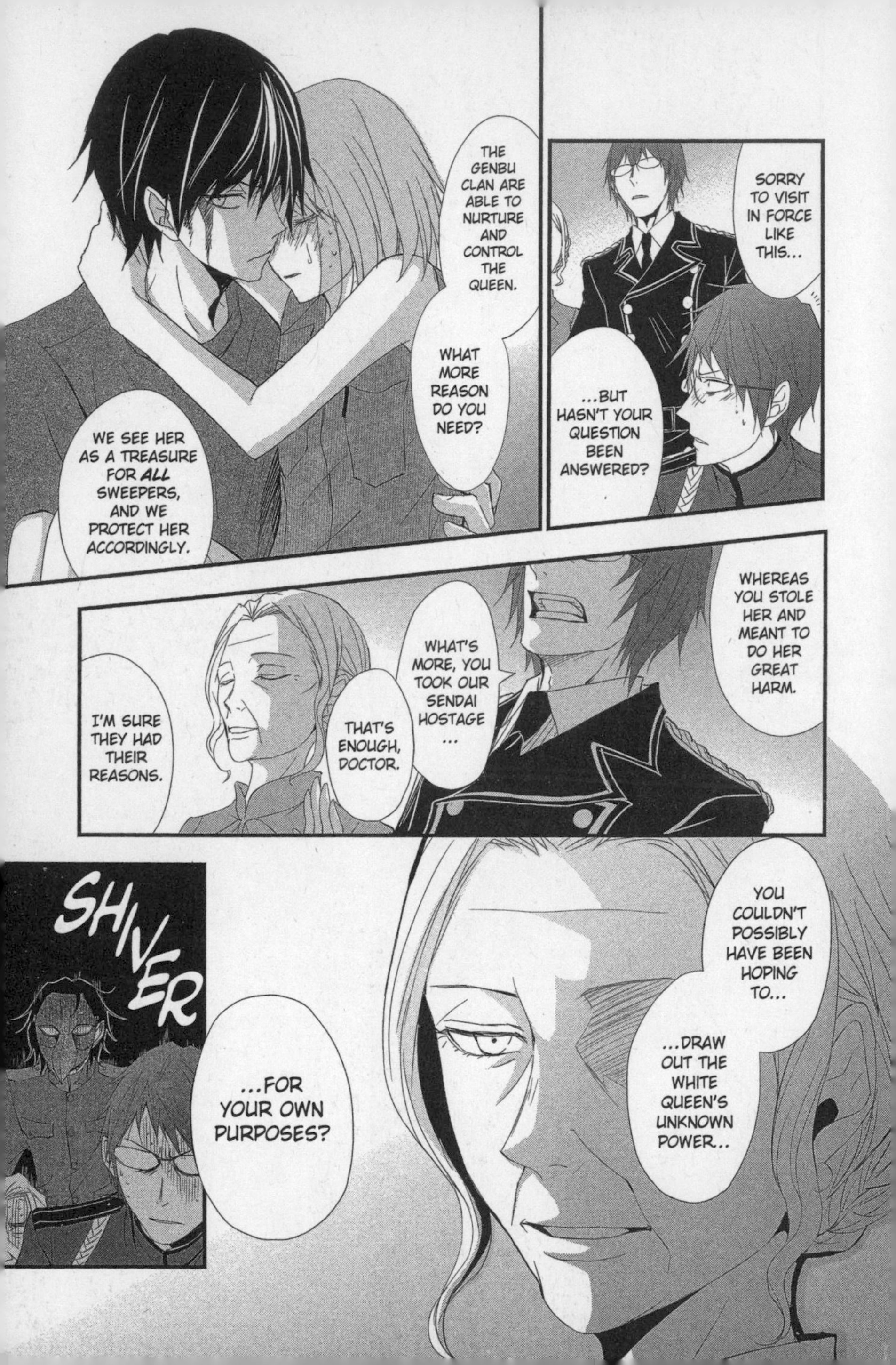
SORRY TO VISIT IN FORCE LIKE THIS...
...BUT HASN'T YOUR QUESTION BEEN ANSWERED?
THE GENBU CLAN ARE ABLE TO NURTURE AND CONTROL THE QUEEN.
WHAT MORE REASON DO YOU NEED?
WE SEE HER AS A TREASURE FOR *ALL* SWEEPERS, AND WE PROTECT HER ACCORDINGLY.
WHEREAS YOU STOLE HER AND MEANT TO DO HER GREAT HARM.
WHAT'S MORE, YOU TOOK OUR SENDAI HOSTAGE...
THAT'S ENOUGH, DOCTOR.
I'M SURE THEY HAD THEIR REASONS.
YOU COULDN'T POSSIBLY HAVE BEEN HOPING TO...
...DRAW OUT THE WHITE QUEEN'S UNKNOWN POWER...
...FOR YOUR OWN PURPOSES?
SHIVER

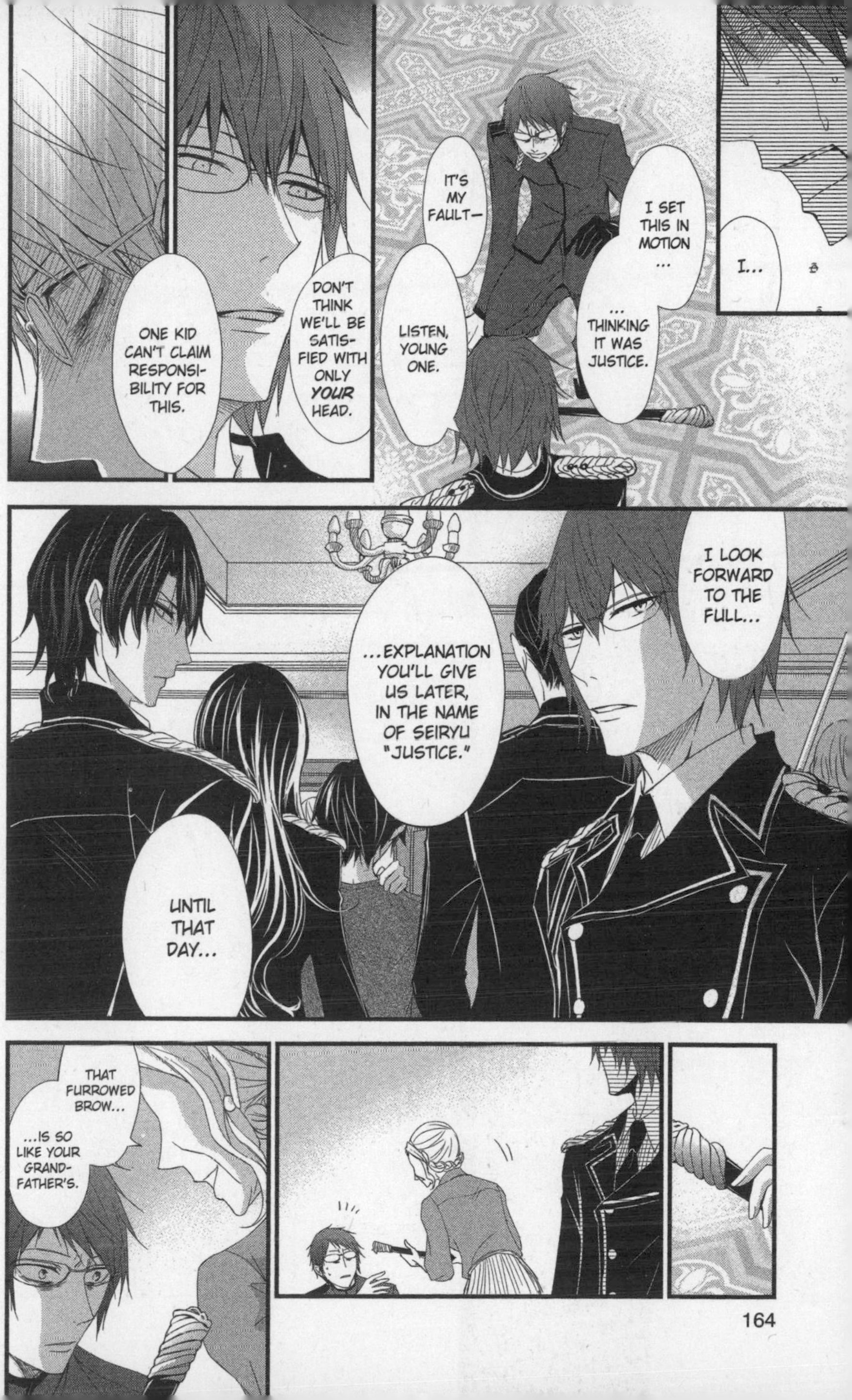
I...
I SET THIS IN MOTION ...
... THINKING IT WAS JUSTICE.
IT'S MY FAULT—
LISTEN, YOUNG ONE.
DON'T THINK WE'LL BE SATIS-FIED WITH ONLY *YOUR* HEAD.
ONE KID CAN'T CLAIM RESPONSI-BILITY FOR THIS.
I LOOK FORWARD TO THE FULL...
...EXPLANATION YOU'LL GIVE US LATER, IN THE NAME OF SEIRYU "JUSTICE."
UNTIL THAT DAY...
THAT FURROWED BROW...
...IS SO LIKE YOUR GRAND-FATHER'S.

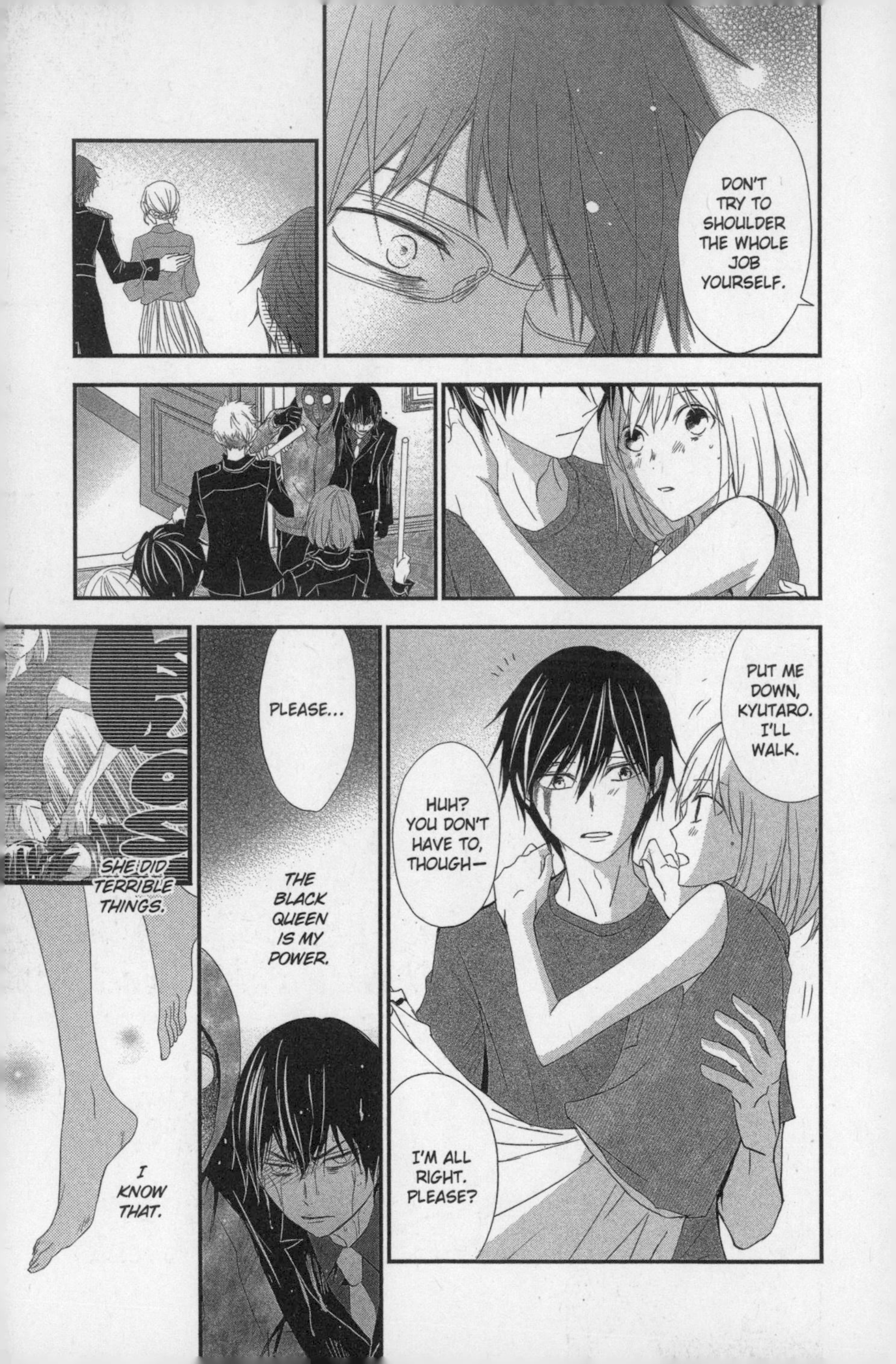
DON'T TRY TO SHOULDER THE WHOLE JOB YOURSELF.
PUT ME DOWN, KYUTARO. I'LL WALK.
HUH? YOU DON'T HAVE TO, THOUGH—
I'M ALL RIGHT. PLEASE?
PLEASE...
THE BLACK QUEEN IS MY POWER.
SHE DID TERRIBLE THINGS.
I KNOW THAT.

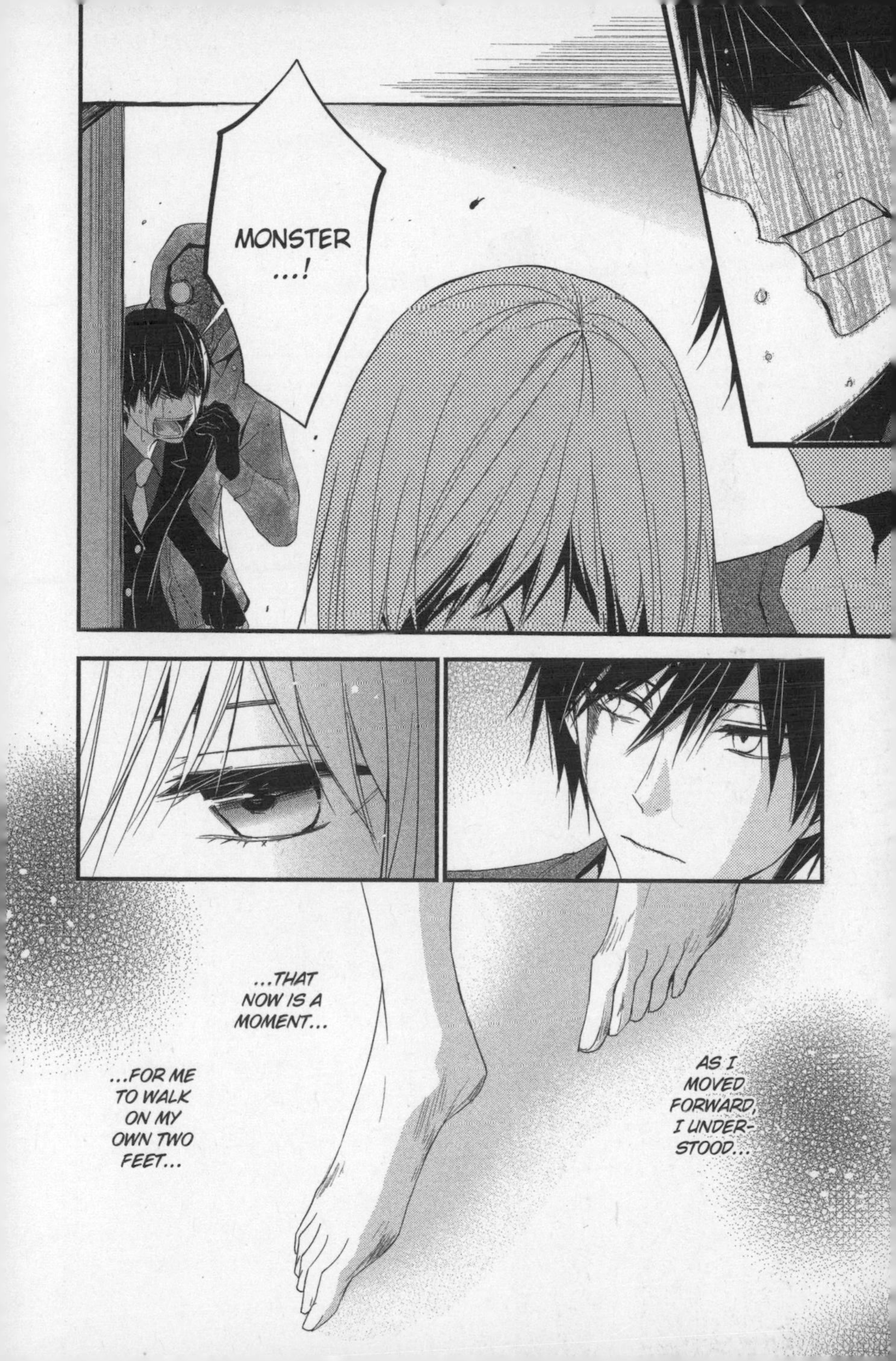
MONSTER ...!
AS I MOVED FORWARD, I UNDER-STOOD...
...THAT NOW IS A MOMENT...
...FOR ME TO WALK ON MY OWN TWO FEET...

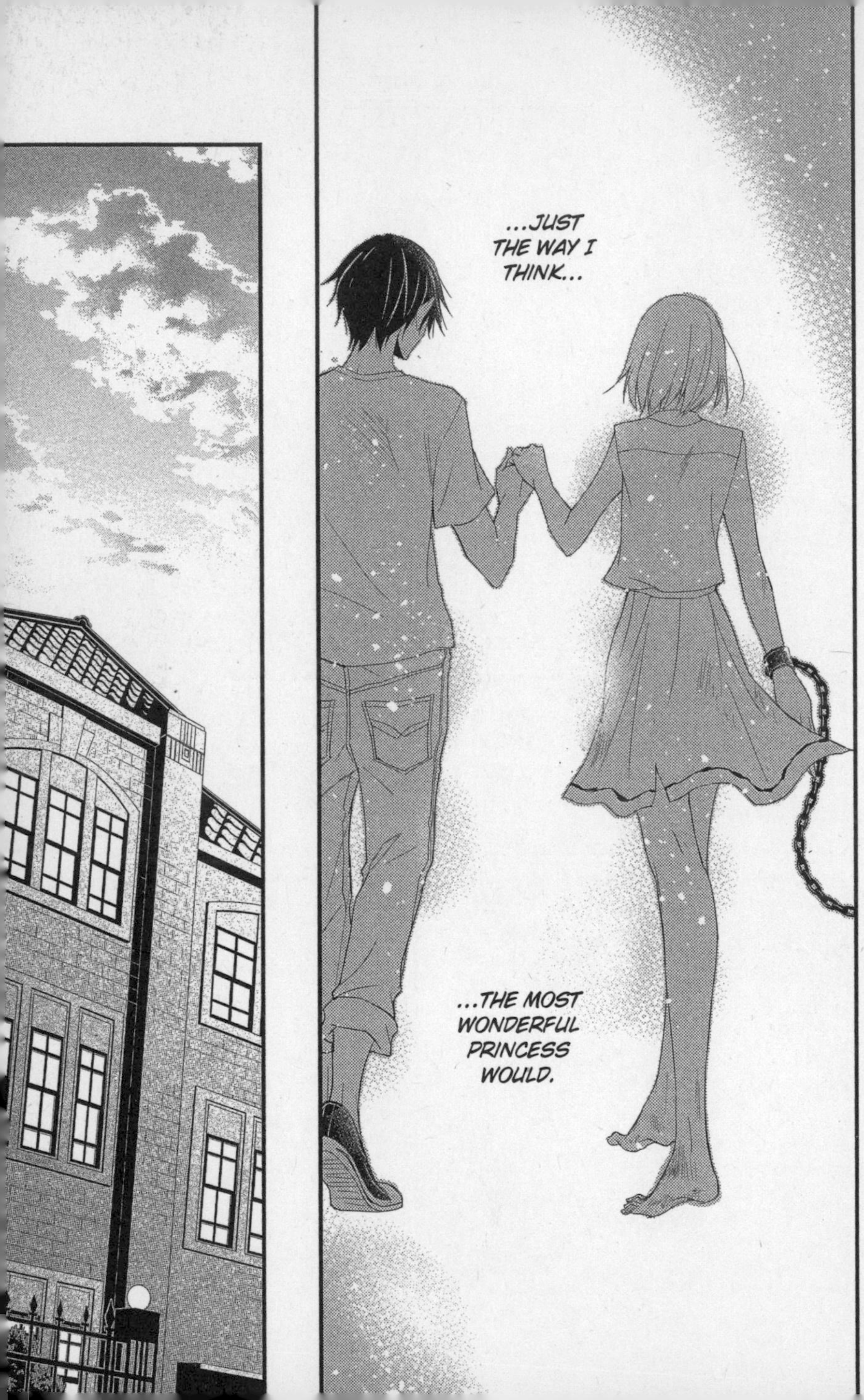
...JUST THE WAY I THINK...
...THE MOST WONDERFUL PRINCESS WOULD.

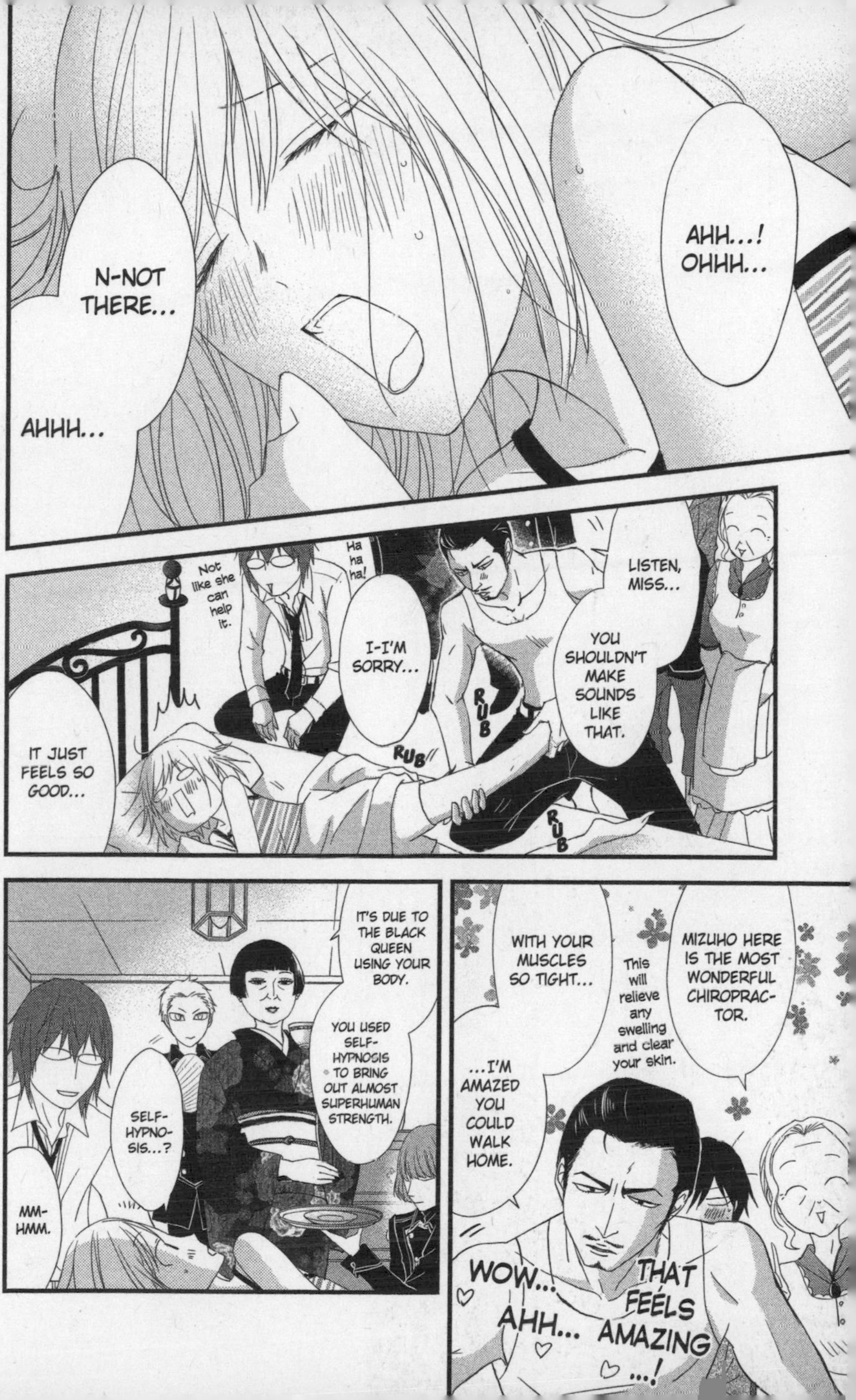
AHH...! OHHH...
N-NOT THERE...
AHHH...
LISTEN, MISS...
YOU SHOULDN'T MAKE SOUNDS LIKE THAT.
RUB
RUB
I-I'M SORRY...
Ha ha ha!
Not like she can help it.
IT JUST FEELS SO GOOD...
RUB
MIZUHO HERE IS THE MOST WONDERFUL CHIROPRAC-TOR.
This will relieve any swelling and clear your skin.
WITH YOUR MUSCLES SO TIGHT...
...I'M AMAZED YOU COULD WALK HOME.
THAT FEELS AMAZING ...!
WOW... AHH...
IT'S DUE TO THE BLACK QUEEN USING YOUR BODY.
YOU USED SELF-HYPNOSIS TO BRING OUT ALMOST SUPERHUMAN STRENGTH.
SELF-HYPNO-SIS...?
MM-HMM.

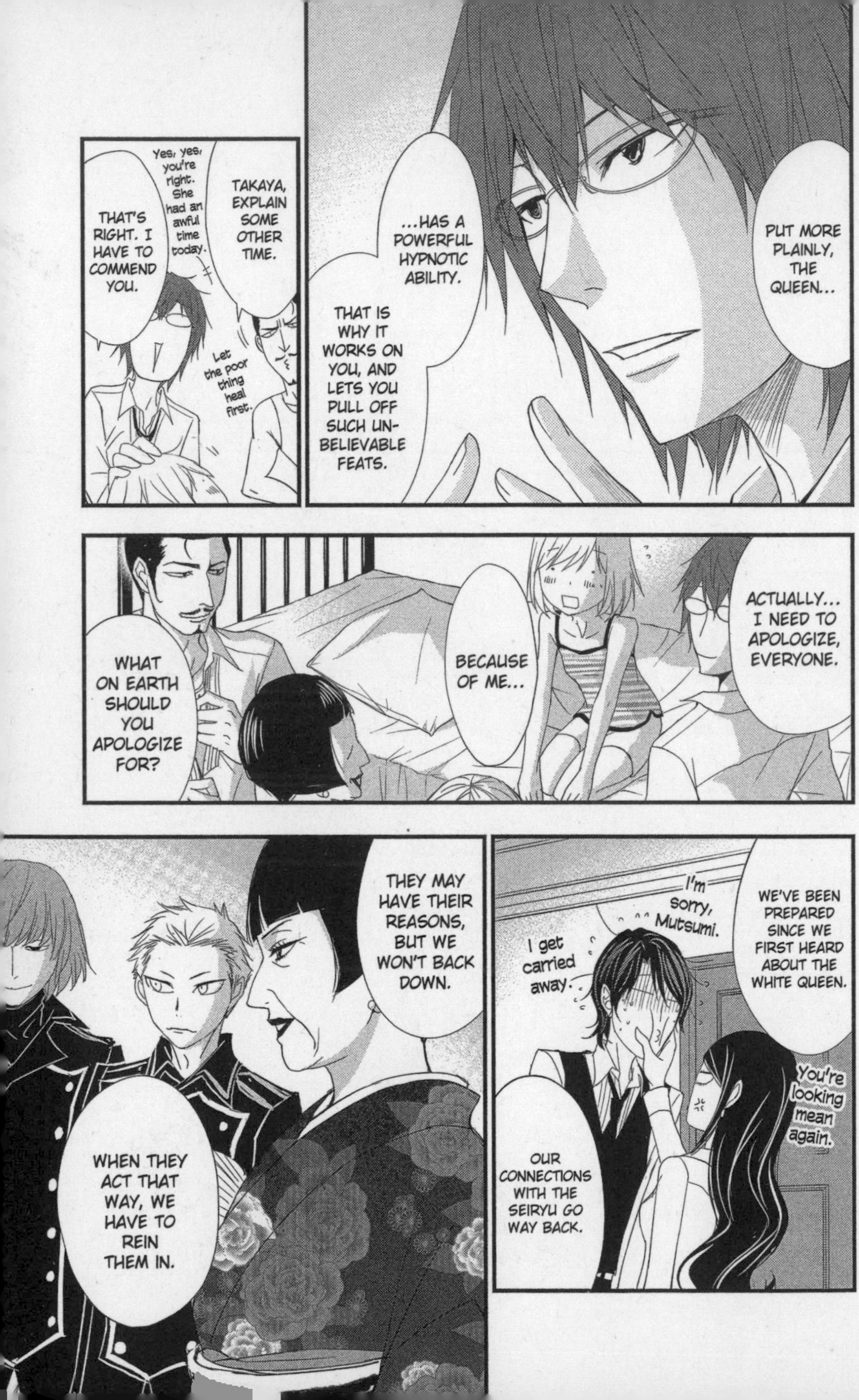
PUT MORE PLAINLY, THE QUEEN...
...HAS A POWERFUL HYPNOTIC ABILITY.
THAT IS WHY IT WORKS ON YOU, AND LETS YOU PULL OFF SUCH UN-BELIEVABLE FEATS.
TAKAYA, EXPLAIN SOME OTHER TIME.
Let the poor thing heal first.
Yes, yes, you're right. She had an awful time today.
THAT'S RIGHT. I HAVE TO COMMEND YOU.
ACTUALLY... I NEED TO APOLOGIZE, EVERYONE.
BECAUSE OF ME...
WHAT ON EARTH SHOULD YOU APOLOGIZE FOR?
WE'VE BEEN PREPARED SINCE WE FIRST HEARD ABOUT THE WHITE QUEEN.
You're looking mean again.
I'm sorry, Mutsumi.
I get carried away.
OUR CONNECTIONS WITH THE SEIRYU GO WAY BACK.
THEY MAY HAVE THEIR REASONS, BUT WE WON'T BACK DOWN.
WHEN THEY ACT THAT WAY, WE HAVE TO REIN THEM IN.

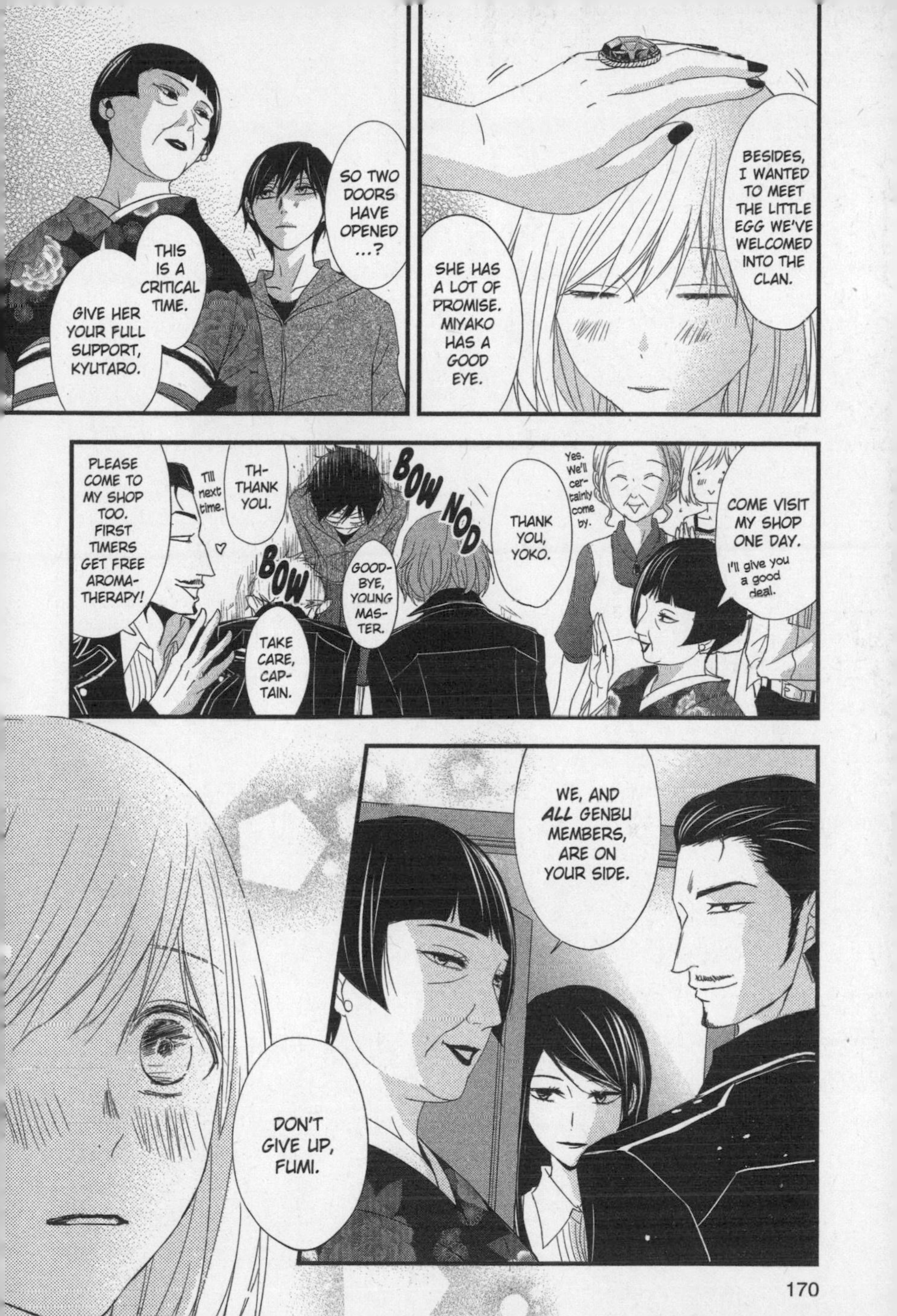

BESIDES, I WANTED TO MEET THE LITTLE EGG WE'VE WELCOMED INTO THE CLAN.
SHE HAS A LOT OF PROMISE. MIYAKO HAS A GOOD EYE.
SO TWO DOORS HAVE OPENED ...?
THIS IS A CRITICAL TIME.
GIVE HER YOUR FULL SUPPORT, KYUTARO.
COME VISIT MY SHOP ONE DAY.
I'll give you a good deal.
Yes. We'll certainly come by.
THANK YOU, YOKO.
BOW NOD
GOOD-BYE, YOUNG MASTER.
TAKE CARE, CAPTAIN.
BOW
TH-THANK YOU.
Till next time.
PLEASE COME TO MY SHOP TOO. FIRST TIMERS GET FREE AROMA-THERAPY!
WE, AND *ALL* GENBU MEMBERS, ARE ON YOUR SIDE.
DON'T GIVE UP, FUMI.

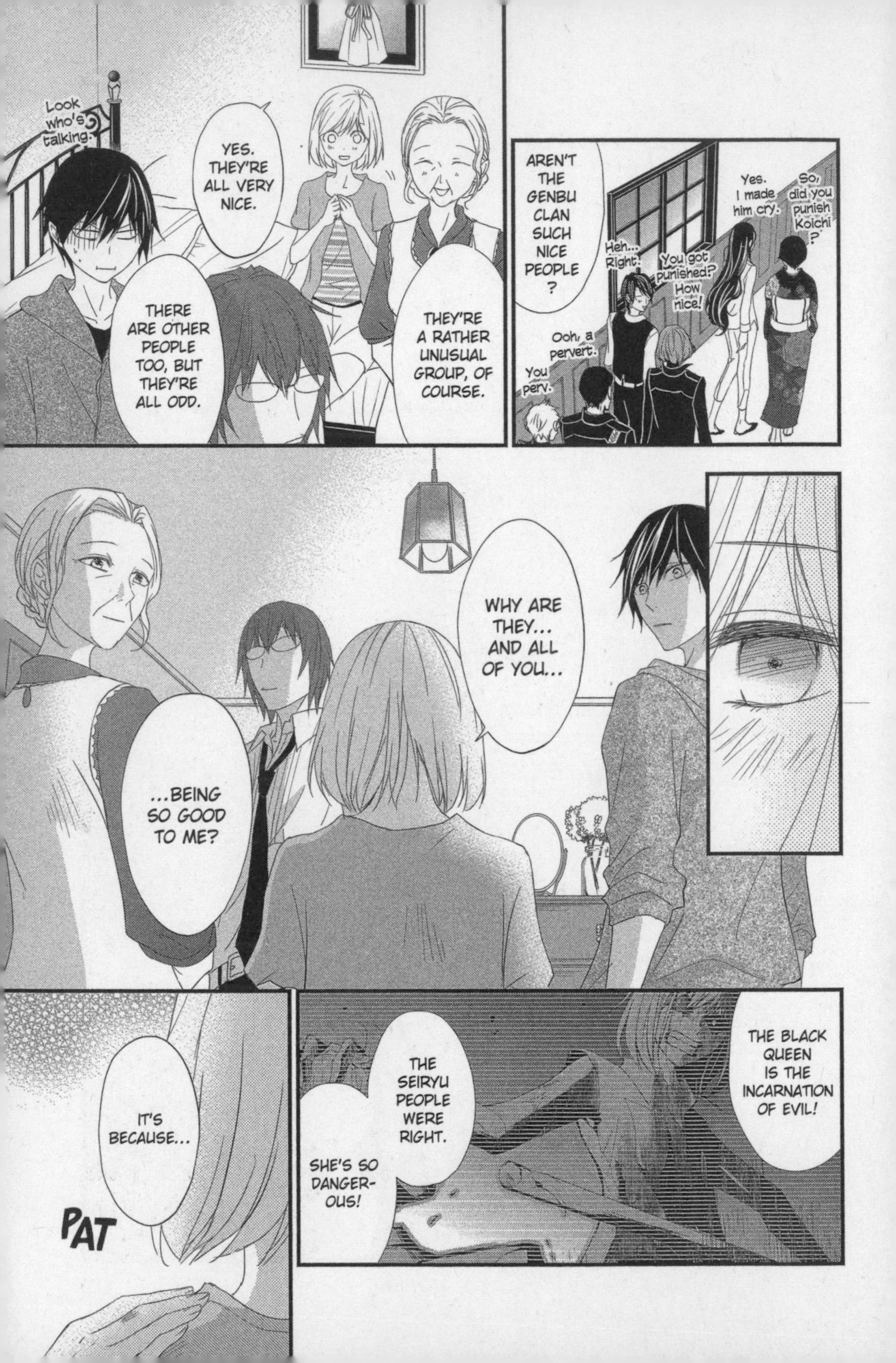
So, did you punish Koichi?
Yes. I made him cry.
You got punished? How nice!
Heh... Right.
AREN'T THE GENBU CLAN SUCH NICE PEOPLE?
Ooh, a pervert.
You perv.
YES. THEY'RE ALL VERY NICE.
Look who's talking.
THEY'RE A RATHER UNUSUAL GROUP, OF COURSE.
THERE ARE OTHER PEOPLE TOO, BUT THEY'RE ALL ODD.
WHY ARE THEY... AND ALL OF YOU...
...BEING SO GOOD TO ME?
THE BLACK QUEEN IS THE INCARNATION OF EVIL!
THE SEIRYU PEOPLE WERE RIGHT.
SHE'S SO DANGER-OUS!
IT'S BECAUSE...
PAT

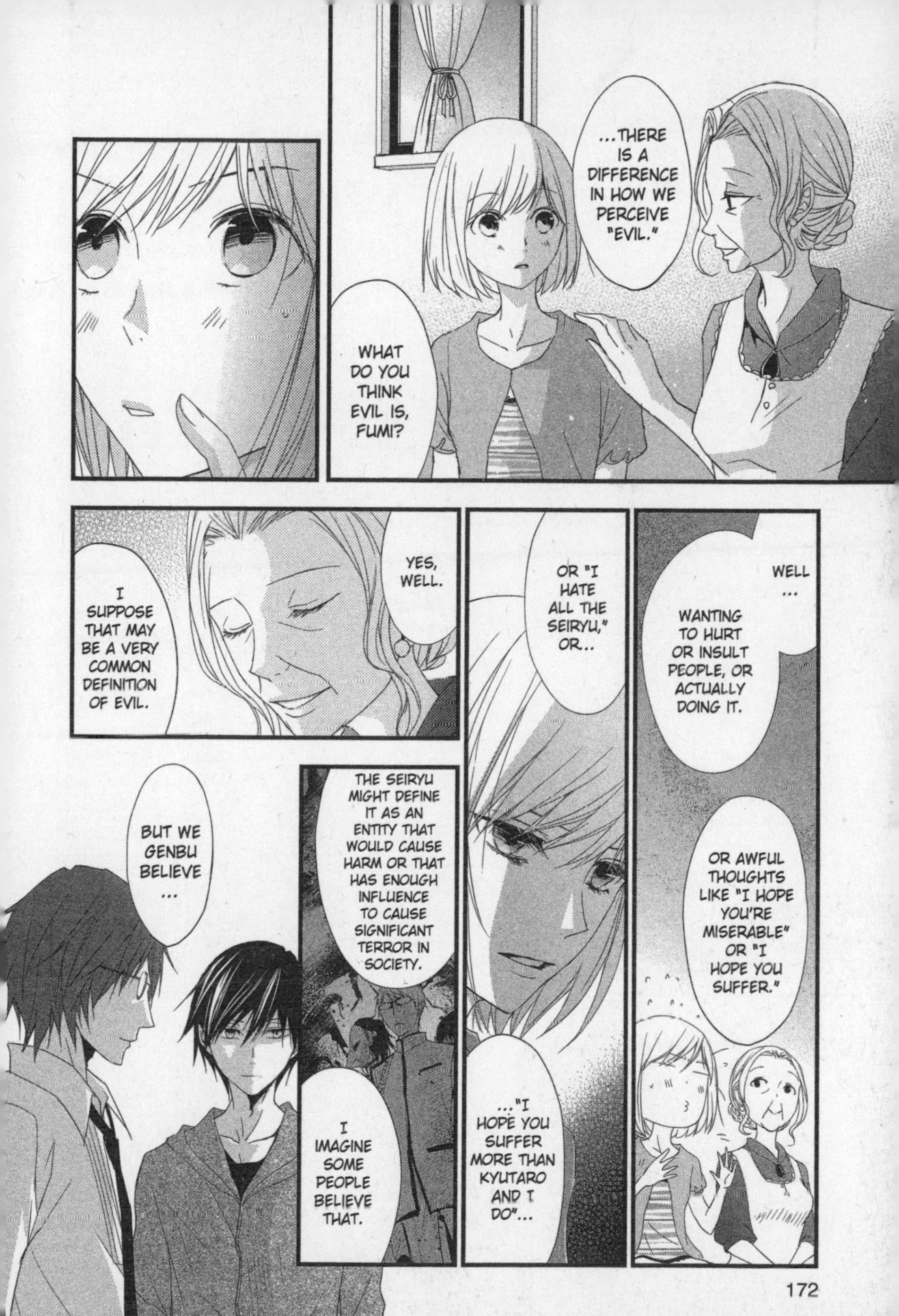
...THERE IS A DIFFERENCE IN HOW WE PERCEIVE "EVIL."
WHAT DO YOU THINK EVIL IS, FUMI?
WELL ...
WANTING TO HURT OR INSULT PEOPLE, OR ACTUALLY DOING IT.
OR AWFUL THOUGHTS LIKE "I HOPE YOU'RE MISERABLE" OR "I HOPE YOU SUFFER."
OR "I HATE ALL THE SEIRYU," OR..
..."I HOPE YOU SUFFER MORE THAN KYUTARO AND I DO"...
YES, WELL.
I SUPPOSE THAT MAY BE A VERY COMMON DEFINITION OF EVIL.
THE SEIRYU MIGHT DEFINE IT AS AN ENTITY THAT WOULD CAUSE HARM OR THAT HAS ENOUGH INFLUENCE TO CAUSE SIGNIFICANT TERROR IN SOCIETY.
I IMAGINE SOME PEOPLE BELIEVE THAT.
BUT WE GENBU BELIEVE ...

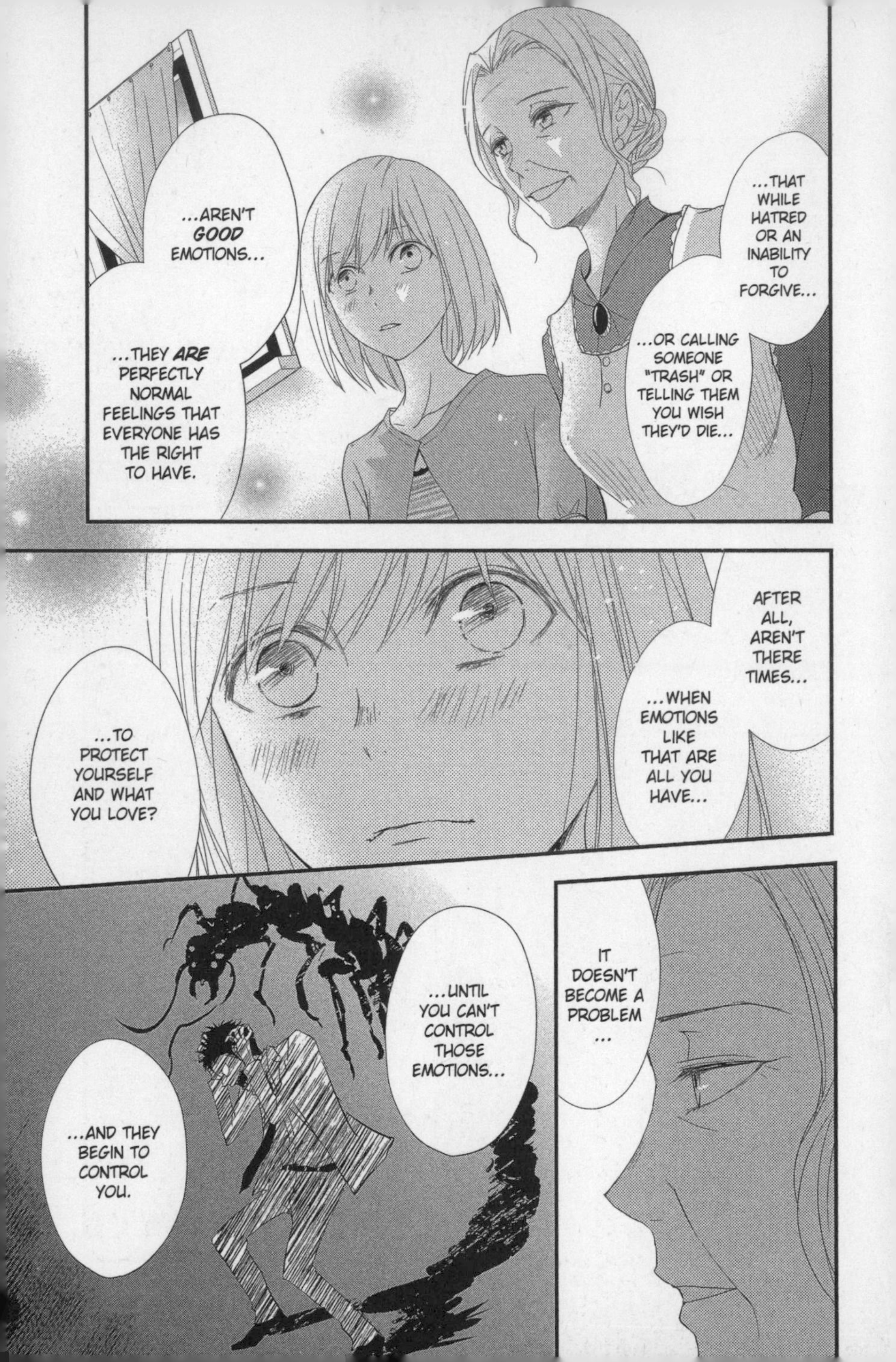
...THAT WHILE HATRED OR AN INABILITY TO FORGIVE...
...OR CALLING SOMEONE "TRASH" OR TELLING THEM YOU WISH THEY'D DIE...
...AREN'T *GOOD* EMOTIONS...
...THEY *ARE* PERFECTLY NORMAL FEELINGS THAT EVERYONE HAS THE RIGHT TO HAVE.
AFTER ALL, AREN'T THERE TIMES...
...WHEN EMOTIONS LIKE THAT ARE ALL YOU HAVE...
...TO PROTECT YOURSELF AND WHAT YOU LOVE?
IT DOESN'T BECOME A PROBLEM...
...UNTIL YOU CAN'T CONTROL THOSE EMOTIONS...
...AND THEY BEGIN TO CONTROL YOU.

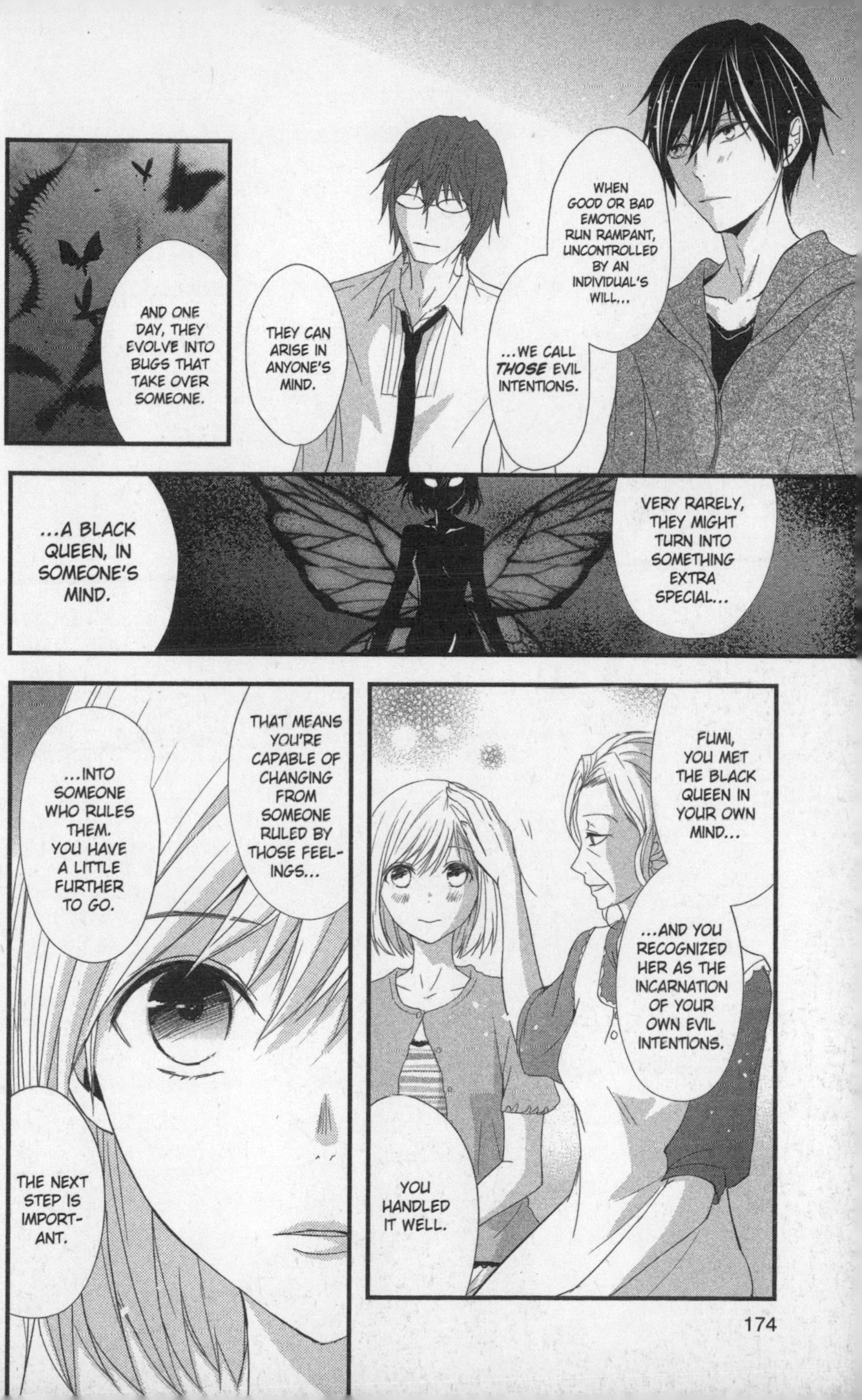
WHEN GOOD OR BAD EMOTIONS RUN RAMPANT, UNCONTROLLED BY AN INDIVIDUAL'S WILL...
...WE CALL *THOSE* EVIL INTENTIONS.
THEY CAN ARISE IN ANYONE'S MIND.
AND ONE DAY, THEY EVOLVE INTO BUGS THAT TAKE OVER SOMEONE.
VERY RARELY, THEY MIGHT TURN INTO SOMETHING EXTRA SPECIAL...
...A BLACK QUEEN, IN SOMEONE'S MIND.
FUMI, YOU MET THE BLACK QUEEN IN YOUR OWN MIND...
...AND YOU RECOGNIZED HER AS THE INCARNATION OF YOUR OWN EVIL INTENTIONS.
YOU HANDLED IT WELL.
THAT MEANS YOU'RE CAPABLE OF CHANGING FROM SOMEONE RULED BY THOSE FEEL-INGS...
...INTO SOMEONE WHO RULES THEM. YOU HAVE A LITTLE FURTHER TO GO.
THE NEXT STEP IS IMPORT-ANT.

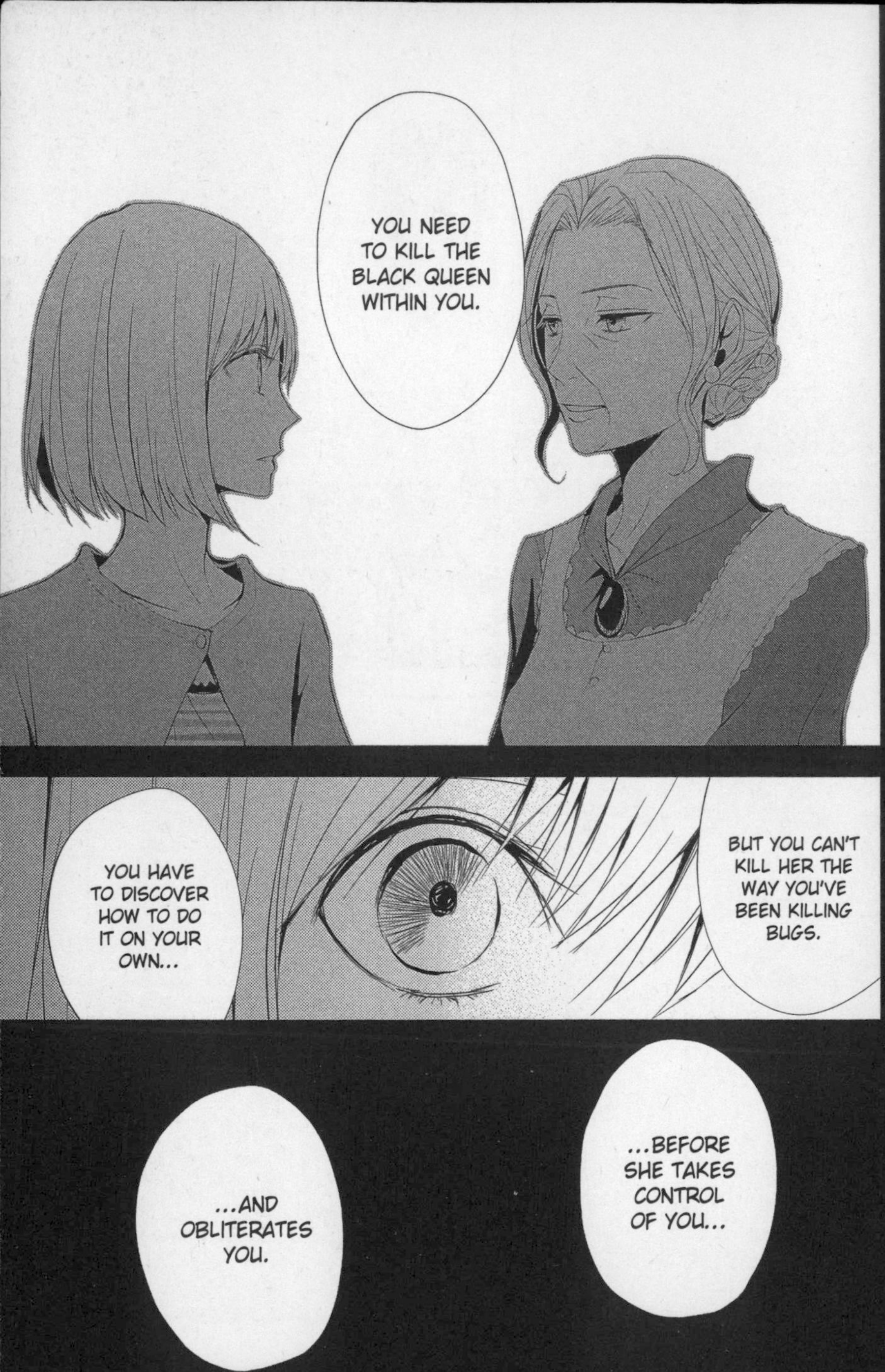
YOU NEED TO KILL THE BLACK QUEEN WITHIN YOU.
BUT YOU CAN'T KILL HER THE WAY YOU'VE BEEN KILLING BUGS.
YOU HAVE TO DISCOVER HOW TO DO IT ON YOUR OWN...
...BEFORE SHE TAKES CONTROL OF YOU...
...AND OBLITERATES YOU.

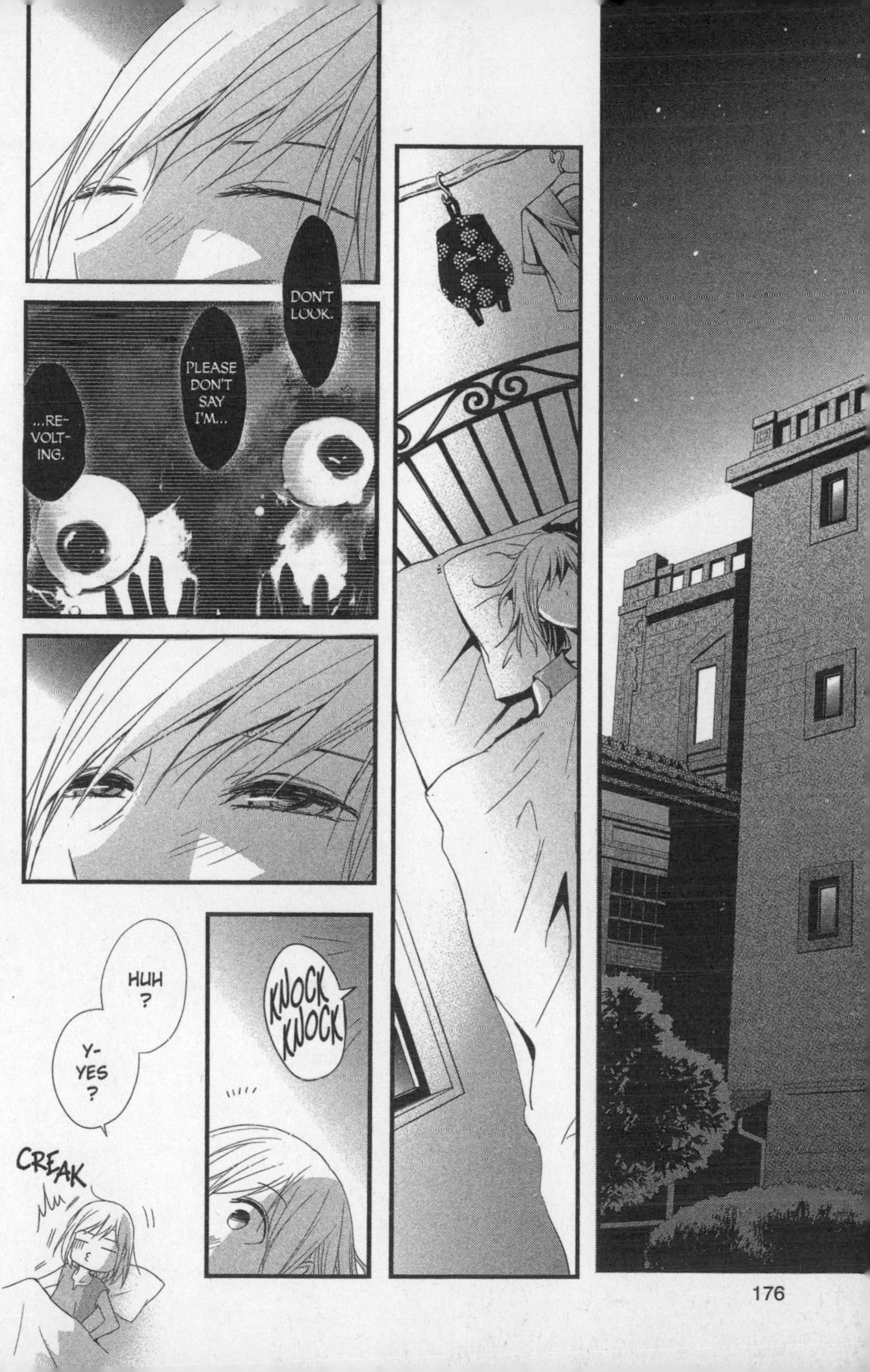

DON'T LOOK.
PLEASE DON'T SAY I'M...
...RE-VOLT-ING.
KNOCK KNOCK
HUH?
Y-YES?
CREAK

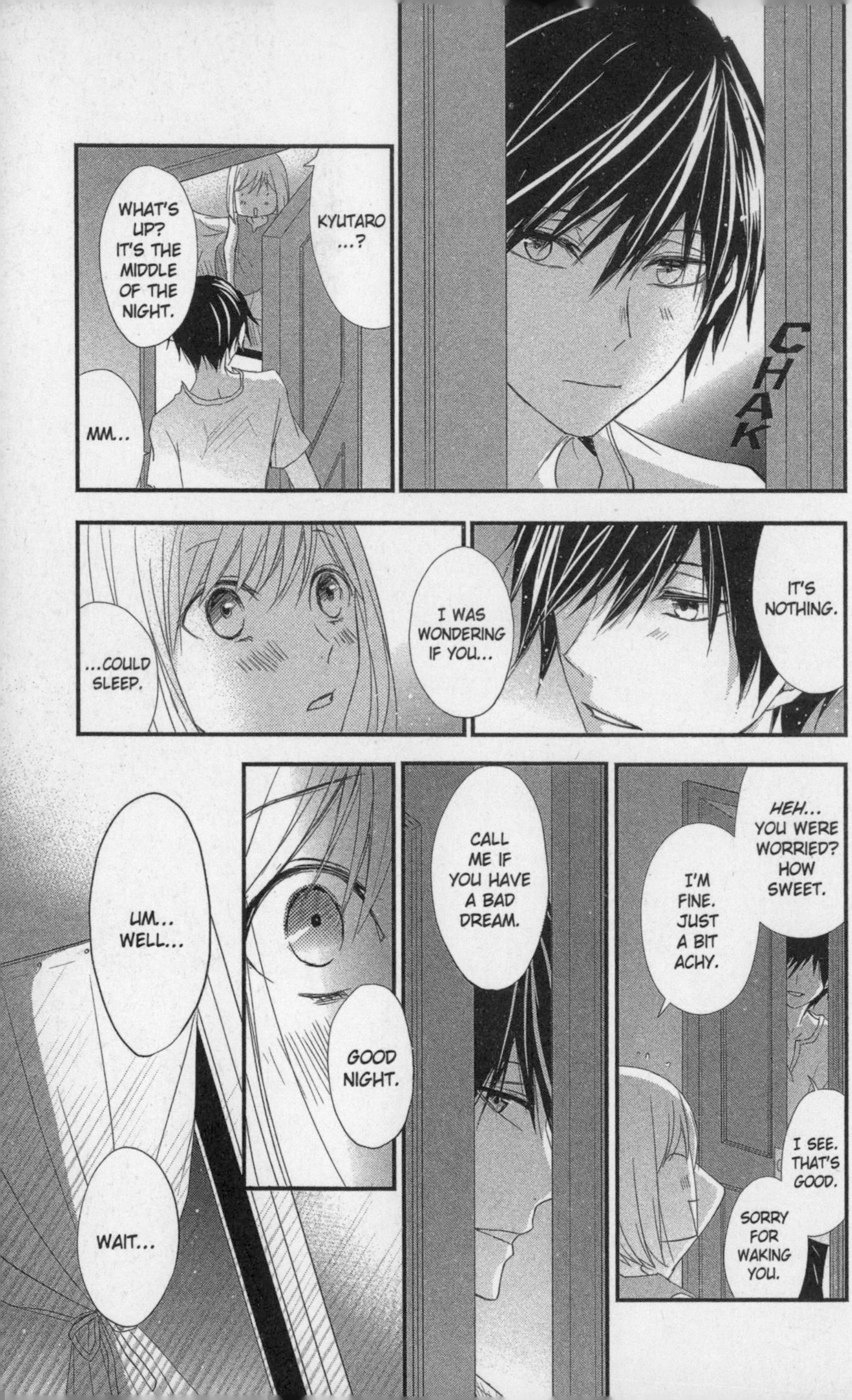
CHAK
KYUTARO ...?
WHAT'S UP? IT'S THE MIDDLE OF THE NIGHT.
MM...
IT'S NOTHING.
I WAS WONDERING IF YOU...
...COULD SLEEP.
HEH... YOU WERE WORRIED? HOW SWEET.
I'M FINE. JUST A BIT ACHY.
I SEE. THAT'S GOOD.
SORRY FOR WAKING YOU.
CALL ME IF YOU HAVE A BAD DREAM.
GOOD NIGHT.
UM... WELL...
WAIT...

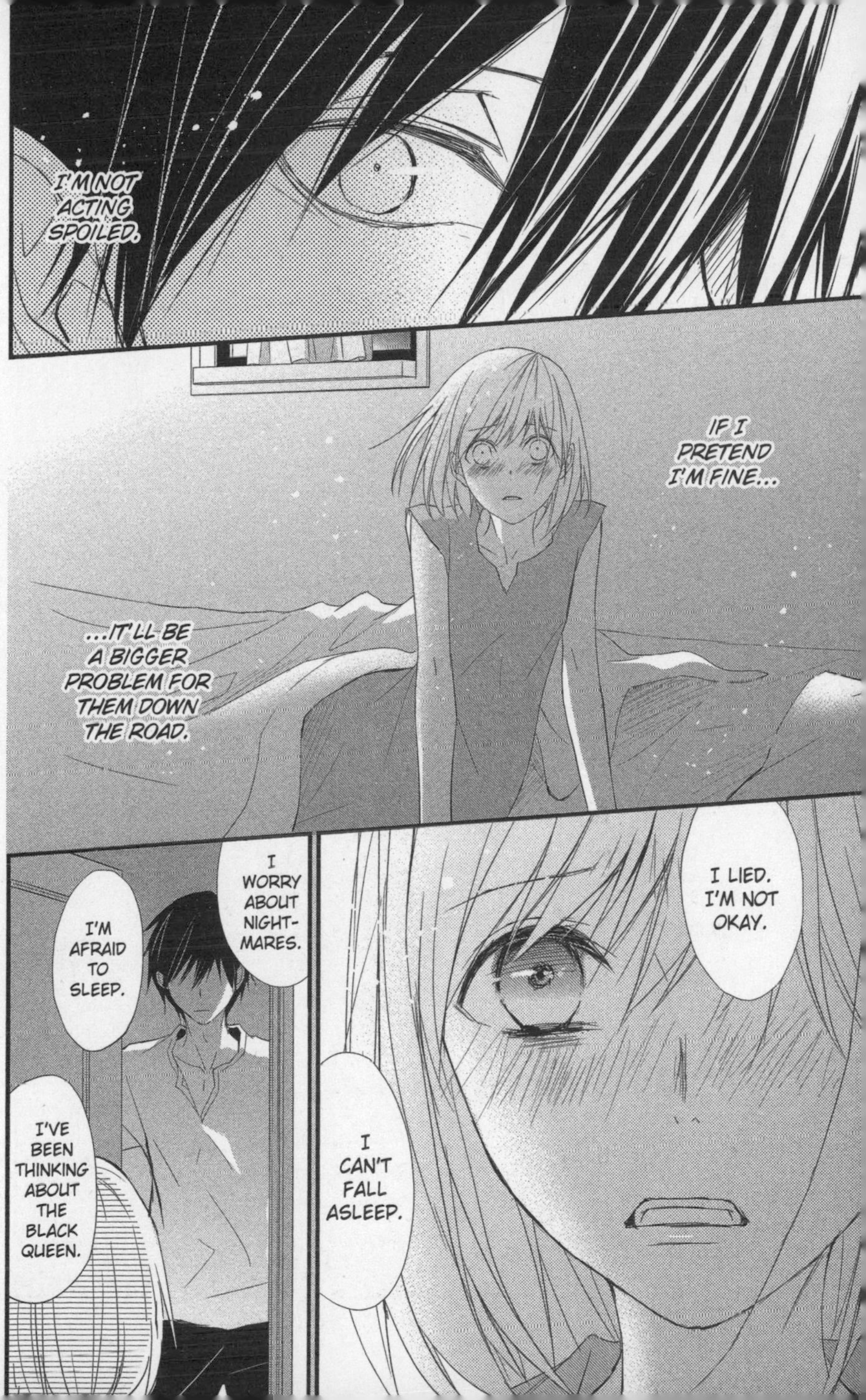
I'M NOT ACTING SPOILED.
IF I PRETEND I'M FINE...
...IT'LL BE A BIGGER PROBLEM FOR THEM DOWN THE ROAD.
I LIED. I'M NOT OKAY.
I CAN'T FALL ASLEEP.
I WORRY ABOUT NIGHT-MARES.
I'M AFRAID TO SLEEP.
I'VE BEEN THINKING ABOUT THE BLACK QUEEN.

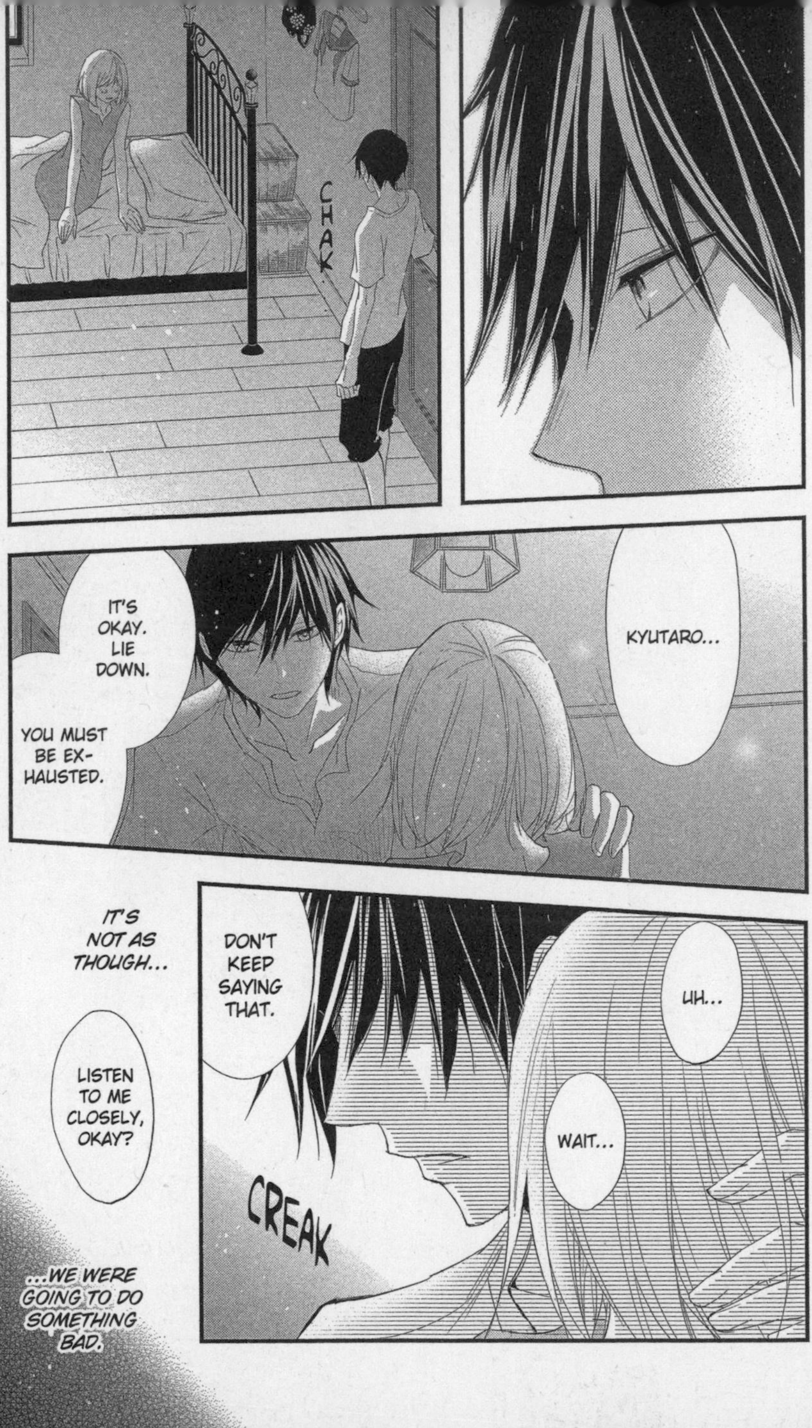
CHAK
KYUTARO...
IT'S OKAY. LIE DOWN.
YOU MUST BE EX-HAUSTED.
UH...
DON'T KEEP SAYING THAT.
WAIT...
IT'S NOT AS THOUGH...
LISTEN TO ME CLOSELY, OKAY?
CREAK
...WE WERE GOING TO DO SOMETHING BAD.

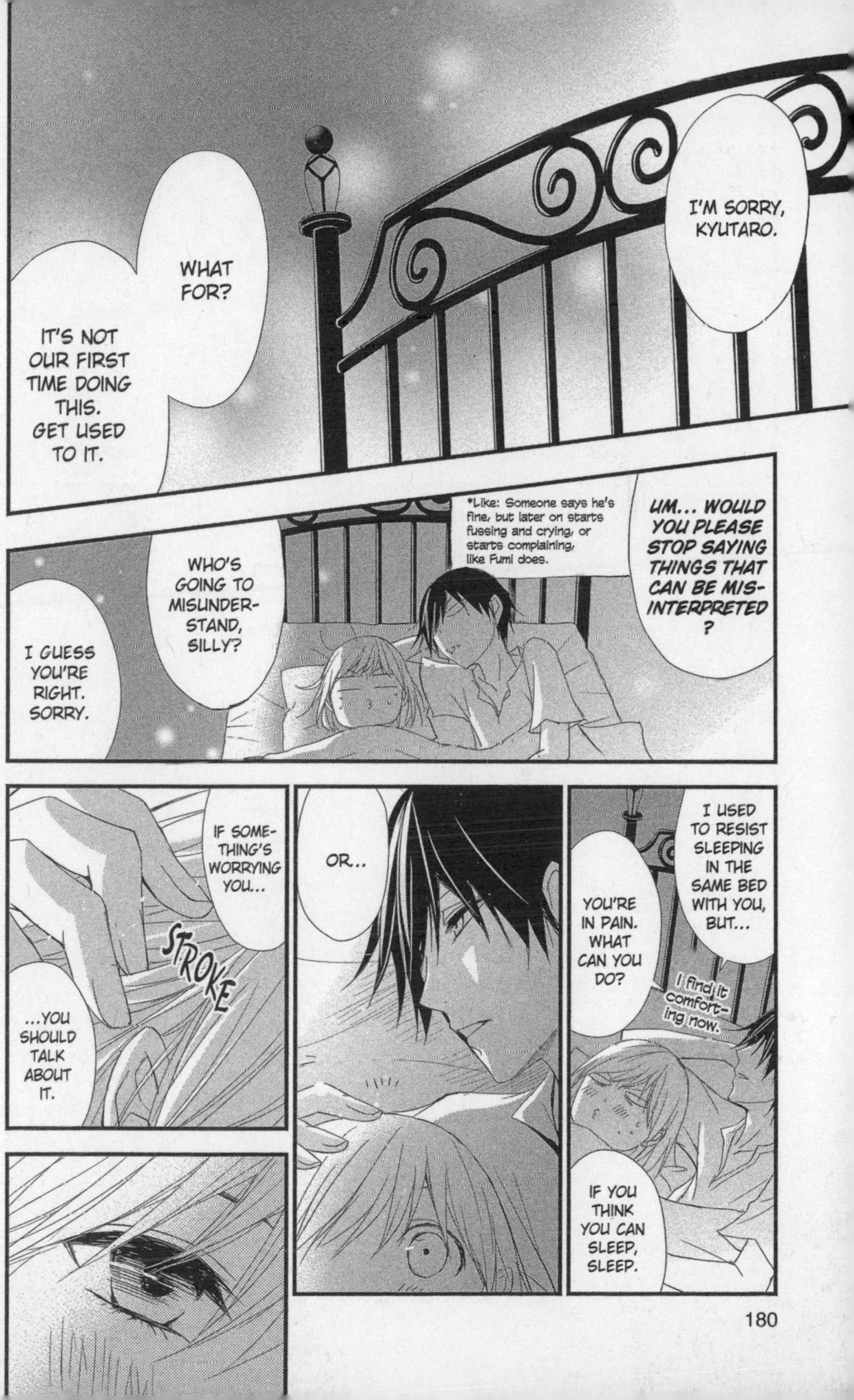
I'M SORRY, KYUTARO.
WHAT FOR?
IT'S NOT OUR FIRST TIME DOING THIS. GET USED TO IT.
UM... WOULD YOU PLEASE STOP SAYING THINGS THAT CAN BE MIS-INTERPRETED?
*Like: Someone says he's fine, but later on starts fussing and crying, or starts complaining, like Fumi does.
WHO'S GOING TO MISUNDER-STAND, SILLY?
I GUESS YOU'RE RIGHT. SORRY.
I USED TO RESIST SLEEPING IN THE SAME BED WITH YOU, BUT...
I find it comfort-ing now.
YOU'RE IN PAIN. WHAT CAN YOU DO?
IF YOU THINK YOU CAN SLEEP, SLEEP.
OR...
IF SOME-THING'S WORRYING YOU...
STROKE
...YOU SHOULD TALK ABOUT IT.

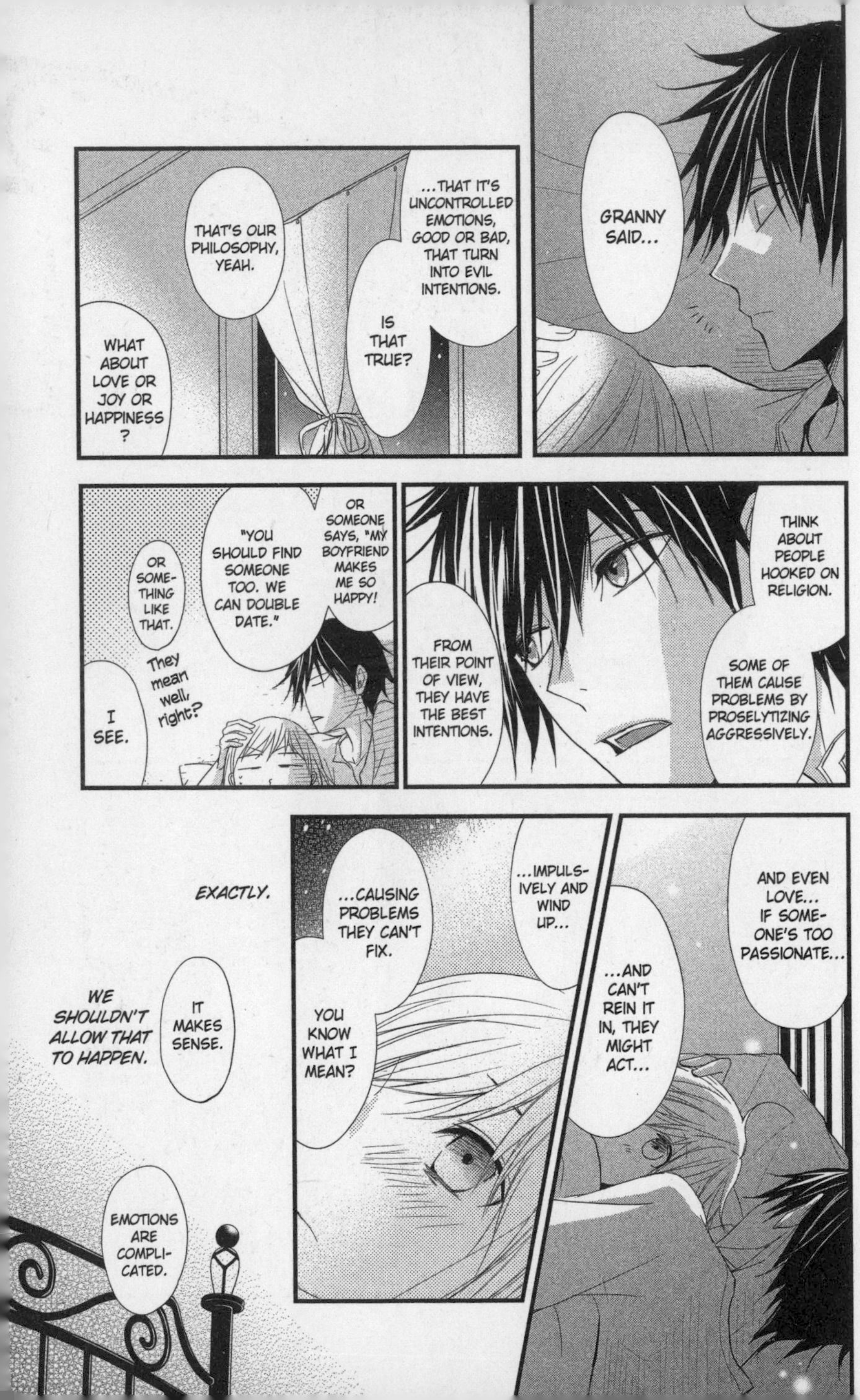
GRANNY SAID...
...THAT IT'S UNCONTROLLED EMOTIONS, GOOD OR BAD, THAT TURN INTO EVIL INTENTIONS.
THAT'S OUR PHILOSOPHY, YEAH.
IS THAT TRUE?
WHAT ABOUT LOVE OR JOY OR HAPPINESS?
THINK ABOUT PEOPLE HOOKED ON RELIGION.
SOME OF THEM CAUSE PROBLEMS BY PROSELYTIZING AGGRESSIVELY.
FROM THEIR POINT OF VIEW, THEY HAVE THE BEST INTENTIONS.
OR SOMEONE SAYS, "MY BOYFRIEND MAKES ME SO HAPPY!
"YOU SHOULD FIND SOMEONE TOO. WE CAN DOUBLE DATE."
OR SOME-THING LIKE THAT.
They mean well, right?
I SEE.
AND EVEN LOVE... IF SOME-ONE'S TOO PASSIONATE...
...AND CAN'T REIN IT IN, THEY MIGHT ACT...
...IMPULS-IVELY AND WIND UP...
...CAUSING PROBLEMS THEY CAN'T FIX.
YOU KNOW WHAT I MEAN?
EXACTLY.
IT MAKES SENSE.
WE SHOULDN'T ALLOW THAT TO HAPPEN.
EMOTIONS ARE COMPLI-CATED.

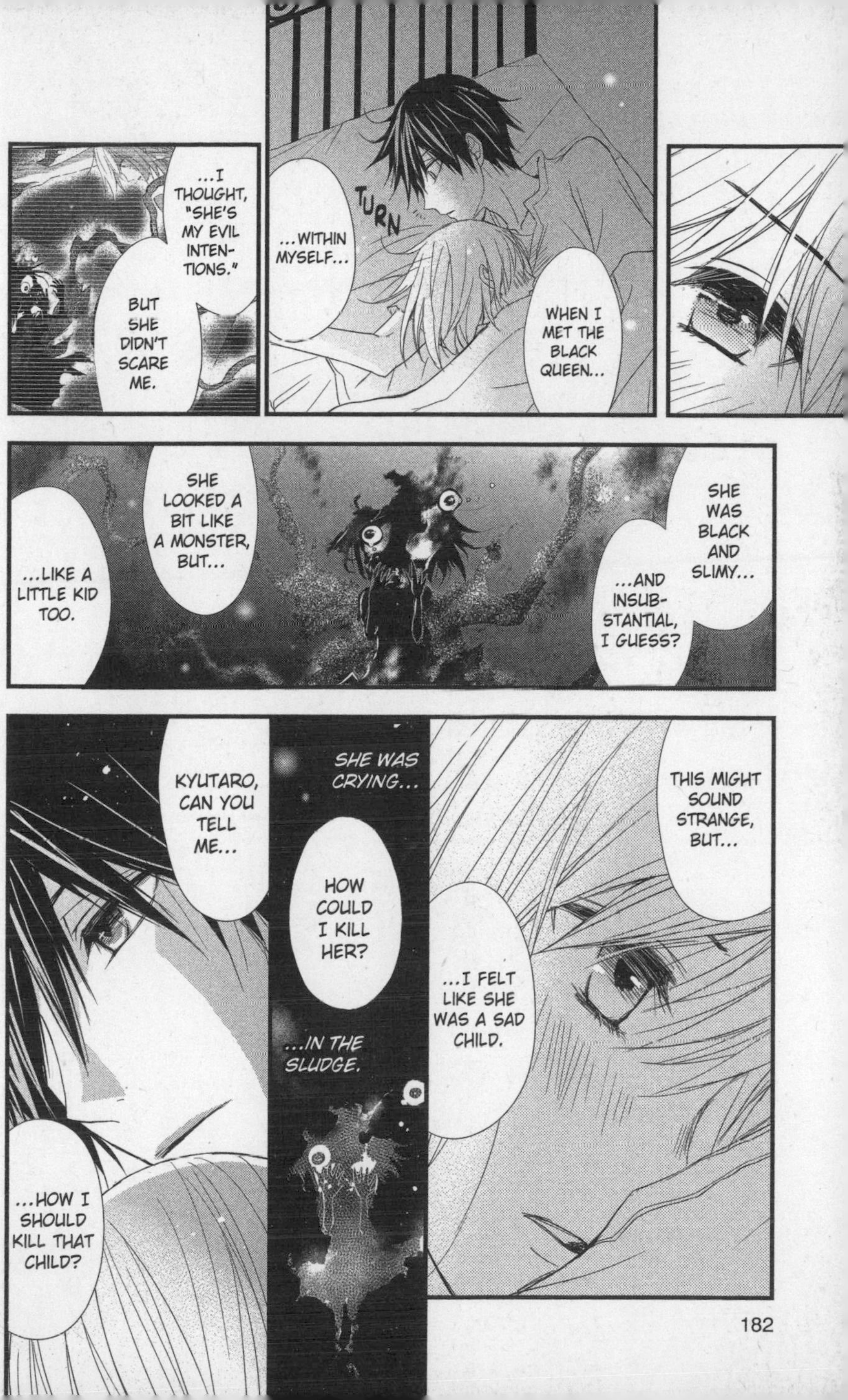
TURN
WHEN I MET THE BLACK QUEEN...
...WITHIN MYSELF...
...I THOUGHT, "SHE'S MY EVIL INTEN-TIONS."
BUT SHE DIDN'T SCARE ME.
SHE WAS BLACK AND SLIMY...
...AND INSUB-STANTIAL, I GUESS?
SHE LOOKED A BIT LIKE A MONSTER, BUT...
...LIKE A LITTLE KID TOO.
THIS MIGHT SOUND STRANGE, BUT...
...I FELT LIKE SHE WAS A SAD CHILD.
SHE WAS CRYING...
HOW COULD I KILL HER?
...IN THE SLUDGE.
KYUTARO, CAN YOU TELL ME...
...HOW I SHOULD KILL THAT CHILD?

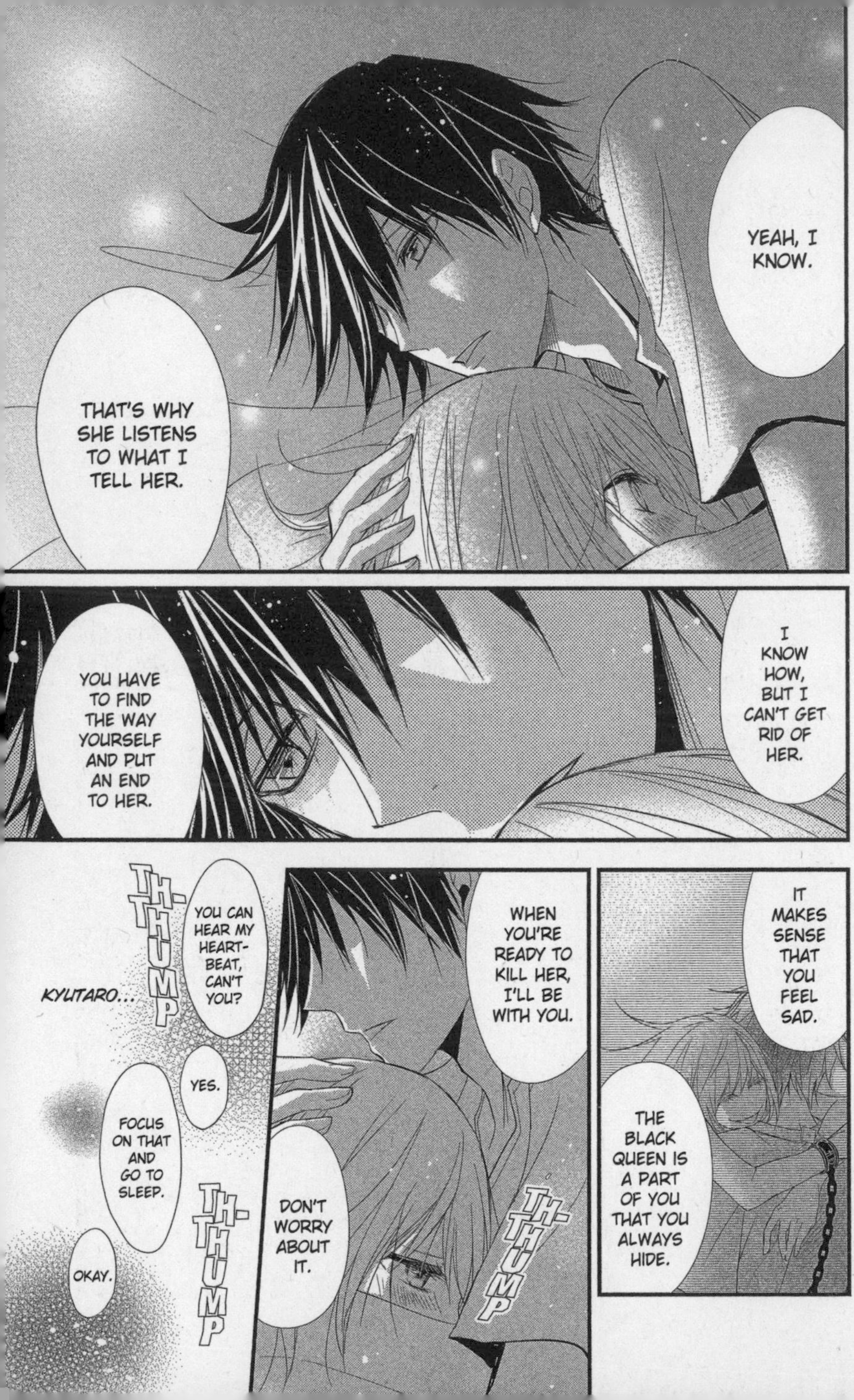
YEAH, I KNOW.
THAT'S WHY SHE LISTENS TO WHAT I TELL HER.
I KNOW HOW, BUT I CAN'T GET RID OF HER.
YOU HAVE TO FIND THE WAY YOURSELF AND PUT AN END TO HER.
IT MAKES SENSE THAT YOU FEEL SAD.
THE BLACK QUEEN IS A PART OF YOU THAT YOU ALWAYS HIDE.
WHEN YOU'RE READY TO KILL HER, I'LL BE WITH YOU.
TH-THUMP
DON'T WORRY ABOUT IT.
YOU CAN HEAR MY HEART-BEAT, CAN'T YOU?
TH-THUMP
KYUTARO...
YES.
FOCUS ON THAT AND GO TO SLEEP.
TH-THUMP
OKAY.

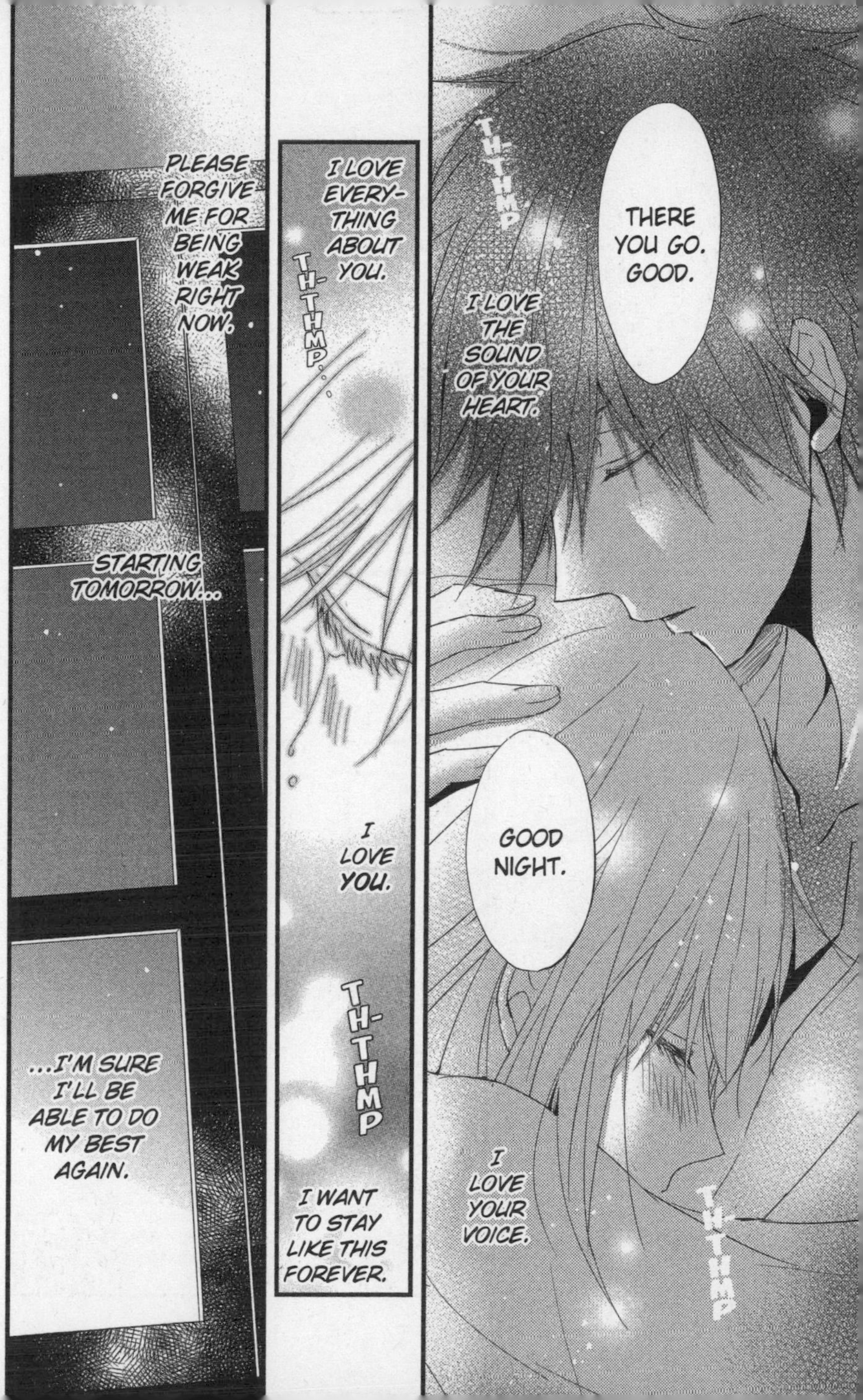
THERE YOU GO. GOOD.
TH-THMP
I LOVE THE SOUND OF YOUR HEART.
GOOD NIGHT.
TH-THMP
I LOVE YOUR VOICE.
I LOVE EVERYTHING ABOUT YOU.
TH-THMP
I LOVE YOU.
TH-THMP
I WANT TO STAY LIKE THIS FOREVER.
PLEASE FORGIVE ME FOR BEING WEAK RIGHT NOW.
STARTING TOMORROW...
...I'M SURE I'LL BE ABLE TO DO MY BEST AGAIN.

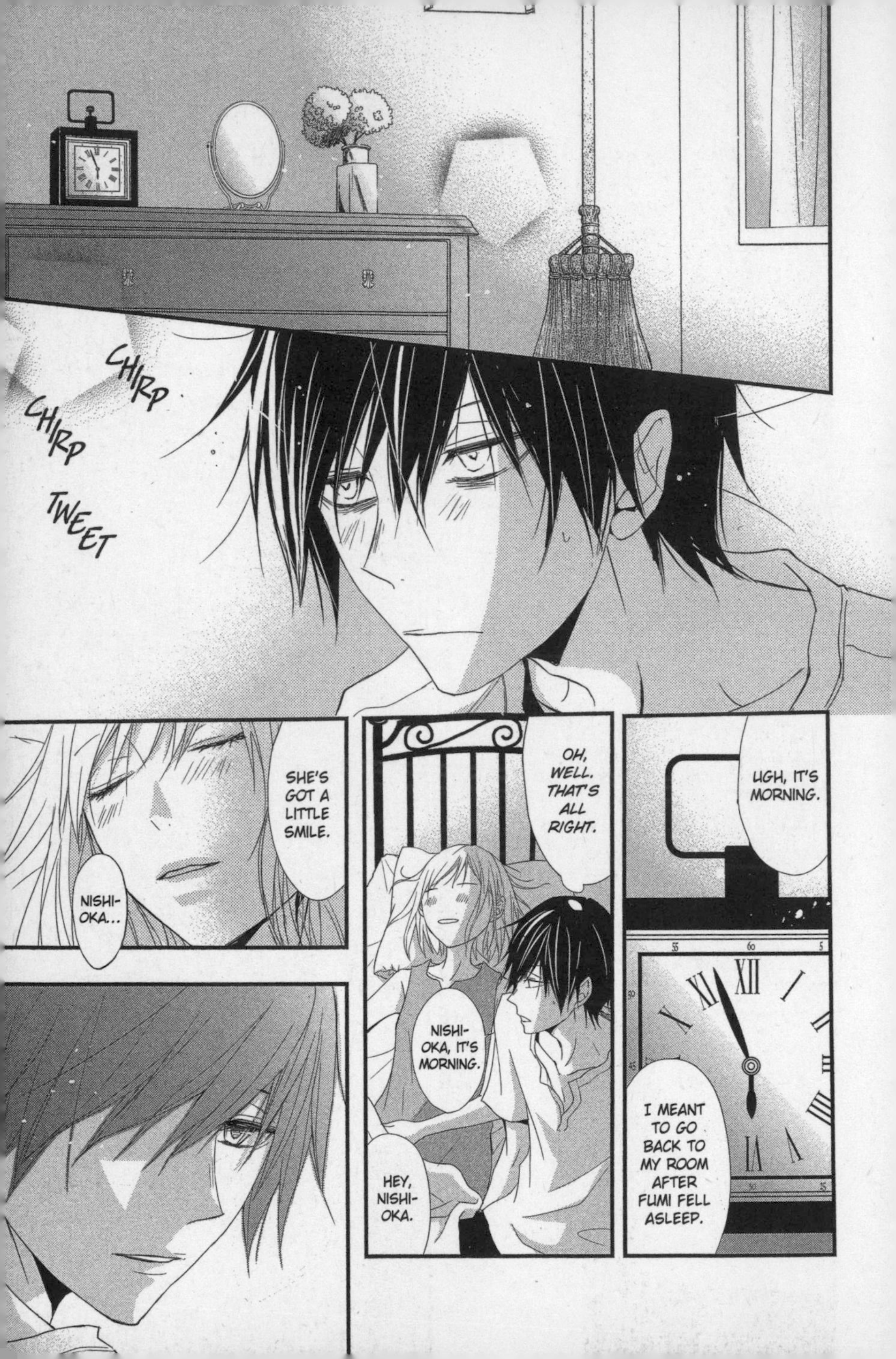
CHIRP
CHIRP
TWEET
UGH, IT'S MORNING.
I MEANT TO GO BACK TO MY ROOM AFTER FUMI FELL ASLEEP.
OH, WELL. THAT'S ALL RIGHT.
NISHI-OKA, IT'S MORNING.
HEY, NISHI-OKA.
SHE'S GOT A LITTLE SMILE.
NISHI-OKA...

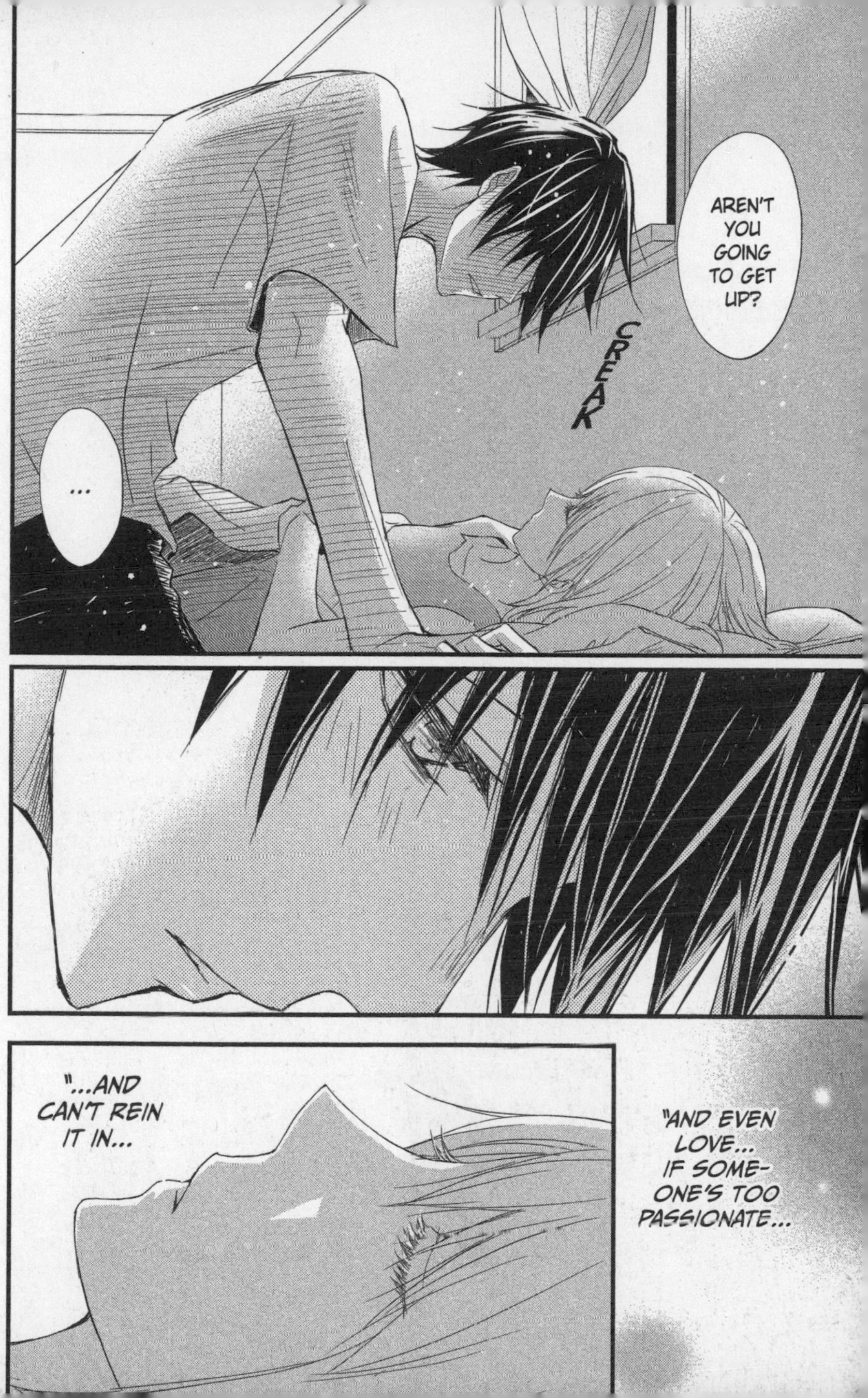
AREN'T YOU GOING TO GET UP?
CREAK
...
"AND EVEN LOVE... IF SOME-ONE'S TOO PASSIONATE...
"...AND CAN'T REIN IT IN...

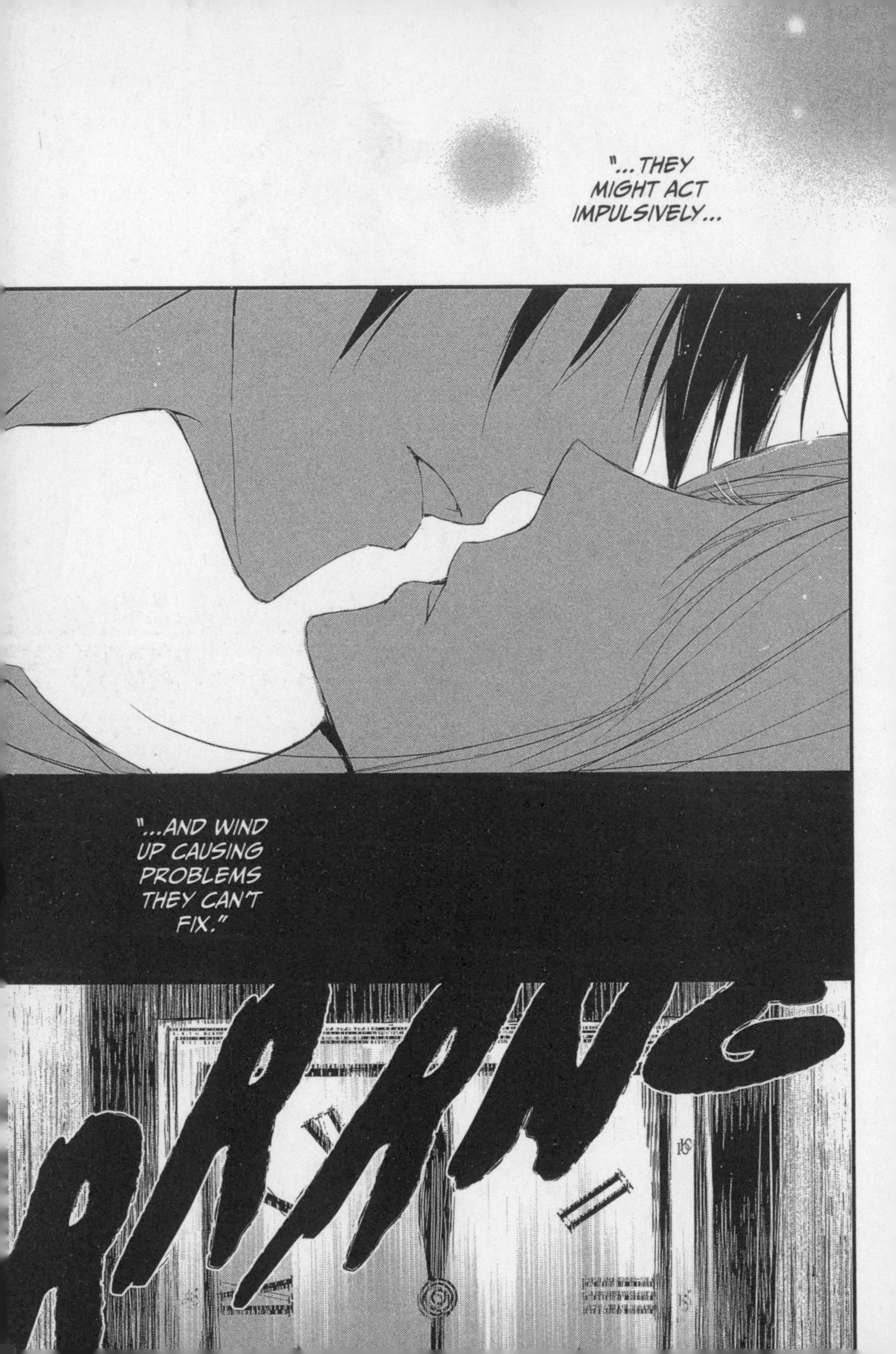
"...THEY MIGHT ACT IMPULSIVELY...
"...AND WIND UP CAUSING PROBLEMS THEY CAN'T FIX."

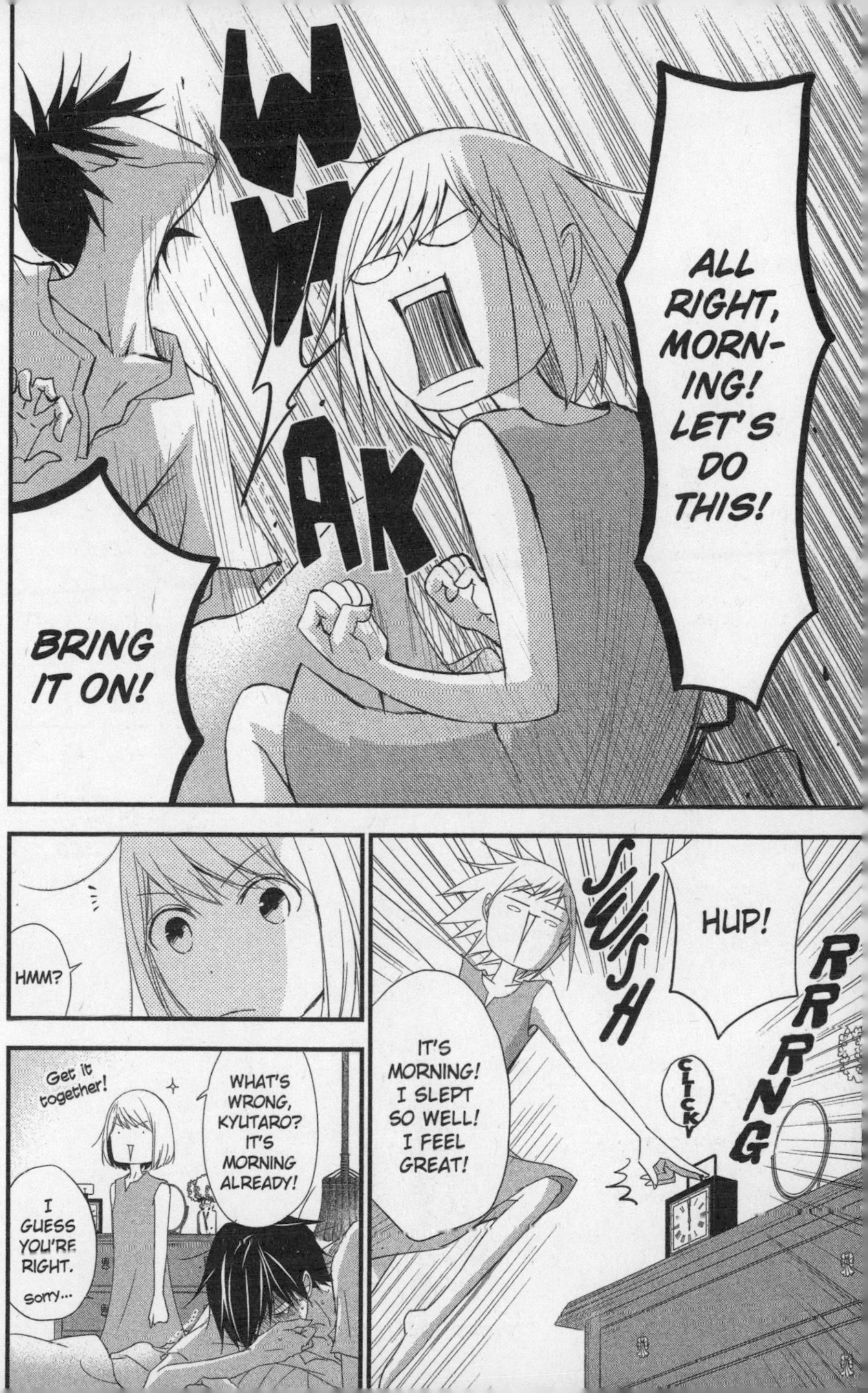
ALL RIGHT, MORNING! LET'S DO THIS!
WHAK
BRING IT ON!
RRRRNG
HUP!
SWISH
CLICK
IT'S MORNING! I SLEPT SO WELL! I FEEL GREAT!
HMM?
WHAT'S WRONG, KYUTARO? IT'S MORNING ALREADY!
Get it together!
I GUESS YOU'RE RIGHT.
sorry...

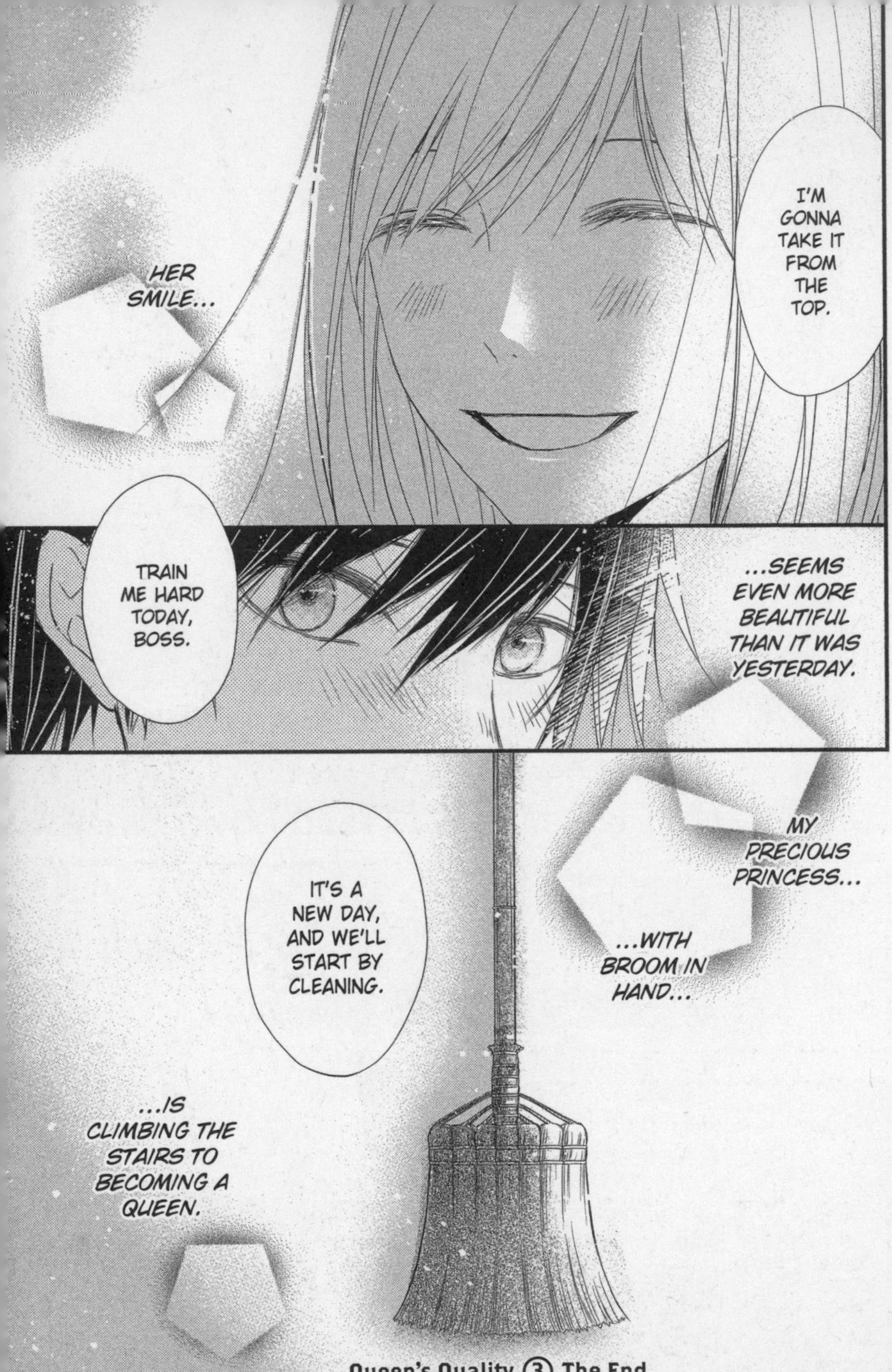
I'M GONNA TAKE IT FROM THE TOP.
HER SMILE...
...SEEMS EVEN MORE BEAUTIFUL THAN IT WAS YESTERDAY.
TRAIN ME HARD TODAY, BOSS.
MY PRECIOUS PRINCESS...
...WITH BROOM IN HAND...
IT'S A NEW DAY, AND WE'LL START BY CLEANING.
...IS CLIMBING THE STAIRS TO BECOMING A QUEEN.

Queen's Quality ③ The End

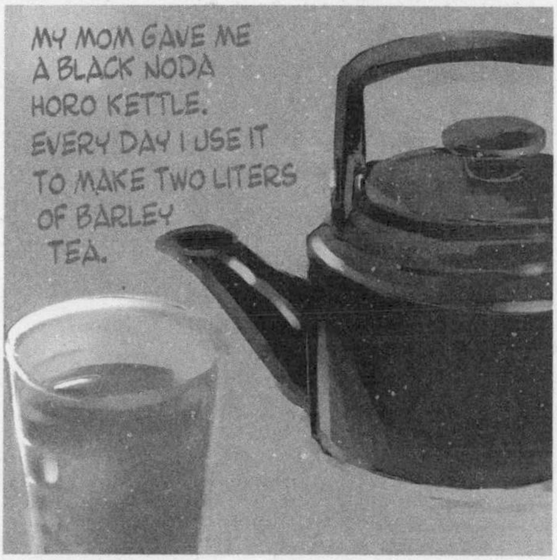
MY MOM GAVE ME A BLACK NODA HORO KETTLE. EVERY DAY I USE IT TO MAKE TWO LITERS OF BARLEY TEA.

For some reason, this summer I've suddenly realized how great barley tea is. Not only is it easy to make, but it's healthy! It's really terrific. So delicious!

—Kyousuke Motomi

Author Bio

Born on August 1, Kyousuke Motomi debuted in *Deluxe Betsucomi* with *Hetakuso Kyupiddo* (No Good Cupid) in 2002. She is the creator of *Dengeki Daisy, Beast Master* and *QQ Sweeper*, all available in North America from VIZ Media. Motomi enjoys sleeping, tea ceremonies and reading Haruki Murakami.

Queen's Quality

Vol. 3

Shojo Beat Edition

STORY AND ART BY

KYOUSUKE MOTOMI

QUEEN'S QUALITY Vol. 3
by Kyousuke MOTOMI

Original Japanese edition published by SHOGAKUKAN.
English translation rights in the United States of America, Canada, the United Kingdom, Ireland, Australia and New Zealand arranged with SHOGAKUKAN.

ORIGINAL DESIGN/Chie SATO+Bay Bridge Studio

English Adaptation/Ysabet Reinhardt MacFarlane
Translation/JN Productions
Touch-Up Art & Lettering/Mark McMurray
Design/Julian [JR] Robinson
Editor/Amy Yu

Printed in the U.S.A.

Published by VIZ Media, LLC
P.O. Box 77010
San Francisco, CA 94107

10 9 8 7 6 5 4 3 2 1
First printing, March 2018

www.viz.com

www.shojobeat.com

RATED T FOR TEEN

PARENTAL ADVISORY

QUEEN'S QUALITY is rated T for Teen and is recommended for ages 13 and up. This volume contains suggestive themes and violence.

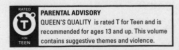

This is the Last Page!

It's true: In keeping with the original Japanese comic format, this book reads from right to left—so action, sound effects and word balloons are completely reversed. This preserves the orientation of the original artwork—plus, it's fun! Check out the diagram shown here to get the hang of things, and then turn to the other side of the book to get started!

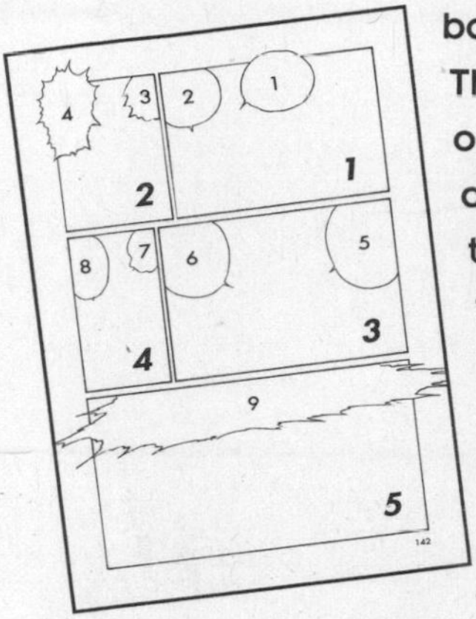
1
2
3
4
1
2
5
6
7
8
3
4
9
5
142

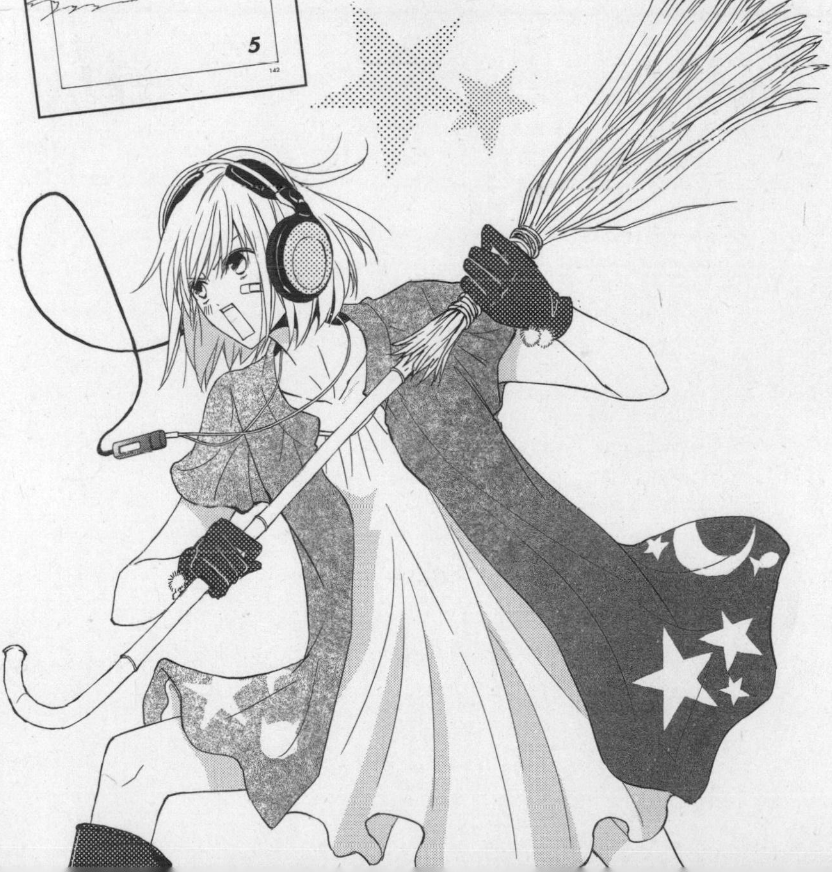